DIASPORA, MEMORY, AN[D IDENTITY:]
A SEARCH FOR HOME

Edited by Vijay Agnew

Memories establish a connection between a collective and individual past, between origins, heritage, and history. Those who have left their places of birth to make homes elsewhere are familiar with the question, 'Where do you come from?' and respond in innumerable, well-rehearsed ways. The diasporic individual often has a double-consciousness, a privileged knowledge and perspective that is consonant with postmodernity and globalization.

The essays in this volume reflect on the movements of people and cultures in the present day, when physical, social, and mental borders and boundaries are being challenged and sometimes successfully dismantled. The contributors, who represent a variety of disciplinary perspectives, discuss the experiences of ethnic and racial groups living in Canada, including those of South Asians, Iranians, West Indians, Chinese, and Eritreans. The volume presents a unique collection of essays, empirical studies, and memoirs that contribute to the development of theories of diaspora, subjectivity, double-consciousness, gender and class, and the nature of home.

VIJAY AGNEW is a professor in the School of Women's Studies and the Division of Social Science and director of the Centre for Feminist Research at York University.

Edited by Vijay Agnew

Diaspora, Memory, and Identity

A Search for Home

UNIVERSITY OF TORONTO PRESS
Toronto Buffalo London

© University of Toronto Press Incorporated 2005
Toronto Buffalo London
Printed in Canada

Reprinted 2008

ISBN-13: 978-0-8020-9033-1 (cloth)
ISBN-10: 0-8020-9033-8 (cloth)

ISBN-13: 978-0-8020-9374-5 (paper)
ISBN-10: 0-8020-9374-4 (paper)

Printed on acid-free paper

Library and Archives Canada Cataloguing in Publication

Diaspora, memory and identity : a search for home / edited by Vijay
Agnew.

ISBN-13: 978-0-8020-9033-1 (bound)
ISBN-10: 0-8020-9033-8 (bound)
ISBN-13: 978-0-8020-9374-5 (pbk.)
ISBN-10: 0-8020-9374-4 (pbk.)

1. Emigration and immigration – Psychological aspects.   2. Emigration
and immigration – Social aspects.   3. Group identity.   4. Identity
(Psychology).   5. Autobiographical memory.   6. Home – Psychological
aspects.   7. Home – Social aspects.   8. Marginality, Social.   9. Hybridity
(Social sciences).   I. Agnew, Vijay, 1946–

JV6091.D528 2005   305.9′06912   C2005-904954-5

Chapter 2 first appeared in the Canadian Journal of Sociology 29(3): 359–388.
© Pamela Sugiman 2004

University of Toronto Press acknowledges the financial assistance to
its publishing program of the Canada Council for the Arts and the
Ontario Arts Council.

University of Toronto Press acknowledges the financial support for
its publishing activities of the Government of Canada through the
Book Publishing Industry Development Program (BPIDP).

For Nicole Agnew,
loving daughter and best friend

Contents

Acknowledgments

After many years of doing research and writing on my own, I decided it was time to leave my solitary habits behind and become more engaged with the work of the university. As director of the Centre for Feminist Research at York, I have had the pleasure of getting to know many academics who were previously unknown to me, and have enjoyed playing host to feminist scholars from different parts of the world who have come to visit the university. In meeting others I have grown intellectually and have learned new skills of communicating with people. *Diaspora, Memory, and Identity* has come out of this phase of my life. The executive of the Centre for Feminist Research wanted to initiate a project that would draw diverse women together, and consequently decided to host a conference on memory and identity. The work of planning and organizing the conference was ably done by the centre's administrator, Annis Karpenko, who has since left us for other opportunities. I thank her for communicating with participants and responding promptly to their concerns.

The conference introduced me to the research of friends and colleagues and suggested new directions for my writings. Editing this volume made it necessary for me to read and reread the papers of the contributors as we worked through the different stages of the publishing process. I gained new insights at each reading and understood patterns and commonalities between the varied experiences of diasporic people of different ethnic and racial identities. Many of the contributors to this volume discuss how memories of the past define our perspectives, help us negotiate our circumstances, and develop new ways of being and becoming. I have greatly enjoyed working and learning from the research of these contributors, and I now think of them as friends. I thank them for their patience with my many queries concerning their essays, and for their prompt and helpful responses. In particular I would like to thank Marlene Kadar and Haideh Moghissi for their engagement with the work of the Centre for Feminist Research, and for their encouragement of my research and writing.

I would like to thank senior administrators at York for their generous support of the work of the centre. I had to raise funds for hosting the conference, and when I passed the hat around it came back with enough to enable me to invite scholars from overseas to come and present their essays. I would also like to acknowledge the support of the Social Science and Humanities Research Council for a three-year grant that enabled me to write the chapters included in this volume.

I am grateful to the anonymous reviewers of this book for taking valuable time away from their own work to read the manuscript. Their comments were both generous and insightful and helped to further improve the book. I thank Diane Young and Jennifer Hutchison for their thorough editing in readying the manuscript for the publishers, and for their very helpful and supportive advice. I also thank Patricia Thorvaldson for editing the final draft of the manuscript, taking us one more step towards completion of this project. I am grateful to Virgil Duff of the University of Toronto Press for his support in publishing my work. Dian Emery, administrator of the Centre for Feminist Research, helped prepare the manuscript for the press, and I thank her for it as well.

I draw courage and sustenance for research and writing from the unfailing love and support of my husband, Tom. Mothers nurture and care for their young, and as Nicole, my daughter, makes her way in worlds that are distant and different from mine, I watch from afar and pray for her well-being. My conversations with her, and with her friends, give me a glimpse into the hearts and minds of young women. As I see these young women plan confidently for their personal and professional lives, I think that the struggles of feminists of my generation were not just a passing phase but have left their indelible print on history. Knowing that gives me enormous satisfaction. I am a mother, full of stories about 'home.' Nicole indulges me by listening patiently, and I thank and love her for it.

DIASPORA, MEMORY, AND IDENTITY:
A SEARCH FOR HOME

Introduction

VIJAY AGNEW

Memories establish a connection between our individual past and our collective past (our origins, heritage, and history). The past is always with us, and it defines our present; it resonates in our voices, hovers over our silences, and explains how we came to be ourselves and to inhabit what we call 'our homes.' Thus, 'what we call the past is merely a function and production of a continuous present and its discourses' (Hirsch and Smith 2002, 9). Those who have left their places of birth to make homes in other parts of the world are familiar with the question 'Where do you come from?' and respond in innumerable, well-rehearsed ways. The past and the present are social constructs that are contested by those with different identities, experiences, genealogies, and histories. This relationship between the past and present is complex and dynamic, with meanings and interpretations that shift with time, place, and social context. In contemporary society, the mobility of people and ideas have been further accelerated, challenging those of us who are interested in the study of diasporas to reflect upon our mental, social, and physical boundaries and perhaps shift and dislocate them. It is as important for us 'to cross metaphorical lines as it is to cross actual ones: not to be contained or defined by anybody else's idea of where a line should be drawn' (Rushdie 2002, 373).

The word *diaspora* was originally used to describe the forced dispersal and displacement of the Jewish, Armenian, and Greek peoples. In his seminal article on this subject, Clifford defines the main characteristics of a diaspora as incorporating a 'history of dispersal, myths/ memories of the homeland, and alienation in the host (bad host?) country, desire for eventual return, ongoing support of the homeland, and a collective identity importantly defined by this relationship' (1994, 305).

Anh Hua, in this volume, discusses the history and theories associated with the term diaspora to argue that the term is useful to study 'the social world resulting from displacement, flight, exile, and forced migration,' enabling us to 'reconfigure the relationship between citizens, nation states, and national narratology.'

Anthias (1998) outlines six criteria that define a diaspora, such as dispersal and scattering, collective trauma, cultural flowering, a troubled relationship with the majority, a sense of community transcending national frontiers, and promoting a return movement. There is no ideal diaspora, nor do all of these elements have to be present to define it, and there is no hierarchy among them that emerges by the absence or presence of one or more of these elements. Importance, however, lies in the shared history of displacement, suffering, adaptation, and resistance.

The term diaspora has been expanded to incorporate situations that are not associated with forced dispersals or a desire to return. For example, the South Asian diaspora is not characterized by its orientation to roots nor its desire for a permanent return to the homeland. Rather, as Rishma Dunlop and I document in this volume, it is defined by its ability to recreate a culture in diverse locations. Diasporas can thus denote a transnational sense of self and community and create an understanding of ethnicity and ethnic bonds that transcends the borders and boundaries of nation states. Yet, the individual living in the diaspora experiences a dynamic tension every day between living 'here' and remembering 'there,' between memories of places of origin and entanglements with places of residence, and between the metaphorical and the physical home.

At the present time, the word diaspora is used in a number of different ways that have more to do with the scholars' disciplines than with any substantive concerns about the term. In this volume, the contributors, who come from diverse academic disciplines – humanities, English, women's studies, sociology, history, social work, contemporary art and theory, and education – use the term in a multiplicity of ways that evoke its original definition as well as its subsequent broader use. The authors are interested in documenting 'how heightened social, economic, and political interconnectedness across national borders and cultures enables individuals to sustain multiple identities and loyalties, create new cultural products using elements from a variety of settings, and exercise multiple political and civic memberships' (Levitt and Waters 2002, 6).

Discourses on diaspora use the term in three distinct but related ways: as a social form, as a type of social consciousness, and as a mode of cultural production (Vertovec 1997). As a social form, the term refers to individuals who live in different parts of the world but identify collectively with one another, with the countries or region from which they or their ancestors originated, and with the society in which they currently reside. Atsuko Matsuoka, John Sorenson, Izumi Sakamoto, and Yanqiu Zhou use the term in this way in this volume. Scholars who define a diaspora by its social consciousness refer to individuals who live in a variety of societies and cultures and who emphasize their sense of belonging or exclusion, their states of mind, and their sense of identity.

In this volume, Pamela Sugiman and Marlene Kadar use the term to show how traumatic and wounding experiences construct identity and shape feelings of community in various social and political contexts. Diaspora, as a mode of production, refers to the reproduction of cultural phenomena through creolization and hybridization. Dunlop, Haideh Moghissi, and I discuss these phenomena in this volume. These categories are not separate and distinct, however; rather, they overlap and intersect with one another.

Migrants use their intellectual, social, and political resources to construct identities that transcend physical and social boundaries, and they are rarely, particularly today, mere victims who are acted upon by the larger society. Ong refers to the experience of ethnic Chinese, of the investor and business class, to argue that their sense of themselves and their community is derived from a variety of locations throughout the world where they live or have lived. The Chinese, who are mobile and move frequently between countries, exercise 'flexible citizenship.' They may experience the oppressiveness of race and gender, but they also intervene in a planned and deliberate manner to contradict conventional racist stereotypes. Instead, they generate new and different images of themselves and their group that correspond more closely to their evolving self-image and self-definition (Ong 1999). Identity thus transcends national boundaries and becomes deterritorialized. Nevertheless, the critical self-defining issue for the migrants may be, in the words of Hawley (1997), 'Who [they] ... expect to be, who they are allowed to be, and who do they choose to be' (183).

Until recently, discussions of diasporas were critiqued for failing to pay adequate attention to the differences of class and for their neglect in studying the gendered experiences of diasporic populations (Anthias 1998; Clifford 1994). All chapters in this volume discuss the gendered and class nature of the diasporic experience. Moghissi analyses whether attachment to the culture and traditions of the homeland that reinforce patriarchy and subordinate women is a response by migrants to the racism and sexism that they experience from the larger society in which they live. The discussions of Sakamoto, Zhou, Matsuoka, and Sorenson in this volume analyse gender in comparative and relational terms to show that being in the diaspora can lead to a positive renegotiation of gender relations. Eritrean and Chinese women who live away from their homelands are compelled to modify conventional gender roles to meet the political and social demands of their new countries. These changes generate new modes of interactions that challenge subordination. Sugiman and I analyse class biases about how different groups of individuals are perceived and treated in the diaspora.

Memory, writes Hua in this volume, is important in studying the diaspora, for it is closely tied to historical and political struggles and in recent time 'has become an object that is gendered, appropriated, politicized, nationalized, medicalized, and aestheticized.' A point of entry into my own history is a portrait of my mother enclosed in a plain wooden frame. This image always hung on a white wall that was devoid of any other decoration, in my father's austere room in our home in Bombay. By the time I was a toddler, my parents and extended family had become refugees as a result of the British partition of India. They fled from Quetta, a Muslim-dominated region in the northwest of India that had been their home for generations and is today part of Pakistan, hoping to escape religious violence and find safety and security with their co-religionists in India. A year later my mother died, and my siblings and I became 'motherless.'

The hurried nature of my parents' departure from Quetta, now part of Pakistan, meant that they carried little with them that was not necessary for physical survival. No albums or pictures of the past survived, other than the portrait of my mother and a photograph of my paternal grandfather. All record of my parents' youth, their celebrations of weddings and births, and joyful gatherings with friends and relations were lost and obliterated. My mother, like many of the women of her class and generation, kept no diaries and journals that recorded her everyday life or her departure from Quetta and arrival as a refugee in India. My only access to her times and her inner self are through the memories of others – my father, siblings, and extended family.

Histories and public archives memorialized, until recently, the lives of the noteworthy and powerful while neglecting, except in broad strokes, the everyday lives and experiences of the majority of the population. Feminists use 'alternate archives' such as visual images, music, ritual and performance, material and popular culture, and oral history to record lived reality, particularly of the disenfranchised, marginalized, and excluded populations (Hirsch and Smith 2002, 10). Memories play a role in the individual's struggle to construct a social and personal identity in a world in which subjectivity is both fragmented and fractured (Giles 2002, 21). Memories that are documented in narratives, life writings, and autobiographies represent individuals and groups with a specificity and particularity that eschew homogeneity and generalizations. Memories recorded in journals, diaries, and life writings are acts of representation, performance, and interpretation (Hirsch and Smith 2002, 5.) If memory is an act of representation and performance, then we can ask what its relationship is to 'fact' and whether memories are 'real' and 'authentic' interpretations of self, home, and history.

In this volume, Kadar examines memoirs and autobiographies in order to determine how survivors of the Holocaust recall memories and how they encode their personal and collective experience of the traumatic events. Women internees who were forced to identify themselves as numbers were traumatized by the imposition of an anonymity that erased their selves. Kadar examines recipes written during the women's internment to illustrate how food texts allowed inmates to recall the flavour of home, fulfil the longing for food, and satisfy the psychological need for familiarity and comfort.

Like Kadar, I question the significance of origins and posit the dismantling of borders and boundaries that enclose identities and heritages. I approach this topic by invoking the symbols of gems and jewels in museums in Britain, North America, and the Middle East. Gems and jewels encode the cultural and political heritage of diasporic populations and satisfy their nostalgia and longing to know and be in touch with their ancestral history. Such symbols of their cultural past enhance the self-esteem and pride of communities that have been eroded by experiences of racism.

Feminists' 'alternate archives' give us access to the everyday lives of women. These archives supplement academic methodologies such as oral histories, interviews, and ethnographic studies. Together, these methods and various forms of evidence shatter anonymity and create a better understanding of what internments, migrations, escapes from danger and violence, and refugee status really mean. The contributors to this volume use various methodologies to document the diasporic experiences of the Eritrean, Iranian, South Asian, Chinese, Trinidadian,

and Japanese peoples. Memories of exclusion shadow their lives and
thwart their feelings of being at home in the diaspora.

As a child, I cared little for my grandmother's and aunts' comments
that pointed out the striking similarity between my mother's facial
features and my own. I did not dwell upon the connection (other than
that of biology) between the woman who gazed sombrely and sternly
out of the photograph, and me. I did not think about my mother as a
woman or ponder her life and circumstances because they seemed to
have no bearing on me at the time. Yet the details of the portrait are
indelibly etched in my mind: she is wearing a sari with a small print on
it, the folds of the garment neatly drawn together over one shoulder
where a gold pin holds it in place. Her hair is pulled back, emphasizing
her stern and unsmiling expression. Now, as a feminist historian who
lives in Canada, I interpret the picture somewhat differently: I attribute
the unsmiling and stern expression on my mother's face to the fact that
she is in a studio and is being portrayed through the lens of a male
photographer. He sees a mother and a housewife and portrays her in
that sombre and somewhat dull mode.

My maternal grandmother's memories of my mother recall a cheerful, confident woman who always had a smile hovering around her lips
and was a loving daughter and a dutiful mother. My brother, who was
my mother's favourite child, strongly disputes my resemblance to my
mother. He asserts authoritatively that he has vivid memories of her,
and that these are more reliable guides to who she was. According to
him, I do not have her sweet temperament and lack the cooking and
sewing talents for which she was well known. My father tells me stories
of my mother that highlight her graciousness, diligence, and modesty
because these are the qualities he wishes me to emulate. My maternal
aunts remember my mother as a feisty and courageous woman who
encouraged them to transgress the boundaries of custom and convention. The memories of others generate images for me that give me
access to my past and history, but I do not try to distil the essence of my
mother through them or try to discern who speaks the truth about her.

Memory is an act of remembering that can create new understandings of both the past and the present. Memories are an active process
by which meaning is created; they are not mere depositories of fact
(Giles 2002, 22). Gayle Greene argues that women writers turn to the
past as a means of effecting change in the present, not for reasons of
nostalgia, which she defines as a form of escape from an unsatisfactory present into an idealized past. She distinguishes between *nostal-*

gia, which she sees as static, and *remembering*, which is a more radical and transformative activity:

> Whereas 'nostalgia' is the desire to return home, 'to remember' is 'to bring to mind' or 'think of again,' 'to be mindful of,' 'to recollect.' Both 'remembering' and 're-collecting,' suggest a connecting, assembling, a bringing together of things in relation to one another ...
>
> Memory may look back in order to move forward and transform disabling fictions to enabling fictions, altering our relation to the present and future. (Cited in McDermott, 2002, 391)

But McDermott (2002) argues that it is impossible to maintain this distinction and indeed it may be unnecessary to do so because nostalgia is a necessary ingredient of memory work. 'When we long for the past, we long for what might have been as well as what was; it is only by incorporating such longing into our narratives that we can suspend the past and ultimately change its meanings in the present' (405–406). Sugiman in this volume reviews the discussion on nostalgia and its relation to memory and history. In her research she found that 'the nostalgic memories expressed by many Nisei women have helped to shape a "secure identity" and to build a "positive image of the self" in both the past and the present.' Memories are constantly made and remade as people try to make sense of the past.

My father, who had more or less retired by the time I was a teenager, often read in his room while sitting in an armchair that directly faced the portrait. As a teenager, I would stamp into his room, stand beneath the portrait of my mother, thus facing him directly, and defiantly assert myself over some trivial grievance I had unearthed. (My physical location was not deliberate or chosen but a mere consequence of the layout of the room.) Perhaps my demeanour or voice evoked memories in my father that made him say quietly to himself, 'She is so much like her mother,' or 'She is not at all like her mother.' When he gazed at her and me, while he was listening to my complaints about his rules, did my mother's silent presence in the room have a role in his negotiations with me? Did he speak for both of them or only for himself? Did the values and norms of our linguistic community in Quetta mediate our interactions and relationship? As a young adult, I resisted the embrace of my father's enveloping memories, asserting instead my desire to define who I was in the present and what I would become in the future.

Memories are not stable and static but fluid and temporal. Toni Morrison (1990) compares memory to water, and notes: 'All water has a perfect memory and is forever trying to get back to where it was. Writers are like that: remembering where we were, what valley we ran through, what the [river] banks were like, the light that was there and the route back to our original place. It is emotional memory – what the nerves and the skin remember as well as how it appeared. And a rush of imagination is our "flooding"' (305). Memories ignite our imaginations and enable us to vividly recreate our recollections of home as a haven filled with nostalgia, longing, and desire; or they compel us, as witnesses and co-witnesses, to construct home as a site and space of vulnerability, danger, and violent trauma. Memories can be nostalgically evocative of imaginary homelands and places of birth and origins as well as an antidote to the struggles of the present. Others who had wounds of memory inflicted on them consequent to horrific dislocations and dispossessions may find travels to the past an involuntary, albeit necessary, journey to come to terms with their present selves.

Kadar notes that 'remembrances of traumatic experiences of the Holocaust have proliferated at the end of the twentieth century, when both wounded speakers and the witnesses seem better able to hear the stories.' Like Kadar, Sugiman in this volume examines memories that are 'surrounded by an emotional aura that makes them memorable.' Sugiman, who is Sansei (third generation), writes about the government internment of Japanese Canadians in camps during the Second World War, and of their subsequent experiences of re-establishing homes and families in different parts of Canada. She comments: 'Though many decades have since gone by, Japanese Canadians continue to live with the injustices and indignities of the past. In response to this act of violence, for years the Nisei (second generation), attempted to filter the painful memories of their internment – by not writing about their stories nor verbally articulating their experiences as part of a public discourse.' Yet their children continue to feel 'haunted' by their 'racial erasure' from history, and it took Sugiman years to 'feel prepared to contemplate and publicly present the past, a past in which [she is] centrally situated.'

Technologies of communication and transportation were not well developed in the early to mid-twentieth century, particularly when my parents became refugees in India. The unavailability of cheap air travel and inexpensive telephone calls, together with the absence of e-mail, constrained their travels away from home and their communications in more than one way. As young adults, they had absorbed the nationalist rhetoric of Indian politicians that defined a nation by its territory and geopolitical boundaries, and accepted as necessary the need to distinguish insiders from outsiders and citizens from non-citizens (for example, Indians from Pakistanis). Besides, citizenship was permanent, stable, and rooted in one nation.

Japanese migrants in the early to mid-twentieth century who lived in Canada were constrained in similar ways and had to settle and adapt to life here without regular contact with their home country and the way of life there. Trips back and forth between Canada and Japan only became common later in the century. These migrants confronted the dilemma of defining who they were and with whom they belonged while experiencing exclusion, racism, and ghettoization. The migrant's self-perceptions and self-definitions were never simply a matter of individual choice and volition; rather, their consciousness was affected by political acts and the behaviour of many white Canadians. Sugiman documents the boundary of racism that encircled Japanese Canadians who had made their homes in British Columbia, and defined them as outsiders, foreigners, and aliens. She analyses memories of the first and second generation that are encoded in stories, letters, and pictures that narrate genealogy and history and tell us from a post-colonial feminist perspective who we, as Canadians, are as a people and a nation.

In the late twentieth century, the speed and frequency of travel and communication transformed the perception and understanding of people living in both original communities as well as in homes in the diaspora. Salman Rushdie (2002) writes that 'the journey creates us' and 'we become the frontiers we cross' (350). The narrowing of physical distances enables migrants to maintain social, economic, and political ties more easily with their countries of origin and with groups sharing similar identities who live elsewhere. The contributors to this volume discuss displacement, cultural hybridity, transnational connections, and 'home,' all within the context of the idea of the 'diaspora.' The contributors articulate, for the group they are discussing, their sense of coming from communities with historical roots and destinies outside as well as inside of the time and space of the settlement society.

Globalization challenges our identities and the social organization of groups and communities. The essentialism and reductionism imputed to groups of people in earlier studies of ethnicity and race have been widely challenged, most notably by Stuart Hall and Paul Gilroy. Gilroy's (1993) writings have been particularly influential in disputing the essentialism encoded in black identities, and he argues instead for the need to conceptualize identities that are locally situated, contingent, and indeterminate. Appadurai (1996) argues that cultures, identities, selves, and traditions change with movement and travel. He has developed the concepts of 'Ethnoscapes, ideoscapes, and mediascapes' to show how media and travel fuel our imagination in the practice of our everyday lives, and he argues our identities, localities, and communities are shaped by travel and images projected by the media. 'The story of mass migration (voluntary and forced) is hardly a new feature of human history. But when it is juxtaposed with the rapid flow of mass-mediated images, scripts, and sensations, we have a new order of instability in the production of modern subjectivities' (4).

Identities are socially constructed, contingent on time, place, and social context, and are therefore fluid and unstable. Defining diasporic identities is complex, and scholars frequently use the term *hybridity* to discuss what is neither indigenous nor exogenous (Code 2000, 260). Hybridity, for Bhabha, comes through constant change and adaptation, and from being marginalized. He would have us all move to hybridity: 'The representation of difference must not be hastily read as the reflection of pre-given ethnic or cultural traits set in the fixed tablet of tradition. The social articulation of difference from the minority perspective is a complex, ongoing negotiation that seeks to authorize cultural *hybridities* that emerge in moments of historical transformations' (cited in Jussawalla 1997, 29). Some scholars, particularly in cultural studies, celebrate hybridity, cultural border crossing, and the production of difference (Ong 1999, 13). Grewal and Caplan (1997) are more sceptical and argue that hybridity 'remains enmeshed in the gaze of the West; Westerners see themselves alone as the ones that sort, differentiate, travel among, and become attached or attracted to the communities constituted by diasporas of human beings … Western culture continues to acknowledge difference primarily by differentiating the "exotic" from the "domestic"' (7).

Not all facets of hybrid identities are equal and symmetrical; rather, they are uneven because they stem from histories that transcend individual intentionality. Thus, the production and representation of the self as a subject in the post-colonial era can be a laborious process that involves taking an inventory of the many facets of gender, race, class, and other socially significant criteria embedded and encoded in one's identity. Although a hybrid identity can be an 'intransitive and immanent sense of *jouissance*,' yet for the postcolonial subject it can often also be an expression of extreme pain and dislocation (Radhakrishnan 1996, 158–159).

Hybridity raises questions about voice, representation, and perspective. For example, I am a refugee from Pakistan, was socialized and grew up in Bombay, came to Canada as an immigrant graduate student, and have lived here since then. Who do I speak for, who do I represent, and where is my home? Moghissi is a refugee from Iran who has lived in Canada since the early 1980s. Does she speak as a Muslim, an Iranian, or as a Canadian woman? If her identity is hybrid, then do her gender, race, and religion play an equal role in her voice and perspective? To what extent do the history and understanding of Islam, particularly in the post 9/11 era, determine her voice and identify her in particular ways? Dunlop came to Canada from India as a young child and grew up in Montreal. In whose voice does she speak? Sugiman is a third-generation Japanese Canadian. Whom does she represent? It may be that the 'diasporic/ethnic location is a "ghostly" location where the political unreality of one's present home is to be surpassed only by the ontological unreality of one's place of origin. This location is also one of painful, incommensurable simultaneity ... that promises neither transcendence nor return' (Radhakrishnan 1996, 175).

'Diaspora consciousness lives loss and hope as a defining tension' (Clifford 1994, 312). Diasporas construct racialized, sexualized, gendered, and oppositional subjectivities, and shape the cosmopolitan intellectual commitment of scholars. Shirley Goek-Lin Lim maintains that the 'contemporary immigrant author' explores, exudes, and perhaps even celebrates a 'bifurcated (though not hybrid) identity.' She writes about the ambiguity that is an inherent aspect of the diasporic experience:

> The immigrant and minority writer who is identified as such is immediately suspicious as to the intentions of that identification. The historical fact of foreign birth, once it is in your hands, can be used for all kinds of purposes ... This knowledge of my other origin allows you to deny me entry into your society on your terms, brands me as an exotic, freezes me in a geographical mythology.
>
> Yet I am proud of my origin. Should you proceed to treat me as if I were not different, as if my historical origin has not given to me a unique destiny and character, I would also accuse you of provincialism, of inability to distinguish between cultures. (Cited in Kain 1997, 8)

The diasporic individual often has a double consciousness, a privileged knowledge and perspective that is consonant with postmodernity and globalization. The dual or paradoxical nature of diasporic consciousness is one that is caught between 'here' and 'there,' or between those who share roots, and is shaped through multilocality. The consciousness and identity of diasporic individuals may focus on their attachment to the symbols of their ethnicity, and they may continue to feel emotionally invested in the 'homeland.' Yet such attachments and sentiments are experienced simultaneously with their involvement and participation in the social, economic, cultural, and political allegiances to their homes in the diaspora. The widespread use and availability of cyberspace and e-mails can further intensify ties, reinforce sentiments, and create differences in consciousness and identity. Thus, diasporas produce multiple consciousness, histories, and identities that generate difference and challenge homogeneity, as Dunlop, James, and I document. Indeed, all contributors to this volume speak from this double consciousness in order to address questions related to deterritorialized identities, gender, class, racism, ethnic origins, and home.

Racism affects our consciousness of ourselves and mediates our continuing attachment to the symbols of our cultural and ethnic heritage. Rushdie (2002) notes:

> The migrant, severed from his roots, often transplanted into a new language, always obliged to learn the ways of a new community, is forced to confront the great question of change and adaptation; but many migrants faced with the sheer existential difficulty of making such changes, and also, often, with the sheer alienness and defensive hostility of the peoples among whom they find themselves, retreat from such questions behind the walls of the old culture they have both brought along and left behind. The running man, rejected by those people who have built great walls to keep him out, leaps into a confining stockade of his own. (356)

In Britain, where 'hybridity is not allowed,' racism has provided the impetus for some diasporic individuals to maintain ties with their homelands, and has encouraged them to 'express their quintessential selves that are rooted in their ethnicities' (Jussawalla 1997, 30).

The experience of loss, marginality, displacement, and exile is intensified through the experience of racism, and adds to the ambiguity that the diaspora generates in individuals. In this volume, James argues that black youth experience racism that makes them feel ambivalent about their lives in Canada and reinforces their attachment to Trinidad as home. Nevertheless, diasporic individuals have skills of survival and find strength within family and community that enable them not only to survive but also to grow, develop, and realize their human potential, as Kadar, Sugiman, Matsuoka, Sorenson, Sakamoto, Zhou, and James document.

Scholars such as Matsuoka and Sorenson use the imagery of ghosts and shadows to discuss the experiences of individuals who were born in one country and live in another. The emotional ambiguity that long periods of residence in Western countries generated in colonized subjects was articulated by Jawaharlal Nehru (1936) in his autobiography. He writes: 'I have become a queer mixture of the East and West, out of place everywhere, at home nowhere. Perhaps my thought and approach to life are more akin to what is called Western than Eastern, but India clings to me ... I am a stranger and alien in the West. I cannot be of it. But in my own country too sometimes I have an exile's feeling' (596).

In contemporary Canada, theoretically at least, there is no social or political compulsion for individuals who were born elsewhere, or for their descendants, to choose to name a nation, state, or territory as home. Yet, the idea of home continues to beguile scholars who write about the diaspora, particularly from the postcolonial perspective. The various contributors to this volume reflect upon or evoke the idea and imagery of home, asking where it is and what it means in their discussions. Homes are made of brick and mortar; that is, they are a physical reality. Yet, they can also be part of our imagination and longing to belong and to be 'at home.' Kain (1997) notes that the diasporic individual lives in a home, but is torn by the need to make it authentic and real.

The flexibility in defining what is home and its location is associated with self and with community identities that are deterritorialized or constructed across borders and boundaries of phenomena such as race, ethnicity, nationality, and citizenship. One can, hypothetically, freely choose and name one's home. Recently, a black student approached me after a lecture on immigrant women. She said her mother was born in Trinidad and had come to live in Toronto. 'I was born here,' she said, and 'I have never had the occasion to go to Trinidad,' yet she noted that she often refers to it as 'home' and uses the term 'back home' in her conversations. Her mother corrects her and says, 'What "home" you are talking of, girl? You were born in Canada!'

But the words of Faiz Ahmed, an Urdu poet, may resonate for other diasporic individuals:

> You ask me about that country whose details now escape me,
> I don't remember its geography, nothing of its history,
> And should I visit it in memory,
> It would be as a past lover,
> After years, for a night, no longer restless with passion, with no fear of
>   regret.
> I have reached that age when one visits the heart merely as a courtesy.
>
> (Cited in Rushdie 2002, 372)

Yet other diasporic individuals may feel constantly torn between 'here' and 'there,' between their countries of origin and their countries of residence. Rushdie (1996) describes their dilemma in these words:

> But I, too, have ropes around my neck, I have them to this day, pulling me this way and that, East and West, the nooses tightening, commanding, *choose, choose.*
>
> I buck, I snort, I whinny, I rear, I kick. Ropes, I do not choose between you. Lassoes, lariats, I choose neither of you, and both. Do you hear? I refuse to choose. (211)

This volume presents a rich and diverse array of essays, empirical studies, and memoirs that contribute to the nuanced development of theories of diaspora, subjectivity, double-consciousness, gender and class experiences, and the nature of home. They, we hope, will help readers to further understand the movements of people and cultures in the early part of the twenty-first century, when physical, social, and mental borders and boundaries are being challenged and sometimes successfully dismantled.

REFERENCES

Anthias, Floya. 1998. Evaluating 'Diaspora': Beyond Ethnicity. *Sociology* 32(3): 557–581.
Appadurai, Arjun. 1996. *Modernity at Large: Cultural Dimensions of Globalization.* Minneapolis: University of Minnesota Press.
Clifford, James. 1994. Diasporas. *Cultural Anthropology* 9(3): 302–338.

Code, Lorraine, ed. 2000. *Encyclopedia of Feminist Theories*. London: Routledge.

Giles, Judy. 2002. Narratives of Gender, Class, and Modernity in Women's Memories of Mid-Twentieth-Century Britain. *Signs: Journal of Women in Culture and Society* 28(1): 21–41.

Gilroy, Paul. 1993. *The Black Atlantic*. London: Verso.

Grewal, Inderpal, and Caren Kaplan, eds. 1997. *Scattered Hegemonies: Postmodernity and Transnational Feminist Practices*. Minneapolis: University of Minnesota Press.

Hawley, John. 1997. Gus Lee, Chang-Rae Lee, and Li-Young Lee: The Search for the Father in Asian American Literature. In *Ideas of Home: Literature of Asian Migration*, ed. Geoffrey Kain, 183–196. East Lansing: Michigan State University Press.

Hirsch, Marianne, and Valerie Smith. 2002. Feminism and Cultural Memory: An Introduction. *Signs: Journal of Women in Culture and Society*, 28(1): 1–19.

Jussawalla, Feroza. 1997. South Asian Diaspora Writers in Britain: 'Home' versus 'Hybridity.' In *Ideas of Home: Literature of Asian Migration*, ed. Geoffrey Kain, 17–38. East Lansing: Michigan State University Press.

Kain, Geoffrey, ed. 1997. *Ideas of Home: Literature of Asian Migration*. East Lansing: Michigan State University Press.

Levitt, Peggy and Mary Waters, eds. 2002. *The Changing Face of Home: The Transnational Lives of the Second Generation*. New York: Russel Sage Foundation.

McDermott, Sinead. 2002. Memory, Nostalgia, and Gender in *A Thousand Acres*. *Signs: Journal of Women in Culture and Society* 28(1): 389–407.

Morrison, Toni. 1990. The Site of Memory. In *Out There: Marginalization and Contemporary Culture*, ed. Russell Ferguson, 299–305. Cambridge: MIT Press.

Ong, Aihwa. 1999. *Flexible Citizenship: The Cultural Logics of Transnationality*. Durham, NC: Duke University Press.

Radhakrishnan, R. 1996. *Diasporic Mediations: Between Home and Locations*. Minneapolis: University of Minnesota Press.

Rushdie, Salman. 1996. *East, West*. Toronto: Vintage.

– 2002. *Step Across This Line: Collected Non-fiction 1992–2002*. Toronto: Knopf.

Vertovec, Steven. 1997. Three Meanings of 'Diaspora,' Exemplified among South Asian Religions. *Diaspora* 6(3): 277–299.

PART 1

Diaspora and Memory

The concept of the diaspora has been widely adopted in academic discourses on forced dispersal, immigration, displacement, and the establishment of reconfigured transnational communities. Memories are the glue that holds the past and present together. They give shape and texture to women's subjectivity, to identities that are fragmented by immigration, displacement, and diasporic living. The past resonates in women's hearts and is reflected in the journeys they have chosen to undertake with hope but also trepidation, mindful of dangers but determined to be courageous. In crossing borders and boundaries, they imagined and then re-imagined their homes and bonded with those they had previously thought of as strangers in order to form new communities. Many pursued their dreams and were caught by surprise when they blossomed in new and different ways.

In chapter 1, 'Language Matters,' I discuss the difficulties encountered by women who do not speak English in Canada, and document them through historical and literary evidence interlaced with personal memories. My discussion of South Asian women contests the homogenization and generalizations that are routinely made of ethnic groups, and shows their diversity with particular reference to the ability to speak English. Colonization of South Asia gave some of its population the privilege of an English-language education, but its undertow was to alienate them from their own culture. Thus, although people come from the same country, their identities are constructed by their knowledge of English, along with history, religion, social class, and regional affiliations.

The South Asian diasporic communities participate in the common culture of Bollywood movies that titillate their imaginations with fantasies of the 'good life,' defined primarily by the consumption of material goods. These images are interpreted with specificity, particularity in local settings, networks, and family relationships that indirectly reinforce fantasies of the affluent West. The hope and excitement of beginning a new chapter in life mitigates the pain of leaving behind the known and the familiar home and homeland. The privileges and the disadvantages encountered 'at home' are transplanted in Canada, stratifying the women in new and different ways. Racial stereotypes prevalent in Canada focus attention on the language, dress, and cultural norms of South Asians and disregard the many talents that these women may have. Sometimes immigrants are successful in realizing their dream of a better standard of living, yet, like many of their compatriots, they feel nostalgic for their cultural and linguistic homes.

Immigrating to a new country and a different culture means crossing frontiers and borders that can intimidate, but, as Rushdie notes, it also allows for possibilities of personal and intellectual growth that shapes the character and tests the mettle. English-language classes are a microcosm of a new culture. The women sit quietly and repeat with great determination words that twist their tongues in new and foreign ways. This, too, is an act of courage.

Memories of the marginalized and subjugated illuminate the past in ways that contest hegemonic memories and raise the question of who remembers, why they remember, and what they remember. Pamela Sugiman's 'Memories of Internment: Narrating Japanese-Canadian Women's Life Stories,' in chapter 2, bridges the dichotomy between historical truth and personal recollection by exploring the sociological concept of memory. Accounts based on memories are mediated by the researchers who bring their personal needs, anger, disillusionment, and moral imperatives to their writings. Sugiman, who is a Sansei, or third-generation Japanese-Canadian woman, has two goals for her essay. First, she addresses the theme of the silence of the past, historically and personally, by moving from a literal silence, an 'unspoken bonding' based on a shared experience, to 'outspoken activity.' Such activity can take the form of the preservation of stories, as, for example, through the movement that sought redress for the internment of Japanese Canadians during the war. Significantly, however, participation in this activity had the unintended effect of legitimizing this group's personal and collective pain. Second, Sugiman explores the selectiveness of memory, its diverse forms and functions, and its shifts and changes within time and social context.

Letters and personal accounts show how memory is encoded in cultural history and artefacts, and how individually experienced activity fuses personal biography with history. Drawing on thirty oral testimonies of Nisei, or second-generation Japanese-Canadian women, they explore the diverse and often complex ways in which Nisei women remember the internment, giving particular attention to the intermingling of past and present; the relationship between narrator and listener; and the layering of personal and public narratives, in the construction of these memories. The themes of silence and telling one's story are also explored, with the understanding that the decision to communicate what one remembers is always a political act.

Marlene Kadar's 'Wounding Events and the Limits of Autobiography,' in chapter 3, explores the relationship between genre and the representation of the personal lives of women and girls who have lived through the traumatic experience of the Holocaust. In order to remember and witness deeply wounding events, Kadar believes the conventional constraints of autobiography must be resisted and even overturned. Sometimes a minimal narrative, such as a recipe or a camp physician's surgical note or list, is the only textual remnant of a life that was lived in a particularly horrific circumstance. To allow these deeply wounding events to be remembered, we need to see how far we can push the limits of the autobiographical genre. Some theorists may resist the further dilution of the laws of genre (Derrida's phrase still holds), whereas others are interested in claiming new autobiographical forms as legitimate genres.

What Kadar finds most interesting is how life writing forms are changed by specific historical circumstances and not how well they represent their subjects according to an erudite measure of adequacy of some kind. 'Measuring up' too often results in the determination that a piece of writing has failed, and thus another significant story is erased. If we are obliged to focus on this question of value, we continue in a vicious circle of genre criticism that restricts our imaginative apprehension of the subject of our study: the individual's life as it is represented during a time of anguish, sorrow, and wandering – in other words, already in a state that is likely to delimit free or public expression.

1 Language Matters

VIJAY AGNEW

Imagine a fall day in Toronto. Let me help you, in case you've never been here. Multicoloured leaves in red, yellow, brown mixed with some green lie on the roads, but as cars drive by they scatter, some flying high into the air while others, entangled in a mass, rise slowly and soon fall to lie in a heap by the wayside. Long-time residents of Toronto would describe the weather for this day as warm and pleasant, but for me – an immigrant from India – it is cold. I am bundled up in a black woollen coat, with socks and shoes, ready to hop into my car. I drive through wide boulevards laid out in a grid while listening to classical Western music on my radio. But somewhere, deep in my heart, lurks a nostalgia for loud film music, pedestrians, vendors, and the noise, soot, and dust of Mumbai (formerly Bombay), rather than these clean, quiet, and well-marked Toronto roads.

I reach a church, one of many such churches that dot residential neighbourhoods in Toronto, and carefully scrutinize its exterior to get my bearings. I see a side entrance with a poster stuck on the door and walk with deliberate steps towards it, and it directs me to the English as a Second Language (ESL) class that I have come to observe. The class is being held in the basement in a room that is large, simple, and functional; there are no pictures, decorations, or plants. In the centre of the room about thirty chairs are lined up in rows, and a flip chart with a chair for the teacher next to it faces the students. On a table against the wall sit an aluminum coffee urn, milk, sugar, styrofoam cups, and a plate of cookies.

A grass-roots community-based organization of South Asians[1] has brought together about twenty-five new immigrants for an introductory class in the English language. The women are wearing *salwar kamiz*,[2] or saris, the dress of South Asians, but in this basement in Toronto they present a curious amalgamation of the needs of the present and the norms of the past. In the tropical heat and dust of South Asia, the salwar kamiz that are worn during the day are made of light cotton fabric and are comfortable to wear and easy to maintain. Usually women wear sandals with them. In Toronto, it is cold, and thus the women are also wearing colour-coordinated heavy cardigans over their salwar kamiz. They're also wearing shoes with socks.

The women's dress marks them as immigrants and newcomers. To my South Asian eyes, this mixture of East and West – light textures with heavy sweaters – represents a curious hodgepodge of styles. But perhaps other white Canadians who are unfamiliar with South Asian dress see the outfits not as an attempt by the women to accommodate themselves to the weather but as foreign and different. After having lived in Canada and studied immigrants for about twenty years, I still have ambivalent feelings about such clothing, and am uncertain what South Asian women would ideally wear in Toronto, and, more generally, in Canada. Sometimes I think these women ought to retain their traditional dress as a symbol of their cultural identity, but at other times I want them to discard their salwar kamiz and adopt pants and jeans and be done with it.

I am jostled by memories that remind me that in the present, as opposed to the past, the ideal is for a multicultural Canada, and that Canadians do not wish to impose any one kind of clothing on the women. Immigrants are free to choose – or so it is said. Sombrely, I wonder how the women are responding to the impolite stares and frowns from some people in public places, people silently expressing disapproval of their dress. Perhaps such stares make the women uncomfortable, and they begin to think about wearing jeans and pants so that they will not, so obviously, attract attention to themselves. But perhaps their lack of confidence and insecurity in their new environment makes them content with the small adjustments in their dress that they must make. Perhaps family norms and religious precepts make them reluctant to adopt new ways of dressing. I hope the women are warm. Their demeanour suggests that they are feeling uncertain, awkward, and ill at ease.

A palpable sense of anxious anticipation fills the room. All of us, with the exception of the teacher, are South Asian. The South Asian counsellor from the area's community organization gives me a brief rundown on the identities of the women present and introduces me to the teacher,

Jane, as a professor who is collecting material for a book on immigrant women in Canada. I talk to Jane, who is dark-haired, fair-skinned, and middle-aged, but my eyes roam restlessly among the other women hoping to make eye contact with them. The women, however, avoid looking in our direction and no one responds by looking or smiling back at me. The women seem to be taking a bit more interest in each other, and some have started making conversation with the person seated next to them, but most are quiet as they wait for the class to begin. The counsellor encourages the women to get themselves some coffee, and, although the women glance toward the table, none gets up. I had expected that the contrast between the larger, culturally alien Canadian environment and the people who look like oneself, despite their social differences, might create a sense of immediate comfort and familiarity. Yet the usual hesitancy and reserve among people who are strangers to one another are still present.

This is the first class in the program of introductory conversational English that is funded by the government as part of its settlement service to new immigrants. Attending the program is free (COSTI 2004). The class is being held in Scarborough, where a large proportion of immigrants from South Asia have settled. In the 1990s, most South Asian immigrants came from India, Sri Lanka, Bangladesh, and Pakistan, and a large proportion of Punjabis from India and Tamils from Sri Lanka settled in Scarborough. Most were economic migrants, like their predecessors throughout Canadian history, while a small proportion were refugees from Sri Lanka escaping ethnic and religious violence there. Judging from the appearances of the women, their style of dress and ornamentation, I would say the class reflects this population mix.

Before long, Jane moves to the front of the class to begin the day's lesson in conversational English, and I walk to the side of the room in the hope of catching the expressions on the women's faces, but otherwise wish to be forgotten by them. Jane tries to put the women at ease by smiling broadly, but their body language reveals their tension as they gaze anxiously at her and focus entirely on what she is about to say and do. Jane tells them slowly and in carefully enunciated English that she has two goals for the class: first, to teach them how to ask a bus driver for directions, and how to tell him or her where they wish to get off; and, second, how to buy a coffee and ask for milk and sugar in it. Jane breaks down the tasks into small segments, providing the words that go with each, and interjecting jokes that the women sometimes respond to with nervous smiles.

Jane asks the women to introduce themselves to the class and to say where they are from. She smiles encouragingly, and the women, who seem terrified, mumble softly, 'My name is Harjeet, Ludhiana, Punjab,' or 'My name is Santosh, Jullunder, India,' or 'Shahnaz, Karachi, Pakistan,' or 'Swarna, Colombo, Sri Lanka,' and so on. The names and places are familiar to me, and they give me clues about the women's regional, religious, and linguistic identities. I follow the women with my eyes as each one introduces herself, and, almost reflexively, I find myself fleshing out a picture of each by mentally adding other details of her social background and identity.

Canadian immigration criteria in the post-Second World War period favoured those South Asians who were upper or middle class. The 1967 immigration policy, which laid the framework for later developments, required immigrants, among other things, to have a certain level of education, knowledge of English or French, and job-related skills, and to be in a profession or occupation that was in demand in Canada (Li 2003, 14–37). Only those with substantial economic, social, and psychological resources were motivated to take on the risks of emigrating and had the financial resources to go through the process of applying for immigration to Canada and leaving their homes.

The ability to immigrate to a new country is a privilege for a few and is vied for and envied by others in South Asia. Although the criteria are weighed heavily in favour of the upper and middle classes, other ideals embedded in immigration policies – such as 'family reunification' and 'humanitarian and compassionate grounds' – vary the picture. A landed immigrant has the right to then sponsor his dependent relatives – his wife and children, for example.[3] The wife, once she too becomes a landed immigrant, can, like her spouse, sponsor parents and siblings under a certain age. Dependent and sponsored relatives are usually referred to as 'family class' immigrants (Li 2003, 14–27). In addition to immigrants, refugees have come from Sri Lanka, though a very small percentage are from the Punjab. The Tamil women in the room are dependants of male refugee claimants, such as fathers, brothers, and husbands. These criteria have spawned a diversified South Asian population in Toronto: some are professional, English-speaking immigrants, while others have limited education and knowledge of English. Consequently, South Asian immigrants are found at both ends of the labour market (Basavarajappa and Jones 1999).

The immigration status of the individual is significant because it entitles her/him to an array of social services, such as this ESL class

(Boyd, DeVries, and Simkin 1994). Some systemic gender biases impact the availability of these social services and have been disputed by community-based organizations, which have lobbied government agencies to remove them. Government cutbacks in the 1990s meant that only those who were thought to be entering the labour market had access to advanced-level training in the English language, while others had recourse to training that would merely enable them to get by in Canadian society.

The age, clothes, and jewellery of some of the women in the class suggest that they are recent brides who have come to Canada consequent to an arranged marriage, while others are older and have come with their families. All the women present are part of the 'family class' of male immigrants, the sponsored dependent relatives of brothers and sisters already here. There are no senior citizens in the class, although they too would be eligible for free language training. The women may have several valuable job-related skills, but their lack of ability to speak English disadvantages them in locating good jobs. Besides, their social integration is impeded by their inability to speak English, and there is some danger of their becoming isolated and feeling alienated. Community groups, such as the one that organized this class, act as mediators between the women and the larger society, and they create venues for them to network with others of their own linguistic and regional communities (Agnew 1998).

All the South Asians in this ESL class had lived in multilingual environments 'back home.' The dominant national language in India is Hindi; in Pakistan it is Urdu; and in Sri Lanka it is Sinhala. There are innumerable regional languages in all these countries. For example, India has seventeen official languages recognized by its constitution; there are thirty-five languages spoken by more than a million people; and in addition there are 22,000 dialects. 'People write books and letters, make films, produce plays, print newspapers, talk, teach, preach, fight, make love, and dream in all those languages' (Kumar 2002, 7). In the class that day, only Hindi, Punjabi, and Tamil were represented.

Since many countries in South Asia were colonized, some European languages have been absorbed locally and have become part of their cultures as well. India, Pakistan, and Bangladesh share a common history of British colonization, and the English language is still used there in governmental institutions, in education, and, to a large extent, in politics as well. The Dutch colonized Sri Lanka, but since knowledge of English provides social and class mobility, it has been widely adopted.

In India, language has been a contested issue and there have been disagreements over the use of English, acceptance of Hindi as a national language, and the division of territory between states (Khilnani 1998, 175). The status of English vis-à-vis the local languages is further complicated because English is identified as the 'idiom of modernity,' and the 'proliferating, uncontainable vernaculars with the "natural" state of things in India' (Chaudhuri 2001, xx). Nevertheless, historically English is the language of the elite and the privileged in India, and continues at present to be a requisite for social and class mobility. Official counts peg the number of English-speaking people at 2 per cent, but others argue that a realistic estimate is closer to 15 per cent (Kumar 2002, 6).

As a young girl, I spoke Hindi, Derawali, and English, and could understand Punjabi, Sindhi, and Urdu. I gave no conscious thought to my knowledge of these different languages, and since many Indians are familiar with several languages I thought it to be unexceptional. In Toronto, when I was required to fill in forms at the university and identify the languages that I could read, write, or speak, I understood the question to pertain to European languages and thus left the space blank. Yet in one incident, a white Canadian professor was annoyed with me for not identifying the languages that she assumed correctly that I knew. Her words made me reflect on how I had unconsciously imbibed the biases of the larger Canadian society, how I had voluntarily declined to take or give credit to people like me for being bilingual and even trilingual. My action can be characterized as a telling example of internalized racism. The women in the ESL class were all bilingual and they knew their regional and national language – almost a necessity in South Asia – but were not conversant with English.

The social and cultural alienation that some Indian women experience in Canada is most easily explained by their inability to speak English. However, in documenting the experience of the women in this ESL class, I am attempting to show how race, class, and gender, along with an inability to speak English, constructs the identity of these women in Canada.

Identity, feminist theorists contend, is socially constructed and it changes with time, place, and context. The process of moving from one country to another and learning to get along in a new society changes the self-perception of immigrant women; however, their inability to speak English takes on significance that is quite unlike that which they had experienced in India. The self-perception of the women is at odds with the way white Canadians know and understand them. Social identity, however, is 'principally the identity which is recognized and confirmed by others'; consequently, it does not matter how strenuously 'individuals may disavow or evade it' (Andermahr, Lovell, and Wolkowitz 2000, 124). Social actions and interactions become meaningful, and although they can be interpreted, much like a text, in many different ways, yet they indicate to the individual 'how to go on,' and give them valuable clues about how to participate in the culture in which they are now living (249). Social actions and interactions thus affect the individual in immediate and tangible ways.

Ethnic groups have conventionally been constructed in ways that homogenize their experiences and erase the many distinctions, such as those of social class and gender, within them. There are commonalities of experience, no doubt, but at the same time there are vast differences that stem from the different identities. The social construction of an ethnic group may emphasize a particular aspect of its identity, such as language or religion (e.g., head scarf), which not only subsumes its other attributes but also blames the victims for the difficulties they encounter in integrating themselves with Canadian society. Yet, as postcolonial feminists argue, women have had to 'negotiate the precarious balance between the tenacious forces of integration and the desire to maintain a sense of their cultural identity as a strategy of self-preservation in their country of adoption' (Code 2000, 396).

Indian women, like other racialized women, experience racism when white Canadians encounter their 'difference' from the norm, whether it is skin colour, different clothing, or an inability to speak English. Everyday racism 'expresses itself in glances, gestures, forms of speech, and physical movements. Sometimes it is not even consciously experienced by its perpetrators, but it is immediately and painfully felt by its victims – the empty seat next to a person of colour, which is the last to be occupied in a crowded bus; the slight movement away from a person of colour in an elevator; the overattention to the black customer in the shop; the inability to make direct eye contact with a person of colour; the racist joke told at a meeting; and the ubiquitous question 'Where did you come from?' (Henry et al. 1995, 47).

Indian women's community-based organizations give the lie to the stereotype that constructs women from their group as passive. Community-based organizations lobby for and hold ESL classes for new immigrants from their communities despite constant threats of non-renewal of funds and government cutbacks (Agnew 1996; 1998). They wish to help individuals adjust to their new environment, and to lessen their cultural alienation by bringing them together in supportive environments such as an ESL class. Working-class, non-English-speaking women have the double burden of not speaking English and not having the language – words – to articulate their dissatisfaction with their marginality and oppression. Consequently, we may well ask, why do they come? I answer this question in the next section.

Imagination as a Social Practice

'I left them all and walked briskly towards the aeroplane, not looking back, looking only at my shadow before me, a dancing dwarf on the tarmac' (Naipaul 2003, 78). Naipaul's description of the first time he left Trinidad to study at Oxford catches the sense of hope and excitement that immigrants experience on leaving their homes to begin a new and different stage in their lives. The process of leaving home is difficult and painful, but at first it is mitigated by hopes, dreams, and fantasies of a new life in affluent Canada.

We often think of ourselves as unique individuals with distinct hopes and dreams, yet our imagination is profoundly influenced by the social context in which we live. The images that float in our minds germinate as a result of where we have been and what we have seen and read. Jawaharlal Nehru, in a letter to his daughter Indira Gandhi, writes:

> For many years now I have been traveling in these oceans of time and space ... It is a fascinating journey ... when the past and present get strangely mixed together and the future flits about like an insubstantial shadow, or some image seen in a dream. The real journey is of the mind; without that there is little significance in wandering about physically. It is because the mind is full of pictures and ideas and aspects of India that even the bare stones – and so much more our mountains and great rivers, and old monuments and ruins, and snatches of old song and ballad, and the way people look and smile, and the queer and significant phrases and metaphors they use – whisper of the past and the present and of the unending thread that unites them and leads us all into the future. When I have a chance ... I like to leave my mind fallow and receive all these impressions. So I try to understand and discover India and some glimpses of her come to me, tantalize me and vanish away. (Gandhi 1992, 121)

Imagination, writes Appadurai (1996), is a social practice that is central to all forms of agency, a key component of the new global order while the imaginary is a 'constructed landscape of collective aspirations' (31). Appadurai has developed the concepts of 'Ethnoscapes, ideascapes, and mediascapes' to show how media and travel fuel our imagination in the practice of our everyday lives, and he argues that our identities, localities, and communities are shaped by travel and images projected by the media: 'The story of mass migration (voluntary and forced) is hardly a new feature of human history. But when it is juxtaposed with the rapid flow of mass-mediated images, scripts and sensations, we have a new order of instability in the production of modern subjectivities' (4). Immigrants' urge to move from one country to another and their settlement in new societies are deeply affected by a mass-mediated imagination that transcends national space.

As an English-speaking woman who lived in Bombay in the 1960s before I immigrated to Canada in 1970, the way I imagined the West was stimulated by the English-language books and magazines that I read, the Hollywood films that I watched, and the music of Pat Boone and Elvis Presley that I heard. (There was no television in those days in India, and the use of personal computers and the Internet was still in the future – even in the West.) Then there were regular stories about America that came in letters from my English-speaking physician brother who worked in New York City. My dream of studying in North America and living away from my family was an unconscious product of the glamorous images that I consumed from the mass media and the ideas that I garnered from English-language books and magazines. In Canada, I began to re-imagine and reinvent myself, although I did so unknowingly.

The imagination and the subjectivity of the Hindi-, Punjabi-, Urdu-, Sinhala-, and Tamil-speaking women who were in the ESL class must certainly be different than mine because they had lived in India, Pakistan, and Sri Lanka during a different period and in different social and political contexts. By the 1990s, television had become a well-established medium of entertainment throughout South Asia among the middle classes, including those who lived in smaller towns and cities. In India, the number and range of programs in different languages (Hindi, English, and regional languages) continued to expand, and television regularly broadcasted English-language serials produced in the West. Television programs and advertising came to be supplemented, as time progressed, by the Internet and cyberspace, new ways to produce and distribute images that inflected the imagination of the people as well. Furthermore, globalization generated a much greater and more constant flow of ideas and goods between countries, and that had an impact on the subjectivities of the people and constructed their sense of self in comparative and relational terms.

Time and social context distinguished the women in the class from me, but their identities were also different from the contemporary English-speaking professional and the entrepreneurial South Asian transnational migrant. These latter migrants leave their countries in pursuit of education, travel, and employment, but they are mobile and may over time live in many different countries to take advantage of the available economic, educational, and social opportunities for themselves and their families (Ong 1999). A vast array of electronic and print images penetrate and inform their imaginations and identities, the possibilities that are available to them in the present, and what and who they might become in the future.

As a student in Delhi, Amitava Kumar was enamoured of the idea of becoming a writer in the West, and his fantasies of life in London were fed by a returning Indian student, a Rhodes scholar from Oxford:

> I imagined trips to libraries, museums, lectures, theatres, parks. I got a gift from him: a pack of postcards showing scenes of life at Oxford. Sunlight slanted across the narrow brick street; bicycles were propped against walls covered with ivy; cricket was being played on the immaculate greens ... Our visitor from London had come bearing other gifts too: shaving cream and disposable razors and duty-free cigarettes. Tepid tea with toast and omelette in the Hindu College canteen on winter mornings had never tasted so good before because awaiting me at the end of the meal were imported Silk Cuts that I had just received. The London that the Oxford man described seeped into the winter mornings and became a part of my dream ... I wanted to be there. (Kumar 2002, 81–82)

The enormous popularity of Hindi-language Bollywood films (i.e., the Indian film industry located primarily in Mumbai) makes them one of the most significant cultural forms in national and transnational South Asian cultural practices (Desai 2004, 35). Mumbai is named after a local deity, Mumbadevi, but 'the real propitiatory deity of the city is Lakshmi, the goddess of wealth. Bedecked in silk and jewels, standing on a lotus flower, a smile on her lips, gold coins spilling from her outstretched hand, pretty Lakshmi beckons her devotees. Glittering and glamorous, she holds out the promise of fortune but extracts cruel sacrifice from her worshippers even as she entices them' (Kamdar 2001, 131). Bollywood 'brings the global into the local presenting people in Main Street, Vancouver, as well as Southall, London, with shared "structures of feeling" that produce a transnational sense of communal solidarity' (Mishra 2002, 238).

Images and values propagated by Bollywood films and picked up in television and advertising filter into the imagination of people living in South Asia and the diaspora, creating thereby a 'community of sentiment' that begins to imagine and feel things together (Appadurai 1996, 8). These everyday cultural practices mean that although people have disparate social identities and live in different social contexts, yet because they engage with the same media and its images, they come to share, to some extent, a similar set of social values and norms. These images and values that pervade popular culture play a role in constructing the dreams and fantasies of people living in different locations (Desai 2004).

People in the movie industry, Mehta argues, are 'big dreamers' and their films give life to the 'collective dreams' of a billion people (Mehta 2004, 340). One message that is often highlighted in Hindi-language films and television is that the 'good life' comprises materialism and consumerism. The West is the epitome of consumerism, and the imagery associated with the West symbolizes wealth, influence, and power. Bollywood films have formulaic plots and elaborate song and dance routines that ask nothing more from the audience than they suspend their disbelief and enter a world of love and romance, wealth and power, and watch individuals who espouse ideal values emerge victorious (Kumar 2002, 30; Desai 2004). For example, a Bollywood movie may evoke fantasy and desire in audiences when they see the handsome and rich hero and his glamorously dressed heroine cavorting on the Swiss Alps. Such images, writes Appadurai (1996), become 'scripts for possible lives to be imbricated with the glamour of film stars and fantastic film plots' (3).

A conventional, if simple, binary distinction is between the materialistic West and spiritual India. (Another similar and not unrelated cliché identifies India as innocent and America as the den of evil.) Such categorizations are often evoked as an apologetic defence of India's poverty, and what can be termed its lack of development. Indians, writes Sunil Khilnani (1997), have over the last century come to 'see themselves in mirrors created by the West' (196). The Orientalist gaze of the Westerner defines India and Indians as the 'Others' (i.e., they use their own culture and society as the norm and define other cultures in comparative terms, perceiving them not only as different but also as inferior; Said, 1979).

Although it is discussed more rarely, India and other countries in

South Asia have also helped shape the self-images of other cultures. According to Khilnani (1997) Western cultures have

> recurringly used India as a foil to define their own historical moments: to reassure or to doubt themselves. And Indians have also, on occasion, tried to work out their own 'indigenous' ways of knowing the West. It is impossible to sever these twisted bonds of mutual knowingness and ignorance: the plunder is constant, and neither side can retreat into a luxurious hermeticism. Any discussion of India is thus inescapably forced on to the treacherous fields of the politics of knowledge. These must be navigated, like any political activity, by one's wits. There is no privileged compass, no method, or idiom that can assist. (197)

The middle classes in India, in the post-independence era, have abandoned their 'traditional moorings' in their avid pursuit of social and class mobility based on the consumption of material goods. Some argue that these goals result from a thoughtless imitation of Western values, particularly among the younger, middle-class generation. Conspicuous consumption has become necessary for enhancing the self-esteem of the individual. 'In a situation where things are difficult to get, and there are so many people around you defining their very existence by the ability to obtain them, the act of acquisition tends to disproportionately dominate the perception of self-esteem' (Varma 1998, 136). The materialistic goals of the middle classes can seem vacuous, debilitating, and immoral in a society where the vast majority of people are poor.

Images of a 'good life' at one level threaten to homogenize the values of South Asians living 'there' and 'here' – in South Asia and in the diaspora. Yet they are consumed and interpreted in local settings and in particular ways that resist standardization and universalism. Furthermore, interpretations of a 'good life' are relative and contextual; a 'good life' for a middle-class Punjabi immigrant in Scarborough may entail access to and the availability of goods and services and a standard of living that differs from a Punjabi woman living in Ludhiana or Jullunder.

Dreams of affluence and well-being mitigate the heartache of emigrating and leaving behind family, friends, and home. In the post-1967 period, individuals who migrated to Canada often had personal contacts that acted as magnets in a process described as chain migration. Once a family left a village, town, or city, they in turn encouraged friends and relatives to migrate as well, by spinning dreams for them of jobs, educational opportunities, and economic security. For example, working- and middle-class Punjabi immigrants living in Canada still write letters and send photographs to their relatives in Ludhiana and Jullunder that describe their lives in terms of the availability of a good education for the children, well-paid jobs for themselves, and the owner-ship of consumer household goods for the family. They also return home periodically, bearing gifts for friends and family. While at home, they tell their family and friends of owning houses and cars, and, since there is no norm in those societies concerning mortgages and consumer loans, it is imagined that these individuals have no debts. In comparison with the lives of middle-class people in cities like Ludhiana and Jullunder, return-ing migrants have discretionary incomes that enable them to consume goods and travel and reinforce the image of the affluent West.

Migrants who return for a visit with their extended families after having lived in the West, the Middle East, or the Far East have some social and economic cachet among the middle classes in South Asia. Furthermore, their children speak fluent English. Given the class and social prestige still associated with that language in South Asia, this accomplishment signals the family's social mobility and well-being. The women in the ESL class undoubtedly had hopes and dreams for themselves and their families when they emigrated. They dreamed of a 'good life' that was perhaps both different and similar to that of the other migrants. If not for the dreams, why would they dismantle their homes and think of rebuilding them elsewhere? Given the option of staying put or leaving, they made a choice according to their own limitations and potentials.

I wonder if the imaginations of the women in this ESL class ever carried them to this church basement where they are now sitting in an alien environment feeling anxious and nervous about learning English? I think not. The trials and tribulations of these new immigrants to Canada bring to mind my very different experiences with the language, despite being an English-speaking immigrant at the university. The words of Azar Nafisi (2004) resonate with me: 'Other people's sorrows and joys have a way of reminding us of our own; we partly empathize with them because we ask ourselves; What about me? What does that say about my life, my pains, my anguish?' (326).

English-Language Education in India

Memory is like the ebb and flow of tides. Imagine I am at a beach sitting on a colourful printed towel on which some sand has blown and accumulated over the last couple of hours. A can of cola lies by my side while my mind is absorbed by the book I am reading. Occasionally, I look up from its pages to glance pensively around or in front of me and watch the waves rise and roll gently into the sand. The waves have lulled me into a quiet, calm, and peaceful frame of mind. I am at one with my environment and am unaware that as the sun has gone down, the water has imperceptibly come closer to me, wetting me a little bit. Sometimes, however, the weather shifts suddenly and unexpectedly and I am awash in the strong waves that come crashing ashore. Memory is like that. Sitting amid South Asian women in the basement of the church in Toronto, I find myself suddenly flooded by memories of back home. I think about, reflect upon, and narrate the experiences of new immigrants, but in the process reinvent myself along with them.

I am a ten-year-old girl dressed in a blue cotton tunic with a white shirt, a navy blue tie, and a matching sash around my waist. On the left side of my tunic, I have pinned a green badge that identifies me as belonging to St Patrick's House at Presentation Convent School in Old Delhi. Daily, I walk to school or am driven there from my aunt's house with whom I have lived since my mother died when I was a toddler. My aunt is a wealthy widow and a devout Hindu. I am privileged, she tells me, to be going to school, especially one that teaches in the English language, for she had no such advantage when she was growing up.

My aunt's parents, and my grandparents, were well off. Nevertheless, in accordance with the prevalent gender norms in the early 1900s among many upper-class Hindu and Muslim families, she received little education and no instruction in English. She could, however, read and write in Hindi and was very familiar with Hindu religious epics like the *Ramayana* and the *Mahabharata*. My father, her brother, was educated in English, and he wanted me to become a 'modern' woman. Unlike the women in our linguistic community and region, he wanted me to have the benefits of an education in the English language. So, although we were a Hindu family, I was sent to a Catholic mission school for girls in pursuit of the dream of an English-language education for me.

Christian missionaries, primarily from Britain and the United States, are to be credited for pioneering the spread of female education in India (Chanana 1996). Social and cultural norms among Hindu, Muslim, Sikh, and other religious communities were a barrier to female education in India historically, and continue at the present time in a modified way to bedevil efforts to promote it widely (Dreze and Sen 1995, 114–116). The norm among upper- and middle-class families in many religious communities was to segregate women, which created the need for single-sex schools and female teachers. But few female Indian teachers were available in the past. The cultural practice of early, arranged marriages usually ended the education of most girls while they were still in grade school. The missionaries stepped in to fill the need by providing instruction for Indian girls and young women. Although the missionaries had the financial and professional resources to start schools in many locations in India, they were viewed with scepticism by the local elites, for it was widely believed that their primary interest in women was evangelical and proselytizing (Chanana 1996).

The work of these missionaries and their criticism of the low rates of literacy among women made Indian social reformers – in Punjab and Bengal, for example – work vigorously to change attitudes and cultural practices to enable women to continue with their education past elementary and high-school levels. In Punjab, the social reformers started schools for Hindu girls that taught them in Hindi and emphasized their own cultural traditions. In comparison, Christian missionary schools taught in the English language, instructed their students in the Bible and the Gospels, and required the reading of British classical literature. They used British and North American cultural norms in the everyday routines of the schools, and neglected, if not devalued, local conventions, traditions, and religions. Consequently, the threat of cultural alienation, which might result from an English-language education in a mission school, made families wary of sending their daughters to these schools.

As a child, my everyday life was compartmentalized. When I was at school, I accepted unquestioningly the nuns, the curriculum, and the church that dominated its premises. I recited Christian prayers at the start of school and before each class, and often my friends and I wandered into the church and unthinkingly repeated the rituals and gestures that we had seen the nuns perform. I read books written by the British and absorbed their ideas, but was hardly aware of the perspective of Indians about their history, politics, and culture. I brought home pictures of Jesus Christ tucked in my books. My aunt, ever vigilant to ensure my continued belief in Hinduism, gave me pictures of Hindu gods to save in my books alongside those of Jesus Christ. She read me stories from the *Ramayana* and *Mahabharata* to socialize me into the idealized Hindu values for females. As a child, I experienced no cultural conflict. Christianity was a religion, like Islam, Sikhism, and others, that was also a part of my everyday experience. I was conscious, however, of my privilege in speaking the English language, for it distinguished me from my cousins and from much of the larger population. It is only after I immigrated to Canada that I realized how much my English-language education had alienated me from knowledge of Indian history and culture.

The introduction of English education in India by the British colonial government had the well-articulated and widely acknowledged objective of training a cadre of bureaucrats for the administration (Brown 1994, 78–82). Such education was formulated in gender-neutral terms, but its intention was to focus on males. In 1835, in the infamous Minute of Education, Lord Thomas Macaulay enunciated the choice of adopting and spreading English-language education among the upper- and middle-classes: 'We must at present do our best to form a class who may be interpreters between us and the millions whom we govern; a class of persons, Indian in blood and colour, but English in taste, in opinions, in morals, and in intellect. To that class we may leave it to refine the vernacular dialects of the country, to enrich those dialects with terms of science borrowed from the Western nomenclature, and to render them by degrees fit for conveying knowledge to the great mass of the population' (Desai 2004, 11).

Throughout the nineteenth and twentieth century, the government founded schools and universities that taught in the English language, and upper- and middle-class Indian males eagerly flocked to them. The choice of English-language education was racist in its perception of Indian languages and literature, but the promise of the economic opportunities that it made possible attracted males to pursue it, regardless (Metcalf and Metcalf 2002, 82–88). The education of females, whether in English or local languages, lacked a clear utilitarian function, and governmental support for it stemmed from a liberal ideology of the advantages to be gained, by society generally and the family in particular, from the presence of knowledgeable wives, mothers, and good citizens. Sometimes cultural norms of sex segregation, however, led to the neglect of women's health because women were reluctant to be attended to by male physicians. This fact propelled the government to create single-sex, English-language medical colleges for women; for example, the Lady Dufferin Medical College for women in New Delhi.

The various initiatives by the colonial government, missionaries, and Indian social reformers laid the foundation of an educational system. After independence in 1947, the Indian government further added to these institutions by starting a vast array of colleges and universities in liberal arts and sciences, agriculture, medicine, engineering, business, and, lately, information technologies, in English as well as in local languages. Universities and colleges, however, are also quintessentially bastions of middle-class privilege (Varma 1998, 56). The urban middle classes have used their political clout with succeeding governments to persuade them to open additional institutes of higher learning, rather than focus their resources on primary education or on rural areas. The priorities of the Indian educational system are thus a reflection of the economic and social power of different groups in India. Some of the cultural barriers to female education persist, despite attempts to overcome them.

The overall rates of literacy in India are low, but there is a surplus of English-educated, well-trained, skilled workers. A comparison of China and India demonstrates some of the structural problems of India's educational establishment. In 1991 in China, the rates of literacy stood at 87 per cent for males and 68 per cent for females, while the comparative figure for India is 64 per cent for males and 39 per cent for females. But India sends six times as many people to universities and other higher educational establishments as does China, relative to its population.[4] Thus, there is a 'necessity of explicitly addressing the questions of both *ancient* and *modern* biases that shaped Indian educational policies' (Dreze and Sen 1998, 15).

In contemporary times, discussions of education by gender usually highlight the disparity in the rates of literacy by region, urban and rural residence, or social class. A number of government policies have highlighted the need to close the gender gap in education, and for the need to prepare women for multiple roles in the home, at work, and in society. The 1986, the government's National Policy on Education (updated in 1992) explicitly recognized the need to provide better opportunities for elementary and adult education, and vocational and technical education, as being equitable and empowering for women (Rajagopal 1999, 268; Velkoff 1998; Government of India 2004). There is little discussion, however, of the need to promote English-language education for women because it remains by and large the privilege of the upper- and middle-class populations, primarily in urban locations. 'The educational inequalities both *reflect* and help to *sustain* social disparities' (Dreze and Sen 1998, 14).

At present, there are vast inequalities by region, urban or rural residence, social class, and gender in the availability and accessibility of schools and colleges. Thus, the question that Jane asked the women in the ESL class, 'Where do you come from?', yields only the minimum facts and does not tell us of the uneven distribution of educational opportunities in the countries of origin that make English-language education available to some and not to others. These differences show up in the mix of immigrants that comes to live in Toronto and becomes part of the larger entity of South Asians. The disparities and disadvantages that originate in the country of origin are thus perpetuated and further aggravated in Canada.

Class and gender biases of Canadian immigration policies favour English-speaking immigrants; thus, women from India come to Canada predominantly as 'dependants' (an immigration category) of their spouses or other male relatives. Their entry status as dependants further heightens the class and gender disadvantages experienced in their countries of birth, since immigration status determines access to social services such as ESL classes. Although all non-English-speaking immigrants have access to some introductory language training, only those who are considered to be destined for the labour market have extended opportunities for advanced learning. Since women have formally entered the country as dependants, it is assumed they will not be joining the labour market and thus will have access to only basic training in the English language. However, most Indian women, like other immigrant women, do take up paid employment, but the lack of language proficiency results in lower economic integration of women into the labour market and imposes what Li refers to as a 'net income penalty' on the women (Li 2003). Often they end up working on the low rung of the occupational ladder in job ghettoes such as the garment industry, working longer hours in more insecure work, and earning lower wages (Fincher et al. 1994). Further, it wastes the skills that the women have acquired with great difficulty and persistence on their part in their countries of birth, and have brought with them. This is a loss both to the individual and to the country.

Gender, race, place of origin, and language facility are cumulative disadvantages that have economic and social repercussions on women's lives. In Toronto, the inability to speak English deters the women from using public transportation, going out alone to buy groceries, or to do other errands for the family, such as driving, or making and keeping appointments at medical clinics and doctor's offices. (There are some community health clinics, such as Access Alliance or Women's Health in Women's Hands, which specifically cater to a multilingual clientele.) The children quickly learn English in school and sometimes act as interpreters for their mothers, but the consequent loss of authority is problematic. Their inability to speak English isolates the women, robs them of autonomy, and reinforces their dependence on their spouses. One positive interpretation of this ESL class might be to view it as indicative of the women's determination to become independent, productive, and contributing citizens of Canada.

The women in this ESL class are intently focused on the instructions Jane gives them. Their tongues get entangled in the strange sounds they are expected to make, the words roll out of their mouths awkwardly, and, though embarrassed, they struggle on bravely, repeating the words that Jane encourages them to say. They are hesitant and self-conscious, yet they carry on.

Linguistic and Cultural Homes

Language is embedded in cultural norms. Lack of proficiency in the English language crystallizes many other forms of cultural alienation and discomfort experienced by new immigrants, but almost all racialized immigrants have subtle difficulties with the language despite their ability to speak English fluently. The linguistic and cultural experience of a new male immigrant from India to the United States (before vegetarianism became a fad) is described by his daughter:

> 'I would like to eat ve-ge-tables. Do you serve ve-ge-tables?' asked my father. (He pronounced the second half of the word like the word 'table' with a long 'a'.)
> 'Huh?'
> 'Ve-ge-tables.'
> 'Oh, ya want vegebles? Why'n ya say so? We don got no vegebles. Ya wanna sanwich?'
> 'Cheese sandwich? Do you have cheese sandwich?'
> 'Ya don wanannie meat?'
> 'I don't eat meat. I am a vegetarian. I only eat ve-ge-tables.'
> 'Okay, kid, I'll make ya a cheese sandwich.'
> (Kamdar 2001, 181)

Although everyone speaks English in the accent that is common to their place of origin and determined by their social class and education, new immigrants from South Asia often feel belittled when they speak English and others have difficulty understanding them. V.S. Naipaul

(2000) felt apologetic that he spoke English in a 'foul manner' after he first arrived in London. He confides in a letter to his sister, 'but now my English pronunciation is improving by the humiliating process of error and snigger' (73). English-speaking South Asians (and other racialized groups) feel disgruntled when they are asked to repeat words and sentences or when white, English-speaking Canadians turn their ears towards the individual to more easily catch his or her words. The latter act is sometimes experienced as a form of racism.

In this ESL class, Jane writes the words *north, south, east,* and *west* on the flip chart and attempts to gauge from the expression on the students' faces whether they understand the concept. She then goes on to tell them to ask the driver of the bus to let them off, for example, at the northwest corner in front of the mall. The cultural lesson for the students is the use of this terminology, for in South Asia they would normally use landmarks, such as a temple, a grocery store, or a bus stop to find their way and to locate themselves. Even I, as a new immigrant, was bewildered when friends asked me to use such terminology to fix a meeting place. Similarly, in South Asia, tea and coffee are commonly brewed with milk, except when requested otherwise. Thus, being served coffee and tea made with plain water was a new experience as well (at least until some coffee shops popularized Chai as a menu item). The ESL class was about language, but social and cultural lessons were being imparted simultaneously as well.

Cultural differences, or the sense of being an outsider or a foreigner, can make the individual feel alienated and heighten feelings of sadness, nostalgia, and create a longing for home. After having been in London for a few weeks that coincided with the Christmas season, Naipaul (2000) wrote to his family in Trinidad:

I have been thinking more and more about home ... Christmas never meant much to me or to any one of our family. It was always so much of a glorious feeling of fun we felt existed somewhere, but we could never feel where it was. We were always on the outside of a vague feeling of joy. The same feeling is here with me in London. Yet there is so much more romance here. It gets dark about half past three and all the lights go on. The shops are bright, the streets are well lit and the streets are full of people. I walk through the streets, yet am so much alone, so much on the outside of this great festive feeling.

But I was thinking of home. I could visualize every detail of everything I knew – the bit of the gate, for instance, that was broken off, the oleander tree and the withering roses. Sometimes the sound of a car starting in the road rouses me. The uncertain hesitant beat of the engine brings back No. 26 [their home] back to me, smells and all. It makes me feel sad. Don't misunderstand. It makes me think about you people in a way I thought of you only rarely at home. (43)

Immigrants, particularly those who are racialized, have raised questions about the nature of Canadian identity and the expectations of the population already here about how subsequent arrivals ought to become Canadians. In the early and mid-twentieth century, the ideal of assimilation and Anglo-conformity was held up as necessary and the only way to become a Canadian. But the continued attachment of immigrants to their culture and their disillusionment with the ideal of assimilation led them to express doubts and raise questions politically. Eventually, the policies of bilingualism and multiculturalism were introduced, but they were critiqued for attempting to separate language from culture. Since the focus of these policies was culture, they left undisturbed the unequal distribution of power and prestige among different ethnic and racial groups in Canada (Fleras 2004). At present, South Asians, along with other racialized groups, increasingly focus on anti-racism and human rights activism. Rushdie argues that a creative imagination can give us the power to construct a better world. He writes that imagination can transform and instill a 'confidence in our ability to improve the world' and 'imagination is the only weapon with which reality can be smashed so it may be subsequently reconstructed' (cited in Needham 2000, 69).

Throughout Canadian history, South Asian women (along with other racialized populations), whether they speak English or not, have encountered formidable structural barriers of race, class, gender, and heterosexuality (Agnew 1996). Although oppressed and victimized, they have survived by exercising their wits. Monica Ali's (2003) novel *Brick Lane* is about the conflicts and tensions that define the immigrant experience. Nazneen, the main character in the novel, is an eighteen-year-old girl from Bangladesh who has an arranged marriage and comes to live in London. On her arrival, she knows only three words in English – *sorry* and *thank you* – and does not know a soul. She lives with her husband, Charu, in Brick Lane, an area exclusively inhabited by immigrants from Bangladesh, whose reference points and values are those that exist 'back home.' Charu sees no reason for Nazneen to learn English, and she accepts his dictum without protest. Nazneen's lack of

English is seldom depicted in the novel as being problematic; rather, it is one of the many characteristics that shape and determine her immigrant experience. Nazneen's life is entirely confined to Brick Lane, where she is happy to make friends, start a family, maintain a correspondence with her sister at 'home,' while she cautiously adapts to the 'strange new contours of life as an outsider in London' (Lehmann 2003).

Nazneen's baby dies, and she is lonely, but in the face of these disappointments she shows courage and initiative in overcoming difficulties. When Charu becomes unemployed, she locates a job sewing garments on a piecemeal basis. She has an affair with the middleman, Karim, who brings her the garments, and through him she is introduced to some young Islamic activists. Nazneen's horizons slowly expand, and when she finally goes on a sightseeing trip to London with Charu and their daughters and utters aloud the word *sorry*, she is taken aback at her own boldness. She picks up English from her daughters and from watching television. Ice skating fascinates her and represents 'exhilarating freedom, frozen false emotion and finally a new world of possibilities' (Maslin 2003). Eventually, Charu desires to return 'home,' but Nazneen is ambivalent and resists him. At the end of the novel, the reader is presented with two epigraphs, one from Heraclitus, 'A man's character is his fate,' and the other from Turgenev, 'Sternly, remorselessly, fate guides us.' Ali's book raises the question, 'Do we, can we, control our own lives?' and 'Should [Nazneen] submit to her fate or make it?' (Gorra 2003).

Immigration is a quest for a better life as defined and imagined by the individual. But for Rushdie (2002), the particulars of the imagined life are less significant than the quest to realize the dream. 'In all quests the voyageur is confronted by terrifying guardians of territory, an ogre here, a dragon there. So far and no farther, the guardian commands. But the voyageur must refuse the other's definition of the boundary, must transgress against the limits of what fear prescribes. [She] steps across that line. The defeat of the ogre is an opening in the self, an increase in what it is possible for the voyager to be' (350–351).

Immigration requires the crossing of frontiers – physical and metaphorical, visible and invisible, known and unknown – and the line that is drawn is fluid and unstable. Language is one such frontier that involves 'shape-shifting or self-translation' (Rushdie 2002, 374). Learning and adopting a new language changes the individual because all languages permit slightly varying forms of thought, imagination, and play. Crossing frontiers can be arduous, and there are innumerable risks but the quest to do so transforms the individual, shapes identity, and enables him or her to realize his or her strengths. The individual changes and his or her presence changes the society. 'The frontier both shapes our character and tests our mettle' (381).

NOTES

1 'South Asia includes a number of sovereign nations – India, Pakistan, Bangladesh, Sri Lanka – with ethnically diverse populations. In Sri Lanka, Tamils and Sinhalese; in Pakistan and Bangladesh, Hindus and Muslims; in India, Sikhs, Tamils, and Parsees (to name only a few). Immigrant women in Canada exhibit vast social, cultural, regional, religious, and lingusitic differences ... The identity of South Asian women in Canada is partly a social construction by hegemonic practices and processes. South Asian women are categorized as a group on the basis of physical appearance (especially skin-colour), with the cultural differences among them disregarded' (Agnew 1998, 118–119).
2 An outfit comprising a long, loose shirt and baggy pants.
3 The sponsoring immigrant can be either male or female but it is usually the male who has the requisite or rather better qualifications than his spouse to gain entry as an immigrant.
4 In 2004, outsourcing of jobs in information technologies was often reported in the news media. One comparison that was routinely and constantly made was between the English-language-speaking workers available in India vis-à- vis China. The presence of these workers gave India a competitive edge in attracting multinational corporations to locate there.

REFERENCES

Agnew, Vijay. 1996. *Resisting Discrimination*. Toronto: University of Toronto Press.
– 1998. *In Search of a Safe Place*. Toronto: University of Toronto Press.
Ali, Monica. 2003. *Brick Lane*. London: Scribner.
Andermahr, Sonya, Terry Lovell, and Carol Wolkowitz. 2000. A *Glossary of Feminist Theory*. London: Arnold.
Appadurai, Arjun. 1996. *Modernity at Large: Cultural Dimensions of Globalization*. Minneapolis: University of Minnesota Press.
Basavarajappa, K.G., and Frank Jones. 1999. Visible Minority Income Differ-

ences. In *Immigrant Canada: Demographic, Economic, and Social Challenges,* ed. Shiva Halli and Leo Driedger, 230–257. Toronto: University of Toronto Press.

Boyd, Monica, John DeVries, and Keith Simkin. 1994. Vol 2. Language, Economic Status and Integration. In *Immigration and Refugee Policy,* ed. Howard Adelman, A. Borowski, M. Burnstein, and L. Foster, 549–577. Toronto: University of Toronto Press.

Brown, Judith. 1994. *Modern India: The Origins of an Asian Democracy.* Oxford: Oxford University Press.

Chanana, Karuna. 1996. Social Change or Social Reform: The Education of Women in Pre-Independence India. In *Social Structure and Change,* ed. A.M. Shah, B. Baviskar, and E. Ramaswamy, 113–148. Thousand Oaks, CA: Sage.

Chaudhuri, Amit, ed. 2001. *The Picador Book of Modern Indian Literature.* Basingstoke, Oxford: Picador.

Code, Lorraine. 2000. *Encyclopedia of Feminist Theories.* London: Routledge.

COSTI. 2004. www.costi.org.

Desai, Jigna. 2004. *Beyond Bollywood: The Cultural Politics of South Asian Diasporic Film.* New York: Routledge.

Dreze, Jean and Amartya Sen, eds. 1995. *India Economic Development and Social Opportunity.* New Delhi: Oxford University Press.

– 1998. *Indian Development: Selected Regional Perspectives.* New Delhi: Oxford University Press.

Fincher, Ruth, Wenona Giles, and Valerie Preston. 1994. Gender and migration policy. In *Immigration and Refugee Policy: Australia and Canada Compared,* ed. Howard Adelman, Allan Borowski, Meyer Burnstein, and Lois Foster, 14–186. Toronto: University of Toronto Press.

Fleras, Augie. 2004. Racializing Culture/Culturalizing Race: Multicultural Racism in a Multicultural Canada. In *Racism Eh?: A Critical Inter-disciplinary Anthology on Race and Racism in Canada,* ed. Camille Nelson and C. Nelson, 429–443. Toronto: Captus.

Gandhi, Sonia, ed. 1992. *Two Alone, Two Together: Letters Between Indira Gandhi and Jawaharlal Nehru 1940–1964.* London: Hodder and Stoughton.

Gorra, Michael. 2003. East Enders. *New York Times,* 7 September.

Government of India. 2004. *Report of the Task Force on Education for Women's Equality.* www.shikshanic.

Henry, Francis, Carol Tator, Winston Mattis, and Tim Rees. 1995. *The Colour of Democracy: Racism in Canadian Society.* Toronto: Harcourt Brace.

Kamdar, Mira. 2001. *Motiba's Tattoos: A Granddaughter's Journey from America into Her Indian Family's Past.* New York: Plume.

Khilnani, Sunil. 1998. *The Idea of India.* London: Penguin.

Kumar, Amitava. 2002. *Bombay London New York*. New Delhi: Penguin.

Lehmann, Chris. 2003. A Long and Winding Road. *Washington Post*, 16 September.

Li, Peter. 2003. *Destination Canada: Immigration Debates and Issues*. Toronto: Oxford University Press.

Maslin, Janet. 2003. The Flavors of a New Land Can Leave a Bitter Taste. *New York Times*, 8 September.

Mehta, Suketu. 2004. *Maximum City: Bombay Lost and Found*. New York: Alfred A. Knopf.

Metcalf, Barbara, and Thomas Metcalf. 2002. *A Concise History of India*. Cambridge: Cambridge University Press.

Mishra, Vijay. 2002. *Bollywood Cinema: Temples of Desire*. New York: Routledge.

Nafisi, A. 2004. *Reading Lolita in Tehran: A Memoir in Books*. New York: Random House.

Naipaul, V.S. 2000. *Letters between a Father and Son*. London: Abascus.

– 2003. *Literary Occasions: Essays*. Toronto: Alfred A. Knopf.

Needham, Anuradha Dingwaney. 2000. *Using the Master's Tools: Resistance and the Literature of the African and South-Asian Diasporas*. New York: St. Martin's Press.

Ong, Ahiwa. 1999. *Flexible Citizenship: The Cultural Logics of Transnationality*. Durham, NC: Duke University Press.

Rajagopal, Shobhita. 1999. Closing the Gender Gap in Education. In *Institutions, Relations, and Outcomes*, ed. Naila Kabeer and R. Subrahmanian, 266–287. New Delhi: Kali for Women.

Rushdie, Salman. 2002. *Step Across This Line: Collected Non-fiction 1992–2002*. Toronto: Alfred A. Knopf.

Said, Edward. 1979. *Orientalism*. New York: Vintage.

Varma, Pavan. 1998. *The Great Indian Middle Class*. New Delhi: Penguin.

Velkoff, Victoria. 1998. *Women's Education in India*. Washington, DC: Bureau of Census.

2 Memories of Internment: Narrating Japanese-Canadian Women's Life Stories

PAMELA SUGIMAN

Basically, my experiences are through the eyes of a thirteen-year-old. And over the years, maybe I've embellished things a bit or been able to rationalize why things had to be done that way, to a point. But I also know that there could have been a better way of doing it. It was truly unthinking politicians who created all this hardship and unnecessary move for ... Japanese Canadians, removing all their property from them. You couldn't even go back home because you had nothing. They'd taken everything away.

(Polly)

The Internment of Japanese Canadians

The most devastating event shaping the lives of Japanese Canadians was the internment and forced dispersal of 'all persons of the Japanese race' during, and in the years immediately following, the Second World War. By now, the rough contours of the story are familiar to many Canadians. After the bombing of Pearl Harbor on 7 December 1941, Japanese-Canadian citizens and Japanese Nationals in Canada were subject to government curfews, personal interrogation, and ultimately job loss and severe economic hardship. The federal government shut down all Japanese-language newspapers, impounded fishing boats, liquidated businesses, and sold vehicles, houses, and personal belongings. The proceeds from the sales were used to pay auctioneers and realtors, as well as to cover the costs of the internment. First interned were 'alien' men; next, Japanese-Canadian men; and, finally, all women and children of Japanese descent. Women and children were initially placed in 'detainment centres' – former livestock pens that reeked of urine and manure. Such violations were not short term. Canadians of Japanese origin were denied full citizenship rights, including the right to vote in a federal election, until June 1948. Furthermore, they were prohibited from returning to the former sites of their homes on the west coast until 1949, four years after the war's end.[1]

These events in Canadian history represent the deliberate destruction of a community, a form of 'cultural genocide,'[2] an erosion of human dignity, and a dramatic disruption of personal lives and family relationships. The last category is especially significant because the family had been the primary vehicle for the acquisition of an ethnic identity and for the transmission of Japanese cultural symbols in Canada. The internment of Japanese Canadians has had profound social, political, and economic implications. Some scholars have described it as an act of political violence (see, for example, McAllister 1999).[3]

A Sansei Researcher Explores Silences of the Past

Though many decades have since gone by, Japanese Canadians continue to live with the injustices and indignities of the past. In response to this act of violence, for years the Nisei (second generation) attempted to filter the painful memories of their internment – by not putting reminiscences on paper, nor verbally articulating their experiences as part of a public discourse. In an effort to shield their own children from the racial hostilities they themselves endured, Nisei parents have furthermore promoted the cultural assimilation of their own children, the Sansei (third generation). Assimilation involved shedding the cultural markers of their Japaneseness: the Japanese language, contact with Japanese-Canadian peers, and an appreciation of traditional Japanese art forms. Japanese-Canadians' fears of again being punished as a culturally and economically distinct group have resulted in what some writers have termed their 'racial erasure' from history (see McAllister 1999).

Marita Sturken (1997, 701) poignantly describes the reverberating impact of such acts of political violence. The children of survivors of internment camps, she explains, experience history as one of many 'untold stories.' Sturken (1997, 698) describes the Sansei as being haunted by the 'silence of their parents and the sense of a memory they cannot quite narrativize.' In the words of Sansei filmmaker Tajiri:

I began searching for a history, my own history, because I had known all along that the stories I had heard were not true and parts had been left out. I remember having this feeling growing up that I was haunted by something, that I was living within a family full of ghosts. There was this place that they knew about. I had never been there, yet I had a memory of it. I could remember a time of great sadness before I was born. We had been moved, uprooted. We had lived with a lot of pain. I had no idea where these memories came from, yet I knew the place.' (Cited in Sturken 1997, 698–699)

Like Tajiri, I am a Sansei, and for a long time I too have been haunted by my parents' and grandparents' past. Though my ancestors had been interned many years before my birth, as a child I had gathered 'fragments and splinters' of stories. Says Anna Neumann (1997, 93), '"protected" stories are often told to a child in bits and pieces ... multiple, mostly unintended tellings.' It is only after years of reflection that I feel prepared to contemplate and publicly present the past, a past in which I am centrally situated. I approached this challenge with the distance of an academic, but the lens through which I view the scholarly product is a deeply personal one.

The Study

This chapter is part of the scholarly product. It is one piece of a larger ongoing study of the Second World War internment as a gendered and racialized event in Canadian history.[4] Drawing on the oral testimonies of thirty Nisei women now living in Ontario and British Columbia, I explore a range of internment experiences, as well as women's ways of relating these experiences.[5] The testimonies of the women who narrated their stories of internment are rich and textured. In this chapter, I will highlight two central points that have emerged from my reading of these testimonies. First, I wish to address the theme of the silence of the past and the attempts of some Nisei to renounce this silence. In recent years, the Nisei have moved from an 'unspoken bonding' based on a shared experience, a literal silence, to 'outspoken ... activity' (see Irwin-Zarecka 1994, 51) and the public preservation of stories through the written and officially spoken word. The shift towards a deliberate and active telling of untold stories is in large part an individual and collective response to the Japanese-Canadian Redress Movement and eventual Redress Settlement with the Canadian government.[6] When groups of Sansei and Nisei activists organized in the 1980s to seek government compensation (or redress) for Japanese Canadians, they attempted to mobilize the community by organizing public forums and community meetings, and by publishing a host of written materials that documented property losses, the violation of rights, and the moments of forced uprooting and dislocation. Some of these moments have, as a result, been etched into the minds of both Japanese and non-Japanese Canadians. In short, the redress activists were successful in publicizing a narrative of the internment, and, in doing so, they mediated the past (see Irwin-Zarecka 1994, 83). They legitimated the pain that it had caused, and thereby unearthed many personal histories.[7]

Second, and most centrally, these personal testimonies present memory as a meaningful sociological concept. While cognitive psychologists, psychoanalysts, cultural theorists, and social historians have written much of the recent literature on memory, sociologists were among the first to explore memory as an object of study (Wachtel 1986, 211; see also, for example, Bastide 1960; Halbwachs 1992). Sociological analysis drew attention to memory as a social act, one that is far more than 'spontaneous,' 'personal' (Zerubavel 1996, 286), and individually experienced. Past events, after all, are very much situated and represented in present-day society. As such, they cannot be accessed in 'unmediated form' (Kuhn 2000, 184). In the words of Annette Kuhn (2000, 186), memory is 'always already secondary revision.' It is neither 'pure experience' nor 'pure event' (189). It reflects personal and historical transformations, ideological shifts, changing relations of power, strategy, and struggle. Memory may be described as a 'fusion of personal biography with the history of groups or communities' (Zerubavel 1996, 290).

Our cultural traditions and artefacts tell us much about memory. Standard history books underscore our 'traditions of remembering,' as do school curricula, war memorials, and museum exhibits (McAllister 2001; Osborne 2001; Zerubavel 1996). Furthermore, as a society, we have social rules that tell us what we should remember and what we must forget, how far back to remember (what to put behind us and how to 'socially partition' the past into recorded 'discoveries' and forgettable 'prehistory'), how deeply to remember, and the ways in which we should 'narrate the past' (that is, the 'conventional plot structure' [Zerubavel 1996, 286–88]).

As a social process, memory then is selective. We remember what we need to remember, what is safe to remember, what we have the cultural tools to express. Memory is shaped by its audience (Tonkin 1992, 9). It is formed and presented for a particular audience, one that may hear or dismiss, listen or ignore, accept or punish. In each of these ways, memory is also a political project.

And, lastly, memory is mediated and shaped by the researcher herself (see, for example, Debouzy 1986; Portelli 1981a, 1981b). The memories I present are undeniably filtered through my own lens, that of an educated Sansei woman of working-class origin. Undoubtedly, they reflect my own intellectual inquiries, personal needs, and moral imperatives – my framework of social justice, my unrelenting anger, the enduring pain of my own family's trauma, and lingering unspoken memories of my mother and father, as well as my comfort with historical chronology, and, at times, the imposition of a feminist logic and feminist sensibilities. The researcher is the narrator's audience, just as the researcher brings the women's words to a wider, lesser known, perhaps imagined community of listeners.

In this chapter, I highlight the ways in which Nisei women's memories bring together biography, history, and sociology. These memories are the product of the intermingling of past and present lives, the creation of a complex dynamic between the individual and the collective, recalling and forgetting, trauma and nostalgia (Hirsch and Smith 2002, 4). Clearly, the ideas I ponder are far reaching, and the literature on which I draw is now burgeoning.[8] But my own aims here are modest. I wish to raise and reflect on these themes and points of inquiry, without claiming to have definitive answers. My intent here is to stimulate thought about the conceptual challenges facing sociologists and social historians. I will introduce these conceptual ideas by presenting a selection of the women's memories.

Nisei Women's Memories

Memory as Constructed Temporally: Prewar Lives and the Negotiation of Racialized Identities

As Elizabeth Tonkin (1992) has eloquently stated, time and temporality are essential to the telling of stories. It is important to remember that narrators are constructing retrospective accounts for audiences who may have very different time scales. Furthermore, both narrators and listeners are 'inescapably formed by their own personal pasts to date' (3). In the act of testimony, each is 'caught at a certain stage of their lives' (66). And this factor will shape the narration in important ways.

Those telling their stories often speak of events long past. Listeners will receive their tales with a different, perhaps distorted, possibly misguided understanding of this past. And the narrator, in turn, may adjust her narrations accordingly (66).

To some extent, the narrators' identification of meaningful events in their lives, their presentation and interpretation of these events, were no doubt shaped by my own (academic) relationship to time and 'sense of history.' As a researcher, I divided up and ordered the pieces of their lives around the Second World War. Indeed, I initially solicited their stories by underlining my strong interest in the impact of war and internment on a woman's personal history. In addition, the women's memories were constrained by cultural conventions around the importance of time to narration. In our society, placement in time lends legitimacy to storytelling. And, I believe that in repeatedly asking the women for dates, for a chronological situation of experiences, and even emotions, I reinforced this convention. My concerns about duration and the punctuation of time (see Tonkin, 1992, 67) were central to the structuring of their memories. 'How long were you there?' 'Was this before or after internment?' 'What year did that happen?' were questions that I and my research assistants frequently used to intervene in and punctuate the women's narratives.[9]

While many women were remarkably quick to recall the dates of marriages, children's and grandchildren's birthdays, or the day that a close friend died, some women felt muted, deficient, indeed unable to remember when questioned about an objective or external historical chronology. Such inquiries generated comments such as, 'Gee, my memory isn't good at all' and 'I can't seem to remember anything' from women who had otherwise been recounting fluid and richly detailed vignettes from the past. This was characteristic of working-class women in particular, who tended not to have rehearsed their reminiscences for public consumption.

Indeed, my efforts to understand the women's lives with reference to linear, historical time now seems almost paradoxical given that during the war, time stood still for most Nisei. Many women spoke about boredom in the internment camps, about the slow passage of time. There wasn't much to do. Time was spent on daily survival, going on walks, leafing through an Eaton's catalogue. Feelings of stasis were no doubt strengthened as they faced an unforeseeable future and grieved for an irretrievable past. For many women, place – that is, geographic location – seemed to carry more meaning than the duration or passage of time. The women frequently made statements such as, 'This was before we moved to Lemon Creek,' 'It happened after my brother was sent to Petawawa,' and 'It was after we moved to Rosebery.' Place, in a sense, punctuated time. Place seemed to bring together or root out 'events' that had no 'logical' sequence or connection. It helped to guide one through the scattered 'montage of vignettes, anecdotes, fragments' (Kuhn 2000, 190).

Clearly, the Second World War did have a dramatic impact on the women's lives, both subjectively and materially. And I do not mean to minimize the significance of documented and dateable historical events in their narratives. Indeed, many women claimed that the internment was the most consequential event in their lives. They themselves participated (with no obvious difficulty, awkwardness, or resistance) in a framing of their lives around broad segments of time: the prewar years, uprooting and dislocation, resettlement, the Redress Movement, the present. It is important to acknowledge, however, that my own ordering of these events may have implied or prompted a sense of causation that may not have otherwise been there.[10]

While I established the women's memories of internment first in prewar times, many of the women themselves constructed a temporal dichotomy based largely on two points in time, broken up by the war. They spoke of a prewar existence – their lives as girls, teens, young women, on the one hand – and of all that followed, on the other: the war years and the postwar worlds in which Japanese Canadians ultimately lived. Notably, some of the women presented a severe, almost violent rupture between the two segments of time.

Most Nisei women talked about their prewar lives in a fairly matter-of-fact, even abbreviated manner, generating simple, perhaps idealized images of youthful innocence and hard work, yet not hardship. They were self-conscious about the ordinariness of their lives. The nature of their accounts reflected an effort to present childhood as normal and conflict free. Their days were filled with activities still popular with Canadian girls: skipping, playing hopscotch, baseball, running, singing, visiting, doing chores, helping mother, and going to school. Absent from the narrations of most women was any mention of clashes with parents, siblings, or friends, or of any restrictions imposed by the gender prescriptions of the day.

Yet unlike their *Hakujin*[11] friends and neighbours, the girls and women were somewhat troubled by their place in a world that was clearly demarcated by geographic, as well as cultural, boundaries and markers. Though most of the women knew very little about Japan (many had never even visited the country), and did not consider themselves to be Japanese, they had a sense of their 'Japaneseness.' This quality was revealed by the food they ate at home (rice, salty pickles, and miso soup), the language they spoke there (most Issei parents, especially mothers, did not speak much English and therefore Japanese was spoken at home), and, of course, by their mothers and fathers themselves.

Family and school reinforced these boundaries. All of the women attended private Japanese language classes after regular public school. Most of them said that their parents had forced them to do so; some of the women claimed to have hated it. In regular school, at the elementary level, some knew many Japanese Canadians; others knew very few. Yet by the time they reached high school, which was typically located beyond the immediate community, many were numerically in the minority. In the public school system, teachers refused to try to correctly pronounce Japanese names. In turn, in Japanese schools, some teachers would reprimand the children for even writing their names in English.

The Nisei thus moved back and forth between their Japaneseness and Canadianness. They negotiated identities as they travelled from public school to home, and from public school to Japanese school. It was difficult for some to navigate these two worlds, though at times, one offered an escape from the other. Kay, for instance, explained that she enjoyed public school because it 'was a place where you grew away from being just Japanese ... When you went to school, you met all sorts of people,' she reported.

Some of the women, both those who lived in and outside of Japanese communities, presented the prewar period as one in which they experienced little racial discrimination. For others, racism was simply part of everyday existence. It too was normalized. For example, Rose commented about racial discrimination prior to the war: 'Well, we just accepted it ... We knew, we grew up with it ... We didn't have time to mingle with Canadian [sic] children.' Polly is one of a minority of women who spoke directly about racial discrimination. '[O]ur parents had always told us that there was this underlying discrimination ... that we were different from the white society people.' Chieko's remarks are more typical of the Nisei women in this study. According to Chieko, 'There was hardly any Japanese in our school. No, I didn't feel any different. All through, all my friends were Hakujin ... I knew nothing about discrimination or anything. I never experienced anything like that.' Similarly, Sue commented: '[High school] was okay. I didn't experience any prejudice or anything. Maybe I didn't realize it. But I think I had a pretty *normal* high school ... My friends were Japanese, *naturally* [emphasis mine].'

This sense of normalcy and stability was severely disrupted, however, with the Second World War. The war brought with it the most dramatic manifestation of racial hostility experienced by the Nisei, and its impact could not easily be minimized in consequence. According to many of the women, as of 7 December 1941, cultural and physical differences took on new meaning. Some women spoke of changes in their relationships with Hakujin, changes that are presented as sudden and immediate. All of a sudden there was racial hostility, they remembered. And this hostility imposed upon Japanese Canadians the mark of racial difference, one rooted in the physical body, in the idea that loyalties and political sentiments were determined by phenotypical racial qualities. With the bombing of Pearl Harbor, Polly recalled: 'Our so-called "white friends" turned completely against us. And we were called all kinds of horrible names like "You dirty, yellow-bellied Japs," and "Go back to Japan where you came from!" ... [O]ur friends turned against us. They didn't want any part of us ... We were friends till last week, but come Monday, we were not anymore.'

Japanese Canadians, as a race, were seen as 'disloyal to the core.' They became the enemy. Their public construction as members of a race, all the same as one another, and so very different from the white race (see Petonito 1992) forced the Nisei to again confront and renegotiate racialized identities. Kay recalled the process by which, as a young girl, she was forced to internalize an externally imposed racialized identity:

We used to go, cross over the bridge, two big bridges ... to where our ... Japanese community was ... They taught Japanese school just to read and write Japanese for one hour after [public] school ... They used to have these huge banners across the bridge ... [I]n those days, 'Jap was a Jap,' no matter who you were. Whether you were born in Canada or from Japan. And I always used to see this banner about 'Go home Japs,' or something like that, or 'We don't want you Japs here.' Great big banners across the bridge ... My dad used to take me to the school because I think he was afraid ... hysteria of war ... And I used to say, 'Oh, who's the Japs?' I never considered myself a 'Jap.' So I said, 'Who are these Japanese, anyways?' And my father said, 'You.' I said, 'Well, I'm not a Jap. I'm not from

Japan.' ... That's the first time my father told me, and when I realized that I was different ... Before we knew it, we were in an internment camp.

A Personal Memory of the Uprooting

About their initial uprooting and dislocation from their homes, the women provided rich detail and spoke with animation. Memories of this episode in their lives seem to have been generated with relatively little effort. These memories seemed to be closest to the surface. The women's readiness to provide details and their ease of verbalization may be a result of their ability to weave their own accounts in and out of the official discourse on the internment. Perhaps the women were comfortable in relating their experiences of uprooting because they were able to draw on this discourse. In other words, some of the information they provided me was already part of the existing and much publicized narrative.

Yet it is important to note that at the same time many of the women personalized the official narrative, by providing the researcher with one specific and highly intimate memory, a memory that held special and particular meaning to them.[12] An abbreviated discussion of the personalization of official narratives appears in 'Understanding Silence: Finding Meaning in the Oral Testimonies of Nisei women in Canada' (Sugiman, 2003). What these women presented to me were images, vivid and lasting, like snapshots, imbued with feeling. These are memories that are surrounded by an 'emotional aura,' which is precisely what makes them memorable.[13] For example, Yoko described an RCMP officer coming into her home in Vancouver, interrogating her family, and, while doing so, lifting the lid from the pot that was simmering on the stove and peering in. She still asks why he needed to do that. She remarked, shaking her head, 'I still remember that.' Kay's most striking and unforgettable memory revolved around her pet dog:

> I still remember the big truck came to pick us up and ... we had a dog too. His name was Tipper ... We used to call him 'nice dog.' Mongrel dog. And the only thing I can remember was leaving the dog behind. We had to leave the dog behind. And you know, that dog, my mother thought that she had put it in the house ... But he must have got out somehow and he followed our ... you know, how you drive off and the dog just ran and ran and ran until he couldn't keep up anymore. I still remember that. And all of us in the truck were all crying. When I think of it I get like this (crying) ...

Gee, I never get like this *(laughing and crying)* ... Dog just threw me off, right now. Going off on the truck and the dog chasing and chasing and couldn't catch up to us. Isn't that awful? I guess it's because we've always had dogs ... Yes, that's the only thing I remember.

These images acted, in a sense, as memory prompts. For some women, they unleashed many more memories. And, importantly, they brought some intimacy to the relationship between speaker and listener. If not closest to the surface, such memories were closest to the heart.

It is also notable that while the official narrative prompted by the Redress Movement activists focused on an accounting of property losses, only some of the personal narratives presented by the women in this study are about property in the form of a house, land, boat, or farm. Moreover, when they did talk about the loss of property, the women again personalized the matter, and thereby internalized the losses. Almost all of the women chose to speak about the small personal items that were left behind. Sachi, for instance, explained how her family burned some possessions rather than have them confiscated by government or stolen by looters: '[We] burned all our toys, we burned our books and things. And you know it was a crying shame. Every day we had to have a bonfire outside to burn all this stuff ... The only thing we sort of hung on to was a photograph album.' Among the burned toys, was the best doll that Sachi ever had.

Often, the loss of personal possessions meant the forfeiture of memory itself, and, as such, the loss of self and identity. In thinking about these losses, it is useful to draw on Iwona Irwin-Zarecka's (1994) concept of memory households. 'Within our memory households,' she writes, 'are both autobiographical reminders and elements of the much more distant past (great grandparents' chest, for example), with a special place often reserved for objects evoking people dear to us who are no longer here.' Highly individualized, 'these symbolic nests represent extensions of our self. Being deprived of them, even if only temporarily, can result in a deep sense of loss. Not demanding our active attention, most of the time, a memory household offers an anchor, the comfort of continuity and identity' (89).

While the contents of our memory household may 'accumulate quietly over time,' during the internment, they were subject to more 'direct and dramatic change ...' Moreover, the uprooting and dislocation constituted a 'time when experience itself' was disrupted (Irwin-Zarecka 1994, 89). It is because of the importance of one's memory household that the Nisei desperately tried to salvage photo albums, wedding gifts, diaries, and dolls. When these items could not be saved, their loss was lamented.[14] Rose explained: 'We had one picture like this, with my father, mother, and both of us. And [anticipating violation of the intensely personal] my mother had cut it up, and I said, "Oh my goodness." So that was sad. Those are the two things that I remember. And now, when you look back, you know, they're trying to set up a museum or whatever ... those two – even now, I feel ... "Gee whiz."'

Furthermore, in their accounting of loss, many women drew on domestic images and themes. The salience of the domestic reflects their position in the gendered familial division of labour. The personal narratives bring to the fore the contributions and responsibilities of mothers and elder daughters within family households – or at least within the remnants of these households. The women spoke of their attempts to hold on to, for example, dishes, stoves, and sewing machines, all of which they felt were indispensable in their efforts to continue to care for their families. Kim recalled: 'I did pack a few dishes that I thought we would really need, and I didn't want to part with some of the china ... Mother thought that we should be able to take our stove with us, but it was taken away from us, anyway ... [S]he thought we should have a stove because we really didn't know where we were going.' Likewise, Mary said, 'Oh, we just packed clothes. And Mom packed. We didn't have much. Just her, she kept saying, "Oh, I need my tablecloth," and the things she used for New Year's, you know. She had one good tablecloth and she took that. And Dad had a knife, a chef's knife. We took that.'

The fluidity of these memories may also be linked to my implicit feminist approach. In introducing myself to the women, I emphasized the value that some researchers place on private experiences – experiences that may have been located in family households, in school playgrounds, in circles of friends. I also made a conscious effort to convey to them my belief that even what is seemingly small and everyday can be of political significance. These assurances were very important to some of the women, especially to those who had never before spoken about their lives to someone outside their family or someone who had not lived through the internment herself. Most of the women felt they had greatest authority over these personal memories. And such memories are central in securing the stories that have never before been told. As noted by Judy Giles (2002), we need to blur the 'distinctions between private and public, fact and fiction' for these binaries have 'functioned to silence women, the working class, and the ethnically oppressed in traditional historiography' (24).

Memories of the Internment as 'Constructed Relationally'

In sharing their memories, many women compared their personal experiences to those of others in the community. In doing so, they sometimes spoke for others; at times, they presented what may be termed a 'shared group memory.'[15] Writing about working-class memory, Marianne Debouzy (1986) describes how narrators express what they believe to be the memory of others 'in one and only one discourse, in one and the same imaginary yet authentic life story.' In this 'dynamic interaction of memories,' says Debouzy, we may trace a collective memory: 'Each individual memory takes its place in a group memory that does not exist by itself but lives through the whole made up of these memories that are at the same time unique and interdependent' (270–271).

In her heartfelt study of Nisei mothers and their Sansei daughters, Mona Oikawa (1999) likewise describes the ways in which women construct memory relationally, within past and present communities. Oikawa demonstrates that in 're-membering,' a woman situates herself in relation to those who 'suffered and lost differently than she' (196). The women who spoke with me similarly presented their stories in relation to members of larger families, families that had been moved to a different geographic location, or to smaller living quarters, mothers who had newborn or very young children. Some women minimized their pain in comparison to that of the men, many of whom faced physical hardship and economic exploitation in road camps as prisoners of war.

The tendency to construct memory relationally is promoted by the official and collective narrative of the internment. Informed by this narrative, the women have a broader knowledge of the heterogeneity of experiences within the community. They have heard by now many different accounts. Contextualizing their remarks in a relational and evaluative statement, some women highlighted small ways in which they felt they were lucky or fortunate. For example, Yoko said, '*Luckily*, we were able to bring a little cot. We were *lucky* we could bring [it]' [emphasis mine]. Jean conveyed similar sentiments: 'We were really *lucky* because ... we got a big house. But part of it was taken by another couple ... Some of the people, they had to have two families in a small place and sharing the kitchen [emphasis mine].' And, comparing the experiences of Japanese Canadians to Japanese Americans, Betty remarked, 'If you get down to the States where they were in these camps in Niagara, and if you go down to L.A., you'll see their museum. You'll see these camps that they lived in with guard towers and guards, soldiers walking all around outside with guns. Then, I think you'd feel it. But [for us] there was no wire, there was no fence. You knew this was your place.'

When first interned, Eiko[16] was in her mid-twenties. Though she had to fend for herself and her disabled son, she expressed sympathy for other mothers. Confused about this, the researcher asked Eiko to explain.

EIKO: I get thinking, well, those people who had small children you know, it must have been pretty hard ...
INTERVIEWER: Was your son with you then?
EIKO: Uh-huh.
INTERVIEWER: So *you* had a small child with you.
EIKO: Well, yeah, but he wasn't in diapers or anything like that *(laugh).* ... They got us on the train. I don't know how they – persons who had babies – survived on that train. I really don't. But we were fortunate.

By referring to others – those who had it worse – the women are able to temporarily withdraw themselves from the traumatic past – take an emotional breather, of sorts, from their own painful memories. And they may dissociate themselves from the narrative. Recall the quoted passage above, when Jean asked herself, 'How could *they* have coped?'

Also prominent in the testimonies is the women's construction of memory in relation to their mothers (and less often their fathers).[17] This is not surprising. With the movement of most men into forced labour camps, the places of internment tended to be feminized. They were places in which mothers were left in charge, often for the first time. Though their sphere of control was very much circumscribed, the family was in their hands. Informed by the historical narrative, reflecting on past lives and identities, Nisei women, now mothers and grandmothers themselves, remember their mothers in new ways. In Kim's words, 'And then the government just took everything ... which broke my mother's heart.'

Just as their own Sansei children wished their aging parents had told them more complete stories of the past, Nisei daughters regret the lack of shared remembrances with their own parents. Furthermore, a few of the women speak of the void created in the absence of a stronger emotional expressiveness between Issei (first generation) mothers and Nisei daughters. The Nisei women themselves take responsibility for this silence. Audrey[18] remarked, 'I regret now that I never asked about family, you know, her [my mother's] upbringing in Japan ... I don't know anything about them. That's the unfortunate thing. And I really regret that. I wish I had asked them more questions and shown more interest.'

Some of the testimonies also uncover a deep sorrow for the mothers and a recognition of their vulnerabilities, but more vividly, their strengths, resourcefulness, and resilience.[19] They conjure up images of maternal strength. Kim remembered how her mother was forced to plead for money: 'The [BC Security] Commission ... she would have to go and beg for the money *(laughs)*. And you know, I think they knew that mother had a bit of money on her, which she sort of kept, and she kept on saying everything is wrapped around my stomach. I don't know how much money she had.'

Yet Nisei daughters' memories of Issei mothers were complicated. The women remembered their mothers empathically, as burdened. In looking back, however, some of them recognized that as children, they themselves added to this burden. Kim continued, 'My mother was so confused, you know. She didn't know what to do ... *I* was happy ... coming across on the train, but I know my mother was very concerned travelling with three girls. And there were a lot of soldiers on the train. We just had to sleep on the coaches or on the bench ... she was forever making sure that we were well covered.'

Like many Nisei, Kay was in her youth during the war, and consequently did not share the same responsibilities as her mother. With some guilt, she remembered the fun times: 'We didn't do any housework ... and we didn't do any cooking. We met a lot of people, and of course I was just getting into the teens, so I was getting interested in boys, too. When I look back ... I thought it was kind of fun. They had programs going for us, and all that. But I know it was a very, very stressful time for my mother, yes, because my father wasn't there.' Chieko similarly recalled, '[In Hastings Park], because we were all teenagers, we all got in a bunch and gathered round and talked and sang ... Who cared what happened then? I mean our parents must have been suffering a lot, but as long as we had three meals a day ... we were only looking for fun.'

Normalcy and Nostalgic Memory

This presentation of the past, notably the sentiment that the internment years were 'fun times' and 'the good old days' was perplexing. Assessing these sentiments through a present-day lens, I was prompted to interrogate the women with some suspicion. One way to interpret memories of this sort is to describe them as nostalgic, as a complex way in which people bring together past and present lives.[20] In much of the literature on memory, critics have charged that nostalgic narratives are conceptually distinct from memory, and detached from the present (see for example, Lasch 1984; Gans 1979; Williams 1974; Rosaldo 1989). Many writers, moreover, have viewed nostalgia as 'inherently conservative, if not reactionary and escapist,' a ' "simplification" if not "falsification of the past" ' (Gans 1979). Nostalgic yearnings for 'uncomplicated times,' according to some, disable political action in the present on behalf of social change' (McDermott 2002, 390). Cultural theorist Raymond Williams (1974; also cited in Spitzer 1999, 91; Vromen 1994, 71) wrote about nostalgia as an 'opiate' that permits individuals to avoid a rational, critical examination of and engagement with the present. As a result, in Williams's view, nostalgia impedes social change and progress. Indeed, in promoting an uncritical acceptance of the status quo, Williams believes nostalgia to be dysfunctional. Historian Christopher Lasch (1984; also cited in Spitzer 1999, 91; Vromen 1994, 73), likewise refers to nostalgia a 'betrayal of history.' Lasch labels 'nostalgists' to be no more than 'incurable sentimentalists' who cannot bear to 'face the truth about the past.' Similarly, Iwona Irwin-Zarecka (1989, also cited in Vromen 1994, 74–75) describes nostalgia as a 'means of conducting a search for the exotic.' In her examination of a 1986 *National Geographic* portrait of the last Jews of Poland, Irwin-Zarecka asserts that what is nostalgically remembered are traditional Jewish rituals and beliefs, the strange and mystical. In such a formulation, 'nostalgia brings to mind the "good old days"; hence, there is no nostalgic memory of anti-Semitism.'

Other writers, however, have recently suggested that the politics of nostalgia may be more complicated than was previously believed (see, for example, Boym 2001; Lowenthal 1989; Steedman 1986; Giles 2002; McDermott 2002). Many of these authors have contributed to a general social theory of memory. Their analyses tend to situate nostalgia in a more positive light and challenge its polarization from memory and history. French sociologist Maurice Halbwachs (1992) led the way in writing about the 'virtue' of nostalgic memory's 'escape from the past' (see also Spitzer 1999, 91). In Halbwachs's view, nostalgia permits a 'transcendence of the irreversibility of time,' thus enabling us to selectively emphasize positive experiences and aspects of the past (Spitzer 1999, 91–92). In this sense, nostalgia has a liberating potential; it permits both an understanding of the past that may not have been originally possible, and allows for an escape from coercive social bonds and from the trials of the present (Vromen 1994, 76).

According to Susan Vromen (1994, 76), nostalgia offers a world in which pain and suffering have been removed. It permits a selective emphasis on the positive, and thereby has important implications for individual as well as collective identity. Fred Davis (1979, also cited in Spitzer 1999, 92) has likewise commented on nostalgia's recuperative value. In Davis's view, nostalgia 'sets up the positive from within the "world of yesterday" as a model for creative inspiration, and possible emulation, within the world of the here-and-now.'

In an insightful analysis, Leo Spitzer (1999, 96) introduces the concept of critical nostalgia, and in doing so underscores its political dimension. Spitzer argues that although nostalgic memory may be viewed as 'the selective emphasis on what was positive in the past,' it is not antithetical to a critical awareness of the negative aspects of one's past. He adds that nostalgia may function furthermore as a means of defiance against efforts to erase or deny the past. Writing about Austrian refugees' efforts to proclaim their 'Austrianness,' to 'reclaim an identification with an Austrian republic after the Anschluss, Nazi rule, and the defeat of the German Reich,' Spitzer observes 'a reassertion of rightful belonging within a body politic and cultural tradition from which the Nazis had attempted to sever them. "You have failed," they seem to assert, "We survive. We have a claim on the best of the past, and we welcome the future!"' (89).

Writing about women and memory, Judy Giles (2002) furthermore notes that regardless of the political sentiments of those who draw on a perhaps idealized past, we must recognize that nostalgia represents a valuing of the past over the present. As such, says Giles, 'while nostalgia can function as a repudiation of an escape from "the modern," it also has the potential to serve as a means of critiquing it.' The figure of one's mother, for example, can offer 'not only psychic regression to maternal plenitude,' but also 'a temporal and spatial return to the secure past of childhood and to the private world of the home' (28). A longing for the 'good old days,' can be read as 'a search for belonging' as well as an attempt to minimize the impact of 'many bereavements' (29–30).

An understanding of the ways in which nostalgia is informed by gendered social processes represents a significant development in the literature (Greene 1991; McDermott 2002, 389; Leydesdorff, Passerini, and Thompson 1996). According to Marianne Hirsch and Valerie Smith (2002), nostalgic narratives perform a 'gendered kind of cultural memory work,' and 'nostalgia mediates narratives and rituals that evolve out of gendered historical experiences' (6). While it is not specific to women, nostalgic memory does have different meanings for women and men. It may serve as one way in which a woman 'actively attempts to make herself at home in a world that continues to deny women like herself power and dignity' (Giles 2002, 30).

For Nisei women, nostalgic memories are firmly rooted in a much earlier life, one that looked dramatically different than later times. Notably, it harkens back to a time that was experienced in youth. Women who were relatively young during the internment described these years as ones of 'adventure.' These women related stories of glee clubs, birthday celebrations, girls' basketball, baseball, skating, tobogganing, going for walks, classes in sewing, cooking Japanese-style, flower arranging, and calligraphy, drama clubs, singsongs, the Hit Parade, Glen Miller, and old Japanese films, as well as Hollywood flicks starring the likes of Clark Gable, Jeannette MacDonald, Nelson Eddy, and Gene Autry. As Gloria recalled, 'The women would get together and they'd have sewing bees. They'd have cooking bees, and they'd tell each other all kinds of recipes they could use, by using what they were able to get. The Japanese had always been fond of making their own food – stuff like tofu and soy sauce and that.'

As well, such memories are placed in the context of a community of people, one that revolved around a shared ethnic and racial identity, as well as a common location within the racialized Canadian state. Notwithstanding its evils, in spite of the pain incurred, the internment brought many Japanese Canadians together in close physical proximity, in a situation of shared oppression. Though families were often separated, groups of Nisei women lived together in forced communities that were characterized by age, sex, and racial/ethnic homogeneity. Isolated in desolate parts of the interior of British Columbia, communities of internees had little choice but to develop bonds based on social support and common experience. In contrast, by the war's end, government policy shifted and the Japanese-Canadian communities that had ironically been affirmed by the internment, were forcibly dispersed. Many social bonds were severed and ethnic identities and loyalties were denied, as Japanese Canadians sought assimilation as a strategy to protect themselves from the harsh racism they had experienced in Canada.

Some women reminisced about these times of mutual support and shared experience, reinforced by gender-based friendships, youth, and a strong identity as Japanese Canadians. Such reminiscences, in some sense, helped the Nisei to define themselves as a group and to perpetuate a collective identity in the face of cultural dispersal in the post-war years.[21] Hideko,[22] for instance, explained: 'Those were very interesting years for me. That's where I met all my friends ... Nobody rich or poor or educated. We were all the same. And we all helped each other ... In fact, the whole of Tashme was ... we were happy. Nobody [was] sad. We all encouraged each other, you know. And helped each other so.'

After the War: Negotiating Racialized Identities

The next set of memories reveal an attempt on the part of the women to reconcile prewar, wartime, and postwar lives. What emerges from these images is the construction of a (Japanese) Canadian national identity, and, in a few women, an almost vehement rejection of the notion of themselves as foreign or 'other.' Nisei women's (albeit limited) understanding of Japan and the Japanese in the postwar years helps them to dissociate themselves from the latter, and, in the process, underlines their Canadianness. But it is equally important to note that this Canadianness has become, for some of the women, a Japanese Canadianness. Many of the women in this study have sought to reintegrate into their lives the previously neglected or denied aspects of their Japanese heritage.

This dissociation from the Japanese (as foreign) was done most effectively, overtly, and resolutely by two of the women who had moved to Japan at the war's end. They drew on their experiences in Japan to define themselves as distinctly Canadian and unassimilable into Japanese society. Chieko left Canada for Japan against her will, on her father's orders. She described this as a devastating event in her life: 'Oh, and I cried every day. When I landed in Japan, I heard American music coming through the radio and then I said, "Oh, I want to go back to Canada." ... Japanese people are completely different from the Japanese that we're used to in Canada ... Oh gosh, I hate these Japanese people, you know' *(laughing).*

An important part of the women's construction of themselves in the current period, the image they presented to me as a researcher/ audience, is embedded in a national identity. Decades after the internment, they continue to declare their loyalty to Canada. They join such statements with the memory of equally strong loyalties in the wartime past. In this way, a nationalism is woven throughout statements about present identities and memories of past identities. For example, as Pat reminded us: 'The Japanese people were loyal. They bought all the Victory Bonds. They supported everything the [Canadian] government did. But it didn't mean a thing in the end.' And Chieko added, 'Every time I go to Japan and come back, I think, "Gee, am I ever lucky to live in Canada." There's no place like Canada. When somebody criticizes Canada, I get so upset. I say, "You haven't lived in any other country, eh?" They say, "No." So, I say, "Don't criticize Canada, okay? This is the best country in the whole world ... and you don't realize it because you never experienced things outside of Canada."'

This allegiance to Canada is spoken by the same women who voice a sometimes implicit, at other times, unabashed critique of the government's actions during the war. This critique was also voiced and legitimated by the Redress activists and their Hakujin supporters. Remembering an incident that occurred long after the war, Eiko[23] poignantly expressed her views:

> EIKO: I cried when they said, 'We'll start the [Christmas] concert with "O Canada."'
> INTERVIEWER: Hmmm. Did you like that or you didn't like that?
> EIKO: Oh! I cried! I didn't like it, hearing 'O Canada.' I've been here ... I grew up with, you know, 'Canada is our home. And that we are Canadians – O Canada, our home and native land.' I really cried. Here it was our home and native land. But we were, you know, in internment camps.

Joining her personal views with those of the community as a whole, Sachi explained, 'We accepted it in our stride ... to Japanese, obedience was foremost. You have to obey what is being said, so if the government says so, that's it (laugh). As I say ... we weren't old enough to fight it. And if you were fighting it then you would have sort of an anger, and all kinds of things going with it as you're doing that. But no. I don't know. We resented it.'

Feeling Memories: Subjectivities of Dignity and Respect

Nearing the end of our conversations, I attempted to situate or move the women into their present lives. One way I did so was by asking them to reflect on their treatment during the war. Looking at the past from the present, some conveyed anger while others volunteered an explanation as to why they did not or no longer could or should feel anger. Anger about the internment, in most of the women, was tempered, sometimes hushed. It was typically, though not always, expressed with calm. And it was most often situated in their past selves. Yet, however conveyed, the articulation of anger by some women is striking insofar as it violates longstanding cultural notions about the Nisei, and Nisei women in particular.

Sachi and Polly both declared moments of outrage. The intensity of their feelings, however, had shifted over the years. Said Sachi, 'I was mad. I was very angry. And, well, after a while, it just grew into you. And you just forgot everything. You just went along with the tide.' Polly likewise remarked, '[I]n hindsight, I think of that and I get very annoyed. In fact, I get mad!' And Kay stated, 'When we got moved into New Denver, I had enough sense and feeling about why did we move there, and I was really resentful, you know. In my heart, let's say, I was really mad ... At home we had all this discrimination and all that ... When I moved out of there, moved out of the coast and went inwards ... and all this interruption and all that, I was really resentful. No, really, I had some anger even at the age of eleven or twelve, or whatever age I was. You could feel all the suffering.'

Many scholars who have written about the internment have long promoted the view that the collective Nisei response was aptly expressed by the phrase, *shikata ga nai*; that is, resignation, to the situation, or what can be done. (For a discussion of this concept, see Nagata 1994, 123.) This world view, along with *Gaman*, a Japanese term that refers to 'stoic patience' and 'the suppression of emotion' (123) was familiar to Kim. She stated, 'There was a wee bit of anger, I guess. But nothing really. We think, "Oh well, it's, you know, the way people see us."'

Read without context, many such statements appear to be consistent with these world views. Yet when understood as part of a fuller narrative, these statements take on a different meaning. They seem to be a crutch, within easy reach, and contained by cultural and gendered views of acceptable behaviour. 'What can be done' helps to neatly and benignly describe a complex, ambivalent, and perhaps dangerous set of emotions. The women's narratives suggest that these sentiments are almost always associated with resignation rather than acceptance. Thus, *shikata ga nai* may be understood as a sentiment that evolves over time. Though it is often written about as an 'essential' cultural trait, we may also interpret it as an adaptive response to a situation of powerlessness.

Ambivalence and multiple meanings can be detected in different parts of Betty's testimony.

Early in her narrative:
You look back now, you realize, yes, you couldn't leave and there were lots of things you couldn't do. But it didn't affect me personally at that time, and at that age. Nobody called me names or anything, you know. I had my friends. Nobody shunned me.

A bit later in her narrative:
It was just racism. And then at that time too the Isseis were very quiet. They thought they couldn't say anything. The Niseis too were brought up that way, to respect your elders, don't make moves. During the war and shortly after, we were told, 'Study hard so you can be better than anybody else. You got to go to school. Don't argue. Don't get yourself in trouble, right? Because you're going to be discriminated against. You're supposed to obey everybody, and just don't make waves.' So, that's the way the Japanese, the Niseis, were brought up. But the Sanseis grew up different. At that time ... you were brought up that you had certain rights. Speak out, right? Is that how you learned in school?

As well, in listening for emotions, the pauses, silences, gaps, and emphases are important. In hearing stories that are emotionally charged, one must attend to the meaning behind the words. The speaker's voice also conveys a message. The written word does not easily impart a whisper. As Childers (2002, 204) explains, in written form, 'memories can assume a depressive posture that hides that which is actually experienced in the act of memory: the pleasure of surprise, the stimulation of thought, the excitement of yearning, and the titillation of the unspeakable.' The significance of tone, pause, voice was powerfully conveyed by Eiko:[24] 'Nowadays, I always think, you know, instead of doing that [interning us], they could line all of us up and ... one of those – what did they call that, machine guns? – and just kill all of us. We all felt like that. It's really much nicer if they had done that. We wouldn't have had to worry, 'Where are we going? What are we going to do?' *(hushed and with strong emotion)*.

It is also important to note that the women presented past suffering with care. While they wanted their pain to be acknowledged, they also did not wish to reduce their status to that of victims (see Childers 2002, 214). They presented their stories in a way that highlighted their endurance, as well as their agency. Judy Giles's (2002, 36) concept of 'composing subjectivities of dignity and self-respect' aptly describes this manner of presentation. Giles notes that working-class women, in particular, relate stories as a means of reinforcing identities for themselves that offer dignity and self-respect in a world that renders them powerless.

In asserting dignity and self-respect, the women gave me many happy endings. The conviction of a happy ending, indeed, was resonant at the conclusion of most of the testimonies. In the words of Mary Childers (2002, 204), an 'ideology of positive thinking and a national myth of triumphant social mobility' could be detected in their narratives. Hideko,[25] for instance, said, 'Everybody has done well because of the suffering. They achieved. It's very hard to be somebody. And they have done well. Most of them.' Rose likewise commented, 'Well, a lot of us, you know, have different ways of interpreting. We always sort of said, "What would we have been doing if it wasn't for the war?" But the war, on the other hand, gave us an opportunity and we measured up to it, you know. So I give credit to the Nisei. They had nothing, you know ... So a lot of people use the term "blessing in disguise" ... There's no poor Nisei ... I give them credit because they're not inheriting anything.'

Hannah, too, explained: 'Well, if this hadn't happened and we were still living at the coast, we'd probably be discriminated [against] ... And people have been able to further their education and they wouldn't be what they are today, a lot of people. So, in a way, maybe it was ... it was terrible to go through that, but I guess in the end ... you look at it now – people are scattered all over and we are a minority group, eh? And maybe that's the way it was. And maybe it was a good thing. Hmmm *(spoken very softly)*.' Finally, Eiko[26] closed her narrative in remarking, 'We coped. That's all. You know, Japanese women are really tough. We survived.' Though they may appear to be fragmented and 'fractured,' remembrances such as these are perhaps 'necessary to a sense of freedom and possibility in the present?' (Childers 2002, 204).

The nostalgic memories expressed by many Nisei women have helped to shape a 'secure identity' and build a 'positive image of the self' in both the past and present. Such memories, moreover, provide 'reassurance and encouragement' to face the future (Davis, cited in Vromen 1994, 78). For many women, memories of internment are no longer dangerous or threatening. In some ways, they feel they have been liberated from the burdens of racial oppression. Most of them now live in greater material comfort than in the past. Many have loving relationships with Hakujin sons- and daughters-in-law, as well as with biracial grandchildren. The Japanese-Canadian community currently has the political voice and legitimacy that have accompanied the upward social mobility of their Sansei offspring. But, importantly, the act of remembering has also helped some women to (re)interpret the violent past. Remembering, in a way, underscores the distinction between past and present. In communicating their personal narratives, some women have symbolically distanced themselves from the past – even though part of themselves will always remain centrally situated in years gone by.

The memories communicated to me were individually experienced and deeply personal. Yet they were, at the same time, very much woven into a shared and collective memory. The personal memories both grew out of, and contributed to, a broader Japanese-Canadian narrative. Indeed, the Redress Movement itself was built in large part upon the concept of memory. While the official, documented history of the internment was by no means simply a compilation of personal memories (nor does it represent the range of individual memoirs), it did draw largely on oral testimonies from certain members of the community. And this history served as a valuable resource in the struggle of some Nisei and their Sansei children to challenge the status quo and ultimately secure financial compensation from the federal government. Given the extremely high rates of interracial marriage amongst Japanese Canadians, as well as their geographic scattering, these memories will serve as an important social, cultural, and political thread. In future years, community bonds may, paradoxically, rest not on 'racial blood' but rather on shared memories and a place in this nation's political history.

Conclusion: Healing and Restorative Memories

When a seventy-nine- or eighty-year-old woman says that, as a twelve- or thirteen-year-old girl, she was angry with the government, what does this mean? It is impossible to ascertain if this statement is 'true' or 'not true.' As a researcher, I cannot prove or disprove the veracity of the women's testimonies. Nor am I interested in doing so. While I began this research in an effort to gather empirical data to support, and to add a human dimension to 'historical truths,' my engagement with the women and their narratives prompted me to reconsider my approach. The value of their words is in viewing them as the memory of lived experience. Rather than as a 'passive depository of facts,' memory may be understood as 'an active process by which meanings are created' (Portelli, cited in Giles 2002, 23).

This chapter calls for a rethinking and problematizing of the process of remembering and the product of that act: memories. There is a need to explore the relationship between personal memory and historical context. Memories, after all, do not originate exclusively within the individual. Memory may be understood as a cultural and social phenomenon, as well as an individual one. Moreover, cultural memorization is a bridging of past and present. According to Mieke Bal (1999), it is 'an activity occurring in the present, in which the past is continuously modified and redescribed even as it continues to shape the future' (vii). Memories, then, are fluid. Collective memories are renegotiated. Personal memories are 'recrafted and rethought' (Sturken 1997, 702). '"Memories," in the sense of a narrative offered to a listener-reader, are constantly made and remade as people attempt to make sense of the past in a changing present' (Portelli, cited in Giles 2002, 23).

This conceptualization of memory is important insofar as it gives agency to the subjects of history. Van der Kolk and van der Hart (1995 cited in Bal 1999, ix) write about memory as an action, '"essentially, it is the action of telling a story."' The Nisei women's memories were framed and bounded by history (certainly not of their own choosing). But these memories actively interpreted, crafted, and recrafted their experience of this history.

To tell history is to act in a verbal mode (Tonkin 1992, 11). According to Tonkin, 'Using language not only involves a choice of "orientation" to a topic and to the person or persons with whom one is in communication: it also involves a "claim" that one should be listened to. To speak at all makes this claim' (39). It is telling that all of the women who shared their testimonies actively chose to participate in this project. They were under no obligation. Some volunteered with eagerness. Others revealed an initial hesitancy. But all of these women, in different ways, located themselves in history. Though some displayed a sense of inferiority, a fear of ordinariness, of insignificance, of invisibility, they agreed to share their stories, with the knowledge that these stories would eventually become part of a public narrative. Moreover, all but a handful of the women made a decision, without any apparent reluctance, to have their names used in print. They have selected memory fragments, filtered their memories for the new audience that I bring to their lives. But in doing so, they have rejected anonymity and silence. Their contribution is of immense value. As stated by Hirsch and Smith (2002), 'forgetting and suppression must be contested by active remembering' (10). The personal act of remembering, woven into an analysis of culture and society, is, after all, a political project. It lies at the heart of political activism and movements for social change.

NOTES

Earlier versions of this chapter were presented at the annual meeting of the Canadian Sociology and Anthropology Association, University of Toronto, June 2002, and as part of the Asian-Canadian Feminist Speaker Series sponsored by the Centre for Feminist Studies and the Centre for Asian Studies, York University. This project was funded by the Social Sciences and Humanities Research Council of Canada and the National Association of Japanese Canadians. For their insights, suggestions, and support, I wish to thank Vijay Agnew, Rose Aihoshi, Gillian Anderson, Candace Kemp, Katerina Deliovsky, Kathryn McPherson, Leah Vosko, Nico Stehr, the anonymous reviewers for the *Canadian Journal of Sociology*, and especially Tomiko Robson. Robert Storey and Tamura Sugiman-Storey, as always, deserve a heartfelt thank you.

 1 Prior to the outbreak of war, in the spring of 1941, the Royal Canadian Mounted Police registered and fingerprinted all Japanese Canadians over the age of sixteen. In the following year, the federal government forcibly uprooted 22,000 persons of Japanese descent. Seventy-five per cent of these individuals were either Canadian-born or naturalized citizens. Many had been given only twenty-four hours to prepare for their departure. As explained by Roy Miki and Cassandra Kobayashi (1991, 16–17), this uprooting was not an isolated act of racism. From the time of early Japanese immigration to Canada, there had been strong anti-Asian sentiments. The war, they say, 'offered the opportune moment for many powerful politicians, business and labour groups, and individuals in BC, to attack the social and economic base of the thriving Japanese Canadian community, under the guise of national security.' According to a Price Waterhouse estimate, the Japanese-Canadian community suffered a total economic loss of at least $443 million (calculated in 1986 dollars). Total income loss was estimated at $333 million. And property loss (including farms, fishing boats, houses, businesses, and personal belongings) was calculated at

$110 million. (Miki and Kobayashi, 1991, 92–93). Japanese Canadians did not secure the right to the federal vote until June 1948 (effective April 1949). They won the right to vote in the province of British Columbia in March 1949.

2 In August 1944, Prime Minister Mackenzie King stated in his House of Commons address: 'The sound policy and the best policy for the Japanese Canadians themselves is to distribute their numbers as widely as possible throughout the country where they will not create feelings of racial hostility' (*Debates*, House of Commons, 4 August 1944, cited in Miki and Kobayashi 1991, 50). In this address, King focused on the visibility of Japanese Canadians as a racial group rather than on issues of national security (the government's officially stated reason for the internment), and claimed that their dispersal either to Japan or east of the Rockies, was in the group's best interests. King's reasoning, write Roy Miki and Audrey Kobayashi (1991, 50), 'endorsed a policy of cultural genocide and disguised it as benign paternalism.'

3 In her study of Japanese Canadian women, Mona Oikawa (1999, 7n14) adopts the term *national violence* rather than *political violence*. Oikawa argues in favour of the latter, in order to underscore how this violence was perpetrated as part of the process of nation-building. As well, she wishes to emphasis how the internment involved a 'nation of citizens,' not only politicians or the state.

4 My larger study draws on the oral testimonies of approximately 50 Nisei women currently residing in Ontario, Quebec, British Columbia, Alberta, and Manitoba; an analysis of the two Japanese-Canadian community newspapers, *The New Canadian* and *Tairiku Nippo*; and a review of various documentary sources housed in archives throughout Ontario and BC. In this chapter, I view the act of testimony itself through a lens of gender and race. I do not, however, present an empirical examination of sex-based differences. Rather than compare female and male, I speculate on how the social and political relations of gender and race 'evoke histories' (Hirsch and Smith 2002, 2).

5 While this group of women may differ from those living in other parts of Canada, my sample does highlight 'in some ways, the heterogeneity of the female Nisei population' At the outset of war, the women were adolescents or young adults. Their fathers were farmers, agricultural labourers, fishermen, small-scale entrepreneurs, a printer, a physician. Most mothers worked at home raising children, farming, sewing, cooking, and sporadically taking on agricultural labour or cannery work for pay. All of the women were born in British Columbia, and, at the outbreak of war,

departed to various parts of the province: Lillooet, Bridge River, Tashme, Greenwood, Slocan (Slocan City, Lemon Creek, Popoff, Bay Farm, Rosebery), New Denver, Sandon, and Kaslo. All had at least one male relative (father, brother, uncle, husband) in a prisoner-of-war camp or general road camp in Angler or Petawawa, Ontario. Upon leaving the west coast, some of the women were forced by parents or husbands to move to Japan. Most remained in Canada.

Though most of the women experienced some economic hardship in their early lives, they could be described as now living comfortably (though not with excessive wealth). A minority of the women in this study eventually attained a university degree, but most did not have a chance to finish high school. The majority eventually married. All but two of the women have children, and of these, all have grandchildren. Notably, their children and grandchildren have become highly educated and successful in employment. All but one of the women's grandchildren, the *Yonsei* (fourth generation), are biracial (that is, Anglo-Celtic/European and Japanese Canadian). All of the women shared their stories with us (myself or a research assistant) in their own homes. The testimonies themselves ranged from one and one-half hours to five hours in duration. More informal conversations with women lasted much longer. About one-third of the testimonies were given in two parts; all were taped and transcribed.

6 The Redress Agreement was signed by the National Association of Japanese Canadians and the Canadian government on 22 September 1988. For more information on the Redress Movement and Agreement, see for example, Ad Hoc committee for Japanese Canadian Redress 2000; Kobayashi 1992; Kurian 1995; Miki and Kobayashi 1991; National Association of Japanese Canadians 1985; Omatsu 1993.

7 The women's words also forced me to think about the relationship between personal testimonies and the larger historical narrative. As I attempted to understand the women's recollections, it became clear that an historical narrative is informed by various sources. The testimonies contributed to the narrative, but represent only one part. The women's recollections should thus be read in conjunction with (or in the context of) the collective, more public narrative of Japanese-Canadian experience: those produced by professional historians, community spokespersons, and the popular media (see, for example, Giles, 2002, 26).

8 See, for example, Alexander 1994; Bal, Crewe, and Spitzer 1999; Bourguet, Valensi, and Wachtel 1986; Butler 1989; Casey 1987; Connerton 1989; Hirsch 1997; Irwin-Zarecka 1994; Kuhn 2000; Leydesdorf, Passerini, and Thompson 1996; Portelli 1988; Zandy 1995.

9 Similarly, Alessandro Portelli (1981a, 172) argues that to date an event is
not only to place the event in linear sequence, but also to 'choose *which*
linear sequences to place it in and by.' Annette Kuhn (2000, 189) notes that
in memory texts, time seldom comes across as fully continuous or sequen-
tial. She writes, 'The tenses of the memory text do not fix events to specific
moments of time or temporal sequences. Events are repetitive or cyclical
("at one time ... ") or seem to be set apart from fixed orders of time ("once
upon a time" ...).'

10 For example, many women make a causal connection between their
current economic status (in most cases, financially comfortable) and the
internment. They reason that they wouldn't have been successful in the
postwar years, if they hadn't been forced to disperse and relocate from BC
to Ontario. I question whether or not the women would have made the
same causal links if they were asked to describe their current economic
position in another social context (that is, outside of an internment narrative).

11 The term *Hakujin* is used loosely by Japanese Canadians to refer to 'white'
people or 'Caucasians.'

12 Yves Lequin's study of the workers of Givors, France (1980, cited in
Wachtel 1986, 219) suggests a distinction between *personal memory* that
emerges from life stories, and *official history*. According to Lequin, personal
memories tend to be 'confiscated or diluted,' in contrast to official histories. While a worker recognizes that certain events are a part of national
history, he has nothing original to say about this past. In the worker's
view, such events are 'the territory of political leaders and professional
historians.' The worker adopts the history of the labour movement as
official, but does not adopt it 'as his own.' National and working-class
memories, therefore, remain 'heterogeneous' and 'outside the personal
story.'

13 The idea of a 'memory snapshot' was inspired by Mieke Bal's writing on
'narrative memory.' Bal describes his narrative memory as distinct from
routine or habitual memories 'in that they are affectively colored, surrounded by an emotional aura, that, precisely, makes them memorable.
Often the string of events that composes a narrative (and narratable)
memory offers high and low accents, foreground and background, prepa-
ratory and climactic events' (Bal 1999, viii).

14 Families who possessed the economic resources could 'choose' to relocate
to sites termed by the federal government as 'self-supporting.' In practice,
in exchange for a very partial family reunification, these families shoul-
dered more of the financial burden of their own internment. Women who
lived in 'self-supporting camps' such as Lillooet, claimed they were able to

bring more personal belongings with them when relocated. They felt this was one of the privileges of being in a self-supporting site.

15 Yves Lequin's study (1980, cited in Wachtel 1986, 219) of French workers highlights the concept of a 'shared group memory,' one in which the narrator adopts recounted events as his own, even though he himself has not personally experienced such events.

16 A pseudonym.

17 The discussion of the construction of memory in relation to mothers may also be found in Sugiman, 'Understanding Silence,' *forthcoming*.

18 A pseudonym.

19 Only a couple of the women in this study were mothers during the war years. They spoke of having sole responsibility for the welfare of their young children. Caring for their children's basic needs was their greatest worry.

20 The term *nostalgia* is taken from the Greek *nostos* (to return home) and *algia* (a painful feeling) (McDermott 2002). The meaning of the word has changed over time. At the beginning of the eighteenth century, writes Susan Vromen (1994, 70), it was considered to reveal a desire to return to a specific place, 'a localized reality.' However, this meaning then gradually shifted to embrace a yearning for childhood itself, and therefore a 'chronic, inconsolable, and incurable condition.'

21 Fred Davis (1979, cited in Vromen 1994) argues that nostalgia is deeply connected to 'a people's historical sense of themselves as a group, because it deflects or attenuates threats to the loss of discontinuity of identity' (78). Furthermore, nostalgia may generate a collective identity insofar as a specific generation shares a specific kind of nostalgia. 'By using selected events from the past symbolically and nostalgically, a demographic cohort becomes an identifiable generation, one with a living sense of history' (79).

22 A pseudonym.

23 A pseudonym.

24 A pseudonym.

25 A pseudonym

26 A pseudonym.

REFERENCES

Ad Hoc Committee for Japanese Canadian Redress. 2000. *Japanese Canadian Redress: The Toronto Story.* Toronto: HpF Press.

Alexander, Sally. 1994. Memory, Generation and History: Two Women's Lives in the Inter-war Years. In *Becoming a Woman and Other Essays in*

19th and 20th Century Feminist History, ed. Sally Alexander, 231–242. London: Virago.

Bal, Mieke. 1999. Introduction. In *Acts of Memory: Cultural Recall in the Present*, ed. Mieke Bal, Jonathan Crewe, and Leo Spitzer, vii–xvii. Hanover: University Press of England.

Bal, Mieke, Jonathan Crewe, and Leo Spitzer, eds. 1999. *Acts of Memory*. Hanover: University Press of England.

Bastide, Roger, 1960. *Les religions africaines au Brésil*, 334–361. Paris: Presses universitaires de France ('Bibliotheque de sociologie contemporaine').

Bourguet, Marie-Noelle, Lucette Valensi, and Nathan Wachtel, eds. 1986. *Between Memory and History: Special Issue of History and Anthropology 2*, Pt. 2 (October).

Boym, Svetlana. 2001. *The Future of Nostalgia*. New York: Basic Books.

Butler, Thomas, ed. 1989. *Memory: History, Culture and the Mind*. Oxford: Basil Blackwell.

Casey, Edward S. 1987. *Remembering: A Phenomenological Study*. Bloomington: Indiana University Press.

Childers, Mary M. 2002. 'The Parrot or the Pit Bull': Trying to Explain Working-Class Life. *Signs: Journal of Women in Culture and Society* 28 (1): 201–220.

Connerton, Paul. 1989. *How Societies Remember*. New York: Cambridge University Press.

Debouzy, Marianne. 1986. In Search of Working-Class Memory: Some Questions and a Tentative Assessment. *History and Anthropology* 2: 261–282.

Gans, Herbert J. 1979. Symbolic Ethnicity. In *On the Making of Americans: Essays in Honor of David Riesman*, ed. Herbert Gans et al, 193–220. Philadelphia: University of Philadelphia Press.

Giles, Judy, 2002. Narratives of Gender, Class, and Modernity in Women's Memories of Mid-Twentieth-Century Britain. *Signs: Journal of Women in Culture and Society*. Special Issue on Gender and Cultural Memory 28 (1): 21–41.

Greene, Gayle. 1991. Feminist Fiction and the Uses of Memory. *Signs* 16 (1): 290–321.

Halbwachs, Maurice. 1992. *On Collective Memory*. Ed. and trans. by Lewis A. Coser. Chicago: University of Chicago Press.

Hirsch, Marianne. 1997. *Family Frames: Photography, Narrative, and Postmemory*. Cambridge, MA: Harvard University Press.

Hirsch, Marianne, and Valerie Smith. 2002. Feminism and Cultural Memory: An Introduction. *Signs: Journal of Women in Culture and Society* 28 (1): 1–19.

Irwin-Zarecka, Iwona. 1994. *Frames of Remembrance: The Dynamics of Collective Memory*. New Brunswick, NJ: Transaction.

Kobayashi, Audrey. 1992. The Japanese Canadian Redress Settlement and Its Implications for Race Relations. *Canadian Ethnic Studies* 24: 1–19.

Kuhn, Annette. 2000. A Journey through Memory. In *Memory and Methodology*, ed. Susannah Radstone, 186. Oxford: Berg.

Kurian, George. 1995. Bittersweet Passage: Redress and the Japanese Canadian Experience. *Journal of Comparative Family Studies* 26: 286–287.

Lasch, Christopher. 1984. The Politics of Nostalgia. *Harper's* (November), 65–70.

Leydesdorff, Selma, Luisa Passerini, and Paul Thompson. 1996. *Gender and Memory*. Vol. 4 of *International Yearbook of Oral History and Life Stories*. Oxford: Oxford University Press.

Lowenthal, David. 1989. Nostalgia Tells It Like It Wasn't. In *The Imagined Past: History and Nostalgia*, ed. M. Chase and C. Shaw, 18–32. Manchester: Manchester University Press.

Miki, Roy, and Cassandra Kobayashi. 1991. *Justice in Our Time: The Canadian Redress Settlement*. Vancouver and Winnipeg: Talonbooks and National Association of Japanese Canadians.

McAllister, Kirsten Emiko. 1999. Remembering Political Violence. The Nikkei Internment Memorial Centre. PhD Diss., Department of Sociology and Anthropology, Carleton University, Hamilton, ON.

– 2001. Captivating Debris: Unearthing a World War Two Internment Camp. *Cultural Values* 5 (1): 97–114.

McDermott, Sinead. 2002. Memory, Nostalgia, and Gender in *A Thousand Acres*. *Signs: Journal of Women in Culture and Society* 28 (1): 389–407.

Nagata, Donna K. 1994. Coping with Internment: A Nisei Woman's Perspective. In *Women Creating Lives: Identities, Resilience, and Resistance*, ed. Carol E. Franz and Abigail J. Stewards, 115–126. Boulder: Westview Press.

National Association of Japanese Canadians. 1985. *Economic Losses of Japanese Canadians After 1941*. A study conducted by Price Waterhouse. Winnipeg: Hignell Printing.

Neumann, Anna. 1997. Ways without Words: Learning from Silence and Story in Post-Holocaust Lives. In *Learning from Our Lives: Women, Research, and Autobiography in Education*, ed. A. Neumann and P.L. Peterson, 91–120. New York: Teachers College Press.

Oikawa, Mona. 1999. Cartographies of Violence: Women, Memory, and the Subject(s) of the 'Internment.' PhD Diss. OISE/University of Toronto.

Omatsu, Maryka. 1993. *Bittersweet Passage*. Toronto: Between the Lines.

Osborne, Brian S. 2001. Landscapes, Memory, Monuments, and Commemoration: Putting Identity in Its Place. *Canadian Ethnic Studies* 33 (3): 39–77.

Petonito, Gina. 1992. Constructing the Enemy: Justifying Japanese Internment during World War II. PhD Diss. Syracuse University, Syracuse, NY.

Portelli, Alessandro. 1981a. 'The Time of My Life': Functions of Time in Oral History. *International Journal of Oral History* 2 (3): 162–80.
– 1981b. The Peculiarities of Oral History. *History Workshop Journal* 12: 96–107.
– 1988. Unchronic Dreams: Working Class Memory and Possible Worlds. *Oral History Journal* 16 (2): 46–56.
Rosaldo, Renato. 1989. Imperalist Nostalgia. In *Culture and Truth: The Remaking of Social Analysis*. Boston: Beacon Press.
Spitzer, Leo. 1999. Back through the Future: Nostalgic Memory and Critical Memory in a Refuge from Nazism. In *Acts of Memory*, ed. Mieke Bal, Jonathan Crew, and Leo Spitzer, 87–104. Hanover: University Press of England.
Steedman, Carolyn. 1986. *Landscape for a Good Woman: A Story of Two Lives*. London: Virago.
Sturken, Marita. 1997. Absent Images of Memory: Remembering and Reenacting the Japanese Internment. *Positions* 5 (3) (winter): 687–707.
Sugiman, Pamela. 2003. Understanding Silence: Finding Meaning in the Oral Testimonies of Nisei Women in Canada. *Selected Proceedings of the Changing Japanese Identities in Multicultural Canada Conference*. Centre for Asia Pacific Initiatives, University of Victoria.
Tonkin, Elizabeth. 1992. *Narrating Our Pasts: The Social Construction of Oral History*. New York: Cambridge University Press.
Van der Kolk, A. Bessel, and Onno van der Hart. 1995. The Intrusive Past: The Flexibility of Memory and the Engraving of Trauma. In *Trauma: Explorations in Memory*, ed. Cathy Caruth, 158–183. Baltimore: Johns Hopkins University Press.
Wachtel, Nathan. 1986. Introduction. Between Memory and History. *History and Anthropology* 2 (2): 207–224.
Williams, Raymond. 1974. *The Country and the City*. New York: Oxford University Press.
Vromen, Suzanne. 1994. The Ambiguity of Nostalgia. *YIVO Annual* 21: 69–121.
Zandy, Janet, ed. 1995. *Liberating Memory: Our Work and Our Working-Class Consciousness*. New Brunswick, NJ: Rutgers University Press.
Zerubavel, Eviatar. 1996. Social Memories: Steps to a Sociology of the Past. *Qualitative Sociology* 19 (3): 283–299.

3 Wounding Events and the Limits of Autobiography

MARLENE KADAR

Apparently nobody wants to know that contemporary history has created a new kind of human being – a kind put in concentration camps by their foes and internment camps by their friends.[1]

(Hannah Arendt, 1906–1975)

When the German philosopher Hannah Arendt made this astonishing claim in a brilliant essay titled 'We Refugees' (1943), she was of course speaking about the banishment of the Jews from Europe and the sense of shame and confusion it engendered in them. But she was also speaking about herself, a woman who fled her homeland of Germany for France in 1933 and fled again to America in 1941. Ten years later, Arendt obtained American citizenship, never to return to Germany. It is wrong to say that Arendt chose her exile, but it is possible to say that she did not choose to repatriate after the period of her wandering. In any case, if we follow Julia Kristeva's analysis, it is in this period of fleeing and seeking refuge that Arendt began to live out her philosophical passion: life and thought are one and the same, and life is at the centre.[2]

Theorists of autobiography often start with the observation that life and narrative are intimately connected, but what happens if they are not or if the narrative is minimal? What interests me is the adaptability of autobiographical genres and how well diverse writers – both the celebrated and 'the socially insignificant and powerless' or 'ordinary people'[3] – use them to communicate traumatic personal and historical events. Indeed, often life is narrative, as Kristeva's title says, or life is represented as narrative, and we have some excellent literary autobiographies to prove this – from Primo Levi's haunting philosophical first-person narratives to Jorge Semprun's *Literature or Life*, both of which are more aptly described as 'half essay, half memoir.'[4]

Nevertheless, not all autobiographical narratives look like Levi's or Semprun's. They may not be as intertextual or as philosophically or formally sophisticated. They may not 'extend beyond' the personal experience of the author/survivor, and thus may be considered inferior as literature. But then how *is* a traumatic historical event represented when the autobiographical cannot extend beyond the 'personal' into a more dense and profound narrative – in the way that reviewers say great literature is profound? Or when the narrators are broken and burdened by haunting and sometimes sketchy memories, but do not have the skill or the intention to reveal these memories? Or, in another context, when the remembrances are not in narrative form, or their source is oral literature? We can assume that life is still at the centre of the representation, but the connection between life and narrative is not necessarily primary. Indeed, the link between the writing and the memory of death or immanent death may be more poignant.

Theorists of autobiography have successfully made the case for a life writing text that does not conform to the more celebrated norm of 'Western civilization during the last four hundred years,' rooted in what Sidonie Smith (1998) has called the Renaissance 'misbegotten man,' a history that erases 'the matrilineal trace of women's subjectivity.'[5] The next step is to see how far we can push the limits of the autobiographical genres in relation to the remembering of deeply wounding events. Some may resist the further dilution of the laws of genre, whereas others will accept a wide variety of writings as autobiographical genres, or, as some theorists prefer to write, auto/biography.[6] It was 1980 when Jacques Derrida issued the warning: 'As soon as the word "genre" is sounded, as soon as it is heard, as soon as one attempts to conceive it, a limit is drawn. And when a limit is established, norms and interdictions are not far behind: "Do," "Do not," says genre, the word "genre," the figure, the voice, or the law of genre ... Thus, as soon as genre announces itself, one must respect a norm, one must not cross a line of demarcation, one must not risk impurity, anomaly or monstrosity.'[7]

Derrida is concerned about the interdictions that result when too much respect is accorded to the limits, and, thus, conventions of genre. Certainly, one could argue that ignoring the victims of the Holocaust because they either cannot write or because their stories are deemed fragmented or irregular or are represented in genres that are impure, anomalous, or monstrous results in misrepresentation. Even worse, it may result in no representation at all, as in the case of stigmatized minorities or small groups of Hitler's victims: children and youth, Jews, Gypsies, blacks, Jehovah's Witnesses, twins, sufferers of epilepsy, the disabled, Roman Catholic nuns, homosexuals, and so on.

Some theorists whose purpose is to emphasize the similarities between biography and autobiography defy the limits of the genre. In spite of Derrida's claims, life writing theorists do not contend that differences do not exist, but that differences are not of primary significance.[8] Regenia Gagnier's study of first-person narratives led her to conclude that 'what is striking about the 'mind' ... is not its uniqueness or autonomy, but rather its profound dependence upon intersubjectively shared meanings and its profound vulnerability to the deprivations of the body.'[9] What is needed, argue Gagnier, Carolyn Steedman, Trev Broughton, and other British theorists, is the 'eschewing of a narrowly textual approach to life writing.'[10] Auto/biographical practices involve interdisciplinary thinking, writes Broughton, but are also a cognizance of the role of auto/biography in the formation of disciplines. In the context of the Holocaust, this cognizance might mean the investigation of how auto/biographical practices work in the larger system of recording lives, and then, deaths, and how they are often constituted as material objects: birth lists, death lists, deporation lists, physician's notebooks, recipe books, and the list goes on.

Life Writing and History

What interests me most is how life writing forms are changed by specific historical circumstances and not how well they represent their subjects according to a specific standard of adequacy (and therefore succeed or fail as examples of the genre). If we are obliged to evaluate life writings, we get stuck in a vicious circle of genre critique that restricts our imaginative apprehension of the subject of our study: the individual life as represented in a specific context. Broughton has expressed this idea clearly: 'It has taken a sustained onslaught from interdisciplinary scholarship, much of it feminist or feminist-inspired, to wrest Life-writing away from these wearying and largely unanswerable questions, or rather to prove that the questions are unanswerable in isolation either from each other or from larger issues of social movement and political process'[11] – such as the traumatic historical events of the Holocaust. As Leigh Gilmore (1994) suggests, we want to call into question the standard form of autobiography and its 'classic hierarchies' by speaking about a 'mark of autobiography' rather than an autobiography proper. Gilmore follows the lead of Monique Wittig when she speaks of 'the mark of gender' as a grammatical category with often unclear ideological implications. The mark of autobiography, writes Gilmore, 'is located provisionally in the always problematical deployment of the I' (6), and does not easily, simply or 'properly refer.'[12] This 'mark' is still an autobiographical practice,[13] and conveys significant details about the self or the personal and the private life, the contours of an autobiographical identity. Gilmore explains that it is first specified in terms of a linguistic function (7). Importantly, however, the mark also 'indicates a disruption in genre, an eruption or interruption of self-representation in genres in which it has not been previously legitimated.'[14] It still has an autobiographer or biographer who functions as the speaker/narrator and whose discourse also shifts the boundaries between self and other, past and present, writing and reading, and sometimes in the most limited sense. Gilmore sees this as an opportunity to read the autobiographical differently because we encounter the creation of 'an enlivening instability in both text and context' (7). Thus, in order to improve representation, we must continually seek the autobiographical in new forms. This task could not be more urgent than it is now, both because the autobiographers who were born before 1945 are dying, and because of the proliferation of autobiographical texts in the last two decades. This chapter, then, will discuss a variety of texts by narrators who both embrace biographical or autobiographical concepts and yet illustrate a certain disruption of the genre that might be tied to the wounding of the subject, a certain disruption of the genre that might be tied to the psychological distress of the subject.

Our knowledge of the personal experiences of victims of the Holocaust and our understanding of what is meant by 'the personal' itself depends on current historical and literary studies. These studies, in turn, are dependent on historical, geographical, racial, and gendered meanings found in both the scholarship and the life writing itself. The life writing has proliferated of late – to the great advantage of scholars. Survivors in the diaspora, for example, have realized late in life that the time has come to tell or recall their experiences, or the climate has changed so much that they are more willing or psychologically able to tell. At war's end, recalls Alicia Appleman-Jurman, she was told to 'forget what happened and go on,' so she did not speak. She says that tragically American relatives, in particular, could not hear their stories:

'They couldn't take us with the Holocaust because we came with the tragedy of their family ... We have seen the unseeable.'[15]

Researchers also seem to feel the time is right for them to further uncover the horrific details of the past or to correct the record that has already been so painstakingly prepared for us before now. We can surmise that autobiographical practices that assist us in learning more about the historical record through personal experience can be enabling and can therefore make their own contribution to an idealistic philosophy of prevention and to the vital 'shaping of Holocaust memory in America' and in Canada.[16]

Gendered Wounding and Memoirs

There is a current proliferation of life writing texts composed by women who are in exile as a consequence of the Holocaust. These texts often speak directly to a 'gendered wounding'[17] that is the product of two separate but simultaneous and/or consecutive traumatic events: the Nazi genocide and numerous methods of heinous persecution, and the simultaneous or subsequent period of wandering. During this period of wandering, the Jewish woman's status changes from stateless Jew once again without a homeland to refugee in another land, exiled in the widening diaspora of the globe. Many so-called 'Holocaust memoirs' end with a reference to the genocide. Aranka Siegal's (1981) polished autobiographical novel for young adults, *Upon the Head of the Goat: A Childhood in Hungary 1939–1944*, serves as a good example. Before the young Piri's mother is able to explain where she and her family were going, 'the German guard yelled, '*Achtung! Rein! Rein!*' And Mother pulled her head back just in time to avoid being struck by the door [of the cattle car] as it closed with a loud metallic clank.'[18] Other very recent memoirs focus on both parts of the experience. Two Hungarian Canadian memoirists introduce the first stage of suffering: ghettoization and deportation. Elisabeth Raab's first night away from home is spent in the nearby ghetto in the industrial city of Györ, after which she is quickly deported to Auschwitz-Birkenau. Ibi Grossman, on the other hand, is hustled into the Budapest ghetto and considers herself luckier than most as the Russian Army liberated her there on Akácfa (Acacia) Street in January 1945. We consider this first violent and shocking exile from the family home the first stage of the women's wounding – trauma or distress – and it is the subject of most memoirs written in the first decades after the war.

The second stage of exile is in the wandering and migration that followed 'liberation.' In an award-winning memoir published in 1997, Raab says to herself in the summer of 1946, 'I can't bear not to believe I have arrived at the end of my wandering,'[19] yet the title of her memoir sadly reveals that the end has not come and likely never will: *And Peace Never Came*. It is during her 'wandering months' in Europe that Raab experiences the consequences of the first trauma of deportation, incarceration, and hard labour most acutely; this is ironically the period of her 'liberation.' This is the effect of trauma, as Cathy Caruth (1996) and Shosana Felman and Dori Laub (1992) have described it; it is a confusing psychological state in which one records the past remembered event as if there were no witnesses. Thus, it cannot be known and cannot be told; it can only be repeated.[20]

Laub writes that the effect of trauma can only be undone by constructing a narrative, reconstructing history, and essentially 're-externalizating the event.' The short version of the effect is: 'This re-externalization of the event can occur ... only when one can articulate and *transmit* the story – literally transfer it to another outside oneself and then take it back again, inside. Telling thus entails a reassertion of the hegemony of reality and a re-externalization of the evil that affected and contaminated the trauma victim,'[21] victims such as Elisabeth Raab and many others who decide late in life to finally tell their stories.

Raab has lost her infant child and her parents to the genocide, and eventually she would have to say that she lost her home and her hometown of Szemere/Győrszemere[22] because she could not tolerate the contradictions of going back to the place she once loved and experienced with a family that no longer exists.[23] Moreover, 'until the holocaust began,' writes another memoirist, Helen Farkas, 'we were very well integrated with our non-Jewish neighbours, friends and their children.'[24] Raab empathizes with the many other 'longing Hungarians who lack a starting address outside the country' in which they were born, but to which they will never return.[25] The choice to join a diasporic Hungarian community is not one that is deliberately made; nor is it one that is always accidental.

The historical example of Hungary is particularly interesting because it is reported by memoirists and historians alike that the Jewish population did not feel threatened by Hitler or Hungary's relationship with the Reich until very late in the war. Hungary was not occupied until 19 March 1944, only months before the German Army began to retreat. Overnight, Hungarian nationals became refugees in a geographical and historical space that was already troubled, that space we know as Hungary, a national space whose linguistic borders are permeable and constantly changing. Disbelieving Jewry – formerly referred to as Hungarian citizens – became enemies of the state in the last six months of the war. They were 'the Nazi's last victims.'[26] As historians Randolph Braham, Attila Pók, and Vera Ranki (1997) attest, Hungary's Holocaust is unique – but all Holocausts are – and its unique features are naturally therefore mirrored in the published narrative accounts we have been bequeathed in various ways.[27]

The specific geography of the land from which the citizen is deported shapes the contours of the wandering and exile, as much as it determines the dates and systems of deportation and incarceration. Eventually Hungary, Germany's last ally, complied with Hitler's racist plan, for which she was richly rewarded with a longed-for increase in territories that expanded the country's borders into what is now the Ukraine and Romania. For Hungarian Jewry, as well as for Hungarian Gypsies, changing political alliances between the Reich and Hungary meant changing linguistic and national borders, shifting the premises upon which their survival was gauged and on which it depended. This shift is illustrated in numerous memoirs by 'Hungarian' Jews, whose ethnicity does not necessarily match their citizenship. Helen Farkas (1995), for example, begins her memoir by telling us she was born in the city of Satu-Mare in northeastern Romania, the province of Transylvania, but it is clear from a later chapter that she considers herself to be ethnically Hungarian. (Transylvania was originally included in Hungary's annexed lands after the First World War, when Hungary lost two-thirds of its territory and three-fifths of its total population, including a large Magyar and Gypsy population.) After leaving an 'unknown camp' near 'a town called Bruno,' Farkas explains how different groups of women, probably Polish and Russian communists, joined the death march that she and her friends had been forced to take from 'Purskau'[28]: 'After joining us, these women did not intermingle with us much because we did not speak each other's language ... Most of us were Hungarians ... Very few of us could speak a Slavic language.'[29] At the same time, however, Farkas associates her persecution with the change of the Hungarian border on 5 September 1940, when Hitler gave Transylvania 'back to [Hungary]' and 'suddenly we became Hungarian residents. It was after this event that the persecution of the Jews began.'[30] And yet, in pre-1940 Hungary, Jews and Gypsies were still relatively safe.[31]

To speak of life writing texts in the context of countries and national borders during the period of the Third Reich is, as we can see from the example of Hungary, already problematic. As the borders of Hungary shift, the identities of its inhabitants necessarily adjust to a greater or lesser degree, and in different ways. The representation of the human trauma and atrocities committed by the state against its own citizenry becomes more complicated, and possibly more delicate, especially as the state's self-definition shifts in response to aggressive acts of the occupier. The memoirist then has to incorporate into what we are calling the personal not only the violence of the atrocities committed against him or her by the homeland and by the homeland's occupier, but also the consequences to the individual of borders shifting. The names of towns and cities might have changed (can one still find the village of Purskau in Silesia, or has its name changed, or is it too small a place to have remembered into the twenty-first century?); the ethnic identifiers may have become uncertain or confused (am I Romanian or am I Hungarian?); the use of language and the language with which one identifies also may have been compromised (should I speak Russian or should I speak Hungarian?). In this circumstance, remembering trauma is not a straightforward event, and can rarely be fruitfully or fairly compared to the autobiographical recalling that is so familiar to us when we read the autobiographies of heroes or celebrities, where we expect an extended life story with a beginning, a middle, and an end, and where the narrator recalls his or her story in order to celebrate individual choices and achievements – as in Augustine's *Confessions*. In the examples by Farkas, Grossman, and Raab, the narrator recalls what she is able to remember in order to recall, in order to survive, even as death may be imminent. It is not that the survivor thinks her story represents a coherent or model experience and therefore can be told; it is that her story needs to be told so that it will not be forgotten. Sadly, the need to tell one's story does not always equate with the need to hear it. It is as Arendt said in 1943: 'Apparently nobody wants to know that contemporary history has created a new kind of human being.'[32] The new human being represents herself as best she can, leaving out what she cannot speak or bear to repeat, or what she cannot remember well enough; or she must be represented piecemeal by others who were her contemporaries, friend or foe. Either way, the wounding event constructs the remembering and the repeating, and trauma theorists tell us that it can also impair the memoirist's and the reader's full response.[33]

Maurice Blanchot's *Unfinished Separation*

Maurice Blanchot suggests that the memoir of trauma makes an incomplete link with the reader and the past, and, as such, it is a fragment. Fragments, Blanchot hypothesizes, are written as an 'unfinished separation.' How do we understand this obscure and poetic claim? Are we speaking about a genre or about an existential alterity that exists in this particularly violent and inhumane circumstance? Blanchot explains that it is 'the disaster' – the subject of the book, *The Writing of the Disaster* – that is separate, 'that which is most separate.'[34] Using Blanchot's thesis, I have reflected on the less celebrated life writing texts produced during the Holocaust. Some are in fact not 'finished' in the literal sense, because narrators experience too much pain as they write about the disaster or because the unfinished version is the only one that is bearable for the survivor, as more than one woman survivor has told me in private conversations, and so the memoirs have secrets, on purpose.[35]

Some life writing texts may also be considered unfinished in a metaphoric sense because their style is poetic and the narration is elusive. Cordelia Edvardson's *Burned Child Seeks the Fire: A Memoir* (1984; trans. 1997), for example, is explicitly identified by the author as a 'memoir,' but is written in the third person about 'the girl' or 'she' who survived, the one who 'became a survivor.'[36] Moreover, the narrator firmly announces that she is 'obsessed with being [a survivor].'[37] Edvardson's third-person prose intentionally distances her from the events she recounts in order both to respect and deny this obsession, yet she intends her narrative to be understood as autobiographical. The reader is not fooled by the persona, and neither is the narrator spared her memories. But the accommodation of the genre to this illusion enables the reader, and, we presume, the writer, to persist in remembering the wound. In this example, writing and surviving are interdependent, as are the relationships between wounding and the accommodation of the autobiographical genre to suit the task.

Stand-ins for Biography

To be included in our historical repertoire, some texts need to stand in for biographical documents and not just autobiographical ones. These texts would be biographies that the subjects did not invite or authorize in any way, and yet we can say they conform in a narrow version to

Dryden's sexist seventeenth-century definition of biography as 'the history of particular men's lives,' detailing at the very least 'the facts of experiences and activities.'[38] If we push this definition to its most radical end, we might consider a vivid, highly 'factual' deportation list as a stand-in for a biographical account, especially when the subject is not literate or is not easily represented by the conventions of the published autobiography. The list can be composed by a variety of authors, often anonymous – from SS officers to prisoner-scribes – who might be accorded some advantages for performing the job, as is common in the world of the camp. This world is Primo Levi's 'gray zone,' where a consistent set of 'ethical' values do not always have the privilege of overcoming necessity.[39] In the example below from the Mauthausen Archives, we learn the names of 62 prisoners (No. 62 is not legible). We also learn when they were born [Geb. Dat.] and what their prisoner number is [Hftl-Nr.], and which nationality they are [Hftl-Art]. The prisoners on this list appear to have been selected for transport to Dachau from Mauthausen on 10 December 1941. The majority of them are identified as Poles, although six are Spanish [Spanier]. The two German prisoners [Deutscher] have a second identity. One is in Protective Custody [Schutz] and one is designated Asocial [AZR]. Often AZR is a synonym for Zigeuner, or Gypsy, but a German Gypsy would likely have more rights accorded him than another nationality. Josef Papay, prisoner no. 12631, is identified as both asocial and Gypsy, although it is likely that his surname is Hungarian. In the case of the Gypsy, nationality did not always matter to the Reich. Twenty-five-year-old Mr Josef Papay was probably young and healthy, and could likely be used for labour purposes at Dachau in spite of what may have been an unsavory identity to the camp guards. An acute shortage of workers meant that imprisoned Gypsies were often requested by companies and farmers for labour.[40]

Figure 3.1 is a deportation list found in the Mauthausen Concentration Camp Archives in Vienna, Austria in August 1999. The document reads: 'List of Prisoners deported to Dachau Concentration Camp on 10 December 1941.'

Tattoos and Numbers

An even more limited biographical account is preserved in a carelessly, or carefully – depending on the skills of the scribe – tattoo that stains the skin with indelible colour and thus replaces a name with a number that

Figure 3.1
Liste der Häftlinge, welche am 10.12.41 nach KLDachau/Hftl.San.ûberst.wurden:

Lfd. Nr.	Name	Vorname	Geb.Dat.	Hftl-Nr.	Hftl-Art	Transp. Liste
1	Bedzinski	Wenzel	18.9.11	4936	Pole	19
2	Blaszczak	Johann	14.1.09	3382	Pole	20
3	Bochenski	Stanislaus	20.3.04	5983	Pole	18
4	Boguslawski	Georg	9.10.11	5984	Pole	20
5	Bralczyk	Kasimir	4.3.17	70	Pole	19
6	Brenda	Ignaz	30.7.01	1191	Pole	18
7	Camons-Portillo	Eduardo	18.3.00	9082	Spanier	22
8	Criado	Jose	27.2.13	9154	Spanier	22
9	Czajkowski	Siegmund	21.1.02	142	Pole	18
10	Dobierzynski	Eduard	17.9.99	3515	Pole	20
11	Danielski	Ignaz	20.5.17	6097	Pole	18
12	Dojnikowski	Johann	10.7.10	1361	Pole	20
13	Dutkowski	Theofil	24.4.18	3449	Pole	20
14	Fiehn	Gustav	16.6.87	7496	AZR/Deutscher	18
15	Garcia	Francisco	4.10.17	9256	Spanier	22
16	Grabowski	Romuald	27.3.14	265	Pole	20
17	Heinrich	Hieronimus	25.3.02	3703	Pole	18
18	Herok	Johann	9.12.81	3705	Pole	21
19	Herweck	Heinrich	3.2.10	2136	Schutz/Deutscher	22
20	Jedrasiak	Stanislaus	7.4.21	3775	Pole	18
21	Jurkiewicz	Georg	10.9.12	7584	Pole	20
22	Kaczmarek	Josef	22.12.93	5203	Pole	20
23	Kaliszozuk	Johann	5.3.14	8052	Pole	20
24	Klimozewski	Johann	29.4.96	402	Pole	20
25	Kozlowski	Thaddäus	14.2.94	459	Pole	20
26	Krysinski	Josef	18.3.19	6543	Pole	20
27	Labedzki	Sranislaus	21.3.01	7655	Pole	21
28	Lange	Siegmund	20.4.15	6598	Pole	18
29	Lossmann	Eduard	12.10.05	1951	Pole	18
30	Luczko	Georg	10.10.06	8586	Pole	22
31	Maczynski	Bronislaus	2.2.02	4112	Pole	21
32	Maniewski	Johann	9.7.17	8601	Pole	20
33	Marchewka	Alexander	2.11.06	5429	Pole	17
34	Markowski	Stanislaus	11.10.14	8104	Pole	18
35	Max	Johann	13.12.03	2038	Pole	18
36	Mazanek	Alexander	15.3.21	4161	Pole	18
37	Migalski	Stanislaus	24.4.09	6728	Pole	21
38	Mirek	Johann	21.1.00	5469	Pole	17
39	Niemczyk	Franz	6.12.16	12690	Pole	17
40	Nowacki	Marian	2.2.09	8665	Pole	18
41	Nowacki	Stefan	31.8.22	5510	Pole	17
42	Odria-Ibarlucea	Jose	11.1.22	9511	Spanier	17

92   Marlene Kadar

Figure 3.1 (*continued*)
List der Häftlinge, welche am 10/12.41 nach KLDachau/Hftl.San.ûbert.wurden:

Lfd. Nr.	Name	Vorname	Geb.Dat.	Hftl-Nr.	Hftl-Art	Transp. Liste
43	Papay	Josef	4.5.16	12631	AZR/Zigeuner	17
44	Parada	Thaddäus	22.12.08	6555	Pole	21
45	Pastewnyczny	Ivan	23.5.13	12292	Pole	22
46	Pastor-Delgado	Antonio	25.12.20	11579	Spanier	17
47	Ratajczak	Leo	2.6.16	6960	Pole	21
48	Rogaoz	Konrad	9.10.16	5637	Pole	18
49	Serwach	Johann	23.11.23	8815	Pole	17
50	Snaglewski	Roman	3.1.96	5700	Pole	21
51	Stefaniak	Johann	9.5.81	7176	Pole	21
52	Tomaszek	Josef	7.2.87	4693	Pole	20
53	Tomczyk	Felix	1.1.14	8890	Pole	19
54	Tost-Planet	Mariano	5.12.20	9746	Spanier	17
55	Turkowski	Siegmund	25.8.11	8896	Pole	21
56	Widynski	Marian	8.12.17	4763	Pole	20
57	Wieczorek	Wenzel	27.10.06	7287	Pole	21
58	Wierucki	Johann	9.2.05	7289	Pole	18
59	Wojciechowski	Kasimir	26.2.93	4788	Pole	21
60	Wojcikowski	Johann	8.6.01	8929	Pole	17
61	Wisniewski	Johann	13.10.03	8921	Pole	22

Copied with permission from Archiv der Gedenkstätte Konzentrationslager Mauthausen, AMM B/75/14.

is one with the body and thus a most visceral identity. Some women memoirists, Raab among them, insist on using their tattoos or *Häftling* (Prisoner) numbers as an unrelenting autobiographical mark. Raab's body was not tattooed, but it was numbered. By the time Raab arrived at Auschwitz, tattooing had ceased or was done irregularly, and prisoners wore their identity *numbers* around their necks, like a necklace. Raab's necklace bore a disc that read '*Häftling 168*,' and, as she says, 'That was all the SS had to know about me.'[41] The number on the necklace is indeed the SS' *biographical* story about Elisabeth M. Raab, and as such it is also insultingly brief, horribly abbreviated.[42]

Eva Langley-Dános (2000) was a Christian member of an underground Budapest resistance group of which Gitta Mallasz (1998) was the leader. The group was called Talking with Angels.[43] Langley-Dános was deported to Ravensbrück and then forced on a death march to Burgau, north of Berlin, and she, too, remembers her self as a number: 92944.[44] Moreover, she recalls that she was required to repeat the biographical act in enumerating her friends for the 'SS-woman [who] enters the wagon' and demands 'the data of the dead person.' Langley-Dános 'stagger[s] forward and recite[s],' as prompted. She is forced to refer to her cherished dead friend by name and number, 'Klara Erdelyi from Budapest, Häftling No. 92952.'[45] The narrator, who wishes she did not recall this traumatic event, has nevertheless remembered Klara's number since 1945, even though there are other dates and facts that elude her.[46] Although the drama is minimal and the denouement unrehearsed, we can argue that the prisoner numbers constitute identity in this circumstance, and no matter how they are produced on the body, they remain in the memory forever. They communicate quickly and sparsely what the trauma felt like, not always exactly what it *was* like. In Langley-Dános's case, the number-identity of the narrator and her friends is embedded in a more conventional narrative; but in the case of a deportation list, there is no memoirist to pad the horror, no narrative to provide a storyline – at least not in the conventional literary sense. Nevertheless, the number is still equivalent to a person whose story is limited by circumstances too wretched to provide for a proper autobiography, or, in the case of Klara, too violent to provide for a proper burial, and the narration that might have come had she survived.

Other 'uninvited' and unauthorized biographical texts give us a glimpse of a portrait that no one would want to hang on a wall, such as Dr Herta Oberhauser's medical reports on the unfortunate Gypsy-girl victims of her sterilization experiments,[47] or 'The Professor's' (Dr Carl Clauberg's) 'gynecological research' documentation from Auschwitz's Block 10, a residence 'created for him and his experimental efforts to perfect a cheap and effective method of mass sterilization.'[48] Erika Thurner (1998) quotes from the chronological deportation list from Ravensbrück for the summer of 1943: 'Professor Clauberg requests three hundred inmates from Ravensbrück for deportation to Auschwitz for the purpose of experimental sterilization.'[49] In a similar list found at Auschwitz a year earlier (7 July 1942), we find the corroborating entry: 'Himmler promises Professor Clauberg to provide women in Camp Auschwitz for his sterilization experiments. Methods are to be found to sterilize many people as quickly as possible in order to exterminate so-called "inferior races," whose labor they still want to utilize.'[50] Ceija Stojka (1989) was twelve years old when, 'shortly before New Year's 1945,' she and her sisters were taken by Ravensbrück guards to the infirmary to be sterilized. Stojka was spared 'because of an electrical failure' that 'her mother attributed to divine intervention.'[51] If it were not for such glitches in the machinery of maiming, there would be even fewer fully formed autobiographical accounts and fewer fragments of stories, that document the Reich's legal measures to prevent 'genetically defective progeny' from forming.

Written in German, Stojka's account was the only one published by a Gypsy woman at the time of Jack Morrison's (2000) study, *Ravensbrück: Everyday Life in a Women's Concentration Camp 1939–45*. There is a need to augment Stojka's story with other personal accounts. Some of these may be embedded in official Reich documents, or in stories written or told by captors or other prisoners. As third-person accounts, one can argue, they become biographical. In no way do such accounts fulfill the biographical contract (in Dryden's sense) of offering a full account of a person's life or any subtleties about her or his character. They do offer something else, though: unadorned facts and information about activities that tell their own halting stories about the subject, underlining the horror she or he experienced, confirming and adding to the historical record, and emphasizing the need for further research and for the further collection of first-person narratives while the survivors are still alive. Apart from these important results of reading life writing texts, the genres of life writing themselves can be re-evaluated, not only to add new forms to the list and to reconsider the scholarly limitations placed on them, but also to acknowledge the difficulty if not impossibility of speaking truthfully about life when death and disaster are ever-present.[52]

Thus, when Holocaust survivors tell their stories, the autobiographical or auto/biographical[53] is sometimes a confused genre inscribed with all varieties of untapped remembering, a genre representing a highly intertextual life not so separate from our own. I don't mean to conflate the suffering or the violations committed against the memoirists with our own experience, but rather to underline their influence on us as contemporary readers of autobiography in our time. Without a doubt, the legacy of the Third Reich reaches indiscriminately into our own time and space. The sense of unfinished separation that emerges in the autobiographical writing about the incarcerated, the wandering, and the interred is one way the Reich's legacy continues to haunt us. In the recent past, Roma have argued for their place in our historical memory, but as Ian Hancock's research would indicate, it is difficult for a largely nonliterate targeted group to re-externalize the event, as Laub advocates, in written texts.

The Roma Song/Lament

Some Gypsy or Roma singers' oral texts have been transcribed and transmitted, especially in the Czech Republic and in France.[54] The Roma song is legendary, and the Holocaust song is generically similar to verse elegies or mournful literary laments that express grief over a personal loss, such as the death of a child (Robbie Burns's 'A Mother's Lament for the Death of her Son'), or the loss of the beloved (Goethe's plaintive 'Mourning Lament,' or the Old English poem, 'The Wife's Lament').[55] The Roma song also expresses deep personal grief for both the narrator and her people who have experienced suffering and persecution at the hands of the Third Reich. In simple language, the four-stanza multi-form lament[56] defies the singer's captors, rails against atrocities committed against the Gypsy peoples, and, though full of emotional expression, does not encourage empathy from the listener. In fact, the lament is addressed to the community of Gypsies, not to the non-Gypsy (*gadje*) audience. One particular lament, 'Oshwitsate,' eludes the gadje[57] listener because the non-Roma is not addressed in the song, and, perhaps in this circumstance, pity for the suffering subject is denied him. Intimacy with the suffering singer is deferred, if not prevented. This distinctive Gypsy Holocaust lament functions as a moveable autobiographical text, one that does not stand still or exist in one multiform variant, and thus appears in many versions without warning, depending on the performance and the performers. In other words, no given version is sacrosanct, although the practice of a single, capable singer can give the lament some stability.

Dušan Holý and Ctibor Nečas (1993) have reported that a four-stanza version of the lament was recorded by one such singer – a survivor of both Ravensbrück and Auschwitz – Ruzena Danielova. Danielova re-composed the lament for performance, adding her own style, and, to some extent, her own lines.[58] The lament begins in the third person – 'Oh, at Auschwitz, there is a big house' – but it is clear that the story in the song is self-referential. It is about the singer's experience during the Holocaust. As we find in most Roma texts, the singer's fate is completely tied to the fate of her community, a fact of Gypsy life that is explained in detail by Michael Stewart in his ethnographic researches in Gypsy communities in Hungary. The link between the individual and her community is symbolized and played out in the progressive use of point of view and addressees in the stanzas. The first stanza is told in the first person singular and is explicitly autobiographical; the second moves into the second person, as the singer instructs the blackbird to take her letter (her song?) to her husband. The third-person point of view is used again in the third stanza: 'Oh, there is starvation in Auschwitz.' It also appears to address the singer's mother. But the voice quickly changes to the first-person plural, 'we,' underlining the preferred, sanctioned community of listeners. Hunger, a common Holocaust theme, is repeated: 'We have nothing at all to eat.' The identification of the individual with the community reinforces the Roma code of group solidarity in the face of long persecution by the gadje.[59] The fourth stanza is again autobiographical and issues a personal curse against the enemy.

We might argue that the Roma lament can be interpreted as a critique of what the editors of *Women in the Holocaust*[60] call 'the Holocaust establishment.' That is, it can be viewed as an attempt to insert the near-lost experience of a Gypsy woman survivor of Ravensbrück into the historical memory of contemporary Europe and Canada through the translation, performance, and transmission of her autobiographical lament. If we understand 'autobiographical' correctly, it refers not only to the identity and story of the 'I' of the song, but also to the identity and story of her community throughout history. In other words, public performances of multiforms of self-identity where the self refers to both a living singer – 'I' – and her people – 'us' – link the personal story of the survivor to the history of the Roma peoples in Europe. Hancock writes that Gypsies use their language and core culture, including their music and songs, as a kind of 'moveable country,' a way for them to maintain their identity and resist fragmentation.[61] Following Kaja Silverman, as Roger Simon (2000) does, we can proceed from the premise that to remember other peoples' memories is, in effect, to 'provide a psychic locus for the foreclosed wounds of the past,' but that this locus derives from the desire of listeners (and readers) to know about the autobiographical subject, who sings her loss because she cannot write it or because it is anathema to do so. Autobiographical texts provide us with one of the few ways by which we can remember other peoples' memories if we are going to build an archive of what Simon so delicately calls a memorial kinship.[62]

The Recipe Book

In addition to the lament, the deportation list and similar reports written about and by incarcerated inmates and deportees to concentration camps, labour camps, and ghettos, we find numerous examples of another 'Holocaust genre,' the recipe, or more often, recipe collections. Recipe books, or *kochbuchs*, are among survivors' most treasured keepsakes, in spite of the traumatic circumstances in which they were written and compiled. Recipe books have been collected and exhibited in Holocaust museums in Canada and the United States, and some have been referred to in memoirs. They are used in memoirs as supporting autobiographical documents. Often the recipe writers are non-Roma women from Central Europe who became refugees in Canada or the United States, or whose families may have become refugees years after the war. In particular, starving, literate Jewish women exchanged recipes in the camps at great personal risk, and they sometimes 'published' these recipes in collections, using meagre found camp materials such as pay slips itemizing German workers' wages, which were retrieved from trash cans. Elisabeth Raab's *Récepték* is one such example. The book of recipes is roughly two and one-half inches wide by three inches long,[63] and one of six items that remains from the months she spent at Auschwitz. Raab attributes considerable meaning to the little cookbook, both as an emblem of her incarceration and as a postwar memorial souvenir: 'I have cherished the recipe book for over 53 years. It served as my only link with freedom and normalcy, even long after the war.' Recipes for Hungarian delicacies such as walnut torte and *gesztenye* (chestnut) purée, reproduced when the writers were being starved, represent an act of defiance and spiritual revolt and ensure Raab's link to home and hearth. In keeping, remembering, and writing about the recipe book, Raab also gives the anonymous recipe writers some semblance of an identity. Raab comments: 'I wrote the ingredients down, hardly able to grip the stump of a pencil, the recipes of nameless women – whoever happened to pass by. I kept writing down the ingredients, words enshrouded in secret meaning and language in my mind. They were accompanied by a distant sound – the promising, bell-like music of my mother's copper bowl as she beat egg whites by hand, coming through the open kitchen door to find me standing in the backyard in the Easter sunshine.'[64] Other memoirists, however, relay a different experience. Farkas says that the exchanges of recipes reminded them instead of pain and hunger.[65]

The recipe may have narrative or storytelling components included in its overall construction as part of the instructions indicated for preparing and cooking the food. This, however, is not storytelling in the conventional sense of the word, but the entire mixed genre does indeed tell a story. Moreover, the act of making cookbooks in Hitler's concentration or extermination camps is itself a telling, courageous story. Commenting on Mina Pachter's cookbook, Cara De Silva (1996) writes: 'Whatever its explicit or implicit functions, Mina's cookbook – and the others [included In Memory's Kitchen] – make it clear that half a century after the Holocaust, when we thought we were familiar with all the creative ways in which human beings expressed themselves during the long years of the horror, at least one small genre, the making of cookbooks, has gone largely unnoticed.'[66] Whether we can argue that the cookbooks are autobiographical is another matter, but De Silva seems to think they can be thought of as a collective autobiographical genre. In other words, the cookbooks can stand in for autobiography where none other exists. The recipes taken as a whole constitute a 'collective memoir that Mina and her friends left behind,'[67] and, as the editor says, they, too, bear witness. The distress of the writers' incarceration is represented in the contents of the recipes – many of them incomplete and muddled, their writers barely able to survive on the minimal calories allotted them in the Terezin Camp, where the cooks in this 'kitchen' were confined. In this traumatic circumstance, the recipes are naturally marked by loss and forgetting. Some recipes are missing key ingredients, such as this Czech or Hungarian recipe for *Milchrahmstrudel* (Milk-Cream Strudel):

> Filling: ¼ liter cream, 2 egg yolks, 6 decagrams blanched, ground almonds, sugar to taste, 1 roll soaked in milk, 4 decagrams butter, all beaten, 2 whites snow [stiffly beaten egg whites]. Sprinkle with raisins, bake lightly. Pour over sugared milk. Let it evaporate. Bake in a casserole [baking dish].[68]

The editor notes that the strudel has no dough, and, in another example, that *Leberknodel*, or liver dumplings, are made and topped with onion and breadcrumbs without ever being cooked.[69] The interrupted life is imitated in the interrupted recipe, which in turn interrupts our usual willingness to identify life story with narrative. There is no autobiography proper here, but there is the mark of the autobiographical both in the individual recipe and in the collection, which serves as a collective memoir. Food is life; food can bring one back to life; imagining food may have the same effect. In their minds, food links the women writers with their memories of the family dinner table, and thus with beloved family members, including children. Within the context of sharing and exchanging, recipe texts may be read as partial narratives that struggle to reproduce a connection with others, especially with loved ones. Educated Hungarian and Czech Jewish women such as Raab and Pachter express the trauma of a starvation they are forced to endure by remembering and writing out their recipes, saving them and decorating them, hiding them, dwelling on what they were missing, and, in so doing, in effect defying their captors. The theme of starvation, it is said, is repeated in all autobiographical genres about the Holocaust. The Gypsy lament, mentioned earlier, condemns the captors as 'bad karma.' Danielova sang about her hunger using very few words and eventually tying it to the hunger of her people. Stanza three of 'Oshwitsate' speaks about the starvation of the Gypsy prisoners:

> Oh, there is starvation in Auschwitz,
> We have nothing at all to eat,
> Mother, not even a piece of bread,
> Those starving us are bad karma.[70]

Pachter, one of the primary authors of the Terezin *kochbuch*, entrusted the little recipe book to a friend just before she died from 'hunger sickness' in 1944, begging him to pass it on to her daughter, Anny, should he and she both survive. Miraculously, Anny finally received her mother's kochbuch in 1969. In a strange way, Anny is indeed connected with her (absent) mother through the recipes, which surely represent foods they had once shared in their family home. It is no surprise that, according to Myrna Goldenberg (1998), food constitutes one of the four major themes in women's camp memoirs.[71] Goldenberg claims that sharing recipes was particularly important among Jewish women in Auschwitz because it reflected a commitment to the future and reminded women of their strengths as homemakers and inventive cooks in an environment where they were forbidden to enact those roles, even forbidden to actively remember them. Yet these minimal narratives call out to us again in the twenty-first century, sixty years after the event, and accomplish the basic functions of other autobiographical genres, if we are willing to allow a much wider range of subjectivities to flourish. In other words, we can argue that women who write about their experiences, or even write during their experiences, inadvertently create an autobiographical text. There is no need to fit the lament or the recipe book into the traditional genre, but rather there is a need to question the restrictions we have used to exclude the voices of the deeply wounded, the refugee, and the survivor. The feature that autobiographical texts hold in common is the remembering of signifi- cant events in the writer's life, whether covertly or directly, whether seamlessly or in interrupted fragments.[72] In minimal narratives, there is no opportunity for a 'seamless I' to evolve and develop her character, but there is an opportunity for us in the current period to apprehend the significant events in the writer's life, or in her community's life during inestimable hardship. It could be argued instead that the lament, the recipe, the recipe book, the deportation list, intertwine the individual's life story with the larger story of the life of the community at greatest risk, thereby swelling the literary and philosophical demands of the genre, not diminishing them. At the very least, we do not want to be the 'friends' Arendt refers to in her 1943 article, the friends who put the wounded in internment camps, or put their words in a secret place that readers of autobiographical texts and fragments may not find. 'Con- temporary history' (Arendt's words) does not have to be that way. There are others who want to hear and who are willing to risk – with Derrida – impurity, anomaly, and even monstrosity.

The Mark of the Autobiographical

In the first chapter of his elusive and careful novel – a novel that is written as though it is an autobiography – *The Emigrants*, W.G. Sebald (1997) tells the story of the narrator's encounter with Dr Henry Selwyn, a man who, like the other three subjects whose names serve as chapter titles, could have been one of Arendt's tragic 'refugees.' Selwyn hints at his confused and vanished life:

> The years of the second war, and the decades after, were a blinding, bad time for me, about which I could not say a thing even if I wanted to.[73] In 1960, when I had to give up my [medical] practice and my patients, I severed my last ties with what they call the real world. Since then, almost my only companions have been plants and animals. I seem to get on well with them, said Dr Selwyn with an inscrutable smile, and, rising, he made a gesture that was most unusual for him. He offered me his hand in farewell.[74]

Soon after Selwyn's death, the narrator ponders the doctor's experi- ence of a deep wounding in his past, as well as his own experience of Selwyn in *his* past: 'And so they are ever returning to us, the dead,' 'unexpectedly,' even after 'a lengthy absence.'[75] So profoundly important to our personal identities and to our histories, such returns, such memories are embedded in the 'mark' of autobiography, if not in the autobiography proper, in life writing texts that necessarily break open and apart under stress, and, in so doing, ask us to think again about the rich and complex relationship between the autobiographical genres and the telling of the long wound of planned atrocities, or the eternal confusion of having to remember them.[76] The mark, as Leigh Gilmore (1994) explains, is a sign of the autobiographical, but will never be the whole thing.

NOTES

1 *Menorah Journal* (winter 1943, 70).
2 Arendt (2001, 3).
3 The words used to describe the non-elite writers of autobiography are inadequate, but these are the words used by Mary Evans (1999, 1–10), in *Missing Persons: The Impossibility of Auto/biography*. London and New York: Routledge.
4 This description is found on the back of the dust jacket of the book; it comes at the beginning of a segment of a review excerpted from *L'Express*.
5 See Smith (1987, 26).
6 Liz Stanley (2000) explains that auto/biographical practices comprise a 'myriad of everyday and frequently fleeting social practices concerned with the articulation of (often competing, sometimes discontinuous) notions of "selves" and "lives"' (40).
7 Jacques Derrida's phrase, 'the law of genre,' in the essay by the same title, first published in *Critical Inquiry* 7, no. 1 (autumn 1980), 55–58), trans. Avital Ronell, 56–7. See also Paul de Man (1979), Autobiography as De-Facement, *Modern Language Notes* 94: 919–930.
8 Liz Stanley (2000) argues that these differences are not generic.
9 Cited in *Feminism and Autobiography: Texts, Theories, Methods* (2000), ed. Tess Cosslett, Celia Lury, and Penny Summerfield (London and New York: Routledge), 242. See also Stanley (2000, 40–60).
10 Broughton (2000, 242–244).
11 Cited in Broughton (2000, 242).
12 Gilmore (1994, 6–18) cites Jakobson, Benveniste, and others, including autobiography theorists Bella Brodzki and Celeste Schenck, *Life/Lines: Theorizing Women's Autobiography* (1–15).
13 See Stanley (2000, 40); also Smith and Watson's (1998) introduction to

Women, Autobiography, Theory, titled Introduction: Situating Subjectivity in Women's Autobiographical Practices (1–42).

14 Gilmore (1994, 7).

15 Cited in Sandy Sims, 'Untold Tales,' *The Sun* (3 April 2002; 16 December 2000). http://www.svcn.com/archives/sunnyvalesun/04.03.02/cover. Appleman-Jurman's (1988) memoir is titled *Alicia, My Story* (Toronto and New York: Bantam).

16 See Alan Mintz (2001).

17 Sara Horowitz (1998) uses the phrase 'gender-based wounding,' or 'gender wounding' in *Women in the Holocaust* as a form of knowing about the Holocaust and specifically the gender implications of trauma for both women and men (366–367). Moreover, Horowitz contends that our understanding of gendered wounding helps to counter 'a master narrative of the Nazi genocide' (367).

18 Siegal (1981).

19 Raab (1997, 131).

20 See Dori Laub's Bearing Witness, in Felman and Laub (1992, 69).

21 Ibid.

22 Szemere is the short form for Györszemere. Raab (1997) uses both names for her home town in her text, although the latter is used in the chronology (ix) and the former in recounting memories of home (3). The village itself is southwest of the industrial city of Györ. The region is called the Transdanubia; it is in the western part of the Hungary, just south of the Danube River. Raab's Szemere is not to be confused with the town named Szemere in the eastern part of Hungary, just south of Slovakia's border in the Puszta region.

23 For an explanation of why there is no witness, see Felman and Laub (1992, 80–85).

24 Farkas (1995, 14–15).

25 Raab (1997, 117).

26 See Braham and Polk, with Miller (1998).

27 See Braham, Pok, and Ranki (1997), and Ranki (1999).

28 I have been unable to locate a town by this name, but Helen Farkas (1995) seems very certain about the name of the town and its location. Chapter 6 is titled Working in Purskau (52–60). As Farkas (1995) says, however, 'It is difficult to remember' how long the prisoners were on the train from Auschwitz, but she is certain that they disembarked in Silesia, and 'from there we were marched to Purskau, a nearby village' (53). It is also possible that the village of 'Purskau' no longer exists, is too small to be included on contemporary maps of Silesia, or has been renamed.

29 Farkas (1995, 61, 77). Is it possible that 'Bruno' is really 'Brno,' a city south of Prague? See p. 76 for mention of the town.

30 Farkas (1995, 15).

31 As Michael Marrus (2000) says, 'The Hungarian case is particularly dramatic because so many Jews survived for so long and because the final result was so catastrophic' (80).

32 See p. 1 of this essay for the quotation, and footnote 1 for its source.

33 Cathy Caruth (1996) writes that the past as reconstructed is burdened by the traumatic weight of the stories. In this circumstance, history is 'no longer straightforwardly referential,' or, in other words, it is not 'based on simple models of experience and reference' (11). See also Susan Brison's (2002) discussion of the self as narrative in *Aftermath* (49–59). Brison, a survivor of the trauma of violent rape, contends that the construction of self-narratives after the trauma requires an audience, or others willing to listen to what survivors have endured. 'Others' need to hear the words of the stories as they are intended.

34 New edition, trans. Ann Smock (1980; Lincoln, NE: University of Nebraska Press, 1985 and 1986).

35 This idea of secrets is reminiscent of the articulation of a secret identity among indigenous peoples who write autobiographically. The Guatemalan activist, Rigoberta Menchu (1984), for example, ends her life story with the comment: 'I'm still keeping my Indian identity a secret. I'm still keeping secret what I think no one should know. Not even anthropologists or intellectuals, no matter how many books they have, can find out all our secrets' (247).

36 Cordelia Evardson. 1997 *Burned Child Seeks the Fire: A Memoir*, translated from the Swedish by Joel Agee (Boston: Beacon Press).

37 Ibid., 104.

38 M.H. Abrams's is just one popular school definition; see *A Glossary of Literary Terms*, s.v. 'biography.'

39 This is not to deny Anna Pawelczynska's thesis that inmates did also, on occasion, successfully look out for their neighbours or resist their captors in numerous small (yet 'moral') ways, and in so doing denied the legitimacy of the camp's corrupt and brutal command. See Catherine S. Leach, trans. (1979), *Values and Violence in Auschwitz* (Berkeley and Los Angeles: University California Press) (1998) 6–14, 139–140.

40 See Erika Thurner (1998) for more information about internal and external forced labour at Lackenbach Gypsy camp (77–78), and other camps.

41 Raab (1997, 85).

42 The serial number, or tattoo, is used in the titles of memoirs. For example,

Fanny Marette, *I Was Number 47177* (Rpt. 1964; Geneva: Ferni, 1979); and Nanda Herbermann, 'The Blessed Abyss: Inmate #6582,' in *Ravensbrück Concentration Camp for Women* (2000), trans. Hester Baer, ed. Hester Baer and Elizabeth R. Baer (Detroit: Wayne State University Press).

43 See the unusual book by the same title, rendition by Robert Hinshaw, assisted by Gitta Mallasz and Lela Fischli, published in 1998. The original English edition was published in 1988. *Talking with Angels* documents Gitta's 'dialogues with angels' who spoke through the mouth of Hanna, one of the group's members who did not survive the camps. Mallasz herself describes herself as the only 'Christian-born' member of the group, and the sole survivor of the Holocaust.

44 Langley-Dános's number, for example, appeared on a white strip above a red triangle, the symbol of political prisoners.

45 Mallasz (1998, 96).

46 Langley-Dános (2000, 96).

47 Lifton (1986, 23–29).

48 See Lifton (1986, 271 and 273–275). A full file of documents is held at the Ravensbrück Memorial Camp Archives under Dr Herta Oberhauser's name: 'Sterilization' Folder 32 (581–598).

49 Thurner (1998, 122).

50 Ibid.

51 Referenced in Morrison (2000, 52–53), based on translations of excerpts from Stojka's memoir in Stojka and Berger (1989), *Wir Leben im Verborgenen* [We Live in Death], 15–40 and 51–53.

52 See Mary Evans (1999) *Missing Persons: The Impossibility of Auto/biography* (London: Routledge), who speaks about autobiography as fiction (26–51), an occasion for the invention of the self and thus a genre that mirrors a 'blinkered perspective' (38).

53 As mentioned earlier, the term autobiographical is split in two with the virgule to indicate two separate genres – the autobiographical and the biographical – and the intimate link between them.

54 Dasan Holy and Ctibor Nečas (1993), *Žalující Písen: O Osudu Romů v Nacistických Koncentračních Táborech* [*Accusatory Song: The Fate of the Roma in Nazi Concentration Camps*] (Brno: ULK), 61–71; lyrics and music for the song, 138–141.

55 See Albert B. Lord's entry on 'Oral Poetry,' in Preminger (591–593). All three literary laments are easily accessible on line: the first two at http://classiclit.about.com/library/bl-etexts/jgoethe/bl-jgoethe-mlament.htm, and the third at http://faculty.goucher.edu/eng211/wifes_lament.htm.

56 Multiforms are versions of the same text or a text that survives in various

renditions. In the case of the multiform lament, an original cannot be determined with exactness, if at all. Multiforms are, in effect, recompositions, not memorizations, and can only be fully appreciated as performances. To underline the importance of preserving oral literatures in gender studies, Elizabeth Meese (1985) writes that 'the only literature of many women of the world today is oral literature' (18).

57 This is the Romany word for non-Roma peoples, sometimes spelled gadže. For information about the etymology of the word, see Hancock (2000) Roma Origins and Roma Identity. See also Hancock's introduction to Crowe and Kolsti (1991, 6).

58 A slightly modified version of this lament was performed by the Common Thread Community Chorus in Toronto on 29 May 2004, conducted by Isabel Bernaus, arranged by Alan Gasser. See the original Romany version in note 70 of this chapter. A full English translation can be found on the website of the Roma Community Centre. http://www.rcctoronto.org.

59 See Ian Hancock (1997) Self-Identity Amid Stereotypes, in *Transitions* (42). Hancock explains that the Holocaust is the second of two 'major events in European Romani history.' The first is 'the five and a half centuries of slavery,' a fact of Gypsy history that is not well known.

60 See Weitzman and Ofer (1998), Introduction.

61 See *Land Of Pain: Five Centuries of Gypsy Slavery*, mimeograph (1982); repr. as *Gypsies in Nazi Germany*, chap. 9 (1985), online Center for Holocaust and Genocide Studies, December 2003. http://www.chgs.umn.edu/Histories.

62 See Simon's (2000) compelling essay, The Paradoxical Practice of Zakhor: Memories of 'What Has Never Been My Fault or My Deed' (9–25). Simon quotes from Silverman's (1996) *The Threshold of the Visible World* (New York: Routledge), 185.

63 An image of the little book appears in Raab's (1997) *And Peace Never Came* (81).

64 Ibid. Most readers notice that Raab refers to 'Easter' sunshine, rather than a more neutral term. Her reference may be a very clear indication of the degree to which Hungarian Jews had been assimilated.

65 Farkas (1995, 55).

66 De Silva (1996, xxxii–xxxiii).

67 Ibid., xl.

68 Ibid., 59.

69 Ibid., 12.

70 Transcribed and translated by Ronald Lee, Roma Community and Advocacy Centre, http://romani.org.toronto, first page. The Romany text is published on the web site. I include all four stanzas here:

Yai, Oshwitsate, hin baro ker
De odoy panglo mro pirano,
Beshel, beshel, gondolinel,
Yoi, opre mande po bishterel.

Yoi, oda kalo chirikloro,
Lidjel mange mro liloro,
Hedjoy, lidjoy, mro romiake,
Yoi, me, beshel, Oshwitsate.

Yoi, Oshwitsate bare bokha,
Na me amen, nane so xas,
Deya, ni oda kotor manro,
Yoi, o bokharis bi-baxtalo.

Yoi sar me yek furkeri djava,
Le bokharis murdarava,
Sar me yek furkeri djava,
Yoi, le bokharis murdarava.

71 Goldberg, 'Memoirs of Auschwitz Survivors,' 335.
72 See Gwendolyn Etter-Lewis's theorization of personal letters as autobiography in Spellbound.
73 Selwyn's inability to speak about his 'blinding' experiences after the war
   is a common theme in witness literature. Susan Engel comments, in *Context Is Everything* (1999), that there are internal as well as external risks to
   bringing 'out a dark memory' and then 'reveal it in the light of day' (157).
74 Sebald, *The Emigrants*, 21.
75 Ibid., 23.
76 I am grateful to Susanna Egan, in Gendered Exile, for her discussion of
   Daphne Marlatt's *Steveston*. Egan claims that the genre becomes stressed
   before it transmutes. See also Egan's *Mirror Talk: Genres of Crisis in Contemporary Autobiography* (Chapel Hill: University of North Carolina Press,
   1999). Many thanks to Alice Pitt and Susan Ehrlich for ongoing conversations about the impossibility of autobiography. For intellectual camarade-
   rie, I want to thank my excellent colleagues in the MCRI group, 'Auto/
   biographical Practices and Questions of Identity.' For financial support, I
   want to express my gratitude to the Social Sciences and Humanities
   Research Council of Canada, to the Humanities Division at York University, and to the Canadian Centre for German and East European Studies at
   York University.

REFERENCES

Arendt, Hannah. 1943. We Refugees. *The Menorah Journal* (winter), 70.
– *Life is a Narrative*. 2001. Toronto: University of Toronto Press.
Braham, Randolph L., Attila Pók, and Vera Ranki, eds. 1997. *The Holocaust in Hungary; Fifty Years Later.* Holocaust Studies Series. New York: Columbia University Press.
– eds. with Scott Miller. 1998. *The Nazis' Last Victims: The Holocaust in Hungary.* Detroit: Wayne State University Press, with United States Holocaust Memorial Museum.
Brison, Susan. 2002. *Aftermath: Violence and the Remaking of a Self.* Princeton, NJ: Princeton University Press.
Broughton, Trev. 2000. Autobiography: The Course of Things. In *Feminism and Autobiography: Texts, Theories, Methods.* ed. Tess Cosslett, Celia Lury, and Penny Summerfield, 242–246. London and New York: Routledge.
Caruth, Cathy. 1996. *Unclaimed Experience: Trauma Narrative and History.* Baltimore: Johns Hopkins University Press.
Crowe, David, and John Kolsti. 1991. *The Gypsies of Eastern Europe.* Introduction by Ian Hancock. Armonk, NY: M.E. Sharpe.
De Silva, Cara, ed. 1996. *In Memory's Kitchen: A Legacy from the Women of Terezin.* Trans. Bianca Steiner Brown. Foreword by Michael Berenbaum. Northvale, NJ and London: Jason Aronson.
Egan, Susanna. Gendered Exile. 2001. Paper presented at the Auto/Biography: Contemporary Issues Conference, organized by the Feminism and Cultural Texts Research Group (FACT). University of Calgary, 7 December.
Engel, Susan. 1990. *Context Is Everything: The Nature of Memory.* New York: W.H. Freeman.
Etter-Lewis, Gwendolyn. 2000. Spellbound: Audience, Identity and Self in Black Women's Narrative Discourse. In *Feminism and Autobiography: Texts, Theories, Methods,* ed. Tess Cosslett, Celia Lury, and Penny Summerfield, 107–127. London and New York: Routledge.
Farkas, Helen. 1995. *Remember the Holocaust.* Santa Barbara, CA: Fithian Press.
Felman, Shoshana, and Dori Laub. 1992. *Testimony: Crises of Witnessing in Literature, Psychoanalysis, and History.* New York and London: Routledge.
Gilmore, Leigh. 1994. The Mark of Autobiography: Postmodernism, Autobiography and Genre. In *Autobiography and Postmodernism,* ed. Kathleen Ashley, Leigh Gilmore, and Gerald Peters, 3–18. Amherst: University of Massachusetts Press.
Goldberg, Myrna. 1998. Memoirs of Auschwitz Survivors: The Burden of Gender. In *Women in the Holocaust,* ed. Dalia Ofer and Lenore J. Weitzman, 335. New Haven and London: Yale University Press.

Hancock, Ian. 1997. Self-Identity Amid Stereotypes. From *Roma, Still Knocking on Europe's Closed Doors. Transitions: Changes in Post-Communist Societies* 4/4 (September): 38–53.

– 2000. Roma Origins and Roma Identity: A Reassessment of the Arguments. Unpublished typescript.

Holý, Dušan, and Ctibor Nečas. 1993. *Žalujīcī Pīsen: O Osudu Romů V Nacistických Koncentračnīch Táborech*. Brno: ULK.

Horowitz, Sara. 1998. Women in Holocaust Literature: Engendering Trauma Theory. In *Women in the Holocaust*, ed. Dalia Ofer and Lenore J. Weitzman, 364–377. New Haven and London: Yale University Press.

Langley-Dános, Eva. 2000. *Prison on Wheels: From Ravensbrück to Burgau*. Trans. from Hungarian by *Mozgó Börtön* 1945. Einsiedeln, Switzerland: Daimon Verlag.

Lifton, Robert J. 1986. *The Nazi Doctors: Medical Killing and the Psychology of Genocide*. New York: Basic Books.

Lord, Albert B. 1965. 1974. Oral Poetry. In *Princeton Encyclopedia of Poetry and Poetics*, ed. Alec Preminger. Princeton, NJ: Princeton University Press.

Mallasz, Gitta. 1998. *Talking with Angels*. Trans. Robert Hinshaw, with Gitta Mallasz and Lila Fischlia. 3d rev. English ed. Einsiedeln, Switzerland: Daimon Verlag.

Marrus, Michael R. 2000. *The Holocaust in History*. Toronto: Key Porter.

Meese, Elizabeth. 1985. The Languages of Oral Testimony in Women's Literature. In *Women's Personal Narratives: Essays in Criticism and Pedagogy*, ed. Lenore Hoffmann and Margo Culley, 18-26. New York: Modern Language Association of America.

Menchu, Rigoberta. 1984. *I, Rigoberta Menchu: An Indian Woman in Guatemala*. Ed. and Introduction by Elisabeth Burgos-Debray. Trans. Ann Wright. London and New York: Verso.

Mintz, Alan. 2001. *Popular Culture and the Shaping of Holocaust Memory in America*. Seattle: University of Washington Press.

Morrison, Jack G. 2000. *Ravensbrück: Everyday Life in a Women's Concentration Camp 1939–45*. Princeton: Markus Wiener.

Raab, Elisabeth. 1997. *And Peace Never Came*, 81. Kitchener-Waterloo, ON: Wilfreid Laurier University Press.

Ranki, Vera. 1999. *The Politics of Inclusion and Exclusion: Jews and Nationalism in Hungary*. New York and London: Holmes and Meier.

Sebald, W.G. 1997. *The Emigrants*. Trans. from German by Michael Hulse. New York: New Direction Books.

Siegal, Aranka. 1981. *Upon the Head of the Goat: A Childhood in Hungary 1939–1944*. New York: Puffin.

Simon, Roger I. 2000. The Paradoxical Practice of *Zakhor*: Memories of 'What Has Never Been My Fault or My Deed.' In *Between Hope and Despair: Pedagogy and the Remembering of Historical Trauma*, ed. Roger I. Simon, Sharon Rosenberg, and Claudia Eppert, 9-25. Lanham, MD: Rowman and Littlefield.

Smith, Sidonie. 1987. *A Poetics of Women's Autobiography*. Bloomington: Indiana University Press.

Smith, Sidonie, and Julia Watson. 1998. *Women, Autobiography, Theory: A Reader*. Madison, WI and London: University of Wisconsin.

Stanley, Liz. 2000. From 'Self-made Women' to 'Women's Made-selves'? In *Feminism and Autobiography: Texts, Theories, Methods*, ed. Tess Cosslett, Celia Lury, and Penny Summerfield, 40-60. London and New York: Routledge.

Stewart, Michael. 1997. *The Time of the Gypsies*. Boulder, Co: Westview Press.

Stojka, Ceija, and Karim Berger. 1989. *Wir Leben im Verborgenen: Erinnerungen einer Rom-Ziegeunerivi*. Vienna: Picus.

Thurner, Erika. 1998. *National Socialism and Gypsies in Austria*. Tuscaloosa: University of Alabama Press.

Weitzman, Lenore, and Ofer, Dalia. 1998. Introduction: The Role of Gender in the Holocaust. In *Women in the Holocaust*, ed. Dalia Ofer and Lenore J. Weitzman. New Haven and London: Yale University Press.

PART 2

History and Identity

The words *haunting, ghosts,* and *shadows* are frequently used in narratives of the past, when people who have confronted the traumas of history attempt to tell us about their genealogy, national history, and themselves. Fragments lodged in memory can, at some critical moments, be brought together by individuals seeking to fill in the gaps of history that attest to their living and memorialize their dead loved ones.

Life writings show us how social and political contexts have impinged on a writer's everyday life and have shaped her consciousness and sense of self. Women's narratives of their sorrows and joys draw us into their lives in memorable ways to reveal the emotional consequences to their identities of the intersection of gender, class, and race. These narratives also show us how they made the homes that sheltered them.

Rishma Dunlop, in 'Memoirs of a Sirdar's Daughter in Canada: Hybridity and Writing Home' (chapter 4) theorizes through poetic texts about postcolonial South Asian women's identities, hybridity, and the evolution of an artist-scholar's identity. Dunlop immigrated to Canada with her family when she was a one-year-old child. The white, upper-middle-class anglophone suburb of Montreal, where she was raised; the Sikh Punjabi heritage of her parents; and the legacies of British Imperialism provide her with a multitude of contrasts and paradoxes within which she explores the construction of her identity. Through engagements with contemporary South Asian diasporic literature, entangled with her own memoir excerpts and poetry, Dunlop explores the loss of *desh,* or homeland, for immigrants who gradually become alienated from their land of birth, despite its entrenched hold on their memory and their embodied longing. The loss of country is aggravated by the loss of a mother tongue that leaves further psychological scarring. Dunlop explores the possibilities of transformed identities through the blurring of creative non-fiction, memoir, poetry, and scholarly theorizing about diasporic and South Asian identity. This remembrance and re-imagining trace her journey from girlhood to artist and university professor. Providing a research model of historiographic poesis, – art-making in response to history – Dunlop includes excerpts from her 2004 collection of poems, *Reading Like a Girl.*

Atsuko Matsuoka and John Sorenson's 'Ghosts and Shadows: Memory and Resilience Among the Eritrean Diaspora' (chapter 5) argues that for those who have been affected by war, the past continues to exert its ghostly, shadowy influence, often in ways that are gendered. Memories of war and commitments to long-distance nationalism shaped the national and gender identities of the Eritrean diaspora in Canada. Nevertheless, long-distance nationalism has not been investigated well in studies of diasporic groups. In the transnational spaces of the diaspora, the patriarchal ideologies of traditional Eritrean society, the determination of the Eritrean People's Liberation Front to challenge these patriarchal attitudes and practices, their experiences of flight, and the gendered structure of Canadian society laid the grounds for the complexity of diasporic narratives. These narratives show how the past continues to shape the present, and how resilient individuals and communities deal with the memory of violence.

In 'A Diasporic Bounty: Cultural History and Heritage' (chapter 6) I reconstruct and reinterpret India's loss of cultural artefacts and art by labelling these objects as a heritage of the world. The collection of Indian gems and jewels, held in British, North American, and Middle Eastern museums and galleries can evoke anger and resentment in formerly colonized subjects, such as myself, and incite us to use words such as *plunder* and *looting*. In this chapter, I document through personal memories and history that homes and heritages do not have to coincide with national and geographic boundaries. The impoverishment that has been imposed upon India also compels its formerly colonized subjects to leave home for a life in the diaspora. Throughout the twentieth century, Indians have left their countries of origin and have chosen to migrate to Britain, North America, and the Middle East. These migrants have settled into their new homes and have established communities that are linked with each other across national and state borders and boundaries through ties of origin, history, and heritage.

Jewels are a symbol of the material and cultural loss that some countries experienced consequent to colonization. The heritage of these countries is now distributed and housed in different parts of the world. Migrant populations thus have a dual heritage: their ancestral cultural heritage, which is sometimes located in museums in their countries of settlement, and their diasporic history. The chapter concludes by noting that gems and jewels, like art, raise many questions about cultural appropriation that are as yet unanswered and unresolved. Perhaps we can now think of these jewels and gems as part of humanity's collective past; they are part of our South Asian heritage, even though they are not owned, controlled, or safeguarded by India. They are the markers of history and the bounty of the diaspora.

4 Memoirs of a Sirdar's Daughter in Canada: Hybridity and Writing Home

RISHMA DUNLOP

I hear them behind me in another continent
across the Indian Ocean
crossing the floors, soft sweep of sandals
in my mother's country. I was born there four
decades ago at 2am. My birth certificate reads
One Living Female Child.

Today my passport reads Nationality: Canadian.

For the writer with diasporic identities, questions of race, culture, identity, and representation are entangled with immigrant memories, shaped by gender, class, education, socio-historic and economic factors, and the unstable notion of 'home.' Ultimately, it is my work as a writer that enables what poet Meena Alexander calls 'a dwelling at the edge of the world.' This sensuous location is a transnational borderland shimmering with the rhythms and tongues of multiple languages: Punjabi, French, English, Spanish, coloured also by Sanskrit, Latin, Italian. Canada is physical geography, my home. India is my birthplace, my origin, the original homeland of my parents and ancestors. The study of diasporic identity opens up a multitude of paradoxes, shifting identities, and intellectual challenges. Diasporic identity shifts into a home I share with other writers from multiple homelands. Within our community of shared artistic practice is a shelter of words, not reliant on national, political, ethnic, or other allegiances and categorizations. Home is in our poems, the identity of the writer shared as a way of speaking to the other across immense global and diasporic group differences, a way of speaking that has the potential to transcend what separates us. This writing is a push against the existing order of things, speech that makes possible new understandings of human differences, writing against the grain of history. Writing against the grain of dualistic polarities enables understandings of global cultures and identities in the twenty-first century at a time when physical, social, and conceptual borders can be challenged and sometimes dismantled.

The reality of where we live and the dislocations of vast populations make the phenomenon of diaspora a commonplace in our time. In the imagining and constitution of diasporic identities and communities, it is critical to include the categories of ethnicity and nation, along with gender, class, religion, and language. In her article 'Two Ways to Belong in America,' Bharati Mukherjee (1996) writes: 'This is a tale of two sisters from Calcutta, Mira and Bharati, who have lived in the United States for some thirty-five years, but who find themselves on different sides in the current debate over the status of immigrants. I am an American citizen and she is not ... She is here to maintain an identity, not to transform it ... The price that the immigrant willingly pays, and that the exile avoids, is the trauma of self-transformation' (3).

Bharati Mukherjee embraces a monolithic Americanness, regardless of ethnicity and class, frequently comparing her discouraging and some-times hostile experiences in Canada to what she sees as a more 'immi-grant-friendly' United States. In the preface to her collection of stories, *Darkness*, Mukherjee (1985) writes: 'Indianness is now a metaphor, a particular way of partially comprehending the world' (3). Though the characters in *Darkness* are or were 'Indian,' most of these stories explore notions of fractured identities, discarded languages, and the will to bond oneself to a new community against the ever-present fear of failure and betrayal. Mukherjee embraces being 'American' – not Indian and American, not hyphenated. Furthermore, she wants to be recognized as 'an American writer' in the tradition of American writers.

Another Indian-American writer, Meena Alexander (1992), allies her-self with the voices of other minority writers, particularly Asian Ameri-cans. She acknowledges her past and links her present and past history as a South Asian American to that of other ethnic groups in the United States: 'The present for me is the present of "multiple anchorages,"' she notes in her essay, 'Is There an Asian American Aesthetic?': 'It is these multiple anchorages that an ethnicity of Asian American provides for me, learning from Japanese Americans, Chinese Americans, African Americans, Indian Americans, and everyone jostling, shifting and sliding the symbols that come out of my own mind' (26). In the same essay, she considers the 'aesthetics of dislocation' as one component of an Asian American aesthetic; 'The other is that we have all come under the sign of America. In India, no one would ask me if I were Asian American or Asian. Here we are part of a minority, and the vision of being "unselved" comes into our consciousness. It is from this consciousness that I create my work of art' (27).

As a Canadian writer of Indian origin, I find myself embracing both Bharati Mukherjee's and Meena Alexander's visions of the diasporic writer's consciousness. I write from that unhyphenated consciousness that Mukherjee speaks of, as well as from the unselved consciousness that Alexander claims. My recent experience of co-editing, with Priscila Uppal, *Red Silk: An Anthology of South Asian Canadian Women's Poetry*, confirmed for me that there would be no homogenizing tendencies as has been the custom of Western scholarship. The submissions of poetry reflected clearly that the category of 'South Asian' is a reductive, constrictive, and false categorization and I use the term in full knowledge of the inadequacy of any such label to express diversities. The terms *South Asian* and *East Indian* include vast linguistic, ethnic and religious differences as well as the historical legacies of markers of class and caste identities. South Asians with origins in the Indian sub-continent include those who are Punjabi, Bengali, Marathi, Tamil, Telegu, Malayali, Parsi, Sikh, Hindu, Muslim, Christian, to name only a few possibilities (Dunlop and Uppal 2004).

The diasporic individual frequently has a double-consciousness, caught between 'here' and 'there,' a privileged knowledge and perspective that is aligned with postmodernity and globalization. For the writer, the initial dual or paradoxical nature of diasporic consciousness moves the mind beyond dualism into a multiple consciousness, cognizant of multilocalities. The exploration of my own autobiographical stories, including my development as a writer, merges with theoretical and actual concerns of South Asian diasporic communities. Writing becomes a vehicle for remembrance and inspiration for artistic and scholarly creation, blurring distinctions and choices between forms as polar opposites.

* * *

My story begins many years ago in India. I am born on 19 October 1956 in a nursing home, in Poona, India, a city close to what is now called

Mumbai, then called Bombay. In Poona, my mother tends to her infant daughter … her maidservant brings her tea and fresh flowers for her hair every morning.

My mother is a teacher, the daughter of a landowner, a farmer in the Punjab region of India. She is a young woman who fought against tradition to get a higher education after attending convent school in Sialkote, Lahore (now in Pakistan), where she was taught by British nuns. She went to Lady McLaughlin High School where half the teachers were British and the principal was Mrs White. She was in Grade 9 when violence and border wars erupted between India and Pakistan, resulting in partition. Her family escaped across the Pakistan border in the middle of the night, taking only the possessions they could carry. She got her bachelor of arts degree at Government College Ludhiana, and then convinced her father to let her go to teachers college in Simla. She married my father only after several years of a career of her own as an elementary school teacher. My father was the son of a Supreme Court judge, university educated with a PhD in biochemistry. My father courted my mother, coming to her school to take photos of his nephew, who was in her class; this resulted in a correspondence of love letters and family negotiations to arrange their marriage.

Ancestors

I hear them behind me in another continent
                    across the Indian Ocean
crossing the floors, soft sweep of sandals
in my mother's country. I was born there four
decades ago at 2am. My birth certificate reads
One Living Female Child.

Today my passport reads Nationality: Canadian.

My mother's land is still there
scooters and rickshaws navigating through crowded streets
full of billboards for Bollywood films,
dreamscapes of floating lotus ponds
lush public gardens, the smells of decay and sweet jasmine,
still the bustling bazaars and stinking alleyways,
cities like Victorian London among palm trees and banyans,
the rivers marking the routes of cranes and egrets

The ancestors are still there, with the last remnants of the
                                                          British Raj
drinking chai scented with cardamom
old women in desert white saris,
turbaned sirdars,

the young women with amber skin, hair and brows as black
as crows wings, eyes of lionesses in heat,
dressed in silks of delirious hues, violent pinks,
                              bangles and anklets clinking

they wander through foreign rooms
in the last daylight of the century
painting their eyes
brush of sandalwood across the collarbone

Somewhere out of them, alive or dead I have sprung
yet no one seems to recognize me.

No one.   (Dunlop and Uppal 2004, 31)

                              * * *

In 1958, Canada is recruiting scientists through the National Research Council, and my father is offered a postdoctoral fellowship to conduct research in Ottawa for the National Research Council (NRC). We set out for Canada, an adventure my parents expected to last for two years. In the beginnings of immigrant memory, I travel across the world with my parents, the Sirdar's daughter in my tiny frocks, in my red smocked dress, riding camels in Egypt, double-decker buses in London. In Rome, the nuns and priests bless me, call me little Madonna. In Canada, the old photographs catch the scenes, freeze-frames of Kodachrome moments.

In my parents' bedroom
the bureau holds the gifts my father gave my mother,
lingerie drawers of lace and silk, peignoir sets of filmy chiffon,
bottles of perfume   *Chanel No.5, Miss Dior, Je Reviens.*

Silver-framed photographs on the nightstand,
lives stilled in sepia and Kodachrome.

There we are, the three of us on Parliament Hill among
tulips, my mother in her red sari, red shoes, red handbag,
my father with his turban, me in my British duffle coat with
the pointed hood, blue like the one Paddington bear wore.

Another snapshot.
My father teaching me to skate on Rideau Canal,
to lie in fresh powder and make snow angels.

In this one I am walking with my mother
in the Gatineau Hills in the flame of maple trees.
We are dressed to match our new country,
my mother in orange printed sari
me in my orange frock sashed at my waist.

A handtinted photo. My mother in her 50's bathing suit,
posing in front of the rounded curves of our blue Ford.
Coke bottles cooling in the sand, lined up along the shoreline.

There is my mother in her sari in front of Niagara Falls.
In another shot the three of us are standing under the falls
in our shiny yellow slickers.

I am the only child then. I am home in Canada and beloved.

(Dunlop 2005, 24)

* * *

After our two years in Ottawa, my father is offered a job with Ayerst
Pharmaceuticals in Montreal. We move to Beaconsfield on the West
Island. Beaconsfield is a white anglophone community.

I speak Hindi and Punjabi and English. Soon I learn French. Gradually, after my two sisters are born, English becomes the main language
of my home and I start to lose my Indian languages.

In Beaconsfield our difference is marked, as we are the only Indian
family. My mother is an exotic bird, her fashionable western clothes,
brilliant saris, her radiant smile.

My turbaned, bearded father has his share of encounters with land-
lords who tell him to go back to where he came from.

I notice my father's difference through other children's eyes. One

Christmas season, we are downtown and a little boy on the street asks his mother if my father is Santa Claus.

We celebrate Christmas in Canada – the parts my father finds magical. In my memory he stands for hours with his little girls in front of Ogilvy's department store on St Catherine's Street. Ogilvy's wrapped their customer's purchases in green tartan boxes and bags, and they had a bagpiper and a tea room in those years. Ogilvy's is renowned for its amazing Christmas displays, complete with moving elves and toy-making scenes. The year I am remembering there is a Santa's Village display. We stand holding our father's hands in the bitter cold, our breath frosting the air, watching the elves hammering and packing Santa's bag with toys, loading it onto the sleigh with sauntering reindeer, red-nosed Rudolph in the lead. We write letters to Santa Claus, letters my father takes and mails to the North Pole. My father fed our dreams and wishes and belief in imagination. He gave us magic.

* * *

I inherit my love of reading from my mother. First the vestiges of a British colonial education ... Enid Blyton, Kipling, Wordsworth's daffodils ... *A Child's Garden of Verses*, *The Arabian Nights*, *Grimm's Fairy Tales*, *Little Red Riding Hood*, Rapunzel letting down her hair ...

First Lessons: Postcolonial

Every morning my mother would
part my hair down the middle, plait
it into long braids reaching down to
my waist. I would walk with the other
neighbourhood kids to the elementary
school, absent-minded, my face always
in a book, reading as I walked, dressed like
the other girls in dark navy tunics, white blouses,
novitiate-like collars.

Those days, my knees were always scraped
and skinned from roller-skating on the concrete
slopes of Avondale Road, my skate-keys around
my neck, flying, weightless
my father continuously swabbing my cuts with

hydrogen peroxide, scabs peeking out over the
tops of my white kneesocks, my Oxford shoes.

In the classroom, we stood at attention
spines stiffened to the strains of singing
God Save the Queen to the Union Jack
recited The Lord's Prayer
hallowed be thy name, learned lessons
from a Gideon's bible.

In geography and history lessons the
teacher would unroll the giant map of
the world from the ceiling, use her
wooden pointer to show us the countries
of the Empire, the slow spread of a faded
red stain that marked them, soft burgundy
like the colour of my father's turbans.
*Ancient history. Crisp whites of cricket
matches at officers' clubs. Afternoon tea
in the pavilion.*

Decades later I can reconstruct the
story, move past the pink glow,
excavate the hollows of history.

I know now that if that surface was scratched
the pointer would fly along the contours of
the parchment world, across the Himalayas,
through emerald coils of steaming rivers.
Under my fingernails, the scents of spices
and teas, the silk phrasings of my mother's
saris, the stench of imperial legacy, blood
spilled from swords on proper khaki uniforms
lanced through the bodies of Sikh soldiers at
the frontlines of her Majesty's British Army.

But our teacher never said, *Remember this.*

(Dunlop 2004, 30)

The 1960s. Only as I look back now do I see the gaps in history. What is never taught. Silences of the colonial and the postcolonial. My mother and father's survival of the Partition of India. My mother's escape in the middle of the night with her family. The bloody violence and inhumane killings on the trains crossing the borders. Trains arriving full of dead bodies. The senseless brutality of religious warfare and ethnic hatred. The loss of a beloved home located on the other side of the Pakistan border.

Only as an adult do I learn of the vastly different immigration experiences in Canada. Of the Punjabi Sikhs who built the lumber industry in British Columbia, of the shameful silences in Canada's immigration history – the *Komagata Maru* incident. Of the waves of farming communities, of poverty, racism, tales of empire and colonialism. In white Anglophone Quebec in the 1960s, these are unspoken stories, absent histories, effaced.

These questions of history, of hybrid realizations, of constructing new maps, new geographies are borne out in South Asian writers' imaginative works. In Jhumpa Lahiri's (1999) story, 'When Mr. Pirzada Came to Dine,' in *The Interpreter of Maladies*, the birth of Bangladesh and the history of the partition of India and Pakistan are seen from ten-year-old Lilia's point of view. For the U.S.-born child, this is a foreign history. While her father is frustrated about what his daughter learns about the world in school, her assimilated mother is defensive: 'Lilia has plenty to learn at school. We live here now, she was born here' (26). Her father categorically says of partition: 'We were sliced up,' the passive voice indicating that the majority of the population had no say over this traumatic event (25). Lahiri sets the story during the struggle for Bangladesh's independence from Pakistan. Dacca-based Mr Pirzada, visiting the United States, is suddenly cut off by the war from news about his wife and seven daughters at home. The daily news is hardly adequate and full of stereotypes disconnected from people's actual lives.

Mr Pirzada seems to be living in limbo, his watch set eleven hours ahead to reflect the local time in Dacca. With a child's sensitivity, Lilia tunes into his anxiety about the fate of his family, and shares the daily ritual of meals carefully prepared by her Bengali mother (who remains tied to homeland tastes and uses the precise kind of mustard oil needed for the fish, or the particular kinds of chili peppers). Still, 'No one at school talked about the war followed so faithfully in my living room.

We continued to study the American Revolution and learned about the injustices of taxation without representation and memorized passages from the Declaration of Independence' (32–33). Lilia discovers what Meena Alexander (1992) describes accurately as the burden 'of carrying our histories within us since they are not visible in the world around us' (27).

At school, when Lilia takes the initiative to look up a book on Pakistan, she is reprimanded: 'Is this book a part of your report, Lilia? ... Then I see no reason to consult it' (33). The reality at home is radically different, as the family tries to be supportive of Mr Pirzada, awaiting 'the birth of a nation on the other side of the world' (34). The whole drama unfolding on the subcontinent – the war for independence, poets and intellectuals killed, refugees flooding into India, and then war declared between India and Pakistan backed by the two superpowers – leaves most Americans untouched. Much of this history remains 'a remote mystery with haphazard clues' for the young child who feels the anxiety that her parents share with Mr Pirzada (40). 'Most of all I remember the three of them operating during that time as if they were a single person, sharing a single meal, a single body, single silence, and a single fear' (41). At last Mr Pirzada is able to return to Dacca and reunite with his family. A new nation is created, and new maps must be made, as the local people redraw the old colonially imposed boundary. As Lilia recalls, 'Every now and then I studied the map above my father's desk and pictured Mr. Pirzada on that small patch of yellow, perspiring heavily I imagined in one of his suits, searching for his family. Of course, the map was outdated by then' (41).

Lahiri's stories capture the humanity of ordinary people struggling with 'traditions,' arranged marriage, food preparation, helping the destitute, people who take diasporic leaps to create new lives even as they keep hold on the small details of their culture: eating with their fingers, enjoying a specific regional pickle, speaking native languages, being dutiful. While Lahiri's characters remain self-consciously aware of their ethnicity, they participate in this U.S. culture through their intimate relationships – married, single – raising children, driving that extra mile to get an absolutely necessary ingredient for a favorite recipe. Even as their ethnicity as South Asian Americans is performed in daily life, they work towards a hybrid realization of their subjectivity as Asians and as Americans.

* * *

My Mother's Lost Places

My teachers and the women in the
neighbourhood would admire the crimson
blooms on my mother's Kashmiri shawls,
exotic, intricate embroideries on the finest
wool the colour of nightfall.

I know they could never imagine,
as I have only just begun to imagine,
my mother's lost places,
laughter in summer houses, wild monkeys
at the hill stations of her youth, peacocks,
the heady profusions of flowers and fruit,
jasmine and roses, custard-apples and
guavas. They could not imagine her with
braids and proper Catholic uniform at the
convent school under the stern eyes of nuns
with their Bride of Christ wedding rings
who taught them all their subjects including
domestic skills such as the tatting of lace and
embroidery stitching. They could not taste the
sweetness of Sanskrit poetry, or the star-flung
nights of Persian ghazals.

In Canada, my mother's young life gets frozen into
the icy winters of my childhood, new stories spun
in English on skating rinks, tobogganing hills and
ski slopes. A new wife, a new mother, she reads
Ladies Home Journal, learns to bake me birthday
cakes and gingerbread houses, wears Western clothes,
pedal pushers and sheath dresses and high heels, sews
me party frocks with sashes bowed in the back.

(Dunlop 2004, 32)

* * *

My mother was a Girl Guide in India. The colonial influences of Lord
and Lady Baden-Powell are felt globally. I too am enrolled in Girl
Guides to become a good Canadian citizen, a capable girl.

The Education of Girls

We learn to recite the Girl Guide promise:

I promise, on my honour, to do my best:
To do my duty to God, the Queen, and my country,
To help other people at all times,
To obey the Guide Law.

We learn the language of semaphore, how to
build campfires and lean-tos and latrines.
We earn badges, pitch tents, learn how to use an axe and chop wood,
how to tie knots, learn first aid and how to survive in the
wilderness. We Learn to *Be Prepared* and to *Lend a Hand*.

We learn the Guide Law.

A Guide is obedient. You obey orders given you by those
in authority, willingly and quickly. Learn to understand that
orders are given for a reason, and must be carried out without question.

A Guide smiles and sings even under difficulty. You are
cheerful and willing even when things seem to be going wrong.

A Guide is pure in thought, word and deed. You look for
what is beautiful and good in everything, and try to become strong
enough to discard the ugly and unpleasant.

We become capable girls, soldiers in our uniforms, with our
companies and patrols and salutes. We learn to build nations and
at the close of the day, we sing Taps, the soldiers' bugle call to
extinguish the lights.

Day is done, gone the sun
From the hills, from the lake
From the sky
All is well, safely rest
God is nigh.

And our mothers kept house, did the laundry and
the cooking and the ironing, drove us to Brownies

and Girl Guides, did volunteer work, refinished furniture,
watched *The Edge of Night* and *Another World*
took antidepressants when their lives did
not resemble the glamorous adventures of Rachel
and Mac Corey, had hysterectomies at 40.

At the close of every day, they had supper ready when
their husbands returned from the city, fresh and slick,
briefcases in hand, polished shoes tapping them home past
manicured lawns along the asphalt driveways.

(Dunlop 2004, 33–34)

* * *

My mother knits us ski sweaters, heavy cable knits that I wear to the
local skating rink and to the ski hills. My father learns to ski, a rare sight
on the hills of the Eastern Townships, St Sauveur, Mont Tremblant, his
turban and ski goggles, among a sea of white faces in Montreal winters.
The newspaper photographs him, writes a story on the Sikh skier in
Canada – the new Canadian. Every Saturday morning in winter, he
drives me to catch the bus to my ski lessons, picks me up at the end of
the day at the Beaconsfield Shopping Centre.

* * *

A curious mix, my cultural education. I am not raised on Indian dance
or music. Chamber music concerts, ballets. Every Christmas, my mother
sews velvet dresses for us, takes us to see *The Nutcracker* at Place des Arts.
And every year those unforgettable ballet classes. The stern Miss Damrol's
ballet classes, our pristine white tunics, powder blue sashes, pink tights,
at the school gym or Stewart Hall, bodies stiff at the barre, our hair in
tight buns at the napes of our necks. I can hear Miss Damrol's voice,
clipped and British: 'Eyes forward young ladies, chin up, stomachs in,
bottoms tucked, *plié, port de bras*, first position, second position, hold it.'

And then there were other forms of dancing.

Slow Dancing: Beaconsfield 1973

Parents away for the weekend
we are in a house like all the others,
freshly painted trim and gabled windows,
brass-numbered door and neatly pruned hedges,

and the basement recreation room is overflowing
with us, sweet sixteens, bodies clutched together in sweat in
the cigarette smoke and beer, slow dancing to Chicago's *Color
My World* and Led Zeppelin's *Stairway to Heaven.*

My girlfriends and I wear angora sweaters our mothers
bought for us in the soft pastel shades of infants: fingernail
pink, baby blue, pale yellow, and cream. We wear drugstore
scents named for innocence and fruit: *Love's Baby Soft*, *Love's Fresh
Lemon*, or the more sophisticated *Eau de Love* or Revlon's *Charlie.*

For years we have danced in ballet studios, spinning, dreaming our
     mothers'
dreams of Sugar Plum Fairies, our rose tight confections, pink slippers
     twirling
pas de deux, jetés, pirouetting our taut muscles until our toes bled. But
     tonight
we dance in our tight blue Levis, our mothers' voices fading as Eric
     Clapton's
electric guitar shivers our spines, the music claiming us and we spill out
under the streetlamps, dancing across equators into the earth's light.

On the streets of suburbia, this is the beginning of hunger.
It catches me by surprise, exploding like a kiss.

(Dunlop 2004, 41)

* * *

Teenagehood. My black hair, olive skin, nontypical features. By Indian
standards I am fair, a whiteness about me. I speak fluent French and
English. In Quebec I am taken for every nationality, Italian, French,
Arab, Egyptian. 'Where are you from?' becomes a repeated refrain.

On our first trip to India with my family, this confusion about identity
is mirrored by Bollywood billboards. The actresses have dyed their hair
reddish brown and their skin is light. In Indian magazines, Lakme
cosmetic creams are advertised, claiming to make the skin fair and
light. Lakme sells Fairever Fairness Cream. The ad reads: 'NOW YOU CAN
CHANGE THE FUTURE! Look fairer, feel more beautiful than ever, with
new FAIREVER! ... Change the way you look, and face the world with
new confidence! Contains no bleach. Suitable for all skin types.'

Lakme also sells Fair and Lovely Fairness Cream and Fairever Mantra Fairness Cream, which is lauded in their ads for being 'India's fairness secret, a fairness cream that combines the power of diverse fairness ingredients to make your skin visibly fairer, naturally.' Other feminine beauty ads market skin bleaches to make the skin fair. My relatives call me beautiful, fair. They call my dark-skinned younger sister *kali*-dark, black, less marriageable, less marketable. I feel the guilt of this difference, even then at sixteen, a growing consciousness of an orientation in the education of girls and women that perpetuates a within-culture racism aimed at women's beauty, a woundedness that moves beyond immigrant identity.

Back in Canada, my girlfriends Colleen, Debbie, Lorrie, and I still baste ourselves in baby oil at the Beaconsfield Swimming Pool, seeking Coppertone tans, the white lines at the edges of our bathing suits the beginning of the sensuous existence of teenage girls.

Sometimes my sister and I dream of being blonde and blue-eyed like the models in *Seventeen* magazine.

My sister is the first child from anglophone Beaconsfield to attend French school. My parents thought it would be the best way for her to learn French. One day, my sister comes home from French school, weeping inconsolably. The French kids call her 'nigger.'

In the most elemental of ways, through my sister's life at school, we are confronted with racism and with our first demonstration of francophone Quebec fundamentalist belief in the notion of 'pure laine.' The term *pure laine* ('old stock', literally 'pure wool') is sometimes taken to be synonymous with *Québécois*, a term referring to someone whose ancestry is almost entirely Québécois. As with any ethnicity in a multicultural country such as Canada, few people can accurately claim to be pure laine. The idea of pure laine has been at the root of some heated polemic battles about ethnicity, culture, and belonging in recent years in Quebec; many find the idea and its linking with Québécois identity and culture to be racist, and belief in the identity of French origins with the Québécois to be by no means universal.

Family Life

In the 1960s they called it *Health Education*
on our report cards. Today they call the subject
Family Life.

At our school, girls are separated from
boys, gathered in the school gymnasium.
The nurse distributes pamphlets about
life cycles and Kotex. There is something
pristine and sanitized about it, the glossy
brochures with the beautiful fresh-faced
girl, her blonde hair swept back with pink
satin ribbon. We know we will soon become
her, young women leading Breck girl lives.

We learn our lessons well, believe we can
hold on to our well-groomed dreams.

It takes us years before we realize how many
things will make us bleed, how easy
for the world to rip us to pieces.

(Dunlop 2004, 38)

* * *

We did not attend a *Gurudwara*, a Sikh temple, on a regular basis – only
if there was a wedding or special occasion. My father did not believe in
organized religion. But he was a spiritual man who lived his life according to humanist principles. So in sixties fashion, my parents took us to
a Unitarian church in Pointe Claire. In 1967 the minister was Fred
Cappuccino. He and his wife, Bonnie, had two birth children and five
adopted children from around the world. I remember Annie from Vietnam and Mohammed from Bangladesh. The church was a lively community, one that perpetuated a Buddhist belief in humans as sacred,
and that this sacredness is not reliant on an external force.

Fred and Bonnie Cappuccino now live in Maxville, in eastern Ontario,
where they run an organization called Child Haven International. Their
family grew to include twenty-one adopted children, some disabled or
of mixed 'race' from Third World countries.

* * *

At Beaconsfield High School, I am on the debating team, the 'Reach for
the Top' quiz show team, a bit of a geek but still popular in a way that
enables me to have a sense of a secret identity. My mother's refrain at

this time of my life is: 'Don't talk so much; a girl should be more reserved.' She wanted me to excel at everything, be strong but reserved, articulate but quiet ...

She wanted me to have a profession she could define – lawyer, doctor, teacher, engineer – something that had a label. I never imagined I would become a poet, and it was mid-life before I pursued writing with the vision of making it a profession or vocation. But a few years ago my mother gave me a tiny notebook she had saved. I had written it when I was twelve – adolescent, excessively descriptive nature poems, full of allusions to classical myth. I had titled the notebook *Poems* by Rishma Singh.

Meanwhile my life was absorbed by books. I spent hours in the Beaconsfield Public Library and eventually got a part-time job there. I read every moment I could steal from the day, and late into the night under covers by flashlight, even though my mother said I would go blind. I finished entire novels in a day. I loved books, devoured them, eating up the words until ink spilled from my mouth. I lived the lives of fictional characters, walking around in my daily life in an absent-minded haze. I read while getting dressed, eating meals, walking to school. Books were my talismans, reading a form of faith.

Little Red

First stories, fragments of colonial texts,
Enid Blyton, Noddy's Adventures, Kipling's Jungle Book
Wordsworth's daffodils
stories full of words like pram, lorry, Wellingtons, nappies.

Then worlds of fairies and witches
Rapunzel letting down her hair from the tower,
princesses and ogres.

The story she loved best was Little Red Riding Hood.
As a young child she learned all the words
                              by heart.
In the storybook her parents read to her,
Little Red is always saved by the woodcutter.

Years later, when she knows the real ending, the Perrault
one where the wolf waits for her in bed, and Little Red takes off

her clothes, lies down beside him and he gobbles her up
                                          it is no surprise.

She is still the red cloaked one, using her words as incantations
against the wolf at the door, the wolf who comes again and again
                                          on nights black as doctrine.

There is no other story, no other text.
                                          (Dunlop 2004, 35)

                              * * *

Reading Wonder Woman

The comic book heroes I loved best
                    were the mutants and freaks.
Spiderman and Batman, Aquaman who was half-fish.

And then there was Wonder Woman. She was glorious,
descended from the Amazons of Greek myth. She had
fabulous breasts, a tiara, a magic lasso and belt, red boots,
as well as those bulletproof wristbands worn by the
Amazons to remind them of the folly of submitting to men's domination.
If a man could bind an Amazon's wrists, she lost all her powers.

In early stories she captures
spies, Third World War Promoters,
sends them to imprisonment on Venus
where they are forced to wear
Venus Girdles of Magnetic Gold to
tame them into peaceful life.
In another story, she defeats the
evil Fausta, Nazi Wonder Woman
in 'Wanted by Hitler, Dead or Alive.'

Wonder Woman was beautiful and powerful as a hero,
understated and reserved in her secret identity as Diana Prince,
the secretary in her smart-chick glasses.

She taught me radical truth.
The geek, the hybrid mutant is a treasure,

so easily misunderstood in real life
a secret identity is necessary. Hold it close.
Protect your wrists.
Put on your red boots   step into fire.

(Dunlop 2004, 36)

* * *

Reading Ladies Home Journal

Reading my mother's magazines
Ladies Home Journal and *Miss Chatelaine*
pictures of women with cinch-waist dresses,
bouffant hairdos. They ride in convertibles
headscarves keeping every hair in place.

These women are so happy with their pink and aqua
kitchen appliances. In one ad for Scott toilet paper,
the woman wears an evening gown in the exact
pastel blue of the toilet paper and Kleenex tissue.

These women use Yardley Lavender and Cashmere Bouquet
talcum powder. They buy new davenports and credenzas. Pictured
in exotic landscapes in their underwear, they dream in their Maidenform
bras and girdles that promise to set them free.

The ad I like best is for the black lace corset called a Merry Widow.
Under the sedate hairdo and perfect makeup of the model, her Max Factor
red lips whisper *It's simply wicked what it does for you. Care to be daring,*
darling?

(Dunlop 2004, 37)

* * *

Girl Detective Chronicles

Long after my mother thought I was asleep,
late into the night, I would read under the
covers with a flashlight.

How I loved them, the stories about the
girl detectives, reading and recording the

world in notebooks – Harriet the Spy
the ones who solved crimes with their
wits, their brains, their All-American good looks.

I drove that blue roadster with Nancy
Drew, dated Ned, looked lovely and charming
and desirable at college football games.

And how I dreamed of being Cherry Ames, student
nurse, with her stylish cap and uniform, her black
hair and rosy cheeks, her boyfriends and her adventures.

And when I grew up, I became them, Nancy and Cherry.
I cut off my long black braids, styled my hair into a bob.

I became the girl detective, the nurse, capable of building
nations and soothing the hearts of men
for awhile.

                                                    (Dunlop 2004, 39)

                            * * *

On the autumn football fields at Beaconsfield High School, the cheer-
leaders chanted and jumped, their pleated miniskirts flipped into the
air, flurries of thighs gleaming. Anything seemed possible for such
young bodies, in such a place and time. I would watch and remain
reading my books under the trees, losing myself in imaginary worlds,
in the tomes of *War and Peace* and *Dr Zhivago*, dreaming of dancing in
evening gowns and elbow-length gloves. Books about revolution excited me, seduced me. I tried to re-imagine the heroines, their perpetual
tragedies. Emma Bovary, Anna Karenina. Anna flinging her body into
the locomotive steam, her red purse on the tracks. I tried to read them
and write them differently, give them different endings, new destinies. I
wanted them to stay alive, to breathe, to be plump with blood and
desire, to believe that anything is possible.

Reading Anna Karenina

The volume of Tolstoy thumbs her open.
She tries to keep the heroine alive.

Outside the library windows
ragged moths beat against the streetlamps.
She feels the heat of locomotive steam
rising from the stacks, weeps when she
sees Anna's red purse on the tracks.

She closes the book with stunned hands
as if she had touched the hem of a final
morning, a sense of going into it alone.
She begins to think she will not be carried
unscarred, untorn into any heaven. Wants
someone to hold her while she burns.

(Dunlop 2004, 40)

* * *

In Chitra Divakaruni's (1993) short story 'Leaving Yuba City,' a second-generation daughter leaves home. The cultural gulf between daughter and parents is so wide that she has to make an escape in the middle of the night, and has to face the question: In which language would she leave a note to her parents? 'The words, the language. How can she write in English to her parents who have never spoken to her in anything but Punjabi, who will have to have someone translate the lines and curves, the bewildering black slashes she has left behind?' (39). She hopes that later, as she learns to make her own space in the world, she will be able to communicate more openly with her parents: 'Maybe the words will come to her ... halting but clear, in the language of her parents, the language that she carries with her, for it is hers too, no matter where she goes' (40).

In Divakaruni's (1993) poem, 'Yuba City School,' a mother struggles with the knowledge that her son is being racially harassed in school. The mother feels helpless because she is not fluent enough in English to argue with the teacher: 'My few English phrases,' she thinks. 'She [the teacher] will pluck them from me, nail shut my lips' (121). Through a few deft phrases, Divakaruni evokes fear and cultural impasse.

* * *

The late 1960s. Lived to soundtracks of Jimi Hendrix, Janis Joplin, Gracie Slick and Jefferson Airplane, the Rolling Stones. These were rebel years when my parents waited up for me at night, smelled my breath for traces of alcohol. My mother would run her hands across my back to make sure I was wearing a bra. She would check the length of my skirts as I left the house. I wore miniskirts, rolled up the waistbands after I left home to make them even shorter ... I wore hotpants and fishnets. My mother stopped smiling in these years – told me I should be modest and show no cleavage.

Prom night was a pale pink gown with rosebuds, corsage, dance at the airport Hilton, drinking what we thought were sophisticated drinks – Pink Ladies, Gin Fizzes, Tia Marias with milk – and then watching the sunrise on Mount Royal ...

* * *

At eighteen, I leave Beaconsfield to study literature, languages, and translation at university. I meet Jim, a young man from New Brunswick. I am in love.

By this time, the dialogues between me and my mother go something like this:

> Sound of the phone ringing/answering machine: 'Hi, I can't come to the phone right now. Leave a message.' Beep of answering machine.
>
> My mother's voice on the answering machine: '*Beta*, we can never reach you. You're never home. Are you studying? Call us back.' Tone at end of mother's message. Click. Hanging up of phone.
>
> Sound of phone ringing: 'Hi, I can't come to the phone right now. Leave a message.' Beep of answering machine.
>
> Mother's voice: '*Beta*, what are you doing? Your uncle has sent letters from India. Some eligible men London-*Angreji* educated who want to marry and come to Canada. One is an engineer and one a doctor – good families and good-looking boys. (Mother gives a big sigh, exasperated tsk, tsk sound.)
>
> 'You are becoming too Western. You should remember your culture. Love you. Stay in touch. Call us. It would be good to hear from you.'
>
> Tone at end of message. Sound of tape rewinding.

* * *

I come home for the summer after my first year at university. It is the time of the 1980 referendum in Quebec. My neighbourhood has been vandalized. I am shocked by the stop signs with the word STOP slashed out with black paint, the word ARRÊT written over top. We are confronted with the notion of 'pure' ethnicity again: pure laine. Everywhere, there is a war of language on our neighbourhood signs. *Langue, ma langue*; in French, *language* and *tongue* are the same word. I always thought French and English were my languages, *mes langues*, my tongues, the tongues of home.

My mother finds my birth control pills, calls me a prostitute.

I move into an apartment with Jim. My parents are beside themselves with worry.

After several years of living together I phone home: 'Mom, Jim and I want to get married. We want a civil ceremony.'

Mother: 'Well, if you want to do that, your father and I will not be there.'

My mother refuses to meet Jim. She talks to him on the phone after some coaxing, and never physically meets him until the wedding. Jim and I decide we will have the wedding my parents want. They can send photos to the relatives in India and make everyone happy. We have a Sikh wedding and a United Church wedding.

The day of the wedding, I realize I can't dress myself. My aunts have to wrap and fold and drape my sari around my body. My sari is not the usual bridal red. I have rebelled against the red, brocade-encrusted, heavy wedding saris. My sari is pale peach-pink, a shot silk like dawn with a deep purple and gold brocade border. I wear a pale mauve orchid in my hair. In traditional ceremonies, the groom rides in on a white horse, but we dispensed with this custom. Jim wears a turban and my mother begins to love him a little.

The *Anand Karaj*, the Sikh wedding ceremony, begins with the sound of chanted prayers in a language I do not understand. I am laden with gold – a *rani-haar* necklace around my throat, my hands painted in henna designs, the bridal head covered and suitably bowed, the Sirdar's daughter walking around the holy book. To signify our union and the giving away of the bride, my father places one end of a scarf in my hand and the other in Jim's hands. The *Adi Granth*, the holy book, is opened and *Lavan*, the marriage prayers, are read. During each of the four stanzas, we walk around the holy book. Still holding our ends of the scarf, we circle around the book four times. I am guided by men – my groom, my father, my cousin, my uncle – as if I could not find my own way. We are seated for final prayers and then given *Kara Parshad*, a holy sweetmeat to share with the congregation.

We sign the official register, Jim takes off his turban, and we are married again in a Christian ceremony, double-ringed, the look of relief on my mother-in-law's face as she hears the English vows she understands.

We leave the church, walking out into the sunshine as friends and relatives place garlands of flowers around our necks, to bless us and congratulate us. We are showered with rose petals.

At the end of the day, I look over at Jim, my sisters, mother, father, everyone dancing at the reception, all beloved, all strangers.

* * *

2004. I am now a university professor of literature and education, a poet, the mother of two daughters. Poetry becomes my migrant home, lit with the many languages that are part of me, a sensuous land, a transnational borderland. Although I write in English, I also write through the rhythms of other languages, French, Punjabi, Hindi, Spanish, Latin, the strut and play of words shimmering with the rhythms and sounds of lines that permit a sense of home even through dislocation.

For many years, I felt distant, foreign from the culture of my *desh*, or homeland of my birth. My home is Canada, my tangled identity is hybrid. My daughters are hybrid mixes, born of my Indian and their father's Scottish-Canadian heritage.

Every Sikh girl is named *Kaur*, meaning princess; it is her name, along with her other given names.

Princess Stories

When I was young my father called me *Princess*.
And princess stories were the ones I loved most,
especially the one about Sleeping Beauty. Her
name was sometimes Briar Rose or Aurora. The
story of the beautiful princess who pricked her
finger on the spindle of a spinning wheel, falling
under the spell of the witch who had been shunned
at her christening.

The curse of a girlchild's birth.
She slept along with the kingdom for a hundred years

until she is rescued by a handsome prince who hacked
through the dense tangle of thorns and wild rose bushes.
The curse lifted with love, his kiss on her lips,
awakening the world.

When my daughters are young, I read them princess stories
The Paper Bag Princess, The Princess and the Motorcycle.
Tales of strong, independent princesses of wit and courage and
intellect who do not depend on princes for survival.

Still, as I watch my girls, young women now, I am filled
with longing, something that mourns the loss of belief
that a beloved would hack through forests of thorns to
sweep a girl off her feet, to bring the world into waking.

(Dunlop 2004, 42)

* * *

Jhumpa Lahiri writes of the post-1965 generation of immigrants who
embark on the psychological and sociocultural journey of becoming
'American,' and their attempts to adopt an Asian-American identity.
Her collections of stories frequently present an ethno-global vision that
transcends narrow nationalism, but celebrates an ethnic heritage along
with evoking an exemplary universalist humanism.

In the title story of the Pulitzer Prize-winning *Interpreter of Maladies*,
the Das family return to India from the United States. While crossing
national borders they are forced to recognize their own dual identities –
more American in clothing, speech, body language than Indian, though
ethnically marked.

Indian North Americans are also described in India as NRIs – Non-
Resident Indians. Although India does not allow dual nationality, the
label of non-resident is a way to retain close emotional ties; even as
American citizens, they are still identified as 'Indian.' As Inderpal
Grewal (1993) notes, the Indian government nurtures the ties to home
since they want to entice NRI financial investments to India; this NRI
population is not interested in forming coalitions with other people of
colour in the United States, and most are uncritical of the country's
'ideology of "democracy" and "freedom."' (226).

The Das family embark with cameras on a journey to see the famous
Sun Temple at Konarack. They want to learn from the ethnic heritage

that is not part of their everyday geography in the U.S. Lahiri (1999) sensitively captures the image of this native-returned-as-tourist in the portrayal of Mrs Das, whose interest in the local guide/driver, Mr Kapasi, is interpreted quite differently by the foreign-returned and by the native. The driver, Mr Kapasi, who works as a doctor's assistant, one who describes the various maladies of patients to the doctor to help him to prescribe medicines, is called 'the interpreter of maladies.' He regards this as 'a job like any other'; to Mrs Das, it is 'so romantic' and 'full of responsibility' (50). He finds 'nothing noble in interpreting peoples' maladies' (51). He works with the doctor in 'a stale little infirmary where Mr Kapasi's smartly tailored clothes clung to him in the heat, in spite of the blackened blades of a ceiling fan churning over their heads' (52).

Lahiri's (1999) representations, on one level, acknowledge the ethnic and national in descriptions of Mr Kapasi and his modest work, as well as in Mrs Das's return to nativism. She can romanticize his job and make it sound grander than it is from her outsider's perspective. Lahiri recreates national identity via ethnicized codes of communication, both spoken and unspoken; culturally defined signals are misinterpreted by Mr Kapasi, who regards Mrs Das as both native and U.S.-stamped. Of course, he does not have her privileges of travel, or of picking and choosing from different cultures – a kind of global entitlement that she and her family have acquired by living in the United States.

When Mrs Das casually asks for Mr Kapasi's address – something tourists do when they take photographs and 'promise' to send them back – he overinterprets the request as signifying real interest in him and his work. Lahiri (1999) subtly weaves in the sexual attraction that he experiences: 'He began to check his reflection in the rear-view mirror as he drove, feeling grateful that he had chosen the gray suit that morning and not the brown one ... He glanced at the strawberry between her breasts, and the golden brown hollow in her throat ... He could smell a scent on her skin, like a mixture of whiskey and rosewater. He worried suddenly that she could smell his perspiration' (53–55).

He fantasizes that since she has asked for his address, they will correspond regularly and he will tell her many more stories of the maladies that he interpreted. He is already anticipating the letter as he calculates how long it would take to get one after their return to the U.S. 'In its own way, this correspondence would fulfill his dream, of serving as an interpreter between nations' (Lahiri 1999, 59). He dreams of crossing national boundaries in his imagination, serving as a kind of cultural ambassador representing his nation to the U.S.-bred and Indian-looking Mrs Das.

As he continues to fantasize and the sexual innuendoes mushroom, and as the others wander off, Mrs Das offers a startling revelation: her son's father is not Mr Das. Mr Kapasi is shocked, but tries to keep his composure. Why tell him? She had kept this secret for eight years and was hoping that his job as an interpreter of maladies would help her feel better, that he would be able to suggest a remedy. Perhaps one reason for this revelation is that Mrs Das is looking for a spiritual, mystical India with healing powers, and sees the interpreter as a vehicle sent to her for that purpose.

Lahiri resolves the story beautifully. The mother's guilt and pain is somehow transferred to the innocent son, who has wandered off alone and is attacked by a pack of monkeys. Bleeding and crying, he needs to be carried back to the car. As Mrs Das tries to comfort him and reaches into her bag, the piece of paper on which she had scribbled Mr Kapasi's address floats away. Her revelation of sexual infidelity to someone who shares her ethnicity but is divided from her in every other way, especially in class privilege, is a reminder that the gap dividing them is more significant than their common ethnicity.

Some stories in the collection unfold in the U.S., while others travel back to India through their characters' imaginations and histories or are set in India with the ever-present West looming in the wings. There are women who have affairs, men who leave their wives, women who choose careers over family, nontraditional women and men. Lahiri's characters demonstrate the diversity of the South Asian American community with their various languages, religions, and regional food cultures. Their daily lives in this diasporic location unfold as they struggle and dream, argue and entertain. These portrayals broaden the representations of Indian Americans, abandoning any fixed notion of North American Indian culture.

* * *

Reading Amy Lowell

Summer and I have returned to the town where
                                    I was a young wife
where we raised our daughters.
The name of the place means *a place to live forever.*
Mythology and daily life. Legends of sea serpents,

ghosts of horses lost swimming in from the island, tangled with
slow pitch tournaments, ball players and Winnebago campers,
tourists on the beaches and lunching at wineries.

Today I am marking freshman English papers in the backyard.
The air is sweet and fugitive. In the garden, wild strew of roses,
pink blooms amidst the silver foliage of planted pathways
                              fragrance spilling from their thorn beds
the morning stillness stung by the
screeching of Steller's jays and flocks of crows
                              singing a crude chorale.

In the distance, the sound of ducks landing on the swimming pool,
                              splashing and flapping their wings.
My daughters laugh and I am struck by that particular radiance
                    again and again/how the laughter of girls
                              cuts through blue air.

How did I come to this place
                    the professor circling sentence fragments,
the occasional leap of the heart when a student writes a beautiful phrase.
My student has written an essay on Amy Lowell.
And suddenly I am transported, back to 1972 at Beaconsfield High
in Mr. Whitman's North American Literature class,
                              yes that was his name.

Fifteen years old, sitting in those straight-backed wooden chairs,
   my legs cramped under the tiny desk with my huge Norton anthology
                    open at Amy Lowell's 'Patterns.'
There have been so many words I have committed to heart. This poem was
   one of them.
I could taste this poetry, feel the rhythms of it beating in my eyelids.
For the first time, reading Amy Lowell,
          I understood that burnt cadence of sense,
                    the quickstep of syllables in my throat.

I wrote an essay on Amy Lowell's 'Patterns'
   something about the Imagist movement, the poet's use of figurative
                              language and form

in a consideration of how societal expectations may
                                  inhibit a woman's actions in society.

Mr. Whitman gave me an A on my essay.

I promptly forgot what I knew about patterns
                                  in the wisdom of my sixteenth year.

I must have known then, something about the effect of patterns,
knowing Lowell's narrator, the feel of her corset, her pink and silver
brocade gown, how she grieves for her dead lover
                  how a heavy-booted lover would have loosened
                  the stays of her stiff correct brocade
in the pink and silver garden
                            the bruise and swoon of it.

I, too am a rare
Pattern.

In dreams I see the husband of my girlhood
                                  my pink and silver time
his arms around me like a familiar blanket.
He is holding something out to me, places it in my palm
                        a scroll, a tablet, some lost history inscribed
                                            unreadable.

And centuries pass and we are still *gorgeously arrayed*
                                  trousseaus of pink and silver
mouths stuffed with bone china
pink and silver, boned and stayed

Christ! What are patterns for?

At sixteen I used to mouth the words
                        swords springing from the repetitions
from the ribs of consonants.

Today, in my forty-sixth year, I reread the poem and the body flies apart,
remembering how a grown woman can brush back her hair in moonlight
watch her husband and daughters inside her house as if in a dream.

Remembering days when the woman wakes up and she understands her skin
doesn't fit her anymore
What she does inside that skin leaves
her outside her house in long nights of crickets
singing and the lake whispering.

Sometimes, she longs to be like characters in a novel or a poem,
the relief of flatness on paper.

The heart is literate.
It wants to read the pages it has unfurled.
It wants the grip of roses on love-ridden afternoons,

the ordinary of tv, chair, table, plate, sneakers
entangled through a sky of blood tracery swept innocent by rain.

I want conversation that is like the stripped truth of the poem,
the way I felt when I first read Amy Lowell's 'Patterns.'
Over the years I wondered what kind of shelter
I could make with words.
I search for the color of home in the extravagance of reading.
I am looking for it still.

This town is not a place for introspection. Such beauty.
The lake, the blue air, the sun, all defy me
to find some fault in this horizon.

Over the years I weaned my babies, got ready to walk
into the pink and silver light.
(Dunlop 2004, 46–49)

* * *

I have learned the stories of my students of Indian heritage, the immensely different immigrant stories of struggle, hardship, racism, and class. I have come to know the huge divides of race, ethnicity, class, gender, economy, and education that mark these differences within cultures.

A dwelling at the edge of the world, this home. The hold of a loved place cannot be taken for granted, and the making of a home and locality, given the shifting worlds we inhabit, might be understood as an art of negativity-praise songs for what remains when the taken-for-grantedness of things falls away.

The question of language always haunts me, brings me back to a memory of a lover who wanted to know about my childhood, my childhood language. He wanted to know my father's words, called me *beta*, little one, child, my father's name for me, as he stroked my hair back from my forehead. And in these moments, I realized how much of this language was deeply connected to a place of soul for me. Punjabi – there is still something beloved about this tongue. Some sense of home, like the poem, a shelter we make of words.

Language uses are a significant part of diasporic experience. In a poem entitled 'Language,' Amita Vasudeva recreates the levels of ignorance about Asian languages and cultures in U.S. society: 'Can you speak Mexican? ... No I am from India ... Can you speak Hindu?' (Vasuveda 1993, 119). Such ignorance compounds a second generation's conflict about learning mother tongues that are not heard in mainstream culture. Yet those languages, especially those mother tongues, cling to them, stuck almost like a second skin that cannot be shed.

* * *

25 May 1990. My father dies young. He is sixty-two years old. My parents had many plans for his retirement in a few years, travels around the world. My mother works at the Beaconsfield Public Library. He leaves my mother cooking dinner. He goes to the Pointe Claire Tennis Club for a game of tennis with a close friend. A blood clot finds its way into his heart, and he dies instantly there on the red earth courts.

My mother gets a call from the Lakeshore General Hospital. Life is never quite the same. We mourn, we gleam.

I find myself remembering my childhood lullaby, the one my father sang to me each night at bedtime, stroking my hair back from my forehead. My father's voice: '*Soja beta*, sleep little one. Sleep child.' The Hindi and Punjabi words, my childhood tongues, lost languages to me now.

At the funeral, it's all I can think about, this lullaby, the childhood words, as I have returned home. My sisters and I have shed our Western clothes and are dressed in the brilliant silk saris my father would have loved. Mine is blue like the lake near our childhood home, the blue of Lake St Louis in Beaconsfield, on the West Island of Montreal.

I know the gleam and smell of the polished
leather of his shoes, buffed every morning
                              before he left for work.
I press my face into the crisp white cotton of his shirts,
brush my cheek against his jackets,
sweaters still warm with him.
I touch my teeth to the metal of his watch, his cufflinks.

I can hear his voice reading fairytales, singing
Harry Belafonte's 'Jamaica Farewell'

But I'm sad to say I'm on my way
Won't be back for many a day
My heart is down, my head is turning around
I had to leave a little girl in Kingston town

I hear him singing Punjabi and Hindi ghazals, lullabies

Soja Rajkumari, soja,
Soja meethe sapne aayen
Soja pyari Rajkumari

Sleep, princess, sleep
Sleep with sweet dreams
Sleep beloved princess

In the hush, I am cradled by the sound of him,
 voice lifting me like birdsong through the pyre.

In my mother's house I enter silence,
wear it as a dress, my father's ashes acrid
in my throat. I remember the days of savage
adoration, child for father, father for child, when
I was tiny enough to stick to his trousers like a burr.
His sudden vanishing a brute sledgehammer blow.
                    (Excerpt from 'Soja,' in *Reading Like a Girl*, Dunlop 2004, 43–45)

* * *

Longing for homes left behind may be intense for first-generation immigrants who seek a community to belong to. A form of culture shock occurs when you live as a citizen in a country for a long time, over forty years; and, still, when someone asks you where you are from and the name of your religion, your first thought is *I don't know*. In becoming diasporic, we need to keep in mind the political parameters of home, community, and nation, as analysed usefully in Chandra Mohanty's 1993 essay, 'Defining Genealogies: Feminist Reflections on Being South Asian in North America':

> What is home? The place I was born? Where I grew up? Where I live and work as an adult? Where I locate my community – my people? Who are 'my people'? Is home a geographical space, a historical space, an emotional sensory space? Home is always so crucial to immigrants and migrants ... I am convinced that this question – how one understands and defines home – is a profoundly political one ... Political solidarity and a sense of family could be melded together imaginatively to create a strategic space I could call 'home.' (352)

The notion of home and ethno-global vision is also explored in the poetry of Agha Shahid Ali (1987), whose recent death leaves a profound gap in the South Asian American literary tradition. His deep and abiding love for his homeland of Kashmir gave the world ways of imaginatively 'finding' home while living away from it. Ethnically grounded and simultaneously embracing a vast humanity, the narrator in the opening poem, *The Half-Inch Himalayas*, startlingly touches his home in a picture postcard. The complex notion of home is constructed through the power of the imagination and through language, through writing home. 'Kashmir shrinks into my mailbox / My home a neat four by six inches. / I always loved neatness. Now I hold / The half-inch Himalayas in my hand. / This is home. And this is the closest / I'll ever come to home' (1).

* * *

In my life as a Sirdar's daughter in Canada, my immigrant journey has proven to be vastly different from immigrant memories of many other immigrants. Canada has allowed me an existence of hybridity, shaped by my individual experiences and all the factors of class, gender, education and circumstance in my life. My work as a writer is driven by the desire to write against such locations as Britain where hybridity has not historically been allowed, where racism has provided the impetus for diasporic individuals to maintain strong ties with their homelands and encouraged them to shape selves and identities that are rooted in their ethnicities.

* * *

The writer's work is not an exercise in nostalgia; rather, the task is to imagine and re-imagine history, memory, the material reality of our lives, testifying to the fact that boundaries of nation, culture, and gender are slippery inventions requiring continuous interrogation:

> And everywhere I travel in life there is still this –
> A small girl in her red smocked dress
> Her father clasps her hand in his, teaches her
> to recognize the convulsive beauty of things ...

(Dunlop 2004, 17)

In my memory and in my writing home, I am in Beaconsfield again. Kissing my father's forehead before we let him go to the crematorium. How the return home can be treacherous, unstable in its imaginings and remembrances. Ultimately, immigrants and others in the world we call home must invent a history of shared space in which to dwell, to know that 'there is tenderness in every geography' (Dunlop, 'Naramata Road,' 2004). And I, in my blue sari, help my mother and my sisters to spread my father's ashes on the waters of the lake he loved, in the place we called home.

Coda

The Poet Contemplates Her Art

But where my moment of Brocade –
My – drop – of – India?

(Emily Dickinson)

What have I expected poetry to do for me? At midlife, poetry has not yielded a God. Poetry is that unfinished thing, some intangible hope. Persistent practice of courage. It is the waiting for a loved one to return home. It is the young woman I was. It is the hue of my wedding sari, shot silk the colour of dawn, brocade border of gold. Not the usual red silk of the Indian bride, some whisper of hope contained there in my rebellion. As the light fades, the mind wanders over books, pen, and paper, even as the hour pulls you into exhaustion. What a scrap of paper gives ... a grocery list, letters, the 2 a.m. fevered composition, Cicero's memory palaces, Book of the Dead. Raw faith in the light of another day, in public records, private histories, the poet unfurling poems like Tibetan prayer flags or the prayers the Japanese tie to trees. The air above the city is saturated with poets' prayers, like the air of industrial towns and dreams, so thick with longing it is hard to breathe. And what resides in the ink but a glimpse of the possible past in memory as you turn off the light, the possible years left to you, written, recorded, your hands a reliquary.

REFERENCES

Alexander, Meena. 1992. Is There an Asian American Aesthetic? *SAMAR* (South Asian Magazine for Action and Reflection) I, 1 (winter): 26–27.
Ali, Agha Shahid. 1987. *The Half-Inch Himalayas*. Middletown, CT: Wesleyan University Press.
Divakaruni, Chitra. 1993. Leaving Yuba City. In *Our Feet Walk the Sky*, ed. Women of South Asian Descent Collective, 38–40. San Francisco: Aunt Lute Books.
Dunlop, Rishma. 2004. *Reading Like a Girl*. Windsor: Black Moss Press.
– 2005. The Raj Kumari's Lullaby. In *Where Is Here? The Drama of Immigration*, ed. Damiano Pietropaolo. Winnipeg: Scirocco Drama, Gordon Shillingford Publishers.
Dunlop, Rishma, and Priscilla Uppal, eds. 2004. *Red Silk: An Anthology of South Asian Canadian Women Poets*. Toronto: Mansfield Press.
Grewal, Inderpal. 1993. Reading and Writing the South Asian Diaspora: Feminism and Nationalism in North America. In *Our Feet Walk the Sky*, ed. Women of South Asian Descent Collective, 226–236. San Francisco: Aunt Lute Books.
Lahiri, Jhumpa. 1999. *The Interpreter of Maladies: Stories*. Boston: Houghton Mifflin.
Mohanty, Chandra. Defining Genealogies: Feminist Reflections on Being

South Asian in North America. In *Our Feet Walk the Sky*, ed. Women of South Asian Descent Collective, 351–358. San Francisco: Aunt Lute Books.

Mukherjee, Bharati. 1985. *Darkness*. Markham, ON, and New York: Penguin.

– 1996. Two Ways to Belong in America. *New York Times*, 22 September.

Vasudeva, Amita. 1993. Can You Talk Mexican? In *Our Feet Walk the Sky: Women of the South Asian Diaspora*. San Francisco: Aunt Lute Books.

5 Ghosts and Shadows: Memory and Resilience among the Eritrean Diaspora

ATSUKO MATSUOKA AND JOHN SORENSON

Violence and terror persist beyond the time and space in which they originally occur. In our recent book, *Ghosts and Shadows*, we employed the concept of a 'ghostly sociology' to discuss the experience of exile, examining the afterlife of war and repression among diasporic populations from the Horn of Africa (Matsuoka and Sorenson 2001; see also Gordon 1997). Here, we focus on the experiences and political subjectivities of those who were driven from their original homes in Eritrea by war, and have settled in Canada. We discuss how the past continues to shape the present and how resilient individuals and communities deal with the memory of violence. For those who have been affected by war, the past continues to exert its ghostly, shadowy influence, often in ways that are gendered. The experiences of the men and women who came to Canada were shaped by a number of factors: their class position in Eritrean society, the patriarchal ideologies of traditional Eritrean cultures, the determination of the Eritrean People's Liberation Front (EPLF) to challenge these practices, their experiences of flight, and the racialized, gendered structure of Canadian society.

Among the defining characteristics of a diaspora are the forced dispersal of people and a collective memory of a lost homeland to which they are committed and to which they feel they should return (Safran 1991). Emphasizing the failure to address class and gender differences in particular, Anthias (1998) points out that in the analysis of diasporic populations generally, theorists tend to take an overly homogenizing view of populations who may be very different, according to the time and circumstances of their departure and the conditions of their lives in different countries (564). Yet for the Eritrean diaspora, the thirty-year struggle for independence from Ethiopia defined their identity, providing a polyethnic population with a unified sense of consciousness of belonging to a distinct community, and it provided the context in which their resilience developed. The commitment and intensity of the nationalist struggle, especially when coupled with the devastating effects of widespread famine, had the effect of at least temporarily displacing or downplaying class, ethnic, and gender contradictions. The nationalist movement encouraged such a downplaying of structural contradictions, emphasizing the duty of all Eritreans living abroad to support the cause and to contribute funds. In order to mobilize this ongoing support, the EPLF created a number of mass organizations that operated in the diaspora: national unions of students, women, and workers. The diasporic population continued to be an important resource throughout the war and after independence.

In the transnational spaces of the diaspora, individuals and communities constructed narratives of the past to explain their current situation to others and to themselves, from particular vantage points. Time and distance increased the complexity of these narratives as exiles remembered and inevitably reinvented scenes and processes of violence. They also reworked their recollections of home, encrusting them with layered accretions of nostalgia, solitude, and longing. The outbreak of a new war between Eritrea and Ethiopia in 1998 (to 2000) over unresolved border issues, and the simmering tensions since that time, have also strengthened the sense of a threatened national identity and intensified the commitments of long-distance nationalism: the enduring attachment to original-homeland politics among diasporic populations (Anderson 1992). These attachments have played a significant role in forming and operating community organizations within the diaspora. Often, these political forces are overlooked in the formation of community organizations, which are viewed as either cultural collectivities or responses to Canadian racism. For example, Bannerji (2000) points out the importance of questioning the assumed naturalness or the essentialism implied in certain ideas of community, but her analysis addresses diaspora associations as if they were formed only in response to conditions in Canada:

> Questioning the status of the community as a natural, social formation does not automatically imply a dismissal of points of commonality among peoples of different regions, cultural habits, nationalities, and histories, or, for that matter, among religious groups from these regions. It is true that such people often tend to seek each other out, to speak the same language,

eat the same food, or display fashions. Very often in the earlier part of their existence in Canada it is a survival necessity for learning the ropes in the new country, getting employment or business contacts, and so on. But if the Canadian society into which they come were non-threatening and non-exclusive, if racism were not a daily reality, this stage of cultural bonding would be short, and more fluid than it is at present. (159)

Undoubtedly, racism is a major factor in forming a sense of solidarity and shared identity within diasporic communities, but it is not the only one. Recollections of political struggles in the original homeland and a continuing attachment to those struggles are also significant factors in how communities operate and define themselves.

These memories of the past are 'situated knowledges,' or memories. These situated knowledges are maps of consciousness produced by Eritrean exiles who have been shaped by their orientation to the categories imposed by the history of colonial domination and superpower intervention (as noted in the following section), as well as by their insertion into gendered, racialized categories in Canada. Meanwhile, our own perspective has been influenced by our involvement with solidarity groups and efforts to provide emergency relief aid to famine-stricken areas of Eritrea during the 1980s (Haraway 1991; Stoetzler and Yuval-Davis 2002). More than a hundred interviews with Eritrean exiles carried out over ten years in five Canadian cities have provided us with access to some of these recollections from Eritreans in Canada; we have also drawn on our fieldwork in Eritrea itself. Giving pseudonyms to some of our participants, we have used their voices here. We do not claim that these voices constitute an exhaustive or completely objective record. The concepts of 'ghosts and shadows' allowed us to capture themes from interviews and organize them to show how the past is not forgotten, but is vitally alive in the present and shapes the experience of exiles today and in the future. The ghostly and shadowy past haunts the present of those in the diaspora as they create new identities on the basis of imagined homelands and play a role in shaping them. We have investigated the shadowy but powerful phenomenon of long-distance nationalism, the process by which political struggles in the homeland structure exile communities, and how those communities participate in those struggles.

In interviews, Eritreans who were physically far from 'the field' but nevertheless involved with events there reconstituted their own versions of conflict. Relaying and replaying these haunted tales were fundamental aspects of the diasporic experience, but also a process that had repercussions internationally, as exiles continued to engage with political conditions in Eritrea.

Eritreans in Canada

War ravaged Eritrea for much of the last half of the twentieth century. The causes as well as the outcome were not only local but global: a distinct Eritrean space was carved out of Africa by Italian colonialism (1869–1941), followed by a decade under a British mandate. After the United Nations imposed an ill-advised and soon-abrogated federation of Eritrea with neighbouring Ethiopia, Emperor Haile Selassie annexed the former Italian colony outright. In 1974, the Emperor was deposed by a military coup and replaced by Mengistu Haile Mariam, who espoused Marxist rhetoric in order to legitimize a dictatorial regime. As the Ethiopians sought to crush the Eritrean nationalist movement that emerged, they were armed first by the United States and then by the Soviet Union as these superpowers attempted to manipulate local conflicts for their own objectives. For their part, the Eritreans received inconsistent support from a number of Arab states and some training in China during the 1960s and 1970s. After a civil war within the nationalist movement, however, the dominant faction – the EPLF – found itself not only isolated from international support but forced to retreat, along with many civilians, into the rugged mountains of northern Eritrea. The retreat was prompted by a massive Ethiopian attack, which was supported by the Soviet Union and Cuba. Forced to turn necessity into a virtue, the EPLF emphasized a policy of self-reliance, and, during the prolonged war, created a remarkable social revolution in its 'liberated areas.' With the aid of a small number of European and North American nongovernmental organizations (NGOs) that provided emergency food aid to the EPLF-held areas, the EPLF carried out programs in education, health care, and agriculture, intended to help the rural population. Much of this activity was conducted at night to avoid bombing attacks by the Ethiopian Air Force. Despite the duration and intensity of the struggle and its extensive international associations, the Eritrean case received little attention from the corporate media in North America and was widely dismissed as a lost cause. Nevertheless, in the late 1980s the EPLF achieved a string of significant military victories, and, in 1991, under the combined pressure of the EPLF and anti-government groups in Ethiopia itself, the Mengistu regime was toppled. In 1993, after an internationally supervised referendum, which included votes from Eritreans in the diaspora, Eritrea became an independent state. The EPLF reconfigured itself as the People's Front for Democracy and Justice (PFDJ) and formed the new government; the EPLF's Secretary General, Issayas Afeworki, became the country's first president.

During the long war for independence, hundreds of thousands of Eritreans were forced out of the area as refugees. These Eritreans were among the vast numbers of international nomads generated as by-products of the Cold War. War scattered Eritreans across the world, and most who came to Canada did so during the mid-1980s, with numbers dropping off sharply after Eritrea achieved formal independence in 1993. Typically, Eritrean newcomers to Canada had spent several years in other countries, such as Italy, Greece, Sudan, and Egypt, after leaving Eritrea. Many men came through resettlement programs coordinated with the United Nations and acquired landed immigrant status. The implied permanency of this status conflicted with how Eritreans saw themselves, as we discuss below. Many women came through family sponsorships and gained landed immigrant status. They became the dependents of sponsors who were often male, and this legal dependency sometimes created another level in gender relationships.

Within most of the ethnic groups that constitute Eritrea's multicultural society, women were regarded as inferior beings. (Interestingly, the Kunama – a minority ethnic population living in western Eritrea – who allow women comparatively more equality, have been regarded as more primitive by those of other ethnic groups.) Women were seen as beasts of burden, lacking any significant intelligence and moral status. Among a generally impoverished population, women were doubly exploited, denied education, excluded from land ownership, and denied a voice in political affairs. Although women contribute essential labour, they are typically the most malnourished, their health problems exacerbated by these conditions. Among the small minority of urban, educated Eritreans, a few women were able to receive some higher education, but the Ethiopians undermined the educational system in Eritrea and reduced their opportunities further.

During the thirty-year war for independence, women's problems were made worse by military violence directed at the civilian population. The Ethiopian military burned villages and massacred civilians to eradicate support for nationalism. Those who stayed in the cities and towns under Ethiopian occupation lived under constant surveillance, harassment, and intimidation, subject to the threat of beatings, imprisonment, rape, torture, or sudden death from the Ethiopian soldiers who lived among them. One woman, interviewed in Asmara in 1998, described her experience of enduring years of Ethiopian military occupation as a civilian in the capital city. She talked about the strain of living under the sense of imminent violence and described being insulted and threatened on a daily basis by the soldiers stationed outside her house: 'We know you are with Shabia [EPLF]. One day we will kill you.'

The EPLF rejected the patriarchal oppression of women, and made women's emancipation a key aspect of its revolutionary program, calling for equal rights and the full participation of women in Eritrean society. Within the EPLF itself, women constituted approximately one-third of the fighters (*tegadelti*), a category that included not only front-line soldiers but also drivers, technicians, and medical personnel. Women's participation in the liberation struggle was promoted as a demonstration of the type of social revolution the EPLF intended to carry out. The Eritrean women we interviewed were proud of the important contributions that women made to the struggle, often pointing out that they had a reputation as the toughest and fiercest of the fighters, ready to risk their lives without hesitation. Many men concurred with these observations and indicated the respect they felt for the women fighters. On the battlefield, women felt compelled to 'prove themselves' by taking on the most dangerous and difficult tasks. Their efforts were seen as an inspiration for women in the diaspora, who pushed themselves and one another to contribute significant portions of their often meagre incomes to the nationalist movement. In both cases, women's contributions spurred greater efforts from men. The national narratives constructed by men, however, are not the same as those constructed by women. Women saw themselves participating actively in decision making and envisioned a more equal division of responsibilities in the state as well as at home. Many men, however, thought women's participation was a temporary aberration and did not believe that women would take a major political role in the new nation; certainly, very few men looked forward to a situation in which they would participate equally in household chores and child care. Women's efforts were undermined and their accomplishments acknowledged only as the consequence of abnormal wartime circumstances. Women's resilience during the struggle for national liberation was thus haunted by the ghosts of past relationships – traditional gender relationships.[1]

For those who fled war and repression in Eritrea, the experience of flight was a gendered process. Women faced all the same dangers as men, but in many cases the men fled singly while women had to care for children. They also encountered the added threat of rape and other forms of sexual violence. The danger came from enemy troops, bandits, other refugees, border guards, and officials of other states. Some women felt forced into relationships with men in order to receive their protection. Women who were captured by Ethiopian troops endured not only the immediate trauma of torture and rape, but also the stigma that endured after such attacks. Since most women lacked higher educational qualifications and economic resources, they were more likely to end up as refugees in neighbouring countries than to immigrate on their own to Europe or North America.

Anti-immigrant and racist discourse proposes that people from the South are eager to leave their own homes for new lives in Canada. No Eritrean we interviewed mentioned having had any specific desire to live in Canada. Most were driven out by war and saw residence here as a temporary necessity rather than a permanent move. Indicative of this was one informant's assertion that 'Every Eritrean is a refugee,' although not all actually had this legal status. During the liberation struggle, Eritreans in Canada asserted that they would return immediately after independence. While appreciative that Canada allowed entry to a few people fleeing a brutal dictatorship and a terrible war, Eritreans were exasperated by the lack of public awareness and concern for the conditions behind their flight. They did not see themselves as immigrants who had chosen to relocate permanently to improve their personal lives, and found it frustrating to realize that the dangerous circumstances they had endured were part of an unseen world.

For many in Canada, the lives of peoples in the Third World are ghostly and shadowy, as invisible as dust. When the first Eritreans arrived, few Canadians knew where Eritrea was located or had any interest in its political realities. Eritreans here did live a shadowy existence: their communities were small in number and their identity was not recognized; they were an invisible minority, subjected to the contradictory pressures of racism, which marked them as different while there was no interest in the nature of that difference or the way in which others defined their own identities. Racism forces people into racialized identities that they do not make for themselves. Before Eritrea became independent, the Canadian government (and much of the public) classified Eritreans as Blacks, Africans, or Ethiopians. Individual Eritreans had different relationships with each of these identities, but most felt a primary attachment to their distinct national identity. This identity was, after all, the basis of their long struggle for independence. Not surprisingly, Eritreans were frustrated, as they were denied the very identity that was central to the wrenching changes they had endured. Being classified by others as Ethiopian was particularly upsetting for many. They found it disturbing to be mistaken for those they considered responsible for their exile, imprisonment, and torture, as well as for the deaths of family members. A number of Eritreans were also frustrated that this externally imposed classification, on the basis of some very general phenotypical characteristics, merged them into extremely broad groups. In fact, some members of this supposedly unified African or Black community actively rejected a distinct Eritrean identity, one based on their specific historical and political experiences. They rejected Eritrean identity on the basis of some differently imagined history which saw the Emperor Haile Selassie as a champion of African freedom, or considered the Eritrean nationalist movement as a secessionist organization that was threatening pan-Africanism. These critics, operating with essentialized categories, dismissed Eritrean nationalism as a distortion of the true identity the Eritreans should properly adopt. Ethiopian nationalists in Canada were enraged by the assertion of a distinct Eritrean identity and characterized it as the arrogance and delusions of a small group who had identified with Italian colonialism and rejected their authentic identity.

These conflicts over identity had practical consequences. In terms of access to the settlement services that were available in the 1980s, Eritreans were referred to agencies serving the Ethiopian community or to organizations intended for Africans in general. As Anthias and Yuval-Davis (1992) note, the politics of community advocacy and representation often assume a commonality of interest that overlooks the interests of different groups subsumed into one category. In this case, Eritreans did not believe that Ethiopians would represent their interests fairly. Tsehainesh, a married woman explained, 'You may think I am stupid or too proud for not getting help from Amhara- [Ethiopian-] speaking professionals. But [pause], I think about my brother, relatives, and friends [who died]. When I remember them, how could I? They [Ethiopians] probably feel the same toward me.' Many Eritreans were extremely wary of these organizations, believing that they would not be treated fairly and that Ethiopians in positions of some institutional power would seek to penalize them for their assertion of a different identity. These suspicions were particularly acute in relation to arranging sponsorship of relatives who wished to come to Canada. While some maintained a sense of self and national identity by avoiding these organizations, this avoidance also meant that they were denied services that might have made resettlement easier. Thus, Eritreans in the diaspora faced ideas about themselves that not only marginalized and denied the national identity that was the basis of their forced migration, but also had material implications.

In Canada, Eritreans encountered a new society with different expectations about gender roles and behaviour. Some found this experience difficult, particularly those women with little formal education, experience working outside the home, and facility with English. Women from a higher class were more prepared to operate in Canada's public spaces, but they faced different challenges in domestic spaces. Some came from homes where servants had done most of the domestic tasks, and they now found themselves without such help. Individuals of all classes, however, supported relatives who had been left behind in dangerous conditions or sponsored others to come to Canada. They had a strong commitment to support the nationalist movement as well as the Eritrean Relief Association, which sent food to famine-stricken areas outside Ethiopian control. Remittances from the diaspora provided a major source of financial support for the nationalist movement and for the new state established after the Ethiopian surrender in 1991. The importance of contributing to the nationalist movement was a strong ethical imperative in Eritrean diasporic communities around the world. This ethical imperative, combined with the need to provide financial aid to one's own relatives in Eritrea or scattered abroad, gave considerable incentives to both men and women to find employment. A strong work ethic pervaded Eritrean communities, and even those who concentrated on furthering their own higher education conceptualized it in terms of their future contribution to an independent Eritrean society rather than as personal advancement. Yet many of those men who had degrees or professional qualifications found themselves suddenly 'declassed,' underemployed, or unemployed because they 'had no Canadian experience.' Furthermore, the qualifications they had achieved in their own society were not recognized, or they were denied jobs they considered appropriate to their status. Some women became the principal earners for their families, and this brought new pressures and threats to gender identity. This crisis of class and gender identity for men had implications for the women who lived with them. These included the challenges of performing new tasks in new circumstances and dealing with husbands whose own gendered identity was threatened by this loss of status. Saba, a mother of two, addressed this point in general: 'It is hard for us. It is hard for everyone. Money is tight so everyone has to work, and long hours. Cleaning, washing, cooking, and taking care of kids, a lot more work on top of that. It is tough. Some husbands cannot take it. Wives cannot take it either, so some argue. Many women endure it ... Some women get more help from husbands.'

These class and gender challenges and pressures led to serious psychological distress and conflict within the home, but other families were more resilient and able to adapt to these new circumstances by providing mutual support and learning to see one another in new ways. Fatima, a woman in her mid-thirties, stated philosophically, 'Life must go on. We have to support each other. We are here for reasons.'

Long-Distance Nationalism

War and the politics of the Horn shaped the diaspora. While long-distance nationalism mobilized diasporic communities, the response was not unified. Indeed, nationalism was experienced through the creation of rival memories and constructions of the past, based on political allegiances. Civil war within the Eritrean nationalist movement, fought between the original Eritrean Liberation Front (ELF) and its more socialist-oriented offshoot, the EPLF, also cast a shadow over the diasporic communities. Most supported the EPLF, especially in the late 1980s, but some Eritrean Liberation Front members remained unsympathetic. In the diaspora, some hostility continued, although this was usually expressed through avoidance rather than confrontation. Commitment to nationalism not only set the prevailing emotional mood in the diaspora but was also a strong organizing principle for diasporic communities. Eritreans across Canada coordinated fundraising activities, tours of EPLF speakers, lobbying campaigns, and cultural events. Personal networks were imbued with the urgency of the political, ecological, and social crisis in Eritrea. Transmission of information about Eritrea also allowed the transmission of attitudes towards the shared experience of exile.

Eritreans abroad found their lives haunted by the war. The conflict they had escaped physically still cast its shadow over the diaspora. Individuals worried about relatives and friends left behind in war zones or living as refugees and exiles in other countries; they also felt a deep commitment to support nationalism. Tsehainesh's experience, stated earlier, is just one example. Eritreans in Canada were haunted by the memory of those they had left behind and the knowledge that a terrible war was ravaging the Horn of Africa while they lived in safety in Canada. Thus, the diaspora was overshadowed by a sense of anxiety and guilt, despite the fact that many had no choice but to flee to save their own lives. The Eritreans' financial contributions to the nationalist movement, the Eritrean Relief Association, and their own relatives meant that many people who already lived below the poverty line in Canada diverted much of their meagre resources to others. Zahra, a single woman in her late twenties who was having difficulty finding a job and had a very limited income, saved some money to contribute to the cause. She explained: 'I am ashamed of not getting a job. But nobody gives me a job. But I am proud to save some for my country.' Amna, a young ex-fighter who worked in a factory, said, 'I will go back to school full time when Eritrea becomes independent. In this way, I can support Eritrea.' Even as people in Canada sacrificed their own material comfort and personal opportunities, they developed a sense of a unified community. Support to Eritrea became a matter of ethical commitment and a source of pride and strength. After independence, it was also a policy that was enforced by institutions of the new state: Eritreans in the diaspora were required to pay a percentage of their income to the Eritrean government for reconstruction of the shattered economy. Such a policy had also existed during the liberation struggle, but after independence it acquired a more mandatory character since it was impossible to obtain a visa to return to Eritrea or to carry out any official transactions there unless one had fulfilled these requirements of citizenship.

Long-distance nationalism and the idea of return helped some Eritreans cope with various disappointments and stresses. Yet, this focus on returning had contradictory effects. Because they saw Canada as a temporary haven, some Eritreans did not seriously try to establish themselves. Many sacrificed personal comfort and opportunities to support nationalism. Nevertheless, nationalist commitments provided self-esteem and pride. Eritreans in Canada repeated the motto of the Eritrean fighters: 'Never Kneel Down.' The EPLF's eventual victory over the larger Ethiopian forces, backed first by the United States and then by the Soviet Union, gave those in the diaspora confidence that they too could overcome impossible odds.

Eritrean nationalism was also a social revolution. The goals included the overthrow of semi-feudal relations, distribution of land to the poor, creation of a multicultural national identity, and the emancipation of women. Protracted struggle created new social conditions, and relations among the fighters provided a model for the development of a new Eritrean identity. Those in the diaspora emulated this model so that Eritrean identity was not simply nostalgia for tradition but an ongoing construction and a challenge to some of the old traditions. An identity, 'Eritrean-ness,' was created in Canada and stemmed from both a rejection of tradition and an assertion against the racism that denied their distinctiveness. The premise of their identity was based on activism, shaped by long-distance nationalism. Just as 'every Eritrean is a refugee,' it is also true that 'being a volunteer is part of being Eritrean.' Eritrean identity in Canada is transnational, enacted by telephone and e-mail, provision of remittances that are vital to Eritrea's economy, volunteer work, lobbying for political and economic aid, and visits to Eritrea. Eritreans are less likely to journey abroad to visit their relatives in Canada because of their financial circumstances and because the Canadian government frequently denies them visas, suspecting that they intend to remain in Canada. In reality, although some might seek to stay on, most of the visitors we have met have been pleased to visit but eager to return to their own homes. This observation is especially true of older Eritreans, such as parents visiting their adult children.

During the first wave of arrivals in Canada, the population included a higher number of men. Those first women in Canada played important practical and symbolic roles for the new diasporic communities. In a sense, they were wives and mothers to those outside their own families. They provided a sense of domestic continuity to many lonely individuals who had been forced out of their own homes and wanted a setting where they could speak their own languages, reflect on shared experiences, and relax in a space that would contain some of the sensory resonance of home – the sounds of their own music, the smells of familiar spices, and the tastes of traditional food. These sensory experiences became important symbols of identity and helped people to briefly embrace the elusive phantoms of their past experiences in their homeland. It became an important task for women to find utensils, ingredients, and the means of cooking something that would approximate the tastes of traditional Eritrean meals. Thus, even the seemingly mundane aspects of domestic life were imbued with symbolic importance and became expressions of resilience.

Women's participation was not limited to these domestic spaces. At rallies and public events, some women took the stage and spoke out. It was usually men, however, who played a more public role in support of

Eritrean nationalism and relief activities, such as lobbying the Canadian government and the NGOs that worked in the region. Nevertheless, women played an extremely important role in creating a sense of identity and solidarity for the Eritrean diaspora. As Eritrean communities across Canada began to grow, women provided much of the labour for political and cultural events, as well as the symbolic 'heart,' by preparing and cooking traditional food. Many feel that these events are not really complete without the provision of a traditional meal, and, through their labour, women supply the means of producing, sharing, and ingesting a sense of identity.

The memory of those left behind, and their struggles, also provided a model for new social relations in the diaspora. During the long war, the EPLF established its liberated areas in the remote northern mountains and a new society developed among the fighters and the civilians who lived in these areas. One significant aspect of this new society was the change to more egalitarian gender relations. These new social relations among the EPLF fighters were promoted as the model for Eritrea's future, and they inspired many in the diaspora. Women in the diaspora found a model for their own resilience in women's activities 'in the field.' In the process of defining an Eritrean identity in Canada, however, the diasporic population found itself dealing with various contradictions as traditional culture clashed with the EPLF's vision of a new society. The key area in which these contradictions emerged was in gender relationships, as diasporic populations attempted to create new communities and households in Canada. Noting that gender relationships are a site in which one's authenticity as a member of a group is played out, Anthias (1998, 572) points out that diasporic groups 'are subjected to two sets of gender relations: those of the dominant society and those internal to the group.'

While this is a significant observation, the Eritreans' experiences further demonstrate the complexity of how gender relationships are negotiated among diasporic populations. In the Eritrean case, such negotiations about appropriate gender relationships have drawn on those accepted in 'mainstream' Canadian society, those defined by the rules of traditional gender behaviour, and those redefined by the EPLF. Faced with such complexity, some Eritreans expressed contradictory beliefs. Some publicly endorsed the EPLF's support for emancipation of women but reverted to patriarchal attitudes within their own homes, justifying this position on the basis of cultural tradition or natural processes. A few individuals openly opposed any reconfiguration of gender relationships and the emancipation of women. Tesfa, a man in his thirties, described the situation as he saw it: 'The main problem is with the women. The women get educated and now they aren't following our culture. Now they want to be equal to the man. Some of them can't even write their names but they want to be equal. This has happened since they came to Canada. They don't want to follow our culture anymore. It's because of the feminists and because of the way of life here in Canada.' Here we see that culture is imagined by some as a closed system that must be preserved from any contamination with others and fixed unchangeably in time. It is typical of this perspective that women are expected to embody these fixed traditions, and changes in women's roles are perceived as a direct threat to cultural identity.

Faced with new circumstances and buoyed by their commitment to a new national identity and a revolutionary ideology that has promoted the emancipation of women, some men made the conceptual leap and modified their own behaviour in the home. Others did not, and some women were required to work outside the home and then return to the full roster of domestic chores. (Of course, this is not a situation that is only limited to the Eritrean diasporic community.) Nebiat, an articulate middle-aged woman, described how the shadows of traditional culture were played out in her home: 'When men came to our house, they expected to have good meals, traditional meals. My husband did not help me. He believed in the EPLF, but he could not bring himself to help me in the kitchen or change diapers ... He could not take more responsibilities at home. I found that Eritrean women accepted new responsibilities and adjusted better than men. Many husbands do not help their wives. They do not help enough.' In other cases, women found space to negotiate new relationships within the home because they did not live within the shadow of all the expectations that would have come with the presence of their parents and in-laws. Although this meant fewer personnel to assist with duties such as child care, it also meant that husbands and wives were forced to develop new arrangements, provide mutual support, and see one another in different ways.

After Independence

Independence marked a turning point for the diaspora, as well as for Eritrea itself. Ideas of return had been constantly reiterated over the past decade. Now that independence had been achieved, it was necessary for people to reassess the feasibility of that much-cherished idea.

Visiting Eritrea became, as one person put it, 'almost a requirement' for those who had been living abroad. Yet those visits presented exiles with a reality many had not wished to face. Relatives and homes they had left behind years ago no longer existed or were completely changed, as were the exiles themselves. Coming to terms with those who were dead, damaged, or had disappeared was no easy process. Those who had endured the Ethiopian occupation, those who had spent years in the 'liberated areas,' and those who had lived abroad were all Eritreans, but their varied experiences had shaped them all in different ways. A few individuals and families did move from Canada back to Eritrea, but most realized that independence would not often provide the opportunity to return. Eritrea's shattered economy could not provide housing or jobs, and many had partially established themselves in Canada and had children in school; children born here lacked the same intense commitment to Eritrea. A telling moment came for some parents who took their families back for a visit: their children asked when they could return home – to Canada.[2]

Just as demobilized EPLF fighters had to reconceptualize their lives in individualistic terms rather than in the collectivist ethos that had existed in the field, independence required many of those who lived abroad to face the fact of permanent diaspora and to think more explicitly about their personal futures and those of their children. For the older generation (in their thirties and forties), long-distance nationalism provided collective space and identity. Those in the younger generation negotiate their space and identity by constructing who they are and how they belong/do not belong in relation to mainstream society, Black youth culture, and their parent's cultural, political, and social world. As one young woman said, 'Parents think we don't behave like respectful Eritreans. Just because we dress like other teenage Canadians, they worry that we are secretly dating or doping. Personally, I do not agree with the traditional marriage. Men and women should be more equal. I respect Eritrean culture, but I won't have a relationship like my parents have.'

Just as the determination of the EPLF fighters to 'Never Kneel Down' had inspired many in the diasporic generation to endure their own struggles in Canada, the victory of the EPLF and the achievement of independence provided a source of pride for the younger generation of Eritreans in Canada. In a context where African cultures are not widely known and where black people are seen through an extremely narrow range of corporate-media images, the success of Eritrean nationalism has provided a source of alternative identity and resilience for the younger generation. While many in this younger generation were not motivated by the same memories and the same urgent emotional connection to Eritrea that had mobilized their parents, long-distance nationalism was not absent: many young people were interested in visiting Eritrea, and a number of them decided to do their term of national service there. In addition, in Canada a new generation of young community activists developed after independence. Although many of them are now concentrated on the challenges their communities face in Canada, they also emphasize their links to Eritrea. The eruption of a new war between Eritrea and Ethiopia in 1998 re-energized the commitments of long-distance nationalism, but its outcome also led to new critical attitudes and a questioning of the PFDJ's leadership.

The 1998 war was devastating, particularly for Eritrea, which suffered under an Ethiopian invasion that killed and displaced thousands. Ethiopia deported thousands of Eritreans, some of whom had spent their whole lives in Ethiopia and did not identify with Eritrean nationalism or speak Eritrean languages. Eritreans interpreted the war as an effort by Ethiopia to reconquer Eritrea, and, indeed, many Ethiopian nationalists did call for this; the demands for further destruction were particularly strong on web sites run from the Ethiopian diaspora (Sorenson and Matsuoka 2001). Ethiopian attacks were deliberately targeted to cripple Eritrea's already precarious agricultural system, so the effects continued beyond the signing of a peace accord in 2000. Along with the huge number of casualties on both sides and the enormous human suffering that still continues because of the conflict, one devastating effect of the war was the creation of a much more repressive political climate in Eritrea. Criticism of the government about its handling of the border conflict was met with a crackdown on and imprisonment of journalists, students, and top-level government officials, including some who had been founders of the EPLF. Just as the ELF-EPLF civil war had split Eritrean communities abroad during the liberation struggle, the PFDJ's harsh treatment of its critics reawakened the memory of these internal struggles from the past and also created new divisions in the diaspora. While some believed that the sacrifices made by the EPLF fighters placed the actions of the PFDJ above any criticism, particularly by those who had been outside Eritrea during the liberation struggle, others were equally convinced that those sacrifices had been made to create a democratic society in which government would be held accountable and open to critique.

To conclude, memories of war and commitments to long-distance nationalism have played a major role in shaping national and gender identities in the Eritrean diaspora. Shadows of the past and the resilience of those in the diaspora keep the community dynamic, and now the younger generation is carving out new spaces of identity.

NOTES

1   Some additional insight into the achievements, challenges and setbacks that Eritrean women have experienced can be derived from considering them in the context of women's participation in other national liberation struggles. There is a growing literature on these matters. Of course, Amrit Wilson's (1991) study of women in the Eritrean revolution can be usefully compared with Jenny Hammond's (1990) discussion of women in northern Ethiopia who joined the Tigray People's Liberation Front, and there is much to be gained from reading Sondra Hale's (1996) analysis of gender and politics in Sudan. Outside the Horn of Africa, itself, studies of women's participation in national liberation movements range from Angola (e.g., Organization of Angolan Women 1984) to Zimbabwe (e.g., Lyons 2004; Staunton 1991). Stephanie Urdang's (1979) depiction of women's involvement in the revolution in Guinea-Bissau shows some similarities to the Eritrean case. Lazreg (1994) provides an interesting discussion of gender and nationalism in Algeria, raising some issues that are particularly relevant to women in Muslim societies. Studies of women's participation in nationalist movements outside Africa also provide some instructive comparisons. For example, Fleischmann (2003), Kawar (1996), Mayer (1994), Peteet (1991), Rubenberg (2001), Sharoni (1995), and Strum (1992) have discussed women's involvement in the Palestinian nationalist struggle. There is considerable material on women and nationalist movements in Latin America, such as Moore (1997), Smith (1996) and Stone (1981) on Cuba; Alegria on El Salvador; and Babb (2001), Collinson (1990), Isbister (2001), and Randall (1981 and 1994) on Nicaragua. Kampwirth (2004) provides a look at feminism and revolution in Chiapas, El Salvador, and Nicaragua. Considerable controversy followed Menchu and Burgos-Debray's (1984) book on Guatemala. Perspectives on women and nationalist struggles in Asia can be found in Smedley (1976) on China, De Mel (2001) on Sri Lanka, and Eisen (1983) on Vietnam. Some general discussion of the issues can be found in Miranda Davies (1983), Jayawardena (1986), and Yuval-Davies (1997).

2   It is also useful to consider, in comparative context, the changes that exiles

had to come to terms with after Eritrean independence. For example, some of those Chileans who had fled repression under the Pinochet regime and returned to Chile years later expecting a homecoming that would heal the wounds of their exile found the experience painful and disappointing (Zarzosa 1996). Like the exiles who traveled to post-independence Eritrea, the Chileans found that the society to which they 'returned' was not the one that had been at the heart of their dreams. Their experiences differed by class, with working-class returnees facing additional difficulties because of a lack of employable skills in the 'new' Chile. For the Chileans, the experience of return was gendered as well; many women had spent years in societies where some of the more obvious features of patriarchy were challenged, and they found themselves constrained in a Chile where the ideology of machismo was still openly enacted. The children of the Chilean returnees, too, faced a number of difficulties, and even those who spoke Spanish found themselves marginalized and frustrated.

REFERENCES

Alegria, Claribel. 1987. *They Won't Take Me Alive*. London: Women's Press.
Anderson, Benedict. 1992. The New World Disorder. *New Left Review* 1 (193): 3–13.
Anthias, Floya. 1998. Evaluating 'Diaspora': Beyond Ethnicity? *Sociology* 32(3): 557–580.
Anthias, Floya, and Nira Yuval-Davis. 1992. *Racialized Boundaries*. New York: Routledge.
Babb, Florence E. 2001. *After Revolution*. Austin: University of Texas Press.
Bannerji, Himani. 2000. *The Dark Side of the Nation*. Toronto: Canadian Scholars Press.
Collinson, Helen. 1990. *Women and Revolution in Nicaragua*. London: Zed.
Davies, Miranda. 1983. *Third World Second Sex*. London: Zed.
De Mel, Neloufer. 2001. *Women and the Nation's Narrative*. New Delhi: Kali for Women.
Eisen, Arlene. 1983. *Women and Revolution in Vietnam*. London: Zed.
Fleischmann, Ellen. 2003. *The Nation and Its 'New' Women*. Berkeley: University of California Press.
Gordon, Avery. 1997. *Ghostly Matters*. Minneapolis: University of Minnesota Press.
Hale, Sondra. 1996. *Gender Politics in Sudan: Islamism, Socialism and the State*. Boulder, CO: Westview Press.

Hammond, Jenny. 1990. *Sweeter Than Honey*. Trenton, NJ: Red Sea.

Haraway, Donna. 1991. *Simians, Cyborgs, and Women*. New York: Routledge.

Isbester, Katherine. 2001. *Still Fighting*. Pittsburgh, PA: University of Pittsburgh Press.

Jayawardena, Kumari. 1986. *Feminism and Nationalism in the Third World*. London: Zed.

Kampwirth, Karen. 2004. *Feminism and the Legacy of Revolution*. Athens: Ohio University Press.

Kawar, Amal. 1996. *Daughters of Palestine: Leading Women of the Palestine National Movement*. New York: State University of New York Press.

Lazreg, Marnia. 1994. *The Eloquence of Silence: Algerian Women In Question*. New York: Routledge.

Lyons, Tanya. 2004. *Guns and Guerrilla Girls*. Trenton, NJ: Africa World Press.

Matsuoka, Atsuko, and John Sorenson. 2001. *Ghosts and Shadows*. Toronto: University of Toronto Press.

Mayer, Tamara, ed. 1994. *Women and the Israeli Occupation*. New York: Routledge.

Menchu, Rigoberta, and Elisabeth Burgos-Debray. 1984. *I ... Rigoberta Menchu*. London: Verso.

Moore, Marjorie. 1997. *Seven Women and the Cuban Revolution*. Toronto: Lugus.

Organization of Angolan Women. 1984. *Angolan Women Building the Future*. London: Zed.

Peteet, Julie. 1991. *Gender in Crisis: Women in the Palestinian Resistance Movement*. New York, NY: Columbia University Press.

Randall, Margaret. 1981. *Sandino's Daughters*. New Brunswick, NJ: Rutgers University Press.

– 1994. *Sandino's Daughters Revisited*. New Brunswick, NJ: Rutgers University Press.

Rubenberg, Cheryl. 2001. *Palestinian Women*. Boulder, CO: Lynne Rienner.

Safran, William. 1991. Diasporas in Modern Societies: Myths of Homeland and Return. *diaspora* 1(1): 83–99.

Sharoni, Simona. 1995. *Gender and the Israeli-Palestinian Conflict*. Syracuse, NY: Syracuse University Press.

Smedley, Agnes, 1976. *Portraits of Chinese Women in Revolution*. New York: Feminist Press.

Smith, Lois M. 1996. *Sex and Revolution*. New York: Oxford University Press.

Sorenson, John, and Atsuko Matsuoka. 2001. Phantom Wars and Cyberwars: Abyssinian Fundamentalism and Catastrophe in Eritrea. *Dialectical Anthropology* 26(1): 37–63.

Staunton, Irene. 1991. *Mothers of the Revolution*. London: J. Currey.

Stoetzler, Marcel, and Nira Yuval-Davis. 2002. Standpoint Theory, Situated Knowledge and Situated Imagination. *Feminist Theory* 3(3): 315–333.

Stone, Elizabeth. 1981. *Women and the Cuban Revolution*. New York: Pathfinder.

Strum, Philippa, 1992. *The Women Are Marching*. Brooklyn: Lawrence Hill.

Urdang, Stephanie, 1976. *Fighting Two Colonialisms*. New York: Monthly Review.

Wilson, Amrit. 1991. *The Challenge Road: Women in the Eritrean Revolution*. Trenton, NJ: Red Sea Press.

Yuval-Davies, Nira. 1997. *Gender and Nation*. London: Sage.

Zarzosa, Helia Lopez. 1996. The Impact of Return Migration: The Case of Chile. *Refugee Policy Network* 21. www.fmreview.org/rpn2112.htm.

6 A Diasporic Bounty: Cultural History and Heritage

VIJAY AGNEW

One day, when I was a young girl, Pitaji, my father, took my two sisters and me to the bank in Bombay where he kept my mother's jewellery. We were excited to see the long-sequestered collection, from which Pitaji was going to let us choose and keep the pieces we found most attractive.

A clerk guided us along a narrow corridor to the back of the bank where the vault was situated. There, bundled together on a table under a dusty white cloth, lay a pile of red ledgers. After solemnly putting on his glasses, the clerk carefully extracted one of the ledgers and flipped through its pages until he identified my father's name. He then picked up a pen with a brass nib, dipped it in blue ink, and handed it to Pitaji while pointing out where he should sign. That done, the clerk led us to a vault lined on all four walls with storage lockers. He inserted his key into one of these vaults and Father did the same, sliding his arm inside its dark interior once the door had been opened and pulling out two boxes. Each was bundled up in a man's handkerchief that had once been white, but had yellowed with age. From under the edges of each handkerchief peeked a tin box that had rusted over the years in Bombay's warm, damp climate.

We withdrew to a small room, and Pitaji handed one of the boxes to us, saying, 'This jewellery was your mother's, and now it is yours. Take what you want from it.' Often when we were with Father, he told us little stories about our mother, hoping perhaps to paint a portrait that highlighted her diligence, modesty, and graciousness – the qualities that he most admired in her and wanted us to emulate. He was also concerned about our 'motherlessness,' and through these stories sought to dissipate our sense of loss by vividly recreating the past. In a way, he seemed to be saying that although we were motherless now, we had had a mother, and we could be proud of her. This excursion to the bank was just one more attempt to connect us, through her jewellery, with our past – our heritage and history.

Much of the jewellery kept in the vault had been given to Mother by her parents as dowry at the time of her marriage, and, conventionally, she would have passed some of it on to each of her children when they married. Perhaps Father thought the jewellery might somehow convey to us a sense of the kind of woman our mother had been, that the design and style of jewellery might give us some idea of the social and familial context in which she had lived. I suppose he thought they might also give us an inkling of her values and her person. Had Mother sought to be different from others, expressing that difference by wearing unusual jewellery? Had she been conventional, accepting the standard patterns and styles of her times? Perhaps Pitaji thought her jewels might enable us to put together our own portrait of Mother's life and times, unmediated by his interpretation of her taste or his memories of her person.

One of the boxes in the vault contained jewellery, the other gold coins. Pitaji told us that when the family lived in Quetta, Mother had, like many upper-middle-class women, avidly collected gold jewellery. Women asserted their social status – or rather their father's or husband's – through wearing such ornaments. My father and both my paternal and maternal grandfathers had indulged Mother in this pursuit because they considered it an aspect of women's frivolous and vain natures. Pitaji was not averse to cultivating that same weakness for jewellery in my sisters and me. He told us that according to Hindu Personal Law, jewels were a woman's *stri-dhan* (wealth); they would always belong to her, and she could do what she wished with them. My sisters and I felt privileged. Many years later, however, I discovered that my father's memory had been a bit selective. He did not tell us that while daughters were fobbed off with jewels in their dowries, sons inherited land and businesses. Nevertheless, Father's stories had subtly conveyed to us the subtext of women's 'weakness' and men's indulgence of it. If a woman fell on hard times, she could always sell or exchange her jewels for cash and thereby ensure a subsistence – no small consideration at a time in India's history when there were no pensions, insurance, or any other kind of state assistance for indigent women. Women like my mother had a bit of education, but no skills that would enable them to support themselves if times got tough.

The partition of India in 1947 had validated women's predilection to collect and hoard jewellery. My parents had lived in the Muslim-dominated region in the city of Quetta, which by the beginning of 1947 had become part of Pakistan, a Muslim country. Wanting to be with other Hindus in India, and despite the pleas of politicians like Mahatma Gandhi to stay put in their homes, they joined millions of their co-religionists and came as refugees to Delhi, leaving behind property, homes, and possessions that they had collected lovingly for generations. My mother and aunts, however, put their jewellery in little tin boxes like the ones in front of us at the bank, or wrapped their valuables in handkerchiefs which they clung to on their journey to Delhi. There the economic and social chaos that accompanied the partition meant that bank accounts were in a state of flux, and once cash had been used up, the women were able to sell their jewels and provide subsistence for their families. Years later, I would hear stories about women who had willingly sold their jewels, the cash they received making the difference between survival and destitution.

My mother's jewels, unexceptional in design and value, were much like the thousands of similar pieces in the collections of upper-middle-class women locked up in vaults throughout India. My sisters and I carefully examined necklaces, bangles, nose rings, and earrings before making our selections. We were familiar with many of the designs, for we had seen them on maternal aunts who had received similar pieces as parts of their dowries. We were amazed to find large circular nose rings decorated with coloured beads; we thought only rural women wore these. Father explained that our mother had worn them at the weddings of her sisters. There were many bangles in solid gold, which we found unattractive, although it was possible that Mother had bought them to accumulate gold rather than for their design or artisanship. We laughed to find tiny bangles that had been given to us at our birth by our grandparents.

Many of the pieces were 'too old fashioned' or 'too grown up' for us, and we had no interest in them. One of the pieces I did choose was an ornate, round pendant in Kundan style encrusted with red stones and pearls. Kundan, which dates from the Mughal period in Indian history, is a style of setting stones unique to India; historians note that its visual effect was copied by other countries in the region. There was also another piece that was most appropriate for me, a small straight pin with a 'V' at the centre, inlaid with small pearls. Since 'V' is my initial, I assumed my mother meant it for me, but as she died so soon after leaving Quetta, I wondered how and when she had bought it. Pitaji remembered her using the pin to tuck up the folds of her sari on her shoulder, but he had no idea how she had come by it. I still have the piece; I am sentimental about it and afraid of losing it, so I seldom take it out. On the odd occasion when I have worn it on a dress, friends in Toronto have expressed an interest in how I acquired an old Victorian pin.

While my sisters and I were examining the jewellery, Father was absorbed in thought over the smaller box containing the gold coins. These coins, referred to colloquially as 'sovereigns' and 'guineas,' had at one time belonged to Lalaji, my grandfather, who had kept them, not as collector's items, as is the norm in the West, but as a form of saving in the early part of the twentieth century when the Indian banking system was not well developed. At that time, branches of the East India Company and later British banks were located in port cities, where they focused on short-term financing of maritime trade. Indian businessmen and farmers met their own need for credit by going to moneylenders or by resorting to informal loans from individuals on the basis of personal trust. Sovereigns and guineas are still often given as gifts to daughters, nieces, and granddaughters on occasions such as engagements, marriages, or the birth of children. Some of Lalaji's coins, dated 1884 and bearing the image of Queen Victoria, are with me now in Toronto. Along with the Kundan pendant and the Victorian pin, these coins are relics of my heritage. I love them, because they have come to me from my mother, father, and grandfather, but they are nevertheless also symbols of foreign rule, domination, and exploitation.

Whose Jewel Is in the Crown?

On one occasion, in the early 1980s, I planned to leave Toronto to visit my father in India, accompanied by Nicole, my daughter, who was then eight years old. In the weeks preceding our visit, I agonized over how to prepare Nicole for the stark poverty she would encounter on the streets of Bombay. My concern, like that of many immigrant South Asian parents, was whether she would take pride in her Indian heritage. I wondered how she would compare Bombay with Toronto, and if she would simply find India crowded, polluted, and poor. Friends had used the strategy of taking their children to the rundown sections of Toronto in order to impress upon them that poverty was everywhere, even in affluent North America. I did the same, but since we were going to stop in London en route, I also planned on taking Nicole to the Tower of London, which houses the British crown with the famous Indian Kohinoor diamond at its centre. I imagined that by taking my daughter to see the diamond, I might provide her with an easy explanation of India's poverty: the Kohinoor would act, conveniently, as a symbol of India's continuing impoverishment through colonization and exploitation. The historian in me knew it was a very partial explanation, but I rationalized that complex economic facts are dry and uninteresting and that a visual symbol would be much more compelling.

The Kohinoor diamond, the most famous gem found in India, left the country as the booty of war and conquest several times before it finally fell to the British. The history of the stone is sketchy. Thought to have been mined in Golconda in central India, the diamond was originally 186 carats in size; its brilliance so dazzled the local people that they referred to it as the 'Mountain of Light.' It came into the possession of the Mughal emperor Babur when he defeated Ibrahim Lodhi for the Sultanate of Delhi in 1526. Later, when his son Humayun's hold on the throne weakened, he traded the Kohinoor, along with some other jewels, to the ruler of Iran in exchange for 1,400 cavalry (Guy and Swallow 1990, 59–62). Nevertheless, the gem was returned to India and was found in the possession of the emperor Aurangzeb. At his death in 1707, the treasury was raided by Nadir Shah, who took the diamond back to Persia – today's Iran – and from there the Kohinoor went to the kings of Kabul, which today is Afghanistan.

Shah Shuja, the ruler of Kabul, experiencing some difficulty in retaining his throne, left for Kashmir in the northern part of India, where he was taken prisoner. His distraught wife managed to find her way to Punjab, also in North India, and gave the Kohinoor to the 'Lion of Punjab,' its ruler Raja Ranjit Singh, as a reward for rescuing her husband. Raja Ranjit Singh was a powerful and expansionist ruler, but his descendants were weak, and by 1849 they had succumbed to the might of the British colonial elite in India, who annexed their kingdom. The defeated rulers of Punjab signed the Anglo-Sikh Peace Treaty and showed their good faith to the new rulers by handing over the Kohinoor to them. Lord Dalhousie, then Governor General of India, presented it formally to Queen Victoria at a ceremony in 1850, and wrote: 'The Kohinoor may be regarded as a historical symbol of the conquest of India, and the Governor General rejoices that it has found fitting rest in your Majesty's crown' (Wolpert 1993). Since that time, the Kohinoor has been the centrepiece of the British crown jewels.

Do origins equate with exclusive heritage and rights of ownership? Some Indian parliamentarians have argued that the Kohinoor was 'misappropriated by the colonial rulers during the British Raj,' and they want it returned to India (BBC News, 26 April 2000). Although the Kohinoor was found in India, it has had many homes in its long history. The Kohinoor encodes the history and heritage of Indians in India, the British in India, Indians in Britain, Iranians, and many other hybrid identities all over the world. We cannot put boundaries around heritages and locate them only in particular geographical contexts because borders are permeable; people leave their homes and evolve new and diverse histories in the diaspora. Yet, the absence of historically significant gems and jewels in India and their existence in museums in Europe and North America are important clues to India's history of being invaded and conquered. As in other contexts, the disposition of such cultural icons marks nations as winners and losers.

History and Heritage

On another of my visits to India in the 1990s, after having lived in Canada for approximately twenty years, I went to visit Lal Quila, or the Red Fort, in Old Delhi. The Mughal emperor Shah Jahan built Lal Quila in 1638 as part of his plan to move the capital from Agra to Delhi. Located on a bluff alongside the Yamuna River, it is built of red sandstone; hence, its name. Although commissioned by a Mughal emperor, the fort incorporates Hindu architectural design and construction methods found in Manasara, a *vastus sastra*, or religious text. Its semi-elliptical design was called *karmuka*, or bow. The wall of the fortress has survived over centuries. In present times, Lal Quila frequently forms the backdrop of major speeches given by politicians to the thousands of people who assemble there. The Lal Quila was often the site of Jawaharlal Nehru's addresses to the nation in the years immediately after India became independent in 1947.

When I lived in Old Delhi as a child, Lal Quila was a familiar landmark, an imposing fortress that by its imperial size dominated the neighbourhood. As a schoolgirl, however, I was taught little about India's historical monuments, even though my Catholic mission school was less than a mile away from the fort. On this particular visit from Toronto, I wanted to learn about it – to satisfy my intellectual curiosity – and I thought Lal Quila might provoke some insights I could share with the students who take my course on India at York University. When I got out of my car at Lal Quila, I was immediately surrounded by beggars, vendors, and tour guides, all pushing and jostling one another in their efforts to grab my attention. The entrance to the fortress was crowded with buses, cars, rickshaws, and scooters. Although the density of the traffic and crowds made me very nervous, I walked through them resolutely to the entrance, purchased my ticket for a few cents, and hired a government-recommended guide to show me around.

I entered the fortress through a large, steel gate and found myself in a lane that was originally called the Mina Bazaar, or gold jewellery market, but was now full of little stores selling souvenirs and knick-knacks to tourists. Storekeepers stood at the doors or sat on stools and loudly beckoned to passing tourists: 'Come here ... Look inside!' Past the stores was a stone wall with an archway. Walking through it, I found myself in a garden alongside a row of rooms that had been at one time the private quarters of the emperor. I noticed that the garden was overgrown and that there were large patches of dried grass. The rooms, from where I stood, appeared dusty and neglected. I was angry with myself for noticing this, for looking at things with 'Canadian eyes.'

Over the years, I have become accustomed to visiting historical sites that are jealously protected and maintained in many European countries. I knew better, however, than to attribute the state of the garden and rooms in Lal Quila to a lack of care or appreciation of history on the part of the local population. Rather, I understood the neglect to be one more aspect of the poverty of the country. The Indian government was confronted with a tough choice: allocating funds for the maintenance of historical monuments or seeing to the everyday, basic needs of its ever-expanding population. I walked towards the back wall of the fortress, hoping to catch a glimpse of the Yamuna River, but saw instead a gigantic flea market, chock-full of people, obscuring the view beyond.

The guide and I walked through the row of rooms, but as many of the walls separating the rooms had long since crumbled, they now formed a long, unplanned hallway. There was not much to see except for some embossed stonework on the floors and the remnants of some fountains. The rooms were bare of tapestries and furnishings. As we walked along, we came to a chamber called the Diwan-i-Am, or the Hall of Public Audience, where Shah Jahan had held court twice a day. On a platform in this hall stood a large marble canopy under which the emperor had sat while meeting his subjects. The wall behind the canopy was decorated with inlaid enamel work with designs carved into the wall depicting flowers and fruits. But amongst these engravings were also some hollow spots that were filled with dust. The gaps in the design – which I have since seen in many other palaces and fortresses in India, such as Shish Mahal in Jaipur – piqued my curiosity.

The guide responded to my queries about these lacunae in an assured and certain manner, saying that they had once held rubies, emeralds, and other gems, but that the precious stones had all been dug out by the British during their rule in India. I did not ask him if he had verified this fact, or if he was merely repeating stories and myths that circulate on the subject. The information, however, did not surprise me. I had read historical accounts of invaders from Kabul, Iran, and Britain looting and pillaging the country, and I was excited to see evidence of it for myself. My immediate reaction was to wrap myself in a cloak of righteous indignation. By doing so, the neglect of the monument and the poverty of the country could be easily explained: India was poor because colonizers had robbed it of its wealth. It felt good to come to such a conclusion, but I was conscious that I had jumped too easily to a simple, monocausal explanation, and that historical facts were many and could be interpreted in a hundred different ways.

Later, back in Toronto, I went in search of textual evidence to corroborate what I had seen, and found *Arts of India 1550–1900*, published by the Victoria and Albert Museum (Guy and Swallow 1990). Shah Jahan had loved jewels, and was himself a remarkably skilled gemologist. Behind the marble canopy, the walls of the Diwan-i-Am, like many of his other monuments, are decorated using a stone-inlay technique. The wall is 'set with an extraordinary combination of small, imported Italian *pietra dura* panels of birds in trees, linked by a tracery of fruit trees in which sit more birds inlaid in the same technique, presumably by Indian craftsmen. At the top is a panel depicting the figure from Western classical myth, Orpheus, who by his music made wild animals live peacefully together' (88). The French merchant-jeweller, Tavernier, wrote after visiting with the emperor that his plan for monuments such as Lal Quila had been 'to cover it throughout with a trellis of rubies and emeralds which would represent, after nature, grapes green and commencing to become red; but his design ... required more wealth than he had been able to furnish, and remains unfinished, having only two or three wreaths of gold with their leaves ... enameled in their natural colors, emeralds, rubies, and garnets making the grapes' (89).

The account does not document the subsequent travels of the gems. For me, a woman who lives in the Indian diaspora, questions of heritage and ownership are significant, but I find few quick and easy answers to them. Some reasonable queries might be: Were the gems taken by Nadir, Shah of Iran, who plundered the country in 1739? Alternatively, perhaps, were they later taken by officers of the East India Company? Or were they perhaps removed by British colonial élites after Delhi became the capital of British India? Where are these gems now? Who owns them, and whose heritages are they now a part of?

I had made a tantalizing discovery, but was no closer to charting the journeys of the gems. In 2001, the Metropolitan Museum of Art in New York hosted an exhibition called Treasury of the World: Jewelled Arts of India in the Age of Mughals. I happened to be visiting the city with Nicole, and was delighted to learn of the show. It was an amazing treat to find exquisite Indian gems and jewellery creatively displayed to their best artistic and aesthetic advantage, and to have the opportunity to admire them in the luxury of an American museum. The three or four rooms in which the exhibition was housed were crowded with white and South Asian visitors. The collection of Mughal jewellery was assembled as a result of the pioneering work of Sheikh Nasser al-Sabah of Kuwait; although Islamic art has been studied, jewels, by and large, have been relatively ignored. Sheikh Nasser is convinced that 'jewellery and jewelled objects generally – and those of the Indian subcontinent specifically – are works of art which are to be taken seriously, and their creators respected in the highest degree' (Keene and Kaoukji 2001, 9).

The jewels and gems were a portion of the al-Sabah Collection that was housed in the Kuwait National Museum. The exhibition catalogue noted that the displayed jewels and gems represented the 'most comprehensive and richest collection of Indian jewelled arts' in the world. 'Indian jewelled objects and royal Mughal gems ... bear witness to the vast wealth of the legendary Mughal emperors of India' (Keene and Kaoukji 2001, n.p.). I saw some exquisite pieces of jewellery, including a Kundan pendant with rubies and a cameo of Shah Jahan that dated back to the seventeenth century. There were emeralds and rubies the size of small rocks, and gems inscribed with the names of several Mughal emperors of the sixteenth and seventeenth centuries that 'reveal their importance as markers of royal legitimacy' (9).

I was grateful to get a glimpse of my history and heritage in New York via the generosity of Sheikh Nasser of Kuwait. The pieces in the show piqued my curiosity about their journeys. The catalogue gave the details of time and design relevant to the pieces, but otherwise simply noted the year each was acquired by Sheikh Nasser from the 'art market.' The journeys of these gems from India to perhaps many homes are now lost to the tides of history, but they have taken root in the Indian diaspora and have become an integral part of their local context and history.

Where Is Home?

Since I am a historian who studies the South Asian diaspora, I like to visit museums in Europe and North America, and especially their Asian and Indian galleries. Such visits dispel, however briefly, some nostalgia for my roots. I am awed by their imposingly high ceilings, huge pillars, and wide galleries lined with invaluable paintings and sculptures. The hushed atmosphere – particularly in the Asian galleries, which normally do not draw huge crowds of spectators – makes me somber and reflective. Sometimes the walls are lined with glass cases that hold artifacts and jewels. When I peer into the cases, I try to imagine the life and times of the collectors who originally commissioned the objects, and of the artisans who laboured long and hard over them. I like to think that these crafts workers were engaged in a labour of love, that they were proud to hone their artistic skills fashioning objects of beauty, even though someone else – most likely someone rich and powerful – would ultimately own their work. I know, however, that some of my friends would not be so kind to the commissioners of these objects, and would argue that the artisans had been severely exploited.

Recently, I went to visit the Victoria and Albert Museum in London, which now possesses 'the oldest and the most comprehensive collection of Indian arts outside that continent' (Guy and Swallow 1990, 9). A small segment of it is also displayed at its Nehru Gallery of Indian Art, which opened in 1990 with an aim of establishing it as 'the major national centre for public education on Indian art and culture' (9). Most of the collection, if not all of it, came to Britain with the officers of the East India Company; British administrators, such as viceroys and governors general; and private individuals who had lived in or visited India from the seventeenth to the twentieth century. Some of the collection was acquired by the museum from the Great Exhibition on design in 1851; other parts, from Indian rajas or bequests from private individuals and trusts. Some parts had anonymous origins. When I visited the gallery, the collection being displayed consisted of Mughal paintings, tapestries, artifacts, jewels, and clothing. Although it occupied three or four rooms, it was a very small portion of the museum's holdings of Indian art.

I was torn by ambiguous feelings – proud to see what I think of as my heritage so beautifully displayed in the gallery, and happy that some aspects of Indian artistic traditions and aesthetic crafts were being shown alongside those of many other countries. But I was sad, as well, because these beautiful artifacts were no longer in India. Their presence in the gallery was a reminder of India's colonial past, and the collection itself a symbol of the country's history of exploitation and impoverishment.

The visit also raised another question about 'home' for me: I wondered if home had to coincide with national and geographic boundaries. Elizabeth Esteve-Coll, director of the Victoria and Albert Museum, notes that they have held the collection 'in trust for present and future generations for many years, but now, with a community of nearly one million people of South Asian origin living in Britain, it is not only time to display more of that collection, but actively to use it to explain the richness and diversity of our multi-cultural heritage' (Guy and Swallow 1990, 9).

People of Indian descent live in many different parts of the world and have made these places their homes for more than a generation. Their art has also been dispersed globally. Perhaps it should be viewed simply as a treasure of the world or humanity, bypassing the concept of ownership altogether. Although I can see the merits of such an argument intellectually, I cannot so easily reconcile myself emotionally with the issues raised over ownership. Besides, the interpretations and meanings given to gems, jewels, and art in general are also dependent on, and influenced by, the social context in which they are displayed. Had I seen the collection at a Nehru gallery in a location in India, surrounded by its present-day sights, smells, and sounds, I think I might have had a different perspective on it, and a different set of questions might have come to mind.

The day I visited the Nehru Gallery, a middle-aged white British woman with an expertise in Hindu art was teaching a class on Mughal paintings that was attended by ten or twelve people. I listened intently to her introductory remarks on the paintings, but then wandered off to examine the jewellery displayed in the glass cases. Since the gallery was small, I continued to listen to what was being said, and the teacher in turn, I think, noticed I was making notes on some of the displays. After a while, I joined the group again and listened to the students finish their discussion of the paintings. The group did not discuss the jewels (and rightly so, since the class had a different objective altogether). At the end, a young woman of Indian descent asked the question that had been on my mind as well: 'How did these paintings come here?' The instructor showed no surprise at the question, and from that I assumed she had been asked similar questions at other times. She was reserved in her response, saying that the paintings had come to the gallery in many different ways: some had been given as gifts to colonial officers, others had been purchased or commissioned by them from local artisans, still others had been sold by the rajas and maharajas to wealthy British individuals in India.

The young woman, however, was not satisfied with this response and enquired bluntly, 'Is it not true that some of these objects were stolen?' Before the teacher could respond, a white male jumped into the conversation to say, amiably, 'Not really. The local people did not value the art, but sold or gave it away for very small sums of money.' I joined the conversation at this point and protested that such assumptions were wrong. After a few more minutes of this talk, the class dispersed, but I stayed back to speak to the instructor. She confessed that the question was intriguing, but remained largely unanswered. This was corroborated by the displays. While some of the paintings, sculptures, weapons, and jewels were accompanied by information identifying their provenance, many others came from unknown, or unnamed, sources. (When I attempted to have a similar discussion a day later with a white British guide and a volunteer instructor while visiting the China and India galleries at the British Museum in London, I was stonewalled.)

The nationalist Indian historian in me saw the displays of jewels in the gallery as proof of the many textbook accounts of the pillaging and looting of Indian gems, jewels, art, and sculpture by British invaders and conquerors. In the seventeenth century, the British East India Company had come to India – initially to Madras and later to Calcutta – to buy spices and cotton textiles. The goods were paid for in the gold and silver bullion used as currency at the time. Historians refer to this early period of the British arrival in India as a time when trade led to the flow of gold into the region, thereby making it rich. The expansion of trade, however, led to rivalries between European nations in India and created the need for them to make alliances with the local rulers. The French East India Company, under Joseph Dupleix, had successfully taken advantage of India's caste, class, and religious differences to play off one ruler against another. It had further exploited local rivalries by offering its favoured rajas both soldiers and armaments to help secure their thrones or expand their territories. The British East India Company used similar tactics brilliantly, and in the conflicts between the French and British companies and the local rulers, the British emerged victorious in Madras. In these battles, Robert Clive, a young lieutenant with the British East India Company, gained a reputation for audacity and daring.

The British, consequent to rivalries in Europe and India, had amassed a large contingent of soldiers and sepoys at their fort in Madras. Although Fort William in Bengal was secure, British expansionist activities there raised the ire of a local nawab, and he engaged them in battle. Panicking, the commander of the fort left hurriedly, along with some of his officers and soldiers. Not all the British residents were able to leave, however, and some of the men and women hid in a dungeon. When news of this reached Madras, it enraged the governor. He dispatched an army under Lieutenant Clive escorted by five warships under the command of Admiral Charles Watson, to rescue the British prisoners and regain control of Bengal. Most of the people died before they could be rescued; the dungeon where the tragedy occurred is referred to in history books as the Black Hole of Calcutta. This event was remarked upon by some British writers of the time as an aspect of the country's barbarism.

In Bengal, Clive and Watson allied themselves with a local magnate, Jagat Singh, and defeated the French in the decisive Battle of Plassey in 1757, consequently becoming the new 'nawab-makers' in the region. They then lent their support to Jagat Singh, to install his candidate as the Nawab of Murshidabad (with its fabled treasury of gems and jewels); Clive personally escorted the new nawab to the throne. The nawab rewarded Clive by giving him an immediate personal fortune and the title of Mansabdar, with all its privileges, and land as well as a salary. 'Overnight, at the age of thirty-two, [Clive] became one of England's wealthiest subjects, first of the reviled 'nabobs' soon to return to London with bags of Indian jewels and gold that he used to buy up shares of company stock and rotten borough seats galore in Parliament' (Wolpert 1989, 180–181).

Some of Clive's jewels and gold were on display at the Victoria and Albert Museum. One, a turban jewel typical of those worn by the nawabs of Murshidabad, was described as having been presented to Admiral Watson by the Nawab of Bengal on 26 July 1757 following the Battle of Plassey. The turban jewel is described on the accompanying plaque as 'enameled gold, the upper section set with diamonds, rubies, emeralds, and a sapphire, the lower with diamonds, rubies, an emerald and a pendant pearl.' There was also a pair of gold armlets set with rubies that were acquired in India by John Johnston of Alva (1734–1795), who fought with Robert Clive at the Battle of Plassey. They are from Thanjavur, South India, and date to the eighteenth century. A necklace displayed at the gallery also caught my eye; it was described as 'enameled gold plaque and pendants, some set with pearls and green glass beads, the strands of the pearls terminate in emerald and ruby beads.' It is from nineteenth-century North India. How it got to the museum is not disclosed. I took an interest in some of the thick bangles decorated with mina, the enamel work studded with diamonds from Jaipur, which is even now copied and reproduced by jewelers in that region. The donor was not identified.

When I saw the jewels, I experienced some satisfaction in knowing that India had not always been poor, but had been made so by its history. I wondered about the extent to which the nawabs and the rajas had voluntarily parted with their wealth, or if they had felt compelled to do so by the threat of dethronement and annexation of their territories by the British. There were many instances in South India and elsewhere where the death of a raja became an occasion for the British to install a puppet raja from amongst the heirs, or to install, in some instances, agents and advisors in the court of a raja and thus become the power behind the throne. Those rajas who were able to retain their thrones often did so at the pleasure of the British. But if some rajas were compelled to trade their heritage for survival, others, like the Maharaja of Jaipur, sold them for profit and pleasure and to acquire estates in Britain. Evidence of that, too, was found at the museum.

The Nehru Gallery also held examples of temple sculptures that had been presented to the colonizers. There were some beautiful examples of large statues of Lord Vishnu in copper alloy that had been excavated at Coimbatore in South India and were thought to belong to the Early Chola period of the tenth century. They had been 'bequeathed by Lord Curzon, Viceroy of India 1898–1905.' There were also large bronze statues of the Goddess Parvati and of Siva Nataraj, also from the Chola period; these had been 'bequeathed by Lord Ampthill, Governor of Madras, 1900–1906.' It is, I suppose, entirely possible that the British who lived in India legitimately patronized Indian art and sculptures, or commissioned jewels and art objects. Some may have acquired them simply as mementoes of their stay in India.

Conclusion

Memory is a key to personal, social, and cultural history and is dependent on time and context. What we remember is articulated by the major political and social narratives of our times; they enable us to reconstruct history by identifying and filling gaps in its many narratives. As a racialized woman, I am sensitive to the negative stereotypes of India and Indians in Canada, and thus my memories of the past are not merely of baubles – gems and jewels – but of the feelings they evoked in me and the images that floated through my mind as I stood mutely in front of them. These feelings and images are my archaeological archives; they enable me to reconstruct my home and heritage – and therefore myself – in new and vivid colours.

In the year 2000, the Royal Ontario Museum in Toronto held an exhibition called The Arts of the Sikh Kingdoms, a most unusual subject for a museum that has seldom mounted shows on South Asia. In the centre of the main exhibit hall sat the golden throne of Raja Ranjit Singh, on loan from the Victoria and Albert Museum in London. Of 'waisted shape,' suggesting the lotus seats of Hindu and Buddhist iconography, it is 'one of the most conspicuous and popular exhibits' in the Indian collection held by the museum (Guy and Swallow 1990, 188). Behind the throne were displayed daggers and swords used for ceremonial purposes or during war, along with many antique tapestries and long brocade coats worn on special court occasions. For me, the most striking thing about the exhibition was the fact that most of the treasures were on loan from the Victoria and Albert Museum.

Feeling disgruntled, I made critical comments about the looting and plunder of India, with this heritage now ensconced in the diaspora. But at the same time I saw some heartwarming scenes at the exhibition. Some Sikh men, who from their appearance seemed to be working class, had brought their children to the exhibition and were proudly showing their Canadian-born offspring their Indian and Sikh heritage. I, too, felt this pride in my cultural history and the accomplishments of my fellow nationals, and took Nicole along to the exhibition, hoping to instil similar sentiments regarding her Indian heritage in her.

Having lived outside India for most of my adult life, I have developed a diasporic sense of myself and my history and heritage. I have had the privilege of seeing gems and jewels from the subcontinent displayed to their best advantage in museums in Britain and North America. Although there are many unanswered questions and unresolved issues surrounding such cultural appropriations, these jewels and gems are now part of humanity's collective past. They are part of our South Asian heritage, even though they are not 'owned,' controlled, or safeguarded by India. They are the markers of history and the bounty of the diaspora.

REFERENCES

Guy, John, and Deborah Swallow. 1990. *Arts of India: 1550–1900*. London: Victoria and Albert Museum.

Keene, Manuel, and Salam Kaoukji. 2001. *Treasury of the World: Jewelled arts of India in the Age of the Mughals*. New York: Thames and Hudson.

Wolpert, Stanley. 1993. *A New History of India*, 4th ed. New York: Oxford University Press.

PART 3

Community and Home

Historically, migrants and refugees from different parts of the world have come to Canada, and made it their home. Scholars describe how the displaced and uprooted individuals transplant the cultures and beliefs they have brought along with them in their new homes. However, over the years they and the societies in which they live are transformed, spawning an identity that distinguishes the individual from their friends and relatives 'back home' and in the diaspora. Migrants and refugees are haunted by the loss of a home and are sometimes nostalgic for a past; however, a close look at what they remember reveals distinct variations by gender, class, and sexuality.

Anh Hua's 'Diaspora and Cultural Memory' reviews the literature on diasporas to reveal the significance of the term as well as the varied ways it has been used by scholars. Hua argues that a study of diasporas can help explain the dispersal of previously oppressed or colonized subjects in diverse locations, and the process by which a sense of community and identity among them is generated and manifested. More specifically, she reviews the theoretical propositions underlying the query concerning how a diasporic community is imagined through collective memory and cultural trauma, and how the homing desire of diasporic subjects is influenced by their gendered identities and sense of belonging.

As Hua documents, diasporas have been formed in many different historical times and conditions, and represent heterogeneous communities that are also internally fragmented and contested along the axis of class, gender, and heterosexuality. The individual who lives in the present, yet remembers the past with nostalgia, may experience a double loyalty and consciousness. She or he may evaluate cultural practices and norms as authentic, or not, based on whether they conform to an idealized norm.

Yet not all diasporic communities remember the past with longing and nostalgia. For example, women's recollections of the past are often tinged with a desire to resist the patriarchal norms of their cultures and class; these norms constitute the cultural baggage brought from 'back home' into the new societies of settlement. (Hua's point is corroborated by Moghissi, Sakamoto and Zhou, and Matsuoka and Sorenson, in their chapters on Islamic, Chinese, and Eritrean communities.) Queer subjects whose presence is unacknowledged or submerged within dominant identities in the nation state do not recall the past with nostalgia; rather, solace for them lies in the act of forgetting. Hua argues that scholars of feminism and diasporas share a common commitment to the ideology of social justice, and their documentation of history and genealogy record testimony of the oppressed that bears witness to their subjugated past. This is a significant activity, since those in power can, and often do, dominate and manipulate memory to serve their own ends. Thus, women, ethnic minorities, and other marginalized groups need to assert their presence in masculinist, hegemonic memory and history.

Moghissi, in 'The "Muslim" Diaspora and Research on Gender,' provides specific examples of problems and prospects encountered in conducting research and educational/training programs concerned with changing gender and family dynamics within immigrant and refugee communities. Those Moghissi works with are of Islamic origin and include Iranians, Afghans, Palestinians, and Pakistanis in Canada and Britain. She identifies methodological and practical problems encountered in the process of interviewing, where the research strategy includes an effort to develop analytic and interpretive capabilities in the communities studied. She describes challenges that arise in developing team efforts and proposes possible strategies for overcoming them.

Izumi Sakamoto and Yanqiu Zhou's 'Gendered Nostalgia: The Experiences of New Chinese Skilled Immigrants' is based on in-depth interviews with twenty-one newly arrived skilled immigrants from mainland China and focuses on the mechanism of their gendered remembrance of the homeland. It examines how gender, as a social axis, is presented in women's narratives of the home that they have left behind, and how their memories construct and reconstruct their imagined homeland. Women's experiences in Canada – the family, work, and society – transform their consciousness of self, which leads them to question and challenge some of the conventional subordinate gender roles assigned to them. Sakamoto and Zhou's essay highlights women's narratives and concludes by suggesting some further directions for additional research on this theme. Carl James's '"I Feel Like a Trini": Narrative of a Generation-and-a-Half Canadian' picks up on the theme of realizing the human potential of individuals in an ethnographic study of an immigrant male. It is also an interpretive account of the complex, pragmatic, sentimental, imagined, dual, and contradictory ways in which home is conceptualized and imagined. James presents a narrative about Mark, a twenty-year-old Caribbean diasporic university student who was born in Trinidad, immigrated to Toronto at the age of thirteen, and, as such, is identified as a 'generation-and-a-half Canadian.' The chapter provides a perspective on how Mark experienced and adjusted to life in Canada, and, in doing so, explores how his Canadian identity (i.e., his sense of belonging) was constructed, the circumstances and structural factors that shaped his life and informed his educational and career aspirations, his perceptions of the opportunities and possibilities that Canada afforded him as a young Black man, and the role his mother played in directing his aspirations. It argues that Trinidad and Canada made him the person he is and expects to become. It was in Canada that Mark discovered his athletic talent and developed the athletic skills that are valuable to him in his career. At the same time, he remains attached to the values he was socialized with in Trinidad, and perceives them to have shaped his aspirations and self-confidence.

In 'The Quest for the Soul in the Diaspora,' I describe my experience of being a Hindu and experiencing different forms of Hinduism in India and Canada. Hinduism, often described as a way of life, has been interpreted and practised in vastly different ways in Varanasi (a pilgrimage site in India), in New York, and in Toronto. In this essay, I argue that social contexts determine the practice of religious rituals as well as shape their meaning and the ways in which they are experienced and understood by their followers. White Westerners in the 1960s and 1970s practised Hinduism by participating in transcendental meditation and by becoming the disciples of gurus and yogis who promised them nirvana. The practices and rituals that have been popularized in North America are vastly different from those integrated into everyday life in India. There is no one authentic practice of Hinduism; rather, there are innumerable rituals that devotees mould to meet their needs and desires.

The discussion of religion provides an opportunity to question the binary distinction often made between the spiritual India and the materialistic West. It questions the performance of religion and spirituality in India and Toronto for the vicarious pleasure of an audience; such performances can only reinforce stereotypes of Indian spirituality versus Western consumerism, rather than convey an understanding of the complex reality embedded in the everyday practice of religion.

7 Diaspora and Cultural Memory

ANH HUA

Diaspora studies conceptualize the dispersions of populations and cultures across various geographical places and spaces. As a result, this discipline is emerging as a cutting-edge area of research, alongside studies on transnationalism, globalization, nationalism, and postcoloniality. Diaspora is one of the most debated terms today, particularly within scholarly discussions on migration, displacement, identity, community, global movements, and cultural politics. Understanding diasporic formations can help us comprehend the relocation and community-making of those people who were previously oppressed and colonized, as well as those who are forced to – or choose to – stay put 'back home.' Diaspora theorizing opens up the discursive or semiotic space for a discussion of many ideas: identification and affiliation, homing desire and homeland nostalgia, exile and displacement, the reinvention of cultural traditions in the New World Order, and the construction of hybrid identities, as well as cultural and linguistic practices, the building of communities and communal boundaries, cultural memory and trauma, the politics of return, and the possibility of imagining geographical and cultural belonging beyond and within the nation-state formation. Here, I will examine what diaspora represents, the usefulness of diaspora as a concept, and some cautionary notes on theorizing. In the latter part of the chapter, I will explore the working processes of memory, and why memory is significant to diaspora studies and to feminism.

Quilting is a metaphor for understanding, from a feminist perspective, the various theories of diaspora and memory. The art of quilting reminds us that theories never stand alone; rather, that they always have a 'dialogic imagination' (Bakhtin 1981) to historical and contemporary theories and languages, within a culture, but also, what Mary Louise Pratt (1992) calls, within an intercultural dynamic exchange or 'transculturation' at the 'contact zones' (4).

Quilting is an activity that has conventionally been done by women, and which has been devalued by masculinist art theorists as 'craft' and not 'high art.' Both quilting and writing require time, patience, imagination, and creativity. A woman puts together, with bits and pieces of fabric and thread, a quilt that has its own history and presents the quilter's aesthetic understanding in ways that resonate with her life. Similarly, scholars, too, make choices about theories or aspects of theories that best suit their version of a story, or represent their perspectives and understandings of the social context in which they live. Like quilting, what is excluded in theorizing is as much an integral part of a story as what is included.

When women get together to quilt or to collaborate on a scholarly project, both activities can provide space for recalling the past as they knew it, and a sharing of memories that can shed a different light on individual experiences further, and help overcome feelings of victimization. Feminist scholars, like quilters, construct new stories that tell from their perspective how their lives were imbued with gender, race, and class hierarchies and testify to their resistance to varied and intersecting oppressions.

The word diaspora comes from the Greek verb *speiro*, meaning 'to sow,' and the preposition *dia*, meaning 'over' (Cohen 1997, ix). The word suggests networks of real or imagined relationships among scattered peoples whose sense of community is sustained by various communications and contacts, including kinship, trade, travel, shared culture, language, ritual, scripture, print, and electronic media (Peters 1999, 20). A diaspora connects multiple communities of a dispersed population, and systemic border crossings may allow this interconnection. Minority and migrant populations share forms of longing, memory, and identification. Once separated from their homelands by geographical distance and political barriers, diasporic peoples find themselves in closer relations with their old countries in ways now made possible by modern transportation, communication, and labour-migration technologies (Clifford 1994, 304). Diasporas subvert nation states. Although they are not innocent of nationalist aims, diasporas are not exclusively nationalistic (307). They exist in tension with the norms of nation states and with nativist identity formations. They are 'dwellings-in-displacement' (310). Diasporic communities live out a mediated tension: 'the experi-

ences of separation and entanglement, of living here and remember-
ing/desiring another place' (311).

When I use the word diaspora, I am referring to the dispersion of a
group of people from a centre to two or more peripheral places, as well
as to the collective memory and trauma involved in such a dispersion.
Diaspora is a historical term used to refer to communities that have
been dispersed reluctantly, dislocated by slavery, pogroms, genocide,
coercion and expulsion, war in conflict zones, indentured labour, economic migration, political exile, or refugee exodus. Diasporic members
frequently feel a sense of alienation in the host country because of
systemic racism, sexism, heterosexism, and socio-economic exclusion.
To resist assimilation into the host country, and to avoid social amnesia
about their collective histories, diasporic people attempt to revive, recreate, and invent their artistic, linguistic, economic, religious, cultural,
and political practices and productions. Thus, diasporic culture involves socioeconomic, political, and cultural transnational exchange
between the separated populations of the diaspora.

Such interconnection is made possible by changes in the new technologies, global communication, and increased travel in our present
world of late capitalism. As a result, collective memories, myths, and
visions of the homeland become manifest. Shared diasporic identities,
consciousness, and solidarities are sutured together, of course, by power
inequality. It is crucial to remember that diasporic identities and communities are not fixed, rigid, or homogeneous, but are instead fluid,
always changing, and heterogeneous. There are always power struggles
within diasporic communities, disjunctures produced by the diverse
intersectional experiences of gender, class, sexuality, ethnicity, age, generation, disability, geography, history, religion, beliefs, and language/
dialect differences. In other words, diasporic communities and networks are not exempted from sexism, racism, classism, homophobia,
ageism, and other discrepancies and prejudices.

Diasporic theory can help to explain the movements of modernity
and postmodernity, from the late colonial period to the era of de-
colonization and into the twenty-first century. Once used to describe a
nostalgic dislocation from the homeland, the word diaspora now has
new political and epistemological meanings, especially in its reference
to independence movements in formerly colonized territories, refugee
exodus, and economic migration in the post-Second World War era
(Braziel and Mannur 2003, 4). As Khachig Tololyan (1991) notes, diaspora
as 'the vocabulary of transnationalism' is a term that 'once described

Jewish, Greek, and Armenian dispersion [but] now shares meanings with ... words like immigrant, expatriate, refugee, guest-worker, exile community, overseas community, ethnic community' (4–5). Diaspora has been analysed from different points of departure: East Asian, Southeast Asian, South Asian, African, Caribbean, Latin American, Central European, and so on. It is crucial to remember that diasporic theorizing should not be separated from historical and cultural specificity; one needs to distinguish between different diasporic formations. As Avtar Brah (1996) observes, it is easy to confuse between diaspora as a theoretical concept, diaspora discourses, and specific historical diasporas. Hence, it is important to differentiate between specific historical diasporas and diaspora as a concept (179). One should also be cautious of 'the uncritical, unreflexive application of the term "diaspora" to any and all contexts of global displacement and movement,' since 'some forms of travel are tourism' and any attempt to demarcate all movements as disenfranchising can be problematic and misrepresent reality (Braziel and Mannur 2003, 3). It is also important to be cautious of diasporic discourses that tend to homogenize difference and multiplicity and to elide power struggles within the community to form what Paul Gilroy (2000) calls 'ethnic absolutism,' in which all individuals of a particular diaspora are perceived as inherently linked by heritage, collective history, and racial descent. Gilroy (1993, 2000), Stuart Hall (1990, 1999), Kobena Mercer (1994), Lisa Lowe (1996), Rey Chow (1993), and other writers are critical of this homogenizing tendency in some diasporas. The lives of diasporic individuals do not transcend differences of gender, sexuality, race, and class, nor can the concept stand alone as a category of analysis separate from these other interrelated categories (Braziel and Mannur 2003, 5). It is crucial to recognize that a diasporic community is not fixed or pre-given: 'It is constituted within the crucible of the materiality of everyday life; in the everyday stories we tell ourselves individually and collectively' (Brah 1996, 183). All diasporas are heterogeneous and contested spaces, differentiated along gender and class lines, generational difference, sexual orientation, language access, historical experiences, geographical location, and so on. Diaspora needs to be understood as embedded within 'a multi-axial understanding of power' (189).

Diaspora, in a sense, is 'this hodgepodge of everyday "out-of-country ... even out-of-language" experience ... and its textual representations' (Lavie and Swedenburg 1996, 14). Diaspora refers to 'the doubled relationship or dual loyalty' that migrants, immigrants, exiles, and refugees have to geography, "their connections to the space they currently oc-cupy and their continuing involvement with "back home"' (Lavie and Swedenburg 1996, 14). Hence, those living in the diaspora have a double perspective: they acknowledge an earlier existence elsewhere and have a critical relationship with the cultural politics of their present home – all embedded within the experience of displacement. For the diasporic subject, home can become 'a mode of interpretive in-between, as a form of accountability to more than one location' (Radhakrishnan 1996, xiii–xiv). Hence, historicizing a diaspora can become doubly complex, since one has to deal with both temporal and spatial discontinuity (xiv). While the diasporic subject may have a double vision and a double consciousness, it is important to recognize, as Radhakrishnan warns us, that 'a diaspora does not constitute a pure heterotopia informed by a radical countermemory. The politics of diasporic spaces is indeed con-tradictory and multi-accentual' (173).

Moreover, it is important to challenge and rethink earlier versions of diasporic narratives with their fixed notion of home, identity, and exile, where the homeland is perceived nostalgically as an 'authentic' space of belonging, and the place of settlement as somehow 'inauthentic' and undesirable. For some of the Chinese and Vietnamese refugees who had painful and traumatic experiences in their homeland and during their exodus as a result of the Vietnam War, returning to their country of origin or looking back with nostalgia may not be a desirable option. Furthermore, some diasporic women may not feel nostalgic because their homelands were the sites of cultural nationalist and transnational patriarchies and violence. Diasporic women are less likely than diasporic men to have nostalgic memories about their homelands because of their painful recollection of patriarchal attitudes, customs, and traditions found in the 'Old World.' As noted by Singh, Skerrett, and Hogan (1996): 'There are reasons for women not to have much to be nostalgic about, "for the good old days when the grass was greener and young people knew their place was also the time when women knew their place, and it is not a place to which most women want to return"' (10).

For queer diasporic subjects, neither the homeland nor the diasporic location can offer spaces of 'safety,' 'authenticity,' and belonging, since queer identities, experiences, and sexualities are written out of the nation and out of the diaspora (1997). As Anita Mannur (2003) explains:

'Issues of home are particularly vexing' for queer diasporic subjects, as many are literally ejected from such spaces. Such subjects experience deep ambivalence towards the notion of home, rather than experiencing it in nostalgic terms as a safe space of refuge or shelter and desiring return ... Clearly, or *queerly* as the case may be, thinking about home and (post)memories of homeland is an arduous, complicated, and ambivalent process for queer individuals and communities. In contexts where the site/sight of home does not allow for an easy entry into a comfortably safe zone of sexual alterity, romanticized metaphors of looking back to a past over 'there' and to a future 'here' need to be interrogated. (286–287)

Radhakrishnan (1996) also warns against the uncritical nostalgia found in some diasporic narratives about the home country. Often when we are dissatisfied with the place of settlement and its unwillingness to change the dominant injustices, we turn our gaze back to the homeland. Yet, as Radhakrishnan notes, this uncritical, nostalgic gaze may ignore the realities of the home country. One may cultivate a memory of an idealized homeland that has nothing to do with contemporary history, or one may pretend that the homeland has not changed since one left its shores (211–212). As Radhakrishnan argues: 'The diasporan hunger for knowledge about and intimacy with the home country should not turn into a transhistorical and mystic quest for origins ... Feeling deracinated in the diaspora can be painful, but the politics of origins cannot be the remedy' (212).

Hence, diasporic theorists, writers, filmmakers, and artists need to 'assert the mobility and fluidity of positionalities and disrupt linear accounts of diasporic subject formation, which privilege singular and unidirectional movement from (a usually problematic notion of) "home" to "not home"' (Dhaliwal 1994, 3). Moreover, one should not celebrate the literal and metaphorical travel movements found in diasporic communities and discourses after 11 September 2001. With the collapse of New York City's World Trade Center, the subsequent attack on Iraq, and the issue of SARS, for example, travel has been made more difficult for Muslim, South Asian, and other Asian subjects.

With these cautionary points in mind, diaspora theorizing is still urgent and important because it allows us to reconfigure the relationship between citizens, nation states, and national narratology. As Paul Gilroy observes, diaspora theorizing can problematize and complicate issues of belonging by providing alternatives to the traditional conceptions of race, nation, and bounded culture. It can help one to understand the social world resulting from displacement, flight, exile, and forced migration. Diaspora theorizing can be used to analyse intercultural and transcultural processes and forms. It can also identify forced dispersal and reluctant dislocation such as slavery, pogroms, indentured labour, genocide, and other social terrors and traumas. Diasporas can subvert nation states because diasporic identification can exist outside of and in opposition to modern citizenship. Diasporas can challenge the family, as a building block of the nation, by recognizing sub- and supra-national kinship. Diaspora theorizing can provide anti-essentialist understanding of identity formation because diasporic identities are often creolized, syncretized, and hybridized (Gilroy 2000, 122–132). In the final analysis, diaspora is a useful concept because it permits feminists, cultural theorists, and social scientists to think through some vexed issues: identity and solidarity, belonging and geography, spatialization and subject positionality, the politics of representation, the relation between roots and routes, transnational and intercultural forms and productions, and the politics of home.

In the next section, I will reflect on the working processes of memory. I maintain that diaspora theorists and feminists need to consider the insights that can be provided from a memory analysis. I will also review the relation between memory and feminism, and how various feminists utilize the politics of remembrance within their feminist theorizing.

Theorizing Memory

> No history can be pure event, pure evolution; each is rather a repetition, a return to a story which must be retold, distinguished from its previous telling. The past is not a truth upon which to build, but a truth sought, a re-memorializing over which to struggle. (Matsuda 1996, 16)

History, Matt Matsuda (1996) reminds us, is not a recording of pure events but a return to or a repetition of a story told with a difference. The past – or history – becomes a site to struggle over individual and collective memories and memorialization. Memory is an important term of analysis for diaspora and feminist theorizing precisely because it is closely tied to historical and political struggles. Memory has become a faculty that is gendered, appropriated, politicized, nationalized, medicalized, and aestheticized. In studying memory, one should pay attention to absence, distance, witness, testimony, tradition, nostalgia, and forgetting (6). Within diaspora studies, an analysis of memory can reveal the incompleteness of the past or history, for both memory and history are forms of partial epistemology. Memory can become a strategy for social justice by recalling the forgotten or suppressed to bear witness, yet it is a strategy that requires reading 'the past as conflictual, evidence as problematic, all positions as suspect.' It requires reading history away from a linear positivist narrative to 'a history of mnemonic traces, each endlessly recited, reiterated, recombined' (15).

Memory refers to 'the capacity for conserving certain information,' or 'a group of psychic functions that allow us to actualize past impressions or information that we represent to ourselves as past' (LeGoff 1992, 51). Rather than mental imprints or iconic likeness, memory is formed through elaborate mental mappings that change over time. Memory is the construction or reconstruction of what actually happened in the past. Memory is distorted by needs, desires, interests, and fantasies. Subjective and malleable rather than objective and concrete, memory is emotional, conceptual, contextual, constantly undergoing revision, selection, interpretation, distortion, and reconstruction (Bertman 2000, 27). Memory does not revive the past but constructs it. The quest for memory is the search for one's history. Sites of memory are collective yet individual, living yet dead, ours yet also belonging to others. In the landslide of commemorative memory, memory shimmers, becomes strange things (Donougho 2002). An understanding of how memory works within diaspora studies and feminism can help us rewrite oblivion. Forgetting is more active than we think. Forgetting is an act, a creative invention, a performance, a selective loss.

Personal and collective memories can be differentiated. Personal memory represents the memory of a single individual, contained within a lifetime, often founded on first-hand experience. Cultural or collective memory constitutes the collective memory of many, encompassing generations (Bertman 2000, 31). Collective memories, according to Maurice Halbwachs (1980, 1992), are memories of a shared past retained by members of a group, class, or nation. They can be found in oral and written stories, rumours, gestures, cultural styles, and institutionalized cultural activities. Collective memories are the shared representation and knowledge of past social events that have not been personally experienced but collectively constructed (Paez, Basabe, and Gonzalez 1997, 150). For Marita Sturken, cultural memory is ambiguous and varied, produced and negotiated through images, sites, objects, and representation. In Tangled Memories, Sturken (1997) investigates various American cultural memory sites in the 1980s and 1990s, including the Vietnam War, the AIDS epidemic, the Kennedy assassination, the Challenger explosion, and the Gulf War. She writes: '[The] process of cultural memory is bound up in complex political stakes and meanings. It both defines a culture and is the means by which its divisions and conflicting agendas are revealed. To define a memory as cultural is, in effect, to enter into a debate about what that memory means. This process does not efface the individual but rather involves the interaction of individuals in the creation of meaning. Cultural memory is a field of cultural negotiation through which different stories vie for a place in history' (1).

Because cultural memory is political, and because different stories and representations struggle for a place in history, memory is crucial to understanding a culture since it reveals collective desires, needs, self-definitions, and power struggles. For feminists Marianne Hirsch and Valerie Smith, cultural memory involves acts of transfer in which individuals and groups construct and perform their identities by recollecting a shared past of contested norms, conventions, and practices. These memorial acts of transfer involve the dynamic negotiation between past and present, the individual and the collective, the public and private, recalling and forgetting, power and powerlessness, history and myth, trauma and nostalgia, consciousness and unconsciousness, fears and desires. These mediated cultural memories are the effect and affect of fragmented personal and collective experiences articulated, performed, and interpreted through various technologies or media of memory (Hirsch and Smith 2002, 5).

Memory analysis is significant to diaspora and feminist theorizing because it can reveal both the inner psychic states of postcolonial diaspora women and men – such as desire, fantasy, repression, denial, fear, trauma, identification, repulsion, and abjection – as well as the social state of diasporic communities. By complicating oral and written histories as sites of struggle, memory studies can disclose the working processes of both hegemonic memory and countermemory. Hence, memory studies can demonstrate how power works, but also give voice and agency to the subjugated. Memory studies aid diaspora and feminist theorizing. Memory is found in historical records, literature, film, television, the visual arts, theatre, the Web, scripture, speech acts, music, national anthems, monuments, souvenirs, museums and galleries, advertisements, journals and letters, rituals and ceremonies, carnivals, architectures, and cityscapes. Memory is one way to pass on traditions, rituals, and group history. Memory analysis can also unfold the working processes of various traumas including transatlantic slavery, the

Holocaust, the Vietnam War, the two World Wars, and 9/11, as well as sexual traumas such as abuse, rape, and incest. Finally, memory can evoke identity formation, the rewriting of home and belonging, nostalgia, mourning, and a sense of lost frequently found in diaspora, exile, and immigrant narratives.

Cultural or collective memory carries with it a certain degree of political force. As Michel Foucault (1975) argues: 'Since memory is actually a very important factor in struggle (really, in fact, struggles develop in a kind of conscious moving forward of history), if one controls people's memory, one controls their dynamism' (25). The accuracy of collective memories has been questioned because national, class, religious, and ethnic memories of various groups have been manipulated and falsified for various political ends (Gross 2000, 1–7). Because memory often works at the unconscious level, it is more dangerously subject to manipulation by time and by societies (LeGoff 1992, xi). In particular, the ruling class frequently dominate and manipulate collective memory for their own gains and interests: 'To make themselves the master of memory and forgetfulness is one of the great preoccupations of the classes, groups, and individuals who have dominated and continue to dominate historical societies. The things forgotten or not mentioned by history reveal these mechanisms for the manipulation of collective memory' (54). However, because individual memory and cultural memory are highly selective and malleable, it is important to identify the principles of selection, how they vary from place to place, from one group to another, and how they change over time and space (Burke 1989, 100). Because of the multiplicity of social identities and different memories – family memories, local memories, class memories, national memories, diasporic memories, women's memories, and so on – a pluralistic model of memory is productive to understand the different 'memory communities,' the different uses of memory for different social groups. It is crucial to ask who wants whom to remember what and why? Whose version of the past is preserved and recorded? One also needs to distinguish between official and unofficial memories of the past, as unofficial memories can invoke 'the geography of dissent and protest' (107).

Remembrance is valuable for marginalized groups such as women and ethnic minorities. These subjects and communities must constantly remind the national masculinist culture of the imperative to witness and to acknowledge the voice, experience, epistemology, and memory of women and postcolonial individuals. As Amritjit Singh et al. (1996)

observe: 'As part of the ongoing argument between history and memory, marginalized groups often attempt to maintain at the centre of national memory what the dominant group would often like to forget. The process results in a collective memory always in flux: not one memory but multiple memories constantly battling for attention in cultural space' (6). For women in particular, remembrance is salient because women are often the keepers of diaries, journals, and family albums. Because they lack resources and outlets in the present, many women live more in the past and hence value personal, familial, and collective memories (10; see also Greene 1991).

Feminists are also concerned with memories. Feminist literature on sexual abuse and violence against women, autobiographies and memoirs, women's oral history, and the gendered politics of migration and slavery disclose insights about the reconstruction and transmission of memory (Hirsch and Smith 2002, 3). Recently, much has been written about memory, in particular on Holocaust trauma and witnesses. Yet few memory studies have considered gender as a category of analysis. Feminists have argued that gender, along with race and class, are important aspects of memory and recollection. Cultural memory is located in specific gender, race, and class contexts, and it evokes particular gender, race, and class identities and identifications. Because cultural memory involves contested claims to power, and because power is always gendered, we need to consider a gender differential in memory. Moreover, cultural tropes and representations are also marked by gender, race, and class. Technologies of memory, frames of interpretation, acts of transfer, and modes of witness are gendered. Experience and the recollection and telling of experience are also gendered. Women's bodies, more than men's, are frequently assigned the cultural work of mourning, pain, witness, and healing. Hence, feminists argue that gender difference and the interrelation between gender, race, and class need to be considered in any understanding of memory, recollection, trauma, witness, and testimony (6–7, 11).

Some feminists are particularly interested in what Bold, Knowles, and Leach (2002) call 'feminist countermemorializing.' Feminist countermemorializing can generate oppositional memorializing by converting individual ownership of memory into collective remembrance, turning personal grief and mourning into a call for social responsibilities, social change, and activism (129). In their study of Marianne's Park in Guelph, Ontario, as a site of feminist memory work for 'Take Back the Night' rallies and the commemoration of the fourteen women killed in the Montreal Massacre, Bold et al. contend that feminist counter-memorializing needs to keep the issue of violence against women visible and on the political agenda. Feminist countermemorializing can pay attention to 'the collective embodiment of individually spoken memory, private pain converted into public rage, action informed by and taking responsibility for remembered trauma without usurping its felt specificity ... and the demand for future change' (138). Rather than remembering the past for nostalgic reasons, feminists are more interested in a critical remembrance that can make women's individual and collective pain and suffering publicly visible. They are also interested in activists producing change for a better future. Feminist interpretation of remembrance is deeply tied to material reality, struggles against national and transnational patriarchies, pragmatic change, feminist organizational strategies, and working towards a hopeful future to end sexism and sexual violence along with racial and class inequality.

Feminists do have their particular strategies of memory work. Feminist studies of cultural memory, as Marianne Hirsch and Valerie Smith indicate, interpret the relation between gender and power in memory work, by applying feminist modes of questioning to the analysis of cultural memory and forgetting. Feminist studies of cultural memory restore the memories and herstories forgotten or suppressed by masculinist historical records and archives. They deconstruct traditional modes of knowing the past by recognizing women's knowledge productions, voices, silences, and lived experiences. Feminists attempt to find 'the testimonies of the disenfranchised' by looking at alternative archives such as fiction and memoir, visual images, music, performance, film, popular culture, and oral history. Feminists have argued the importance of women 'reading against the grain' as oppositional readers and viewers, thus challenging dominant masculinist ideological assumptions. Feminists also interpret everyday life experiences, asserting that the personal is always political. Feminist strategies of memory work recognize the importance of active listening, 'empathetic identification,' 'nonappropriative identification,' intersubjective relations, coalition building across difference, modes of knowledge production that are material, embodied, located, and responsive to the disenfranchised. Finally, feminists denote that active remembrance, as well as the analysis of personal and cultural memory, can be forms of political activism (Hirsch and Smith 2002, 11–13).

Memory can be reconstructed and transmitted for some feminists: to rewrite notions of home and belonging, to develop various performative identities, to retell one's located life history, to recognize the importance of embodied memory and countermemory, to document a genealogy of resistance, to derive a new knowledge of self-growth and self-recovery, and to differentiate memory as nostalgic yearning from an archaeology of lived, critical, and intentional remembrance. Feminist M. Jacqui Alexander (2002), for example, contends that the need to differentiate between memory as nostalgic yearning and memory as an intention to remember critically, to understand our relation to the past, history, and time:

> Can we *intentionally* remember, all the time, as a way of never forgetting, all of us, building an archeology of living memory which has less to do with living in the past, invoking a past, or excising it, and more to do with our relationship to time and its purpose. There is a difference between remembering *when* – the nostalgic yearning for some return – and a living memory that enables us to re-member. (96)

Black diaspora feminist bell hooks (1990), who frequently begins her feminist theorizing with a recollection from her own personal history, also argues for the importance of a remembrance that is not a passive, nostalgic longing. In *Yearning*, she writes:

> In *Freedom Charter*, a work which chronicles resistance strategies in South Africa, the phrase 'our struggle is also a struggle for memory against forgetting' is continually repeated. Memory need not be a passive reflection, a nostalgic longing for things to be as they once were; it can function as a way of knowing and learning from the past, what Michael M. J. Fischer ... calls 'retrospection to gain a vision for the future.' It can serve as a catalyst for self-recovery ... collective black self-recovery. We need to keep alive the memory of our struggles against racism so that we can concretely chart those places, those times, those people that gave a sense of direction. (40)

For bell hooks, critical remembrance can function as a way of knowing and learning from the past, as a catalyst for self-recovery and community-building, and as a documentation of the genealogy of resistance. Recollection can keep alive the memory of our collective postcolonial struggles against racism as well as sexism, heterosexism, and global capitalist exploitation. As a methodology of the oppressed, remembrance can resist the erasure of the aesthetic legacy produced by women of colour and women in general (1990, 115). The struggle for memory can help 'to create spaces where one is able to redeem and reclaim the past, legacies of pain, suffering, and triumph in ways that transform present reality.' Remembrance is not simply to document but to construct the new, 'to move us into a different mode of articulation' (147). The struggle for memory against forgetting requires the politicization of memory, distinguishing nostalgia from 'remembering that serves to illuminate and transform the present' (147). Remembrance is a necessity to retrace one's life journey, to reconsider the choices one has made, and to arrive at the destination of feminist and diasporic theorizing.

The recovery of the memory of one's past through autobiographical writing or feminist theorizing offers both 'a sense of reunion and a sense of release' (hooks 1989, 158). Writing from personal recollection permits one 'to find again that aspect of self and experience that may no longer be an actual part of one's life but is a living memory shaping and informing the present' (158). Writing down one's memory can provide clarity and witness, as well as liberating the unconscious and the past to the present. Finally, memory writing can help one to understand one's psyche and different perspectives through narratives, as well as generate new knowledge and self-growth (159).

Conclusion

Diasporas are grounded in historical and cultural specificity that are heterogeneous and contested sites differentiated by gender, class, sexual orientation, generational difference, language access, historical experiences, and geographical locations. Diasporas are fluid, changing with history, not fixed or pre-given.

Scholars who study diasporas have documented how cultural memory can be negotiated, claimed, and invented. Diasporic writers, poets, and artists have deployed collective memory to document the traditions, rituals, and history of their communities and groups. Such remembrance is particularly important to marginalized groups, as for example the Chinese, South Asian, Afro-Caribbean, Eritrean, and 'Muslim' women who have a history of subjugation in Canada. In subsequent chapters of this volume we hear the voices of diasporic scholars whose joys and sorrows enable us to know, from their perspective, the past of their families, communities, and societies. These accounts demonstrate the dynamic negotiation between the past and the present, the individual and the collective, power and powerlessness, nostalgia and trauma, consciousness and unconsciousness, fears and desires. The authors recall the forgotten and the suppressed, to bear witness and to give testimony of their pasts; they are countermemories and a quest for social justice.

Through the act of recalling and documenting memories, some diasporic women have been able to resist the definition of Others about themselves and their histories. The critical remembrances of women, included in this volume, show how women from marginalized, ethnic, and racialized communities define themselves and how memories can act as a catalyst for self-recovery and community-building. Their accounts point to new ways of knowing and learning from the past and show how remembrances can help reclaim the aesthetic legacy of subjugated groups and keep alive the memory of their collective resistance against sexism, classism, racism, and heterosexism. However, memories do not simply document the past but move us to new ways of articulation, thus liberating us from the past as it has been known to the present and the future.

A metaphor for remembrance, displacement, and what Paul Gilroy calls 'roots/routes' of diasporic transnational communities can be the Ginkgo biloba tree. The Ginkgo, a fan-leafed, ancient Asian tree, was brought to North America by immigrants and is sometimes used as an herbal supplement for enhancing memory. In *A Thousand Plateaus*, Deleuze and Guattari (1988) argue that the Enlightenment privileging of 'The Tree of Man' as found in evolutionist and liberal progressive discourses and representations can be replaced by the 'weed' which grows everywhere. The weed can be deployed as a symbol for interventionist political theorizing. The Ginkgo biloba can similarly represent an oppositional way of remembering the history of colonization and the subsequent displacement of individuals, groups, and communities. It speaks against the socialized forms of forgetting and the historical amnesia of nations. Drinking Ginkgo biloba tea permeates our bodies, and thus memories can be inscribed onto and into our gendered and racialized bodies.

As an Asian woman interested in and haunted by the negotiation of individual and collective memories, I feel that

Memory is a trickster, shape-shifting fox or coyote.
Memory is the soft footsteps of a tiny warrior woman,
leaping from terra-cotta roof to terra-cotta roof,
stealing insights in the night.

Do you see her fly,
vaporize, transform, metamorphose,
blue smoke over a serene lake?
Are you fascinated by her sensuous recall,
robed in black, veiled in black,
disguised in magic?
She is memory; she is remembrance.

(Anh Hua)

REFERENCES

Alexander, M. Jacqui. 2002. Remembering This Bridge, Remembering Our-
    selves: Yearning, Memory, and Desire. In *This Bridge We Call Home: Radical
    Visions for Transformation,* ed. Gloria Anzaldua and Analouise Keating,
    81–103. New York and London: Routledge.
Bakhtin, Mikhail. 1981. *The Dialogic Imagination.* Trans. C. Emerson and M.
    Holquist. Austin: University of Texas Press.
Bertman, Stephen. 2000. *Cultural Amnesia: America's Future and the Crisis of
    Memory.* London: Praeger.
Bold, Christine, Ric Knowles, and Belinda Leach. 2002. Feminist Memorializ-
    ing and Cultural Countermemory: The Case of Marianne's Park. *Signs:
    Journal of Women in Culture and Society* 28(1): 125–148.
Brah, Avtar. 1996. *Cartographies of Diasporas: Contesting Identities.* London and
    New York: Routledge.
Braziel, Jana Evans, and Anita Mannur. 2003. Nation, Migration, Globaliza-
    tion: Points of Contention in Diaspora Studies. In *Theorizing Diaspora,* ed.
    Jana Evans Braziel and Anita Mannur, 1–22. Malden, MA: Blackwell Pub-
    lishing.
Burke, Peter. 1989. History as Social Memory. In *Memory: History, Culture and
    the Mind,* ed. Thomas Butler, 97–113. New York: Basil Blackwell.
Chow, Rey. 1993. *Writing Diaspora: Tactics of Intervention on Contemporary
    Cultural Studies.* Bloomington: Indiana University Press.
Clifford, James. 1994. Diasporas. *Cultural Anthropology* 9(3): 302–338.
Cohen, Robin. 1997. *Global Diasporas: An Introduction.* Seattle: University of
    Washington Press.
Deleuze, Gilles, and Felix Guattari. 1988. *A Thousand Plateaus: Capitalism and
    Schizophrenia.* Trans. and foreword by Brian Massumi. London: Athlone
    Press.

Dhaliwal, Amarpal K. 1994. Introduction to The Traveling Nation: India and Its Diaspora. *Socialist Review* 24(4): 1–11.

Donougho, Martin. 2002. On the Advantages and Disadvantages of Cultural Memory: Pierre Nora and The 'Lieu de memoire.' Paper presented at The Future of Cultural Memory, a program in comparative literature, University of South Carolina, Columbia, SC, 15 February.

Foucault, Michel. 1975. Film and Popular Memory: Interview with Michel Foucault. Trans. Martin Jordan. *Radical Philosophy* 11:24–29.

Gilroy, Paul. 1993. *The Black Atlantic: Modernity and Double Consciousness.* Cambridge, MA: Harvard University Press.

– 2000. *Against Race: Imagining Political Culture Beyond the Color Line.* Cambridge, MA: Harvard University Press.

Gopinath, Gayatri. 1997. Nostalgia, Desire, Diaspora: South Asian Sexualities in Motion. *Positions: East Asia Cultures Critique* 5(2): 467–489.

Greene, Gayle. 1991. Feminist Fiction and the Uses of Memory. *Signs: Journal of Women in Culture and Society* 16(2): 290–321.

Gross, David. 2000. *Lost Time: On Remembering and Forgetting in Late Modern Culture.* Amherst: University of Massachusetts Press.

Halbwachs, Maurice. 1980. *The Collective Memory.* Trans. Francis J. Ditter, Jr. and Vida Yazdi Ditter. New York: Harper and Row.

– 1992. *On Collective Memory.* Ed. and trans. Lewis A. Coser. Chicago: University of Chicago Press.

Hall, Stuart. 1990. Cultural Identity and Diaspora. In *Identity, Community, Culture, Difference*, ed. Jonathon Rutherford, 222–237. London: Lawrence and Wishart.

– 1999. Thinking the Diaspora: Home-Thoughts from Abroad. *Small Axe: A Journal of Criticism* 6 (September): 1–18.

Hirsch, Marianne and Valerie Smith. 2002. Feminism and Cultural Memory: An Introduction. *Signs: Journal of Women in Culture and Society* 28(1): 1–19.

hooks, bell. 1989. *Talking Back: Thinking Feminist, Thinking Black.* Toronto: Between the Lines.

– 1990. *Yearning: Race, Gender, and Cultural Politics.* Toronto: Between the Lines.

Lavie, Smadar, and Ted Swedenburg. 1996. Introduction to *Displacement, Diaspora, and Geographies of Identity*, ed. Smadar Lavie and Ted Swedenburg, 1–25. London: Duke University Press.

LeGoff, Jacques. 1992. *History and Memory.* Trans. Steven Rendall and Elizabeth Claman. New York: Columbia Press.

Lowe, Lisa. 1996. *Immigrant Acts: On Asian American Cultural Politics.* Durham, NC: Duke University Press.

Mannur, Anita. 2003. Postscript: Cyberscapes and the Interfacing of Diasporas. In *Theorizing Diaspora*, ed. Jana Evans Braziel and Anita Mannur,
283–290. Malden, MA: Blackwell.

Matsuda, Matt K. 1996. *The Memory of the Modern*. New York and Oxford:
Oxford University Press.

Mercer, Kobena. 1994. *Welcome to the Jungle*. London: Routledge.

Paez, Dario, Nekane Basabe, and Jose Luis Gonzalez. 1997. Social Processes
and Collective Memory: A Cross-Cultural Approach to Remembering
Political Events. In *Collective Memory and Political Events: Social Psychological
Perspectives*, ed. James W. Pennebaker, Dario Paez, and Bernard Rime,
147–174. Mahwah, NJ: Lawrence Erlbaum Associates.

Peters, John Durham. 1999. Exile, Nomadism, and Diaspora. In *Home, Exile,
Homeland: Film, Media, and the Politics of Place*, ed. Hamid Naficy, 17–41. New
York: Routledge.

Pratt, Mary Louise. 1992. *Imperial Eyes: Travel Writing and Transculturation*.
London and New York: Routledge.

Radhakrishnan, R. 1996. *Diasporic Mediations: Between Home and Location*.
Minneapolis: University of Minnesota Press.

Singh, Amritjit, Joseph T. Skerrett, Jr., and Robert E. Hogan. 1996. Introduction
to *Memory and Cultural Politics: New Approaches to American Ethnic Literatures*, 3–18. Boston: Northeastern University Press.

Sturken, Marita. 1997. *Tangled Memories: The Vietnam War, the AIDS Epidemic,
and the Politics of Remembering*. Berkeley: University of California Press.

Tololyan, Khachig. 1991. The Nation-State and Its Others: In Lieu of a Preface.
Diaspora: A Journal of Transnational Studies 1(1): 3–7.

8 Gendered Nostalgia: The Experiences of New Chinese Skilled Immigrants in Canada

IZUMI SAKAMOTO AND YANQIU RACHEL ZHOU

On 16 October 2003, the *Toronto Star* carried a large photograph of the first Chinese astronaut to complete a successful twenty-one-hour flight in outer space. Immediately beneath the photo was the story of a thirty-four-year-old skilled immigrant who came to Toronto from Beijing. 'Making Buns Not Quite Rocket Science,' declared the title. The caption under her picture read, 'Former aerospace engineer Ivy Zheng left China two years ago and now earns her living making Cinnabons in a subway shop' (Ross 2003, A10).

Skilled immigrants are admitted to Canada on the bases of educational and occupational abilities. The successful resettlement of skilled immigrants is imperative to Canada's continued economic growth, to counterbalance the aging population and the Canadian 'brain drain' to the United States (Li 2003). Under current Canadian immigration policy, highly educated, skilled adults are encouraged to apply for immigration 'to address the needs of Canada's knowledge-based economy' (Citizenship and Immigration Canada [CIC] 2003). The number of immigrants, however, is often greater than the availability of employment in the immigrants' fields of specialization, often posing challenges of underemployment and unemployment for newly arrived skilled immigrants (Man 2002; Reitz 2001), as in the case of Ivy Zheng.

Chinese ethnic individuals comprise the largest group of newcomers and visible minorities, both in Canada and in the City of Toronto (Statistics Canada 2003). As the proportion of new immigrants from Hong Kong declined in the late 1990s, the People's Republic of China has recently become the largest source country of immigrants to Canada (CIC 2003). In 2002, over 33,000 individuals from mainland China immigrated to Canada, accounting for 15 per cent of all immigrants who came to

Canada during that year (CIC 2003). Of the immigrants from China in 2002, just under one-third (9,349 principal applicants) immigrated as skilled workers, making China the main sending country of skilled immigrants, with India second and Pakistan third (CIC 2003).

Chinese immigrants who live in Toronto are an exciting population to examine. They are the largest group of immigrants in Canada, and encompass much diversity *within* that group in terms of language, culture, country of origin, socioeconomic class, and immigration categories. Many cultural, social, and economic resources are established by and for these diverse communities. On the one hand, discrimination is still a daily reality for many Chinese immigrants (e.g., Ornstein 2000; Statistics Canada 2003); on the other hand, Chinese communities, on the whole, are strong presences within larger immigrant communities as well as being the largest visible minority immigrant group. How then do these educated professional immigrants from China, the largest group of skilled immigrants, fare in Canada?

Unfortunately, many immigrants in Canada are unemployed and/or underemployed, despite their high education and skill levels (Chinese Interagency Network of Greater Toronto 1994; George, Tsang, Man, and Da 2000; ISPRPC 2000; Li 2003; Man 2002; North Chinese Community of Canada 2003). Various secondary issues such as poverty, family conflict, and mental health have been found to be associated with these employment challenges (e.g., George et al. 2000; ISPRPC 2000; Man 2002). Much of the research on all visible minority, skilled immigrants in Canada has focused on structural barriers, such as the devaluation of foreign credentials (e.g., Li 2003). Research is lacking, however, on the everyday experiences of immigrants as they relate specifically to the multiple cultural contexts in which these individuals lead their lives. Existing psychological literature[1] does not fully capture how structural issues affect these individuals' and families' day-to-day experiences. For example, what are the experiences of recent skilled immigrants who may be unemployed and/or underemployed? How would an underemployed immigrant like Ivy Zheng describe her employment experiences in Canada? How do these immigrants perceive their home countries in the face of employment challenges? How do various factors, such as gender and family relationships, affect their experiences?

The research study presented in this chapter is part of a larger grounded theory[2] study project aiming to document and theorize the subjective cultural negotiation experiences of mainland Chinese skilled immigrants (Sakamoto and Zhou 2003). The project is informed by the aforementioned psychological literature and Sakamoto's (2001, 2004) previous research with Japanese academic migrants; it also utilizes a constructivist-oriented grounded theory approach (Charmaz 2000) in which the process of the research is inductive. As such, several important themes emerged from the participants' narratives. Although not the initial focus of our study, one interesting theme arose concerning how our study participants described their home and homeland. This theme was interrelated with other factors, such as gender, employment status, family relationship, and aspirations, which led the authors to ask the following two research questions: How is 'homeland' constructed or reconstructed by Chinese skilled immigrants vis-à-vis their life experiences in Canada? and How are gender and family relationships as social axes presented through their narratives?

Methodology

Twenty-one semi-structured, in-depth interviews were conducted in English or Mandarin Chinese, depending on the preferences of the participants. Purposive and snowball sampling techniques (Patton 1990) were used to recruit Chinese adults from mainland China who were now living in the Greater Toronto Area (GTA). Participants included skilled immigrants who had come to Canada from 1998 to 2003, as well as their spouses. Three e-mail lists for Chinese professionals and graduate students in the GTA were used to recruit potential participants for the study. When the potential participants contacted the researchers, the procedures were explained and individual appointments made with one of the interviewers in the participant's language of choice. Upon arriving at the interview site, the interviewer explained the study again, and obtained informed consent from those who agreed to participate.

Sample questions included: What has your experience been like living in Toronto? How is your family doing? and Why did you decide to immigrate? While an interview guide with key and probing questions was prepared, the specific questions asked in each interview varied, depending on the experiences of the participants. As the research process proceeded, some of the questions were modified.

The data collection and analysis process for the current study was informed by grounded theory, as described earlier (Charmaz 2000; Strauss and Corbin 1998). After each interview, the interviewer wrote a memo summarizing the main points of the meeting, as well as her preliminary thoughts and impressions.

Participants

Twenty-one people (13 women and 8 men) from 11 cities in mainland China participated in this study (please refer to Table 8.1 for summary of participant characteristics). Participants' ages ranged from 25 to 48, with a mean age of 33.4 years. Their lengths of stay in Canada were between 4 and 36 months, with a mean of 19.4 months. All participants but one (who did not discuss her/his educational background) had high educational backgrounds; 1 participant had attended college, 10 had bachelor's degrees, 5 had master's degrees, 2 had doctorate degrees, and 1 was currently working as a post-doctoral fellow. In terms of marital status, 17 participants were married, 1 participant was divorced, and 3 participants were single or unmarried. Three married women were living separately from their spouses, who had remained in China.

Ten participants (7 women and 3 men) were unemployed and the other 11 participants (6 women and 5 men) were employed. Among those who had jobs, 3 were working part-time (all women) and 8 full time (3 women and 5 men). Among those currently working, 7 (4 women and 3 men) held professional jobs and 4 (2 women and 2 men) were working as general labourers (e.g., in a factory or restaurant). When asked about the possibility of permanently living in Canada, 2 participants (one woman and one man) were 'very sure' (100 per cent) or 'sure' (90 per cent) that they would stay in Canada, and 12 (8 women and 4 men) indicated that this was 'very possible' (80 per cent), while 7 (4 women and 3 men) responded that this was 'possible' (50–60 per cent).

Findings

The purpose of this study is to understand how skilled immigrants from mainland China who are now living in Canada construct or reconstruct their 'homeland.' The narratives of the immigrants in our study elucidated the fact that a concept of homeland is malleable, and defined by these Chinese skilled immigrants in relation to their experiences in Canada. In other words, these immigrants' constructions of homeland largely depended upon how they perceived and evaluated their lives in Canada in relation to the goals they set before immigration. Shedding light on their life experiences in Canada, particularly their employment experiences, is therefore imperative. Through such life experiences, Chinese skilled immigrants have developed a variety of goals and

Table 8.1: Characteristics of Interview Participants (N=21)

Characteristics	Frequency/Range/Mean
Gender	
Male	8
Female	13
Age	
Range	25–48
Mean	33.4
Marital status	
Single	3
Married	17
Divorced	1
Months of being in Canada	
Range	4–36 months
Mean	19.4 months
If have children	
Yes	11
Currently expecting	3
No	7
Educational level	
College	1 (female)
Bachelor's degree	11 (7 female & 4 male)
Master's degree	6 (3 female & 3 male)
PhD	2 (1 female & 1 male)
MD	1 (female)
Current employment status	
Unemployed	10 (7 female & 3 male)
Employed	11 (6 female & 5 male)
Type of current jobs (among 11 who had jobs)	
Full-time	8 (3 female & 5 male)
Part-time	3 (all female)
Current occupation status (among 11 who had jobs)	
Working as labourers	4 (2 female & 2 male)
Professional jobs	7 (4 female & 3 male)
Possibility of permanently living in Canada	
Very sure (100%)	2 (male)
Sure (90%)	1 (female)
Very possible (80%)	12 (8 female & 4 male)
Possible (50–60%)	7 (4 female & 3 male)
Not sure (20–30%)	

strategies for adapting to life in Canada. Their relationships with mainstream culture, their marital relationships, and their employment status all have a significant impact on the construction and reconstruction of their memories of China as the 'homeland' vis-à-vis their experiences of Canada as 'the West.'

Based on inductive analyses, the following three interrelated themes have emerged: (1) employment-related challenges experienced by these recent Chinese skilled immigrants, and their strategies to cope with these challenges; (2) gendered experiences of sociocultural adaptation in Canada that were largely influenced by their employment situations; and (3) construction and reconstruction of home and homeland, and the conditions of homesickness experienced.

Employment-Related Challenges and Strategies

Underemployment and/or unemployment have historically been primary challenges and frustrations for mainland Chinese skilled immigrants in Canada (Li 2003). The situation amongst our study participants was no different. As stated previously, of the 21 people we interviewed, 10 were unemployed and 4 were clearly underemployed, working as general labourers in factories or restaurants. Seven participants held professional jobs, but none of them held jobs as advanced as those they had held in China. For this highly educated group of immigrants, employment-related frustrations had significantly affected many other aspects of their daily lives (e.g., income security, social position, and marital relationship), and had negatively influenced their inner worlds (e.g., self-perception, perceptions about homeland and the host country). Having had a 'good life' in China, the skilled workers from mainland China in our sample often saw 'going abroad' as an option to realize self-improvement and to 'see the world outside of China.' Going to Canada was one way to go to 'the West' and achieve such aspirations. Unfortunately, the difficulty in obtaining professional jobs in Canada has had a harmful effect on the daily lives of this group and their families. In China, most of these individuals enjoyed privileges related to their higher social positions. During the early part of their immigration to Canada, however, these same individuals often reported *luo cha* – the sense of living a life with lower quality – compared to their previous life experiences in China.

Under various financial pressures, an individual or a family may employ temporary short-term strategies to help them attain their long-term goals. For example, an individual may work temporarily as a factory worker and wait to see if an opportunity for professional employment arises, or an individual may be employed temporarily as a labourer so that his or her spouse is able to go to graduate school. In our study, those who held less than ideal jobs, including non-professional positions or low-skilled jobs in factories, often viewed these jobs as a temporary means to secure income until better employment opportunities materialized. A male participant, who had a bachelor's degree and was working in a bakery at the time, commented: 'I used to have another job from afternoon to midnight ... I was washing dishes there. The work is not heavy, but the working schedule is not good. You know, I couldn't rest well after midnight; I couldn't get my energy back, even though I sleep during the daytime. It is troublesome for people at our ages [in his late 40s] ... I felt not well at home.' (Interview conducted in Chinese.)

Employment-related challenges were also often reported by female participants in this study. With regard to educational background, 12 of 13 female participants in our sample held bachelor's or higher degrees and all had held professional jobs in China, yet in Canada they were either unemployed, or, if they were employed, it was not at the level they had held in China. Notably, the women also faced non-employment-related challenges that the men did not (e.g., in their roles as women, mothers, and wives). For instance, in a situation where a wife enjoyed a higher social position than her husband in Canada (e.g., the wife attended graduate school while her husband worked as a general labourer or the wife had a professional job while the husband was unemployed), the potential for marital conflict was more likely. Specifically, the wife's successful employment, especially professional employment, resulted in a potential redistribution of power between husband and wife within a family. At times, a change of power was resisted by the husband, possibly jeopardizing the solidarity of both marital relationship and family. The following description was given by a female participant who was able to find a professional job while her husband could not. In fact, the husband couldn't fully commit himself to immigration for fear of losing his privileged status in China, although both had discussed and applied for immigration together:

You see, when I'm in China, I always obey him, but here when he says something, I don't agree with him. Like I said, no smoking in the house, no smoking in the car. So we quarrel[led] again, we quarrel[led] about everything. And he said Canada is not good, it's cold, the house is small. And when we go [to] swim, he says this is not a good swimming pool, [it's] so small ... He complained [about] everything [here in Canada]. I prepare a dish, and he said it's not as good as what he eats at home. Of course, I don't have enough time to cook. I work, I didn't complain when he complained. We quarrel[led] … He's the kind of person who always thinks he's the man; being a Chinese man means you should have a [better] position than a woman. If I find a job and he couldn't find a job, he could not bear that, you know, so he's afraid of that. (Interview conducted in English)

This narrative highlights the impact of this woman's professional development on her marital relationship. It also reveals her perceptions about herself as a woman and her husband as a man as well as their perceptions about their lives back in their homeland. Despite difficulties, the wife is willing to accept and adapt to Canadian society while the husband idealizes Chinese society and resists his wife's acculturation to Canada, indirectly challenging her womanhood and motherhood in general. For example, the husband's various complaints might imply she was not a 'good' wife, as she could not make him happy or satisfied. As illustrated in this case, a professional employment opportunity for a husband as head of a Chinese family is often perceived as a success for the entire family, because such an employment status (i.e., the husband having a professional job) barely jeopardizes the traditionally desirable gender roles within the family. However, the same opportunity for a wife, if her husband remains unemployed or underemployed, might result in the change of a privileged role for the husband in their family and in society in general. When the privileges (either gender-based or employment-based) that they used to enjoy in China are in jeopardy or lost, the nostalgia for their previous lives (including their professional lives, social privileges, conjugal relationships, etc.) is likely present in their narratives, though such narratives can be very much gendered. (We will discuss this point more fully later in this chapter.) At the same time, a change in gender roles within a family may also be unsettling to some women. For instance, one woman was bothered by the fact that she went to graduate school while her husband worked as a labourer. She would have preferred the opposite situation:

I wished he could go to school and I could go to work to support this family. Because I am female, I think I should be [in] an inferior position in terms of things [external to the family]. I really hoped he could do something, but he was unable to … So, as usual, I keep being disappointed [by] him. I thought, I came here and studied here, but all [this] hard work should be conducted by him rather than me. Perhaps he felt very wronged

... In China, at least he didn't work as a labourer. He may feel uncomfortable and discouraged. But he looked for it. Didn't he deserve it? This is the life he chose by himself. He can choose to go to school, but he is lazy. He can't study English; he would fall asleep when he read English books. (Interview conducted in Chinese)

This woman's narrative highlights her frustration with her husband for not meeting her standards as an educated man and head of the household. She wished he would study English, even after coming home from laborious work at a factory, so that he could go to graduate school. She saw his further education as a way of achieving a gender-based, 'appropriate' status within the household, a belief she held firmly, and which, in turn, structured her high expectation of her husband.

Consistently, the men in our sample, more so than their female counterparts, seemed to miss the social positions in China that had afforded them the multiple privileges associated with being a successful, professional husband, father, and head of the family. For instance, one man described many 'good' things – including the good job, the good salary, the good relationship with colleagues, the good boss, the good working environment, and the strong sense of belonging, commitment, and achievement – that he used to have when he was in China:

Before coming here, my salary in China was very good, my relationship with [my] colleagues [was] very good. In our company, the salaries were very good. Most colleagues were young people ... We shared the same interests. They were very kind. [Occasionally], one or two people were tough, but you didn't need to deal with them all the time. Our CEO was from a big American company, very educated, with high integrity. The managers in our company, a foreign company, were very nice. Even though we sometimes had to work overtime without payment ... there were also other benefits, like [the company paid] our dinner or taxi fare. After 9/11, the business in China was ... affected. So we had to work overtime. This was also for our company; actually [working hard] for [our] company was also [working hard] for ourselves. This company offered the best working environment [I've ever experienced]. I felt it [i.e., the working environment] became so bad after I came here. (Interview conducted in Chinese)

The individual's employment status – whether she or he was unemployed or had a professional position – also influenced the identity construction of these mainland Chinese immigrants. Their pride in being skilled workers or intellectuals combined with their long-term goals of resuming their privileged social positions in this new land was often reflected in their narratives. Consistently, the drastic drop in social privilege due to their inability to procure professional employment in Canada caused them to compare their previous lives in their homeland to their present lives in Canada. Our participants often discussed Canadian immigration and resettlement policies in terms of 'false advertisements' and how they felt somewhat deceived by the way they were solicited to immigrate to Canada, but then were not able to attain professional employment once they were here. Educational background and professional attainment (in which many of them took pride) were supposed to be transferable to Canada; in fact, these credentials were the very basis of their successful immigration applications. However, these skilled immigrants had to find out the hard way that local businesses, agencies, and professional accreditation bodies do not necessarily value their credentials as highly as Canadian Immigration did. In other words, on the one hand, the globalization of capital and information prompted these highly educated professionals to move relatively easily from mainland China to Canada; on the other hand, their lives in Canada, including their employment, social position, and conceptualization of home and host country were still affected by various inhibitors, such as their English proficiency and societal devaluation of their foreign credentials and professional experience.

This point was well highlighted in the narrative of a Chinese skilled immigrant who had been a computer technician in a joint venture in Beijing and was working as a labourer in the Chinese community in Toronto at the time of the interview:

> My parents and my brother are living in China. I am thinking my immigration may be of help for my younger brother ... I think he can come here to study. But he may not need to consider immigration (laughter). Why? In my opinion, for all Chinese who shared my current situation, they really should rethink if it is necessary to immigrate [to Canada]. If you have a very good career in China, do you need to immigrate? Like us, though we were [psychologically prepared] before we came, we still feel the life here is very hard sometimes. Like my wife, she often cried because she couldn't bear it. Men seldom cry, though they do feel [a lot of] pressure. It's like a torture ... My wife felt that the life pressure is too huge. She looked at things from my angle. Like I searched for jobs for two months. I got some

interviews, but no further news. I had no idea at that time. So I thought I should go to work ... She felt what I experienced was very difficult. She used to work [in a] marketing department [in China]. The language requirement is quite high if she wanted to resume her career here ... So she felt that life pressure [here] is so huge. (Interview conducted in Chinese)

Gendered Experiences of Adaptation

When migrating, mainland Chinese skilled immigrant couples often discussed various strategies to achieve their long-term goals of securing jobs in their fields of expertise. After a thorough investigation, each couple adopted what they thought was the best possible strategy. In order to achieve the long-term goal of family success in Canada, sacrifice by one or both members of the couple was often thought necessary. Although these couples role-shared (Sakamoto, in press), the individuals who sacrificed their professional aspirations were not necessarily the female spouses. For example, if a wife was seen as having a better chance of succeeding, a couple might decide that she should be the first one to study for entry to a graduate program while her husband worked in a factory. Significantly, though, when the wife sacrificed her time or professional aspirations, it was taken for granted, when the husband sacrificed his time or professional aspirations, however, it was seen as a great concession on his part. As suggested earlier, couple role-sharing was implemented and viewed differently across the gender line. One woman, for instance, was struggling with her relationship with her husband, who had chosen to live in China due to career-related difficulties in Canada. She thought she might need to change herself or even sacrifice her position in order to resume the previous 'balanced' marital relationship in which she was more obedient to her husband. She said:

> [I]f I go back to China ... I can change myself. I couldn't change him, [but] I can change myself, so I might feel our relationship [is] getting better ... Since I came back here, I found myself, I know myself more, [know] much more [about] what I need, so I think I pity him better. I didn't quarrel with him over the phone, so he feels that he is changing and I am changing. Even his patience is changing. If I say I don't want to take [his] phone call, he says, 'Okay if you don't want to take [my] phone call, I will hang up now but I will call back again' *(laughter)*. So I didn't get angry, I calm[ed] down and his reaction change[d] a little bit. I don't think he will change,

but I can change myself. So if I change myself, I can accept him and he will feel better. If I accept him, that means he will come and he might have more confidence in himself ... Being a woman, you should sacrifice. Many people told me, you should sacrifice. (Interview conducted in English)

In our study, families seemed (or seemed to try) to function as units, within which wives and husbands worked as collaborative partners for the long-term immigration objectives of the family (e.g., ensuring income security and resuming higher social positions). When the family did not function in this way, it was a source of stress, as seen in the narrative above. The power relationships within the family played a key role in reforming and adjusting the division of labour between the husband and wife and the short- and long-term family immigration goals. Often the division of labour within the family and the short-term family adaptation goals became more or less negotiable. This adaptive behaviour was a direct result of such challenging realities as financial pressures (commonly reported by the participants of this study) and/or opportunities (or lack thereof) of employment and advanced study. In most cases, such negotiations led to gendered results, with women's interests more prone to be compromised for the family's good.

In fact, for most families in this study, the traditionally held Chinese value of gender power balance (wherein the husband has a higher position than the wife) remained largely intact. However, the method through which the gender power balance was achieved did vary among couples. In some cases, the husband's privileged position was not evident in the division of labour within the family, but rather indirectly realized through 'good' in-law relationships. For instance, in one participant's case, it appeared a husband tolerated his wife's higher social position because of her dedication and obedience towards his mother. A male participant had this to say about his wife:

From my perspective, many years ago I did think that, as a 'big man (da nan ren)'[3] [it is hard to accept that] what I earned was less than hers. I had such an idea ... I am sensitive to this issue ... Sometimes I told her that we can use our incomes separately because you make more than I do. She is good. I can feel she is very careful not to hurt me in this regard. She never says her wages are more. She always says the money belongs to all of us. Just as I told you before, I didn't expect her to be that nice to my mother.

My sister said my wife was even better than her [i.e., my sister], which is true. It is not that I praise my wife. It is my sister, my mother, and my brother-in-law that praise my wife. (Interview conducted in Chinese)

In other words, the wife's dedication to her mother-in-law counterbalanced the power 'imbalance' between the wife and the husband, even though the husband earned less than the wife.

The existence of children in a family can also function as a balancing point to readjust the power relationships between husband and wife. For instance, educational or developmental concerns about children often enable the gender roles of the parents to be negotiable and thus more flexible. Securing a better education and better futures for their children – a common theme in many immigrant narratives – was one of the main reasons why many of our participants said they wanted to immigrate. In contrast, the life objectives and relevant adaptation strategies for those who were single or divorced were more individually oriented and flexible. In some cases, this may have resulted as well in less interpersonal support/assistance.

Consequently, gender and marital status also complicated the idea of home and homeland. For the participants in our study, home and homeland were concepts constructed in relation to lives that had often proven more challenging than our participants had expected before migration. The 'homesickness' of their narratives reflected home as a place with better jobs, secure income, social status, family, and friends. For the men in our sample, successful lives in Canada seemed beyond their capabilities. As noted earlier, whereas they were once privileged in China by their education and gender, they were suddenly discounted here as lacking Canadian experience, credentials, English proficiency, and so on. Thus, in comparison to women, more men tended to talk about their home and homeland in an idealized manner. In contrast, for married women, while home could still mean an idealized location, it also meant a place where there were stronger social powers to regulate their lives (e.g., social rules, family or community pressure). These sociocultural norms included prescribed gender roles that were monitored by parents, mothers-in-law, and people in the community. For these women, now in Canada, the relative absence of regulatory powers, which enforce tighter sociocultural norms, has given them more personal space in a foreign land. For example, such social regulatory powers may include sociocultural rules in general, but also kinship networks and family/community pressure such as stigmas associated with divorce. It is worth noting here that we attribute the increased freedom for the women more to the immigration experience and the distance from familiar social regulatory powers than to the effect of Canada's social climate, which is assumed to have more gender equity, at least in some areas. Despite their homesickness, home was not necessarily where these women wanted to return.

Construction and Reconstruction of Home and Homeland

On the one hand, the undesirable reality in the previously desired land provides mainland Chinese skilled immigrants with a different perspective on the West, enabling them to re-examine their previous aspirations and idealization about life in the West. For instance, after experiencing various hardships in Canada, including working as a waitress in a restaurant and continual sexual harassment, a female participant sighed and called herself 'naïve' for having dreamed about 'going to the West' since childhood.

Such observations about Canada or the West also have led to simultaneous retrospections about the participants' previous lives in China. Those participants who were frustrated by their current daily lives in Canada often described their 'good lives' in China. A simple quote by a female participant – 'We had everything [in China]' – crystallizes the new-found sentiments of many after experiencing frustrations in Canada. Though the definitions of 'everything' they used to have in China varied for different participants (e.g., a professional job, a privileged social position, an expensive car, and/or a maid), the underlying dynamics of their idealization of their homeland may be thought to be somewhat similar. That is, they regretted not being able to have their 'dream lives' in this new land, although they had already lost what they used to have in the homeland. At this point, it may be less important to scrutinize whether or not they really had 'everything' or what their 'good lives' were really like in China. A more important question is why these immigrants have such an idealized collective narrative about their homeland, which gives meaning to their feelings of nostalgia or homesickness.

On the other hand, the construction and representation of homeland and homesickness appeared to vary by gender, as seen in the case of the women and men in our sample. In other words, the narratives about their homeland that mainland Chinese immigrants construct are somewhat gender-specific. Women in this study seemed to have more fluid ideas of these two locations (China and Canada). Though their narrated lives in Canada are far from perfect, these women attribute their immigration experiences with having afforded them an opportunity for personal development in this new country. For instance, one woman, who had not dared to divorce her husband in China, finally obtained a divorce in Canada. Here, far away from home, family, and relatives, she felt the influence of sociocultural norms (or, the regulatory powers of those close others who would enforce these norms) to be much weaker. Another woman, mentioned earlier, felt sufficiently empowered by her career development in Canada to be 'disobedient' to her husband, an option not available to her in China.

Favourable perceptions about the host country (Canada), however, did not necessarily translate into intentions to 'stay here.' The above-mentioned woman (who was happy with her divorce) was planning to 'go back' after finishing her graduate degree in Canada. She came to this decision largely because her family was expecting her to come home, and because she believed her future career in China would be as good, if not better, than in Canada. This case, along with other cases in this study, illustrates that the construction of homeland can be a much more complex mechanism than a simple clear-cut weighing of 'which one is better.'

Last but not least, silence was seen as a way in which these skilled immigrants could respond to uncontrollable reality. Our participants were struggling with multiple conflicts: between their original immigration goals and the present hardships experienced in Canada, between deciding to 'go back (to China)' and 'staying (in Canada),' and between the desired 'new home' and the sometimes unspeakable pain found therein. Various forms of silence 'expressed' by the participants included their sense of hopelessness, their invisibility to current social services, their alienation from mainstream society, their ambivalent feelings about 'going back' versus 'staying,' and their uncertainty about their lives. All of these realities were part of their day-to-day lives. Again, various sociocultural elements permeated those moments of silence, the concrete experience of which can vary individually, contextually, and by gender. Despite disillusionment, most of the immigrants in our study reported that they would likely stay in Canada, but their reasons for doing so varied with each individual. Sometimes such a decision could be difficult to make. For instance, a man and his wife were both in an MBA program at the time of their interview.

The husband illuminated the complexity of such decision making as follows:

> My basic idea is that, after I graduate, we may go back to China to develop our careers. So our kid will be educated in China for a while. Based on the [current] career market here, people who have MBAs can just do some very simple work, and some people even do not have a chance ... But in China, you can get a much better job and better salary. Also in China, the space to develop my career and the sense of achievement is big ... If you stay here, with a stable job, you can buy a car and a house, do the garden after work – but this is not our dream. So we think it's better to go back. When our kid enters junior high school, we will bring him here [Canada] to go to school. We can go back and forth at that time ... Or, it is okay that both of us, after we get our citizenship, to stay here. I haven't yet thought about it very thoroughly. (Interview conducted in Chinese)

Conclusion

This chapter has presented the themes that emerged from a qualitative study investigating how new skilled immigrants from mainland China constructed and reconstructed the notions of home and homeland, and how gender and family relationships affected the processes. Homeland and home were found to be relational concepts, defined primarily through these immigrants' experiences of coming to Canada. The unemployment or underemployment perceived by many was a major factor influencing how they defined home and homeland. Furthermore, gender and family relationships played a key role in how both home and homeland were constructed. Overall, the Chinese skilled immigrants' construction and reconstruction of these concepts was a complex process which consistently changed vis-à-vis their various life experiences in Canada, including micro (e.g., couple dynamics) and macro (e.g., employment-based discrimination) factors. This finding is reminiscent of Aihwa Ong's (1999) argument in her book, *Flexible Citizenship*: 'Although increasingly able to escape localization by state authorities, traveling subjects are never free of regulations set by state power, market operations, and kinship norms' (19–20). In a way, these Chinese skilled immigrants' reconstruction of home and homeland was affected by transnational capital forces that prompted them to migrate, but at the same time was coloured by how the local market was operated (e.g., local business practices, the devaluation of foreign creden-

tials by professional accreditation bodies) and family norms were renegotiated (e.g., men's position as head of the family). At the same time,
the participants in our study negotiated with and resisted these multiple forces in various ways, and it is important to note that they are not
passive players in these transnational experiences.

This study was limited in several ways. The fact that both interviewers were women may have affected the data in terms of gender dynamics. Furthermore, the researchers may have had other general traits that
prompted participants to offer certain kinds of information. For example, the lead investigator is Japanese, which may or may not have
deterred some Chinese participants from participating. Second, although
diversity of participants was sought as much as possible in the absence
of the sampling framework, it may not have been possible to tap into a
certain segment of mainland Chinese skilled immigrants. For example,
those who were successful in attaining professional jobs may not have
had the time or interest to participate in an interview study. As this is an
inductive qualitative study, the experiences described here should not
be seen as representing the broader Chinese skilled immigrant population in Toronto. Instead, the focus of this chapter was to explore the
meanings of these Chinese skilled immigrants' experiences. Therefore,
transferability of the findings should be approached with caution. Since
the earlier study focused on recent immigrants, future research will
include older skilled immigrants with five to ten years of resettlement
history, to see if their narratives change over time. In addition, comparative research across various skilled immigrant populations will
illuminate the commonalities and differences of the experiences of diverse skilled immigrant populations in Toronto.

In conclusion, we would like to revisit the issue of homesickness.
Often, questions are posed to immigrants in a casual manner, such as
'Which do you like better, Canada or China?' and 'Will you ever go
back to China?' However, as these questions are not as simple as they
might sound to the questioners, we would like to share the narrative
of an informant whose feelings regarding his immigration process
may have remained hidden if we hadn't approached him and listened: 'Sometimes I also think that we shall go back to China. But my
wife is face-loving *(yao mianzi).*[4] She doesn't know how to respond to
people if we go back. So she doesn't want to go back ... I just talk about
it with her. I said, see our life quality decreased by many levels; life
here is so laborious and hard ... but she said no.' (Interview conducted
in Chinese)

Although this participant's experience is not necessarily representative, it nonetheless reveals the complexity and silence related to homesickness that is experienced by many Chinese skilled immigrants. As such, missing home may or may not have to do with the decision to go back, even for these professionals whose skills and jobs are supposedly transportable. As is clear in the narrative above, these skilled immigrants may choose to stay in Canada not necessarily because of macro forces (e.g., market demands) but also because of perceived sociocultural norms imposed upon them from communities and families back home (e.g., saving face). Listening more often to the voices of these skilled immigrants would lead to a richer and more nuanced understanding of their experiences in Canada. Furthermore, listening to these often unspoken voices would shed light on the social policy and service delivery in today's Canadian society, whose imperative includes the continued absorption and integration of skilled immigrants.

NOTES

1 Please see Markus and Kitayama (1991), Fiske et al. (1998), Berry (1997), and LaFromboise et al. (1993). See Sakamoto (2001, 2004) for a more detailed review of these bodies of literature.
2 Grounded theory is a qualitative research methodology first developed by Glaser and Strauss (1967), and further refined by many researchers such as Strauss and Corbin (1998), Chesler (1987), and Charmaz (2000). In grounded theory approaches, data collection and data analysis take place simultaneously, one informing the other. Grounded theory approaches emphasize that prior knowledge should be suspended so that themes from the data are allowed to emerge freely. Thus, grounded theory researchers generally start with general areas of inquiry, not from existing theories, and theories are often introduced at a later stage of inquiry for comparison.
3 The Chinese expression *da nan ren* ('big man') is often used to figuratively highlight masculinity or the pride and privileges of being a man (over being a woman). However, now this specific expression is used relatively less by the young generation of men.
4 *'Yao mian zi'* ('face-loving,' or 'saving face') constitutes a distinct characteristic of Chinese traditional culture, referring to that one's caring about how others look at his/her image or reputation. This term is often seen in studies and articles related to Chinese culture. In *A Modern Chinese English Dictionary* (1988), for instance, the Chinese term *'yao mian zi'* translates into 'be keen on face-saving' in English (Editorial Division, 1988, 1032).

REFERENCES

Berry, J.W. 1997. Immigration, Acculturation, and Adaptation. *Applied Psychology: An International Review* 46(1): 5–68.

Charmaz, K. 2000. Grounded theory: Objectivist and Constructivist Methods. In *Handbook of Qualitative Research*. 2d ed. Ed. N.K. Denzin and Y.S. Lincoln. Thousand Oaks, CA: Sage.

Chesler, M. 1987. 'Professional' Views of the 'Dangers' of Self-Help Groups. CRSO Working Paper No. 345. University of Michigan, Ann Arbor.

Chinese Interagency Network of Greater Toronto. 1994. *A Study of Psychological Distress of Chinese Immigrant Women in Metropolitan Toronto*. Toronto: Health and Family Services Subcommittee, Chinese Interagency Network of Greater Toronto.

Citizenship and Immigration Canada. 2002. *Facts and Figures – Immigration Overview 2001*. Ottawa: Strategic Policy, Planning and Research, Citizenship and Immigration Canada.

– 2003. *Facts and Figures – Immigration Overview 2002*. Retrieved 30 April 2004 from http://www.cic.gc.ca/english/research/menu-fact.html.

– 2003. Retrieved on 1 March 2003 from http://cicnet.ci.gc.ca/english/irpa/fs-skilled2.html.

Fiske, A.P., S. Kitayama, H.R., Markus, and R.E. Nisbett. 1998. The Cultural Matrix of Social Psychology. In *Handbook of Social Psychology*, ed. D.T. Gilbert, S. Fiske, and G. Lindzey. Vol. 2, 4th ed., 915–981. New York: McGraw Hill.

Foreign Language Teaching and Research Press, Editorial Division. 1988. *A Modern Chinese English Dictionary*. Beijing: Foreign Language Teaching and Research Press.

George, U., K.T. Tsang, G. Man, and W.W. Da. 2000. *Needs Assessment of Mandarin-Speaking Newcomers*. Toronto: The South East Asian Service Centre.

Glaser, B.G. and A.L. Strauss. 1967. *The Discovery of Grounded Theory: Strategies for Qualitative Research*. New York: Aldine de Guyter.

ISPRPC (Integrated Settlement Planning Research Project Consortium). 2000. *Re-Visioning the Newcomer Settlement Support System*. Toronto: Integrated Settlement Planning Research Project Consortium.

LaFromboise, T., H.L.K. Coleman, and J. Gerton. 1993. Psychological Impact of Biculturalism: Evidence and Theory. *Psychological Bulletin* 114(3): 395–412.

Li, P.S. 2003. Destination Canada: Immigration Debates and Issues. Toronto: Oxford University Press.

Lim, I.-S. 1997. Korean Immigrant Women's Challenge to Gender Inequality at

Home: The Interplay of Economic Resources, Gender and Family. *Gender and Society* 11: 31–51.

Man, G. 2002. Globalization and the Erosion of the Welfare State: Effects on Chinese Immigrant Women. *Canadian Women Studies* 21/22(4/1): 26–32.

Markus, H.R., and S. Kitayama. 1991. Culture and the Self: Implications for Cognition, Emotion, and Motivation. *Psychological Review* 98(2): 224–253.

Markus, H.R., P. Mullally, and S. Kitayama. 1997. Selfways: Diversity in Modes of Cultural Participation. In *The Conceptual Self in Context: Culture, Experiences, Self-Understanding*, ed. U. Neisser and D.A. Jopling, 13–61. New York: Cambridge University Press.

North Chinese Community of Canada. 2003. Will 130,000 Mainland Chinese Immigrants Go Back Due to Adjustment Problems in Canada? Retrieved from http://www.is4u.net/blocks/show.php?id=165. 10 October 2003. (Original in Chinese, trans. Yanqiu Zhou)

Ong, A. 1999. *Flexible Citizenship: The Cultural Logic of Transnationality.* Durham, NC: Duke University Press.

Ornstein, M. 2000. Income Inequality in Toronto. Toronto: Access and Equity Office, City of Toronto.

Patton, M.Q. 1990. *Qualitative Evaluation and Research Methods.* 2d ed. Newbury Park, CA: Sage.

Peston, V., and G. Man. 1999. Employment Experiences of Chinese Immigrant Women: An Exploration of Diversity. Paper presented at the annual meetings of the Association of American Geographers, Honolulu, HI, 23–27 March.

Reitz, J.G. 2001. Immigrant Success in the Knowledge Economy: Institutional Change and the Immigrant Experience in Canada, 1970–1995. *Journal of Social Issues* 57 (3): 579–613.

Ross, O. 2003. Making Buns Not Quite Rocket Science. *Toronto Star.* 16 October, A10.

Sakamoto, I. 2001. *Negotiating Multiple Cultural Contexts: Flexibility and Constraint in the Cultural Selfways of Japanese Academic Migrants.* Phd diss. University of Michigan, Ann Arbor.

Sakamoto, I., and Y. Zhou. 2003. New Skilled Immigrants from Mainland China: Family, Income Security, and Cultural Negotiation. A paper presented at the Interdisciplinary Conference on Subethnicity in the Chinese Diaspora, University of Toronto, 13 September.

– 2004. Cultural Negotiation and Transnationality: Family-Based Cultural Adaptation and Gender Roles of Academic Migrants in the United States. Manuscript submitted for publication.

Sakamoto, I. In press. A Model of Cultural Negotiation and the Family:

Experiences of Japanese Academic Migrants in Michigan. In *Cultural Psychology of Immigrants*, ed. R. Mahalingam. Mahwah, NJ: Lawrence Erlbaum.

Statistics Canada. 2003. *Ethnic Diversity Survey: Portrait of a Multicultural Society*. Ottawa: Statistics Canada.

Strauss, A., and A. Corbin. 1990. *Basics of Qualitative Research: Grounded Theory Procedures and Techniques*. Newbury Park, CA: Sage.

– 1998. *Basics of Qualitative Research: Techniques and Procedures for Developing Grounded Theory*. 2d ed. Thousand Oaks, CA: Sage.

9 'I Feel Like a Trini': Narrative of a Generation-and-a-Half Canadian

CARL E. JAMES

CARL: How do you identify, as Trinidadian or Canadian?
MARK: Definitely Trini.
CARL: Why?
MARK: I think it has to do with the way I was raised, and the different values I have; the way I see life. And I think my whole perspective on life and education is all different. So I can't really say I am Canadian in that sense.

In my first three questions to Mark (a pseudonym), I established that he was born in Trinidad and had immigrated to Canada in March 1995 at thirteen years of age. In asking Mark how he identified himself, I sought to learn where he stood on the question of national identity – a question often posed to immigrants and Black people (immigrants and non-immigrants alike), especially by white Canadians (Agnew 2003; James 2001; Palmer 1997; Shadd 2001). Mark's response was unequivocal – 'Definitely Trini' – that short, familiar, nostalgic, and colloquial expression to assert his sense of kinship and nationality. And he reasoned that his values, perspective on life, and education were 'different,' hence he could not be considered Canadian. What are these differences? And what are the perceived Canadian norms that Mark believed he did not possess and therefore made him 'different'?

Mark was one of twenty young Black Canadians living in the Toronto area who participated in our study[1] entitled Product of Canada![2] in which we explored the settlement processes and experiences and the educational and occupational outcomes of Caribbean Canadians between the ages of eighteen and twenty-nine. We sought to understand how, in the face of the public discourse in which young Black Caribbean males were constructed as 'foreigners,' these young people constructed, understood, and articulated their sense of Canadian identity and belonging (see Boyd and Grieco 1998; Foner 1997; Handa 2003; Minichiello 2001; Norquay 2000; Park 1999; Statistics Canada 2003; Waters 1999; Zhou 1997). To this end, we explored how the experiences of generation-and-a-half Caribbean Canadians informed their sense of family, their expectations of societal institutions, and the social and cultural construction of themselves as Black Caribbean Canadians. (We defined 'generation-and-a-half Caribbean Canadians' (or the 1.5 generation) as those who immigrated to Canada between the ages of eight and twelve, with and without their parents.)[3] We perceived that while many of the experiences of generation-and-a-half and second-generation (those born in Canada) Caribbean Canadians were likely to be similar, there were also differences. The most notable differences were the early schooling and parenting that these Canadians had received in the Caribbean, and the fact that, as immigrants, they had undergone an adjustment process as they settled in Canada.

I present this narrative of Mark, who was a twenty-year-old first-year university student at the time of the interview (fall 2001), in an effort to provide a perspective on how one young Caribbean diasporic male experienced and adjusted to life in Canada. I want to explore his understanding and construction of his identity as Canadian; that is, his sense of belonging (Norquay 2000; Statistics Canada 2003), his educational and career aspirations, and the role his parent – in this case, his mother – played in directing his aspirations (Gitlin et al. 2003). In my audiotaped interview with Mark, I was struck by the way he made sense of his values and experiences as a generation-and-a-half Canadian, the circumstances and structural factors that shaped his life and informed his educational and career aspirations, and his perceptions of the opportunities and possibilities that Canada afforded him as a young Black man. More compelling was the role that sports played in Mark's adjustment to life in Canada. This factor is significant, for as research has shown, many Caribbean Canadian youth have used sports to negotiate and navigate high school in an effort to attain an education and develop their athletic abilities and competence. These young people believe that by excelling at sports, they will win athletic scholarships to American universities and colleges and eventually 'make it' in the sports world and in society generally (James 2003; Spence 1999; Solomon 1992). But for Mark, while sport was central to his adjustment to life in Canada and to his career plans, unlike his Caribbean Canadian peers, it was Trinidad that provided the opportunities to showcase his talent and gain the inspiration and satisfaction he needed to maintain his ambitions. In fact, Canada was where he lived, received his education, 'found his athletic talent,' and developed his athletic skills, but it is Trinidad that provided the foundation for his values, self-confidence, and aspirations. In fact, both countries have made him the person he is and expects to become.

This interpretive account of Mark's sense of home provides insights into the complex, pragmatic, sentimental, imagined, dual, and contradictory ways in which home is conceptualized or imagined. The emphasis on 'interpretive' is germane, since Mark's story is layered by his interpretations (not mere descriptions) and analyses of events, as well as the social, political, economic, and cultural contexts of the societies that have shaped and structured his life (Denzin 1996; Munro 1998). It is also layered by my own interpretation and experiences as a Black Caribbean Canadian educator and researcher. Furthermore, Mark's story cannot be considered a static product that represents his life at a particular point in time; rather, his story captures the developing processes and changing pictures of his life journey (Coleman 1991), as well as the confusions, contradictions, ambiguities, fluctuations, and transitions that are part of his lived experiences (James 2002). And as Munro (1998) points out, the tensions and contradictions that are inherent in how individuals construct their stories signify the power relations and practices against which they write their lives. In such a context, the personal stories of minority group members like Mark can be an effective source of counter-hegemonic insights because they expose the viewpoint embedded in a dominant ideology as particular rather than universal, and because they reveal the reality of a life that defies or contradicts the rules as well as essentialist constructions. Researchers, then, writes Lincoln (1993), 'can provide [an] active counterpoint by describing historical and social contexts in which silenced groups have traditionally found themselves' (35).

In the first section of this chapter, I explore Mark's early life in Canada and what moving to Canada meant for him. In the second section, I examine his high school experiences, noting his educational and career aspirations. In section three, I discuss the pivotal role his mother and grandparents play in influencing faith in education as a mechanism for success. But in the short term, as I discuss in section four, Mark perceived that a career in sports was a viable option. This perception proved to be influenced by his connection to his Trinidad 'roots,' the implications of which are discussed in the fifth section. I conclude with a discussion of how being a generation-and-a-half Caribbean Canadian has informed Mark's life in terms of his experiences, identification, aspirations, opportunities, and sense of belonging or home.

The Move to Canada

'... to give us an opportunity to get a better education'

Mark came to Canada to join his mother who had immigrated here five years earlier, leaving Mark and his younger brother to live with their maternal grandparents. According to Mark, his mother 'moved from Trinidad with the plan to bring us here, to set up a home and stuff, and give us an opportunity to get a better education.' The idea of emigrating from the Caribbean to North America to ensure a better life for one's children is well documented (Henry 1994; James 2002; Plaza and Simmons 1998). There is good evidence that young people can and do attain the better education that their parents had hoped for when they immigrate to Canada. Nevertheless, for Mark, who at thirteen years of age was attending 'the second best' school in Trinidad (having passed the entrance examination) and 'was enjoying school there,' it took some persuasion from his mother to convince him to immigrate: 'Well, she had us pretty convinced that it's a better standard of living, and basically the main reason is to look out for your future. She wanted us to have an opportunity – It's sort of like a rat race in Trinidad, where even students with great grades and high marks are not getting the high jobs that they want, so they have to settle for the jobs they get. But it's a different situation up here. So I wanted to come for two reasons: to live with her and to make a better future for myself.' For Mark and his mother, Canada was an escape from the Trinidadian 'rat race.' It was a place where a better future was possible because of the opportunities he would have to get jobs which were commensurate with his level of education.

Mark admitted to weighing what he would gain by immigrating to Canada against the fact that he was leaving his grandparents, with whom he had 'a closer relationship,' and his friends. 'It was tough,' he said. 'My father was never around, so my grandfather was basically my father. My grandma was much more loving [and] comforting ... I didn't really want to leave them, but I wanted in the same sense to come with my mom because I was missing her as well. She would come back and forth from Canada to Trinidad. So she was moving back and forth and it was kind of emotional. Like I would see my mom for a couple of weeks and then she is going back to Canada. Yeah, it's a fine balance there too.'

It would appear that having decided to immigrate, and despite what he was leaving behind, Mark was confident and satisfied that in return he was coming to Canada to establish a family life with his mother and secure a 'future' for himself. But at the time of the interview, Mark, who had been living in Canada for more than seven years, conceded that he had a strong allegiance to Trinidad 'because, I guess the effect that being raised there has on me, and you are taught to be basically loyal; and all my values remain the same, I can say. Maybe my accent has changed, but if I were to go back down there it wouldn't take two days before you would hear me talk in the same way again.' Hearing this comment, I sought to establish the factors that kept Mark from claiming a Canadian instead of a Trinidadian identity. Was it because he was repeatedly asked, 'Where are you from?' Or because he was told that he 'had an accent'? As Palmer (1997), a Caribbean Canadian, writes, 'This probing of our ancestry keeps us forever foreign, forever immigrants to Canada ... Their faulty [or racist] premise assumes that because you are not White you could not be Canadian' (v–vi; see also Agnew 2003). Furthermore, were experiences with racism the reason for Mark's assertion that he was Trinidadian? Again, Palmer contends that 'systemic racism in all its many guises ensures that no matter how long non-White Canadians are here, we will always be treated differently. No matter how much we assimilate, we will never be accepted as being Canadian' (viii). In light of these questions, I proceeded:

CARL: Are you a Canadian citizen?

MARK: Yes.

CARL: So why don't you consider yourself Canadian?

MARK: Why the difference? I think that living here I am not fully submerged into the Canadian culture because there are many Trinidadian people who I meet here, who cling strongly to their values as well, and to their own heritage, especially at [this university].

CARL: So how has Canada been for you so far?

MARK: Canada has been great.

CARL: Do you like it here?

MARK: Yeah, I like it here.

CARL: Would you move back to Trinidad?

MARK: Yes, I would, but I don't think I could build a good future there; only if I could have, like, the same type of life. So I am kind of enjoying the best of both worlds.

Mark perceived that he had not changed his values or made that cultural shift that would make him a Canadian; he felt this was not necessary, nor did he wish to do so because he was 'enjoying the best of both worlds.' This meant that he was taking advantage of the educational and athletic opportunities that Canada provided while remembering and using his Trinidad-inspired and socialized values and aspirations to keep him focused on his educational and career ambitions. Furthermore, not being Canadian meant that he would be different from his Canadian peers, and hence should not be expected to fit the existing social, cultural, and educational profile or stereotype of Black Caribbean Canadian youth. His idea, then, was to keep distancing himself from such characterization – that is, not to assimilate – because to the extent to which assimilation was possible, the result was not going to be in his favour (see also Garrod et al. 2002, 64; Minichiello 2001; Noguera 2003; Park 1999; Waters 1999). Alternatively, being Trinidadian meant he had a commitment to doing well academically, and, in this regard, had the personal and familial values and aspirations that gave him the confidence and optimism he needed to succeed in Canadian society. So, pragmatically speaking, 'both worlds' constituted Mark's constructed home. With his culturally imagined Canada – the society in which he resided – he had access to the educational and occupational opportunities he wished for, and knew that his aspirations could be realized. Meanwhile, with his culturally imagined Trinidad, he knew he had the social and cultural capital to be able to take advantage of the opportunities in Canada. In a way, then, physical residency aside, Mark's 'home' was a fluid mixture of both Trinidad and Canada, for it was in both places that he resided emotionally, and sought, through a network of supportive individuals and structures in both countries, to sustain his values, understanding of life, and ambitions, particularly as he navigated and negotiated high school.

School, Teachers, Coaches, and Peers

'I found my talents through high school here.'

Having arrived in March, Mark was initially placed, or, as he said, 'dropped' in Grade 8 in a Toronto school and proceeded to high school the following September. His use of the word 'dropped' is a hint at his dissatisfaction with the fact that he was placed in an elementary school when he already had been attending high school in Trinidad. During his short time in Grade 8, however, he 'met a teacher from Trinidad' who, as Henry (1998) would say, functioned like his 'other mother' and ensured that he maintained his focus on his education. He explained: 'She saw me starting to change a bit, trying to fit in with the crowds and stuff. She saw my change in attitude and my focus shifting away from schooling because I thought it was not as difficult as Trinidad at that point in time. And she would always give me pep talks and try to keep me on the right track, and really that was very supporting.' Similarly, in high school, Mark met 'other black teachers' who were also supportive, and, in his words, 'always looked for me, told me ... not to undermine your talents, try to achieve and fulfil that potential.'

As part of his adjustment to school life in Canada, like many Caribbean youth who enter the Toronto school system, Mark participated in sports upon entering high school. 'I had coaches' (all of them white), he said, 'pushing me on, trying to help me recognize my talents.' And, like many other Caribbean students, he started with basketball, a sport to which he, like many others, was unaccustomed (James, 2005). But in Mark's case, despite his ability 'to jump pretty high and block shots,' he was unable to transcend, as he saw it, his limitation in 'size,' height (he was 5 feet 11 inches), and 'handling skills to be a guard.'[4] He opted, therefore, to participate in track and field, something he was also doing for the first time. He explained that in Trinidad the emphasis in school was to 'get as high marks as you can,' but in Canada the emphasis was more 'on sporting life ... So,' he continued, 'that's where I kind of filtered into sports and I found my talents through high school here. So in that sense I was very lucky to be able to recognize my talents and focus in on some sports.' Mark recounted with satisfaction the 'motivation' he received from both his white and his Black teachers, who saw him as 'really special' and having lots of 'potential.' And he insisted that the potential his teachers and coaches saw in him was just as much related to his competence in sports as in academics. For, as he noted, sports did not play a central role in his school life; they were 'extracurricular activities.' Hence, participating in sports did not prevent him from maintaining an 'overall A average' while also doing 'well on the playing field.' 'School,' Mark said, 'was a breeze until OAC [the last year] ... [and] they [the teachers] respected me as an athlete and student.' He also pointed out that the size of the school was a factor in helping him to gain recognition and support: 'Well, I was lucky enough to go to a small school where I was the one who was making an impact on the school. So if I went to a bigger high school nobody would have really known your name, you would just be one of many who are talented.'

According to Mark, friendships did not detract him from his academic work during high school. In fact, as he said, 'I didn't really have a chance to form many significant relationships in high school. I think partially because of racial differences, they just weren't that many Black Caribbean people. Most of them were either born here, or have been here for a long time. So they were different from me when I came. I couldn't really relate to them in any way ... I couldn't relate to many of the white kids either, so I pretty much stuck to myself.' For Mark, the cultural differences between himself and other Black Caribbean students who were either born in Canada or had been living here for a long time were just as significant as the racial differences between him and white students, hence his inability to relate to both groups of students (see also Garrod et al. 2002, 65–73; Park 1999). The 'only person' to whom he could relate and with whom he mostly associated was his brother (two years his junior), who obviously shared and supported his values and aspirations.

During high school, then, Mark's social network – his Black Caribbean teachers and brother – played a significant role in helping him sustain his perceived Trinidadian cultural values and his ambition, as an immigrant, to get a good education. From Mark's perspective, being a Trinidadian and an immigrant contributed to his 'cultural difference,' which set him apart from his peers; this distance seemed to have helped him to keep his perceived values and aspirations intact. Sport, then, was merely, as he put it, 'an extra something' that occupied his time, since he did not find the schoolwork as demanding as it had been in Trinidad. Here Mark was identifying yet another difference between himself and his peers: the academic work to which he was accustomed in Trinidad was seen as 'very intense' in terms of the strict enforcement of discipline compared to what he experienced in Canada.[5] Coming from such a context, Mark perceived that he was better prepared than his Canadian peers to deal with the academic work here. Thus, the sound academic foundation he believed Trinidad provided him likely contributed to his continuing fondness for, and identification with, the country. As well, his claim to liking Canada was a reflection of his belief that in Canada he would be able to realize his educational and other aspirations without becoming Canadian like his peers, for doing so would mean being like them and fitting a stereotype in which school was not considered a priority. Mark notes, 'I would say that stereotype doesn't fit me because I was doing well in school. I wasn't responding to any stereotype; I was making my own decisions. If school were suffering because of that, then I would have to give up the sports.'

Expectations, Aspirations, and Parental Influence

'Education ... that's what I came here for.'

Confident that he could participate in sports and maintain high academic standing throughout his years in high school and now university, Mark participated in track and field, and also swimming for a short time in high school, and aspired 'to get into sports medicine, but if that doesn't work out, then definitely the career in running will.' To this end, he was pursuing 'a double major in psychology and kinesiology,' having received an academic scholarship to a university in Toronto.[6] That he decided upon a university education in Canada is significant, for there is the tendency among African Caribbean Canadian athletes to seek an athletic scholarship to American universities and colleges (James 2003), a practice as popular among generation-and-a-half Caribbean Canadians as among the second generation. But in this case, Mark did not appear to be typical in that, while he wished to attain a scholarship to an American university, it was more the education he sought rather than the opportunity to participate in sports. He would only accept scholarships from 'big schools' (universities) for, as he reasoned, 'The type of level of education that you are getting from these smaller schools, it wouldn't be accepted; it wouldn't be respected as much as a degree here [in Canada]. And you are working your butt off running every weekend with somewhat of a non-guarantee. There is no guarantee with regards to having four years of education there. So it was a more simple decision I made.'[7]

That simple decision was to accept the academic scholarship from a Canadian university rather than either one of the 'two athletic scholarships' he was offered by two 'small' American universities. In deciding not to accept these scholarships, Mark was listening to his mother and his coach, who were advising him to accept the scholarships: 'The other school coaches were saying, "Why don't you; it seems like a good school"; but I already had my mind convinced that it's a small school, and you are not going to get a respectable degree, and my mom was saying the same thing. They wanted me to go, but I didn't want to risk having to perform for them every single weekend and not get a good education anyway.'

As Mark saw things, going to American schools, at least the ones to which he won scholarships, would have been at the expense of his academic success – something on which he was not prepared to gamble. It is not surprising that his thinking was informed by his mother's expectations that he remain focused on his education and not just on sports: 'My mom was, like, why would you go away and have to be running every single week, your marks would suffer, plus you don't come back here with a respectable degree. Why not just go to [a Canadian university] and still be able to train and get a good education at the same time? So just that alone, with my mom not pressuring me into having to go away to get a so-called free scholarship, was very good for me because I was able to still focus on the education. That's what I came here for and that's what I am doing.'

That Mark would give such considerable attention and credit to his mother's advice is related to his belief that his mother, and not his peers, had the necessary insights and wisdom about what it would take to successfully negotiate the structures of the society. After all, she was an immigrant who, like him, had had to learn how to survive in the system. In contrast, his peers did not have to learn to survive; they were 'Canadians,' as he said. In reiterating that he came to Canada for an education, Mark was also signalling the centrality of education to his existence in Canada. Consistent with his mother's ideas, he believed he would be able to gain the respect and acceptance needed to be successful through the education he would get at a reputable Canadian university. Furthermore, he saw education as his security – something he could revert to if his athletic career did not materialize, particularly in the long term. Convinced that the scholarship did not really mean obtaining a 'free education,' he was not prepared to take any chances. So he opted for security.

CARL: You said 'so-called free scholarship.' You don't believe that scholarship was free?

MARK: No way, I hear too many of my own teammates who went down there come back in two years because they all run out, they have injuries, they are off the team. And they get sent back as soon as they are not able to run and perform for the school anymore. They are sent back. I know that my body would most likely not respond all the time, so it's not worth the risk wasting time out of school. Having to meet new coaches, having to have new people understand your body, the way you perform, what works for you. It's too complex. I just decided to stay here.

From my other research on Black student athletes, I have found that these students mostly listen to their coaches, and are less critical and discriminating about accepting scholarship offers; they feel they can 'bounce back' and do well athletically after injuries (in fact, they tend not to consider or talk about injury as a possibility); and they rarely consult or take the advice of their parents (James 2003). Mark, on the other hand, 'educated' himself and critically assessed the 'many options available' to him, as he said, by listening to people's good and bad athletic stories, talking with coaches, and forming his 'own opinion' – with his mother's guidance. As noted earlier, this difference in the way Mark cautiously approached his athletic, educational, and career ambitions is largely informed by his situation and experiences as a generation-and-a-half Caribbean Canadian, one who was still very strongly connected to his mother and grandparents. He looked to them for guidance, willingly complied with their expectations of him, and was comfortable with them living vicariously through him:

Both my grandparents always talked about not being able to achieve because they had to work from when they were younger in order to build this. So they built something; and then my mom moved a step forward. She was able to build something, but she didn't get her university education either. And she is encouraging me because she sees it everyday in her workplace, where, as long as you have that piece of paper, you are able to get more money and are able to make decisions. Although she has the brains to do things, they just don't respect you unless you have that, so that's my encouragement, that's what I remember, and that's what I am doing right now.

Like his parents and many other immigrants (Anisef and Kilbride 2003; Gitlin et al. 2003; Li 2001), Mark was convinced that as long as one has the 'brains,' like he did, then education – 'that piece of paper' – was ultimately what would enable him to make money and gain respect in this society. As he repeatedly said throughout the interview, that is what he knew and that is what he was doing, which also meant taking agency and putting into place a plan of action.

A Plan of Action and Opportunities for Success

'I cling to my roots.'

While Mark made pursing his university education a priority, as indicated above, he also had a short-term plan to pursue a career in track, especially since he had been 'doing well [in track] at the national and international levels.' In fact, Mark had also been participating in an athletic club while in university, and his achievements and the support he was receiving made him feel confident that devoting about eight years to a career in athletics was a possibility. As he said, 'We reach our peak at the age of, say, around twenty-eight ... and I am twenty years old.' It does seem somewhat contradictory that Mark would talk about investing so much time in sports, especially when he understands the precariousness of a sports career. Is it possible that he is like the other Black Caribbean Canadian youth who see sports as their ticket to success (James 2003), those from whom he had distanced himself? Perhaps not. Through sports, Mark was able to stay connected to his 'roots,' become nationally and internationally known, and to gain respect. As he stated,

> This past summer [2002], I competed as a junior, meaning under twenty, at the national level here. I won Canadian junior nationals, and I was in contact with one of the coaches in Trinidad ... And I was asking him if I could be a part of the Trinidad team to compete at the Pan Am Junior games in Argentina. I wanted to compete for Canada, but Canada was charging ... So you had to come up with [money] to run for Canada – and Trinidad was going to pay for me to go for free. So after telling him that I achieved this and this, and these were my PBs [personal best] before, they were very grateful to have me on the team. They did a whole story in the newspaper; I had a whole big article on me in the newspapers there. I went down and travelled with the team, and I was there with the team and I saw some of my friends from here who were competing for Canada, and it was kind of weird. This year I'm going to the Commonwealth Games for Trinidad and to another competition in the States.[8]

It is worth noting that Mark was interviewed in the autumn following his participation and success in the Pan American Junior games and the publicity he received in Trinidad. With his enhanced reputation, it is understandable that Mark would feel confident that a career in track was a possibility and within his reach. This success might help explain

242 Carl E. James

his passionate and seemingly unbending identification as a Trinidadian, not the fact that he had only been living in Canada for seven years. For him, Trinidad might not have been able to provide the education he sought, but it provided the opportunity for him to get on the path to his athletic career – a career based on a talent discovered in Canada. Furthermore, insofar as the competition for a position on Trinidad's national sports teams was less acute than in Canada, it is logical, given Mark's athletic interest and aspiration, that he would use his contacts in Trinidad to seize the opportunity to run for that country. Mark had expressed a similar logic earlier, when he spoke of the benefits he gained from having attended one of the smaller high schools in Canada; that he was known there, and was 'not just one of many [students] who are talented.' Ostensibly, Mark accepted that Trinidad and Canada were both useful and important to his ambitions. So, it was not that he did not feel some affinity to Canada, or rejected Canada as home – indeed, as he admitted, he felt 'weird' when he saw his friends competing for Canada. Instead, his comments reflected his practicality, pragmatism, and criticism of the way Canada treated athletes like him. He reasoned, 'If Canada was to support their athletes the way that other countries do, then people would want to compete for them. But if you have other options, you should explore them. Similar to what Ato Bolton did, he was American and he decided to run for Trinidad, and that was my decision. And Ato just happens to be one of my role models.'

Hearing this reasoning, I asked Mark if Canada offered the very same opportunities as Trinidad, would he then run for Canada? He replied, 'It's a very, very tough question, but I already know that Canada doesn't have the finances to do that, and they never will. So I would stay with Trinidad. You are asking me to totally blank out the fact that I know that Canada cannot do it. I would still run for Trinidad if it was even. [Why?] Because I cling more to my roots there.' I pursued this line of questioning seeking to ascertain if racism was a factor in why Mark 'clung to his roots,' or why he might reject Canada as home. But, as he said, 'I think both societies are almost the same with multiculturalism and stuff like that. The white culture here is more dominant obviously, but I haven't experienced any racism here, so I can't say that.' Later, to a series of questions, he added:

> MARK: I don't see colours when I see people, I see people. So I look at the way people react to me. Sometimes you see, like, say, you're walking down the street at night-time, you see the differences or

reactions. I don't really see racism as a factor in Canada; at least not in my neighbourhood or where I was raised.

CARL: And do you ever see in the future that race could possibly influence your life changes?

MARK: No.

CARL: Do you think racism could make it difficult, or become a barrier for you in the future?

MARK: Not in the field of sports. No. [Why?] Because in the field of sports, we all follow the same rules, and it's a level playing field. That's why Jessie Owens was able to showcase his talents.

CARL: And you think Canada compared to the U.S. could give a black person the same possibilities and opportunities as the U.S. gave to Jessie Owens?

MARK: The U.S. gives more financial support to their athletes, and that's a known fact. But I think Canada can make something out of you, but they can easily put you down just as Ben Johnson was. They can lift you up to making a lot of money and being a well-known figure as Donovan Bailey, but they can easily put you down the same way.

CARL: So do you have any fear of that?

MARK: No. I need to make my right decisions. I'll make the right decisions when they come up.

CARL: You sound very confident. Why are you so confident?

MARK: You can't beat destiny.[9]

Like many Canadians, Mark understood Canada to be multicultural, and, as he said, 'almost the same' as Trinidad. This thinking is likely a product of his belief that in seven years in Canada, he had managed to maintain his 'Trinidadian' culture. Such imagined cultural maintenance is consistent with the premise of multicultural discourse, which holds that assimilation to Canadian culture is not necessary, and that racial and ethnic minority group members are 'free' to indulge in 'their' cultural practices. Underlying this premise is the idea that culture is static and demarcated by such things as the national, racial, and ethnic affiliation and origin of people who are members of minority groups. At the same time, there is the claim that in Canada individuals are not identified by race or skin colour, and neither are their opportunities and achievements mediated by these characteristics (James 2003; Dei and Calliste 2000). Mark's 'colour-blindness' and his belief that racism will have no effect on the realization of his ambitions are consistent with the multicultural discourse of Canada, something he has obviously incorporated into his belief system as a resident of this country (see also Minichiello 2001). Furthermore, that Mark believed equal opportunity existed in sports[10] is not only in keeping with his coached sports values, but is also informed by the discourse of multiculturalism and the related notion of colour-blindness. Like many other athletes, especially marginalized young people who are looking to make it big in sports, Mark displayed his optimism, faith, and belief that he would be assessed and rewarded with opportunities to compete solely on the basis of his skills, abilities, and competence in track. Accordingly, Mark believed that regardless of skin colour, his success in sport is possible because he 'made the right decisions' and it is his 'destiny' (see James, 2005).

Ironically, while Mark claimed to be colour-blind, and claimed not to 'really see racism as a factor in Canada,' the individuals he mentioned in his discussion of equal opportunities here were black males – Ben Johnson and Donovan Bailey – who, like himself, were of Caribbean origin. In saying that opportunities exist in Canada for athletes, like Johnson and Bailey, to 'make something' of themselves – that is, make 'a lot of money' and become 'well known,' he also admitted that 'they [implying non-Black Canadians] can easily put you down the same way.' With these illustrations, also that of Jesse Owens, Mark in fact was making a case that, structurally, race does matter in Canada. Thus, contrary to what he said, Mark *was* 'seeing' colour and was alluding to the racialized ways in which structures operated in affecting individuals' outcomes. But, while on the surface, Mark's assertions – that, he did not 'see colour' and had not 'experienced any racism here' – can be considered contradictory; in fact, from his perspective, there was no contradiction, for through his 'blindness' to colour and racism, he had maintained and expected to continue to maintain his self-confidence and conviction that he could achieve what he came to Canada for. In his comments, Mark was expressing confidence in the fact that he understood how the system worked and was therefore quite capable of effectively negotiating and navigating the structures of racism that otherwise would operate as barriers to his success. Thus, it was not that he was colour-blind, but rather – in accordance with his youthful optimism, his immigrant drive, his Trinidad-referenced, generation-and-a-half Caribbean Canadian identity – like many other immigrant, marginalized, and Black youth, Mark believed he could sidestep the structural barriers of racism, and with his high performance in education and athletics would be able to realize his ambitions. After all, as he said, 'You can't beat destiny' (Anisef et al. 2000; Desai and Subramanian 2003; James 2003; Seat 2003).

Conclusion

'You can't beat destiny.'

Growing up, my mom would always encourage me not to follow people, first of all – not to follow this group, not to follow this person because they are doing something. Do what you think is right. So in that sense I was sort of pushed into being one who makes my own decisions and doesn't like to follow. In another sense, I always liked the thought of being somebody who is known for something, who is notable and who can be recognized, so I am forming my own destiny and I like that idea.

In his article, 'I Really Do Feel I'm a "1.5" Korean American scholar,' Kyeyoung Park (1999) makes the point that 'although biologically the notion of a "1.5" generation is absurd, the sociocultural characteristics and psychological experiences of the pre-adult immigrant are distinct from either the first or second generation ethnic American' (140). And with reference to W.E.B. Du Bois's concept of 'double consciousness' that is to be found among African Americans, Park posits that Korean Americans live a dual existence in the United States in the same way. This duality, Park argues, is especially evident among 1.5 generation young people who 'are neither Korean, American, nor Korean American,' while they are, at the same time, all three. The simultaneity of their being 'neither/nor' and 'both/all' distinguishes the 1.5 generation from both immigrant Korean and American-born Korean Americans (142). The same could be said of generation-and-a-half (or 1.5 generation) Canadians (Desai and Subramanian 2003; Minichiello 2000; Norquay 2000), especially Caribbean Canadians (James, 2005) and Mark as examples. Mark, on the one hand, emphasized that he is Trinidadian – 'I feel like I am a Trini' – but he liked being in Canada: 'Canada has been great.' His Trinidadian identification seemed to be related to what Trinidad had been able to offer him – a good grounding in, and respect for, education, and the opportunity to participate in national and international athletic activities and work towards realizing his athletic aspirations. In addition, he noted that it was in Trinidad where, in his formative years, he learned the fundamentals of discipline, respect, and politeness, which he claimed his Canadian peers did not have. The skills and mindset that were drilled into Mark in Trinidad explain his feelings for the country. Seemingly, then, his identification is related to how he felt about Trinidad and is not necessarily a rejection of Canada. For, after all, Canada provided the opportunity for him to escape the 'rat race of Trinidad'; to attend school, where his latent athletic talents were revealed, tested, and nurtured; and to attend university, where he was able to pursue the necessary education for his career in sports medicine. And it is in Canada where, like his role model Ato Bolton of the United States, Mark enrolled at the university in 2000 and is receiving his training to compete in both national and international sport arenas.

Mark's seeming reluctance to identify himself as a Canadian likely has to do with what he does not wish to become. He does not want to be like his Canadian-born (second-generation) peers of Caribbean origin, whom he views as fitting a stereotype: putting sports before their education, and hence doing poorly in their academic work, and paying more attention to the advice of their coaches than their parents, often because of the strained relationships they tended to have with their parents. As noted previously, Mark demonstrated how much he weighed his mother's advice in making a decision not to accept athletic scholarships to U.S. universities. Clearly, Mark wanted his mother and grandparents to be proud of him, and it did not matter that his mother did not 'have the time to come and watch' him run: 'I'm not one of those who would be angry because my mom can't [watch me],' he said, 'because she is a busy woman. She is trying to handle all the finances and be responsible for everything. So she is proud, and she supports me anyway.' In essence, Mark has appreciated the time, effort, and money that his mother and grandparents have invested in him, and seemed to feel morally obligated to meet their expectations. Compared to his Caribbean Canadian peers, Mark presented as a practical, pragmatic, careful, and cautious young man who wanted to be known, not because he fit the stereotypes but because he broke the stereotypes, exercised agency in establishing his own meaning in life, and demonstrated leadership. As he said, 'Well, I think most people are searching for their own meaning and essence in life. They want to be noted for something, whether it be in your studies or in your field or profession. I want to be noted for my athletic career, or, if that doesn't work out, then at least people can remember me as being able to achieve in school and achieve on the field.'

That Mark recognized the stereotypes and essentialism that apply to

Black youth, and took steps to contradict and challenge them, indicated that he was certainly not oblivious to individual and systemic racism as they might affect him. Here the 'double-consciousness' about which Du Bois writes in relation to Black Americans might be applied to how Black Canadians, and, in this case, Mark, understand and deal (or cope) with racism knowing it could be a barrier to the achievement of their career ambitions. 'It is,' writes Du Bois (1994), 'a peculiar sensation, this double-consciousness, sense of always looking at one's self through the eyes of others,' and a feeling of 'twoness – an American, a Negro; two souls, two thoughts, two unreconciled strivings; two warring ideals in one dark body, whose dogged strength alone keeps it from being torn asunder' (3). The duality and the dogged strength, as Mark revealed it, could be said to be his consciousness that racism exists, while simultaneously pretending that it would not be a barrier to his success. Such conceptualization must be understood in relation to Mark's status and experiences as a generation-and-a-half Caribbean Canadian who has not yet become cynical about the opportunities that exist in Canada. Mark's confidence and optimism that racism is not an insurmountable barrier might be explained by the fact that, at the time of writing, he had lived in Canada for only seven years, had the support and example of his immigrant mother, siblings, and grandparents, with whom he has a close relationship, and had achieved some successes. Hence, in Mark's mind, his future in Canada is secure, because it is his destiny.

Further, the double-consciousness is also evident in Mark's sense of home. If home is the place where comfort and confidence are nurtured, and safety, security, and stability are provided and attained and a perspective of the world is formulated and sustained, then, for Mark, as a diasporic Canadian, and specifically as a generation-and-a-half Caribbean Canadian, home necessarily involves a combination of his 'two worlds': Trinidad and Canada. Hence, it is through his understanding and imagination of both societies that we must understand Mark's constructed story, or stories, of his life, identity/ies, and aspirations. The 'twoness,' or duality, is represented in his perception of Trinidad as his birthplace, or 'roots,' a place that provided the foundational values upon which he has built his life and aspirations, and a place of belonging and cultural reference; and Canada as his place of residence, a place he 'likes,' that 'has been great' to him, and that has provided and continues to provide the opportunities on which he can base his future. This conceptualization means that home is not a fixed entity, space, or place with boundaries and/or borders, but is a fluid construction that is

informed and mediated by an individual's life-stage, context, and situation. Within this context, then, Mark's identification as a 'Trini' – intend-
ing to represent his Trinidadian roots and his Canadian existence –
should not be seen as confusing, erroneous, or irreconcilable; for it is the
strength of this duality that gives him his sustenance, nurtures his
ambitions, and, hence, his sense of home as demonstrated in the comfort, confidence, stability, and security he expressed in his 'feelings'
about his life and future.

Addendum

Upon completion of this essay, more than three years after he was first
interviewed, I gave it to Mark for his comments on my reading of his
life narrative. I also wanted him to further consider the consent he gave
me to tell his story, since his subsequent national profile in sport and his
unique status as a generation-and-a-half Caribbean Canadian would
make it difficult to strictly maintain his anonymity. As Sparkes (2000)
points out, it is difficult in a biographical study 'to disguise somebody
when they have a national profile in a specific sport' and at the same
time provide the necessary and sufficient details or 'thick description'
for the individual to be recognizable to himself and to others (20). Upon
returning the essay a day later (2 March 2004) on his way to track
practice, Mark and I talked for about an hour about its content and his
many notes, which explained or rationalized his earlier comments and
updated his activities further. He stated that he was comfortable with
the essay's content and agreed that I should proceed to submit it for
publication. We then went on to talk about his education and athletic
activities. He reported that he was doing well in university and still
working towards his degree in psychology and kinesiology, with the
expectation of going on to medicine afterwards. His mother has moved
to Europe, and he continues to live with his other siblings who are also
in university. He visits Trinidad annually to see his grandparents. Mark
recently competed in the OUA (Ontario University Championship)
indoor track meet and won his event. He figures that making the
Canadian team would be 'out of reach' for him given the standard here.

   In his notes on the essay, and the points which were reiterated in our
conversation, Mark pointed out that his identification as a 'Trini' is
because he thinks that 'there is no real Canadian identity.' He continued, 'I think Canada is about two or three generations away from a true
national identity. Many people you speak with in Toronto rarely say

they are Canadians. They're born somewhere in Europe, family is from somewhere in Asia or the Caribbean. Canada is different from the U.S. where national identity is firmly established.' He emphasized that it was not that he did not like Canada; in fact, he said he does not think he would return to live in Trinidad – 'maybe just to vacation for a month.' Thus, Canada, a country where he believes he will be able to realize his dreams while identifying as a 'Trini,' remains home for Mark. So this imagined culture and identity he insists he has been able to retain can be regarded as representative of the Canadian cultural value system. But given the complexity and elusiveness of culture, Mark, like many Canadians, will continue to live his Canadian 'imagined-Trini' existence while culturally participating and integrating successfully into our society, as evidenced by his keen knowledge of Canada's societal structures and how to navigate and negotiate them, and his questioning of the existence of a national cultural identity. In essence, despite his insistence otherwise, Mark has learned to be culturally Canadian, and he lives as such.

NOTES

1 Prof. Dwaine Plaza was the co-investigator on this study, which was conducted in 2000–2002. Of the 20 participants, 10 (5 males and 5 females) were second generation and the same number were generation-and-a-half Caribbean Canadians. The study was funded by the Centre for Excellence in Research in Immigrant Settlement (CERIS) in Toronto. A selected number of parents were also interviewed in an effort to triangulate the data.

2 This title is taken from the headline of a *Toronto Star* newspaper article, which read: 'Their fair day in court: Born in Jamaica, the three men accused in the death of Georgina Leimonis were a product of Canada' (8 December 1999). Two weeks later, the *National Post* reported on the deportation of a 22-year-old Guyanese male who was classified as a 'danger to the public.' The federal court judge noted that the individual had been living in Canada since he was 11 years old, hence 'an individual who has spent all of his youth and early adulthood in Canada and who can perhaps appropriately be described as a product of his environment in Canada rather than of the environment of his early life in Guyana' (23 December 1999).

3 1.5 generation is another way in which generation-and-a-half is represented. In doing so, scholars such as Park (1999) and Myers and Cranford

(1998) emphasize the unique experiences of this generation who immigrated prior to high school or early to mid-adolescence. But for the most part, scholars tend to lump these youth into the first- or second-generation group of immigrants. Park (1999) noted that 'immigration between the ages of six and ten places one as 1.7 generation; between eleven and twelve, 1.5 generation; between thirteen and fourteen, 1.2 generation. After graduating from high school, one is classified as the first generation' (p.140).

4 Mark also pointed out: 'I quickly realized that you needed to start younger in order to have the sort of handling skills with the ball.'

5 This explanation came in our follow-up conversation (2 March 2004) in which Mark 'retracted' his earlier statement in which he claimed that his schooling experience in Canada was 'easier' than in Trinidad. 'In retrospect,' he said, 'the main difference in schooling was the discipline [which] was strictly enforced in Trinidad.'

6 Mark reported that he received an entrance scholarship to the university based on his 'high 80s' high school grades, and it was renewable annually if he maintained the high grades.

7 Having been encouraged by some of his other coaches to try for a scholarship from an American university, Mark admitted that he 'sent down packages' to two big-name universities, but 'they didn't work out'; he never did hear from them.

8 In our follow-up (March 2004), Mark reported that he was injured and unable to go to these competitions.

9 In the follow-up (March 2004), Mark noted: 'I wouldn't be so confident if asked this question again. Let's just say, if you have talent, you should use it to the best of your abilities.'

10 In making this point, Mark asserted that 'it's a level playing field,' and that is why it was possible for Jesse Owens, a black American, to succeed in his sport. In referencing Owens, Mark was indicating that race was not a barrier because athletes 'all follow the same rules.'

REFERENCES

Agnew, Vijay. 2003. *Where I Come From*. Waterloo, ON: Wilfrid Laurier University Press.

Anisef, P., P. Axelrod, E. Baichman, C. James, and A. Turrittin. 2000. *Opportunities and Uncertainties: Life Course Experiences of the Class of '73*. Toronto: University of Toronto Press.

Anisef, Paul, and Kenise Kilbride, eds. 2003. *Managing Two Worlds: The Experi-*

ences and Concerns of Immigrant Youth in Ontario. Toronto: Canadian Scholars Press.

Boyd, Monica, and Elizabeth M. Grieco. 1998. Triumphant Transitions: Socioeconomic Achievements of the Second Generation in Canada. *International Migration Review* 32(4): 853–876.

Coleman, P.G. 1991. Aging and Life History: The Meaning of Reminiscence in Late Life. In *Life and Work History Analysis: Qualitative and Quantitative Developments,* ed. Shirley Dex, 124–136. New York: Routledge.

Dei, George S., and Agnes Calliste, eds. 2000. *Power Knowledge and Anti-Racism Education.* Halifax, NS: Fernwood Publishing.

Denzin, Norman K. 1996. *Interpret Ethnography: Ethnographic Practices for the 21st Century.* London: Sage.

Desai, Sabra, and Sangeeta Subramanian. 2003. Colour Culture and Dual Consciousness: Issues Identified by South Asian Immigrant Youth in the Greater Toronto Area. In *Managing Two Worlds: The Experiences and Concerns of Immigrant Youth in Ontario,* ed. P. Anisef and K. Kilbride, 118–161. Toronto: Canadian Scholars Press.

Du Bois, W.E.B. 1994. *The Souls of Black Folks.* New York: Dover Publications.

Foner, Nancy. 1997. The Immigrant Family: Cultural Legacies and Cultural Changes. *International Migration Review* 32(4): 961–974.

Garrod, A.C., L. Smulyan, S.I. Poweres, and R. Kilkenny. 2002. Adolescent Portraits: Identity, Relationships and Challenges. Boston: Ally and Bacon.

Gitlin, Andrew, Edward Buendia, Kristin Crosland, and Doumbia Fode. 2003. The Production of Margin and Center: Welcoming-Unwelcoming of Immigrant Students. *American Educational Research Journal* 40(1): 91–122.

Handa, Amita. 2003. *Of Silk Saris and Mini-Skirts: South Asian Girls Walk the Tightrope of Culture.* Toronto: Women's Press.

Henry, Annette. 1998. *Taking Back Control: African Canadian Women Teachers: Lives and Practice.* Albany, NY: State University of New York Press.

Henry, Frances. 1994. *The Caribbean Diaspora in Toronto: Learning to Live with Racism.* Toronto: University of Toronto Press.

Humphreys, Adrian. 1999. Guyana Doesn't Want Dumped Deportees. *National Post* (23 December) A1, 7.

James, Carl E. 2001. Encounters in Race, Ethnicity and Language. In *Talking about Identity: Encounters in Race, Language and Identity,* ed. C.E. James and A. Shadd, 1–8. Toronto: Between the Lines.

– 2002. Achieving Desire: Narrative of a Black Male Teacher. *International Journal of Qualitative Studies in Education* 15(2): 171–186.

– 2003. Schooling, Basketball and U.S. Scholarship Aspirations of Canadian Student Athletes. *Race, Ethnicity and Education* 6(2): 123–144.

– 2005. *Race in Play: Understanding the Socio-Cultural Worlds of Student Athletes.* Toronto: Canadian Scholars Press.

Li, Jun. 2001. Expectations of Chinese Immigrant Parents for their Children's Education: The Interplay to Chinese Tradition and the Canadian Context. *Canadian Journal of Education* 26(1): 477–494.

Lincoln, Y. 1993. I and Thou: Method, Voice, and Roles in Research with the Silenced. In *Naming Silenced Lives: Personal Narratives and the Process of Educational Change*, ed. D. McLaughlin and W.G. Tierney, 29–50. New York: Routledge.

Mascoll, Philip. 1999. Their Fair Day in Court: Born in Jamaica, the Three Men Accused in the Death of Georgina Leimonis Were a Product of Canada. *Toronto Star.* 8 December, C1, 3.

Minichiello, Diane. 2001. Chinese Voices in a Canadian Secondary School Landscape. *Canadian Journal of Education* 26(1): 77–96.

Munro, P. 1998. *Subject to Fiction: Some Teachers' Life Narratives and the Cultural Politics of Resistance.* Philadelphia: Open University Press.

Myers, Dowell, and Cynthia J. Cranford. 1998. Temporal Differentiation in the Occupational Mobility of Immigrant and Native-Born Latina Workers. *American Sociological Review* 63(1): 68–93.

Noguera, Pedro A. 2003. Joaquin's Dilemma: Understanding the Link Between Racial Identity and School-Related Behaviours. In *Adolescents at School: Perspectives on Youth, Identity, and Education*, ed. M. Sadowski, 19–30. Cambridge, MA: Harvard Education Press.

Norquay, Naomi. 2000. Where Is Here? *Pedagogy, Culture and Society* 8(1): 7–21.

Palmer, Hazelle. 1997. *'... But Where Are You Really From? Stories of Identity and Assimilation in Canada.* Toronto: Sister Vision Press.

Park, Kyeyoung. 1999. 'I really do feel I'm 1.5': The Construction of Self and Community by Young Korean Americans. *Amerasia Journal* 25(1): 139–163.

Plaza, Dwaine, and Alan Simmons. 1998. Breaking Through the Glass Ceiling: The Pursuit of University Training Among African Caribbean Migrants and Their Children in Toronto. *Canadian Ethnic Studies* 30(3): 99–120.

Seat, Rajko. 2003. Factors Affecting the Settlement and Adaptation Process of Canadian Adolescent Newcomers Sixteen to Nineteen Years of Age. In *Managing Two Worlds: The Experiences and Concerns of Immigrant Youth in Ontario*, ed. P. Anisef and K. Kilbride, 162–195. Toronto: Canadian Scholars Press.

Shadd, Adrienne. 2001. 'Where Are You Really From?' Notes of an 'Immigrant' from Buxton, Ontario. In *Talking about Identity: Encounters in Race, Language and Identity*, ed. C.E. James and A. Shadd, 10–16. Toronto: Between the Lines.

Solomon, R. Patrick. 1992. *Forging a Separatist Culture: Black Resistance in High School*. Albany, NY: State University of New York Press.

Sparkes, Andrew C. 2000. Illness, Premature Career-Termination, and the Loss of Self: A Biographical Study of an Elite Athlete. In *Sociology of Sport: Theory and Practice*, ed. R.L. Jones and K.A. Armour, 13–32. Essex, UK: Pearson Education.

Spence, Chris. 1999. *The Skin I'm In: Racism, Sport and Education*. Halifax, NS: Fernwood Publishing.

Statistics Canada. 2003. Ethnic Diversity Survey: Portrait of a Multicultural Society. Ottawa: Minister of Industry.

Waters, Mary C. 1999. *Black Identities: West Indian Immigrant Dreams and American Realities*. Cambridge, MA: Harvard University Press.

Zhou, Min. 1997. Segregation Assimilation: Issues, Controversies, and Recent Research on the New Second Generation. *International Migration Review* 31(4): 975–1008.

10 The 'Muslim' Diaspora and Research on Gender: Promises and Perils

HAIDEH MOGHISSI

In any project, turning ideas into workable tools and implementing abstract concepts within a practical organizational and administrative framework is a challenge for researchers. In large-scale comparative and collaborative projects, the integration of research activities, team members, and research results adds excitement as well as distress to the research process. Maintaining the focus while fostering creativity and allowing imaginative responses to the specific circumstances and opportunities that arise is a challenge. Incorporating suggestions and new insights as the project progresses can also be a difficult task. The researcher's sense of responsibility towards participants and about the outcome of the research, particularly when any type of marginalized community is involved, makes every step in the process both more rewarding and more demanding. Part of the difficulty in community-focused research is the need for accountability to those whose voices will be interpreted and who will be directly or indirectly affected by the research process or its findings. In a revealing example, Kathleen Rockhill (1986) describes the difficulty and the importance of bringing her own subjectivity to bear in the research she conducted. In re-examining transcripts of interviews from a research project she had done several years earlier, she realized that she had not considered or perhaps unconsciously she did not want to use the information female respondents had provided about violent experiences in her study of literacy programs for a group of Hispanic women. At the time, she had not found the information relevant to the subject of her research and had not included it in her analysis. She writes that she was alarmed by the potential interference of the researcher in the research findings. In her study, she had the power to determine what was and was not significant in the interview transcripts, and inevitably it affected her analysis of the data collected (Ristock and Pennell 1996, 66). In this case, the researcher acknowledged what she called a power play in her research, and was troubled by it. The point, however, is that not all researchers are as self-reflective and honest about their work as Rockhill. We all need to be alert to the possibilities of the abuse of power in the act of research.

In studying communities with distinct cultures, such as Islamic communities, we deal with people whose realities have remained hidden beneath official refugee documents, resettlement reports, and statistics that more often than not are influenced by prejudicial ideas and perceptions. We have the daunting task of capturing their overlooked lives, realities, activities, ideas, and feelings, and being mindful of harmful analysis and conclusions. We need to recognize and validate the agency of people whose voices are recorded. We also need to avoid speaking for them and justifying this act in the name of helping to expose discriminatory and demeaning practices. At the same time, as Joan Scott (1987), among others cautions us, researchers who work with marginalized groups should be active listeners, that is, they should not uncritically accept the respondents' perspective as representing the truth. To avoid essentializing the identity of the speaker, Scott argues, the researcher should be concerned as to why the speaker says what she says, whom she believes she is speaking to, and why.

In any case, working with a marginalized community is usually related to the researcher's hope that the findings will benefit the community in some way. At the least, the research should help demystify the activities, ideas, and practices of groups whose cultures are the subject of irresponsible theorizing and procedural and policy formulations. We need to engage in a dialogue with the researched, keep them informed about the goals of the project, and share the findings. It is also in the interest of the research to do so. From beginning to end – that is, from developing appropriate methodological tools for collecting data to analysing that data – we are repeatedly challenged by uncertainty, unanticipated nuances, and differing views and suggestions. We face new circumstances and events that need to be incorporated into the initial research plan, and we need to be prepared to make revisions to that plan. Keeping community researchers informed is not only necessary, it is also useful for making changes as painlessly as possible. In what follows, I will discuss some of the barriers and constraints encountered in a process of ongoing research that studies family dynamics in the process of migration and relocation.

Studying the effects of displacement on gender relations and the change in family dynamics among four disaporic Islamic communities is the goal of the Diaspora, Islam, and the Gender Project. The communities include Iranians, Afghans, Pakistanis, and Palestinians. All four communities are studied in Toronto and Montreal, but to identify the impact of specific exit and entry conditions on each dislocated community, each one is also studied in a different setting. For example, we also consider Iranians and Pakistanis in Britain, Afghans in Iran, and Palestinians in Jordan, the West Bank, and Gaza. With the Palestinians, we focus on life under social and economic conditions that arise from occupation and the impact of these conditions on family relations. Using a systemic and comparative method allows us to identify the impact of specific conditions on each community's experience and to compare and contrast their experiences with those of their counterparts outside the West.

The impact of gender on the experience of diasporic groups and the difference between men's reactions to the changes in gender roles that are inevitably part of life away from home are recurring themes in studies of diaspora and homeland (Kandiyoti 1977; Ali 1992; Afshar 1994; Grmela 1991; Nielson 1992; Walli 1995; Buijs 1996; Eastmond 1996; Flynn and Crawford 1998; Moghissi 1999; Mousavi 1999; Ashrafi and Moghissi 2002). We propose that gender as a differing factor in adjusting to relocation might be directly linked to the greater difficulty men have in re-establishing themselves in a new society in which every aspect of social life seems to conspire against their authority and sense of self-worth. Many men in the diaspora have to make a living under very difficult and often demeaning conditions; their jobs and pay are often at a lower level than their educational achievements and technical skills would indicate. Many face reduced standards of living and lose control over household money and children's conduct. Economic hardship and the loss of friends and social status provoke a deep emotional vulnerability. Many men rely more on family members, particularly their spouses, who are themselves struggling to adjust to new conditions in their lives and thus are sometimes unable to provide the necessary moral and emotional support. This lack of support becomes a new source of tension, straining family relations. To camouflage their sense of insecurity and the loss resulting from the inevitable changes in gender roles, many men try to blunt the demands for more egalitarian family and gender relations by resorting to religion and to a traditional cultural heritage that has sexist undertones.

The structural racism of the host countries and their interaction with patriarchy both within and without the family and the community is central to men's painful experience of dislocation. In contrast, the diasporic experience for women can be transformative. This observation is not meant to excuse the manipulation of culture, tradition, and religion by conservative men who are determined to maintain the structures and relations of male dominance. We hope to identify the forces from which conservatives in the diaspora draw strength. By so doing, we will also draw attention to dissimilarities rather than similarities among diasporic communities from Islamic cultures, and the great variety and complexity of practical experiences between these communities as well as among individuals within each community. That is to say, apparent similarities among Muslim societies in the application of the *Shari'a* often cloud significant differences between peoples of Islamic cultures in their ways of life and in the family and social relations that result from the complex web of class, ethnic, gender, religious, and regional factors. (Shari'a is the canon law of Islam that has evolved through time. Different versions of Shari'a govern all aspects of Muslim behaviour in different Islamic societies.) Thus, challenging homogenizing perceptions about cultural values and practices of diaspora from Islamic cultures, we suggest that one's attachment to cultural and religious values (including values that may be hostile to gender justice and equality within the family) must always be considered together with a range of differentiating variables.

To capture the experiences of the four communities, we analyse an individual's experience in the home as well as in the host country, together with the socioeconomic conditions and policies of the host. In the case of Palestinians, we look at the conditions of living under occupation that make them a diaspora in their homeland. To conduct this research, we have chosen a multiple method combining two major methodological perspectives: the comparative and the systemic. Our research instruments include oral interviews with immigrants and refugees, as well as with social workers, service providers, and informants in the community; questionnaires, administered in the communities; content analysis of community publications; and census data analysis. But to understand the environment in which we are conducting our study, we need to place it in the larger context in which studies that deal with Islam and gender are situated.

Islamic Diasporas

Despite the differing material conditions of displaced groups in adopted countries, and regardless of where the adopted country is, diasporic populations struggle with the feeling of not belonging. The sense of not belonging, or feeling like an eternal outsider, is perhaps most acute for migrants who are 'visible' as a result of their skin colour, dress code, publicly observable cultural practices, or simply their names. These aspects of their identity make them targets of stereotypical imagery and exclusionary practices. Migrants of Islamic cultures are among such groups. In fact, the rise of Islamic movements in the Middle East and South Asia has made migrants from Islamic cultures the target of renewed anti-Muslim sentiments and stereotypes about Islam's rigidity in the area of women's rights. This imagery has been deliberately promoted and politically manipulated by the media in the post-September 11 period. But even prior to the hyper-anti-Islam climate of 9/11, many individuals from diasporic Islamic cultures felt trapped by the essentialized and pre-given notions of cultural difference that prevented them from achieving a stable and dignified identity in their new country – an identity that would retain aspects of the moral and cultural practices of their homelands, but would do so under the protection of enforced legal equity. In the absence of a rigorously enforced ideal of equality that also makes room for cultural diversity, the individual migrant's psychological security and stability become fragile. The sense of insecurity is sometimes expressed through hostile reactions to the host country and its social values. This situation often occurs when those values appear to infringe upon the assumed 'private' sphere of life and family relations in the form of public policies and legal practices.

The outcome has been devastating for substantive and objective research in Islamic and gender studies. In this climate, homogenizing ideas about Islam and about Muslim women impose a fixed and non-negotiable identity on diasporic Islamic communities, and often create a strong sensitivity or resistance to becoming the subjects of research. Associated with this resistance is a sense of self-consciousness among researchers who are studying Islam and Islamic gender politics. Convinced of the biases involved in such studies – a conviction promoted by some religious leaders, certain Muslim scholars, and political elites in Islamic states – more conservative Islamic groups tend to boycott or dismiss scholarly work on Islam and gender practices that is of a critical nature. Sometimes respondents in such research projects may turn on the field researcher and make her the target of their anger and frustration. As one of our research partners in the United Kingdom stated, some Muslim communities feel they have been over-studied, and suffer from a sort of research fatigue. This situation has had a profound effect on researchers in the field. Afraid of being accused of Islamaphobia and critical of the racism that targets Muslim diasporas in Western cities, they tend to limit themselves and their research to less controversial issues.

This approach has not been ours. Our study uses what feminists have called 'conscious partiality,' as opposed to making claims of being 'value-free' and 'objective' and stressing the separation between researcher and researched. Our concern has been to document significant differences in how the sexes deal with dislocation as well as differences among various Islamic communities in their gendered cultural practices. We are conducting this research not only to understand and explain why these differences exist, but also in the hope of assisting, in some modest way, in bringing about change for the better. While aware of the complexities of the study and the sensitive nature of the issues that form the intellectual core of the project, we never thought we should shy away from asking hard questions in order to avoid offending our respondents. We hope the project's findings will help policymakers understand what prevents community members from different classes and strata from selectively accepting the social values of their adopted country, and what they consider as barriers to their participation in the new country's civic and political life. We also hope that by probing into these communities, the study might help provide its members with empowering tools of knowledge about their own social and cultural hang-ups and mental blocks that prevent them from adjusting to life in a socially, geographically, and temporally different setting. Acquiring such knowledge should lead to the development of 'a sense of collective influence over the social conditions of one's life,' which is the true meaning of community empowerment (Young 1994).

Including researchers from the community and representatives of the local population in the research process is a major step in the direction of making a study's results useful to both policymakers and the respective communities. It would certainly be reassuring to the users of any community-focused analysis to know that the subjects of the study have not been only targets of research, but its partners. This means providing the possibility for the communities to research themselves through active participation in the research process; to appreciate their struggles, sufferings, and triumphs; to recognize their moral agency; to validate the different sources of scholarly and practical knowledge and experiences they provide; and, as Cook and Fonow (1990) would have it, to allow the respondents to 'talk back' to the investigator (76). It also means being consistently open to new ideas and the feedback coming from the field researchers and the communities involved. In other words, doing research within communities requires a great degree of modesty and openness. We go into the research with certain leading ideas, but we have to be ready to rethink certain points. We don't know for sure. We conduct research in order to acquire knowledge, but to do so effectively we need to win the trust and confidence of the individuals and communities involved, without which we cannot explore the issues at hand and produce a reliable and ethically supportable analysis. Furthermore, as researchers we need to be aware of and committed to the fact that the qualitative and quantitative analyses may help prove or disprove the hypotheses that shape the conceptual framework of our study. We can discover unexpected factors that affect our respondents' lives provided we keep in mind that the purpose of the research is to investigate our subjects' experience and not merely to find evidence in support of ideas and hypotheses. Above all, we need to look at our research as a learning process for all, both the researchers and the researched.

In doing research among diasporic Islamic communities, we were very fortunate to succeed in securing the participation of a broad range of research partners, both from academe and from the communities themselves. This participation helped us to provide a clearer understanding of the objectives of the research, an understanding that has been shared with all those involved, and thus has been instrumental for the effective integration of research activities and findings. For example, our research among Afghan refugees in Iran was entirely conducted by members of the community in the country, under the supervision of a research partner who is also a staff member at the office of the United Nations High Commissioner for Refugees (UNHCR) in Tehran. The research in Palestine has also been conducted by community members and supervised by the research partners in the territories. Some of the field researchers have roots in the refugee camps. After participating in brainstorming sessions at the start of the research, and subsequently participating and organizing workshops on the site, our partners were able to supervise the data-collection processes with a great deal of flexibility and imagination, without losing sight of the main objectives or altering key questions that are central to the study. This has also been the case with the four communities in Canada, where the coordinators of the field research for each community are from these communities. Student researchers in fact conduct research under the supervision of community team leaders, whose participation in various consultation and training sessions organized by the project has prepared them for the task.

Unplanned opportunities and difficulties are part of any large-scale research project. For example, almost immediately after funding for our project was secured, we were faced with changing circumstances under which the research had to be conducted. The eruption of further violence in the Palestinian Territories, particularly in the West Bank and Gaza during the summer of 2001, imposed some changes in the process of research. In a sad and sharp contrast to the optimistic moods which prevailed during the summer of 1999 and the spring of 2000 when we discussed our research goals and plans with our Palestinian counterparts, we had to strategize on how to complete our research in what had become a war zone. Clashes at road junctions, raiding helicopters, explosive squads, and the systemic destruction of Palestinian infrastructures directly affected the work of international projects and nongovernmental organization (NGO) activities. Research activities in Palestine were postponed for a while, and even then they were continually interrupted because of the incursion by Israeli forces into Palestinian towns and cities during the second intifada. The imposition of travel restrictions, roadblocks, and closures made it difficult for the coordinator of the field research to meet appointments. Communications were cut off in a critical period between core project personnel and our Palestinian coordinator. Nonetheless, data collection progressed, under enormous difficulties and often under life-threatening conditions. The research was also affected by the increasingly volatile political environment of post-September 11. In fact, the day-to-day experiences of refugee and migrant communities underwent dramatic changes in Canada and elsewhere as a result of regressive measures such as 'security' and 'anti-terrorism' acts in the host countries that targeted Muslims and diasporas from Islamic cultures in particular. The restrictive measures fuelled anti-immigration sentiments and induced suspicion and distrust of the 'Muslims' in terrified citizens of Western government, causing frustration and anger among members of diasporic communities, and making them reluctant to speak freely of their experiences. We had to spend more time on some steps in our research, partly because we were obliged to take energetic but more cautious measures to work with members of Islamic communities. Such challenges are not unusual in research undertaken among dislocated communities. Nevertheless, when our project was funded, no one expected the tragedy of

September 11, which occurred only a few months later. Nor did anyone anticipate its social and political consequences for diasporic Islamic cultures – ironically, the very subjects of this study. The question of winning the trust of the target communities became even more important in the aftermath of September 11, as the 'war on terrorism' appeared to many to have become a war against citizens of non-European ethnic background. An extensive buildup of intelligence and surveillance apparatuses, racial and ethnic profiling, widespread questioning and the detention of individuals of Middle Eastern origin, the blockage of bank accounts or businesses owned by persons from the Middle East, and racist depictions of the Middle East, Islam, and Muslims by the media have all continued to create fear and distrust among the groups who are the subject of our study. We tried to address these concerns and overcome self-consciousness in the communities, as well as a certain defensiveness that we felt as researchers, through various means such as organizing workshops and mini conferences on these issues. We also revised our pilot questionnaire to take the new situation into account, and extended our consultation with community members to test further the appropriateness of certain questions.

Preparation and administration of the questionnaires in different countries also posed certain problems. For instance, in addition to the written translations of the questionnaires in five languages, for Pakistanis living in the United Kingdom the questionnaires needed to be translated orally into Punjabi as well as Urdu. Generally, each translation required several drafts to disentangle cultural knots and get the appropriate equivalencies. Some questions did not make much sense in a non-Western context. For example, asking about the use of the Islamic dress code or the consumption of halal meat made no sense in Muslim societies and environments. In addition, changes were required, conceptually and operationally, in the Arabic questionnaires administered in the West Bank and Gaza under military occupation, to achieve equivalencies between the meanings of 'dislocation' and 'diaspora' there, and among refugees and migrants in the West. Subtle cultural differences emerged, as well, in the actual administration of the questionnaire, as we discovered a number of fascinating but potentially daunting intragroup peculiarities. Among Pakistanis, for example, Ahmadi Muslims would not accept Sunni interviewers, and Sunnis would not sit for interviews with Ahmadis. The Urdu translation in Canada also created some problems, since one translator from a Pakistani community took it upon himself to change the questions that he found un-Islamic. He also tried to discourage the student researcher from joining the research team because he thought some of the questions regarding domestic violence infringed upon the community's sense of dignity and would tarnish its reputation. In addition, strategies had to be developed to ensure privacy during interviews, when spouse and family intruded. Before interviews could proceed with some groups, such as Afghans and Iranians, the community team leaders would not suffice, since it was felt, culturally, that approvals had to be negotiated at the higher level. The project director and co-investigators had to participate in initial meetings with the communities' respective associations to prepare the ground for subsequent meetings with field researchers. In addition, before Palestinians could be interviewed, special efforts were required to establish communications, since the community was widely dispersed throughout the Greater Toronto Area (GTA) and included Christians as well as those of Muslim origin. (The study is restricted to individuals of Muslim origin.) Locating potential Palestinian respondents took more time than anticipated. The reason was that until the establishment of the Palestinian Authority in the occupied territories, following the Oslo Accord, Palestinian refugees came to Canada as citizens of various Arab countries. Finally, some of the researchers found that without regular attendance at community centres and local mosques, it was sometimes hard to win the trust of the more religious respondents.

Interview: The Site of Interaction or Tension

Anyone who has been involved in an interview process for a specific research project, either as a researcher or a respondent, knows that the process can be either an enjoyable or a stressful experience – or both. It can also become the site of tensions between the researcher and the researched. Obviously, the interview and what the researcher draws from it can affect the accuracy and reliability of the analysis. Many interesting points have been raised by researchers in our projects, arising from their experiences in working with the communities involved. For example, sometimes interviewers would lose the chance to conduct an interview simply because it had to involve two individuals who were in a potentially conflictive or contradictory relationship. This has been the case when a husband insisted that his wife be interviewed in his presence, or that children and youth be interviewed in the presence of parents. Our approach has been to refrain from conducting an interview if it can only take place in the presence of a second party. Nevertheless, we have always explained why it is important to conduct interviews in this way.

Another recurring issue among some minority communities, but specifically among the camp refugees in the Palestinian territories, has been the overeagerness of the interviewees to talk. While many participants in an interview session need encouragement to talk, others often like attention and appreciate having their opinions sought, as they find an opportunity to express their joy, frustration, or simply their experiences in a particular situation or process. For many, this may represent the rare occasion when they feel their thoughts and opinions are sought and recorded, or simply that they are listened to. Sometimes the information about family history, current marital status, the number of children, and so on, which was recorded, far exceeded what the questionnaires required. These cases caused problems for the data-inputting process. At other times, family members would join the session, offering their own perspectives, or 'correcting' the information provided by the individual respondent.

In our training and consultation workshops, we remind the researchers that although one wants to encourage an honest, determined, and even passionate response to questions, they should find a way to keep the conversations on topic so that key questions do not remain unanswered after one or two hours of talking. Aggressive behaviour has also been reported in some cases. For example, one man volunteered to sit in for an interview with one of the female researchers only to give fake answers to all questions as a way of dismissing the research and humiliating the interviewer. In another case, after responding to the questions, the respondent exploded with anger and became verbally abusive, and the researcher had to flee the site before being physically assaulted. Obviously, some questions may cause discomfort for respondents; in particular, questions about interpersonal dynamics in the respondent's family, roles (and role changes), family members' responsibilities, sources of tension and conflict prior to and after migration, and changes in the hopes and aspirations shared (or in dispute) within the family may be problematic. Respect for the respondents, transparency, and honesty about intentions and research goals go a long way towards easing such tensions. It must be noted that the extreme cases mentioned earlier have been exceptions. Generally, the researchers' experiences in working with the communities have been instructive and the respondents courteous.

We emphasize the importance of being an interested listener, as well as a focused and sensitive one, particularly when asking questions that require some emotional commitment and make respondents think again about their lives. Generally, interviewees will be more forthcoming if they feel their opinions are shared by the interviewer, or at least are fully understood and appreciated. Obviously, this means showing solidarity and empathy, but it also helps when the interviewer's role is closely related to being part of the community to which the interviewees belong, and when respondents know that the researcher shares some of their experiences, although not necessarily in the same context or situation. This is of course a point that needs careful consideration, as, in some cases, individuals do not wish to share humiliating experiences, failures, and the intimate details of their lives with members of their own communities. This reluctance is more profound in cultures where saving face and keeping up public appearances are very important to individuals. In these cases, the acceptance by and approval of the community define the individual's psychological health and sense of security.

We have also been mindful of the fact that many participants in our interview sessions or focus groups have to deal with the practical difficulties of displacement, and that they will sometimes call upon us in capacities other than that of interviewer. Our approach has been that we do not do counselling. On the other hand, we are prepared to provide simple advice on certain practical matters, such as how to contact appropriate organizations and individuals, immigration lawyers, legal aid, training classes, specific social services, women shelters, and so on. Therefore, basic information about relevant available services in Toronto, Tehran, or other sites of research is needed by the interviewer. It is always a question of knowing how far to go and avoiding an intrusive approach. While it would be ethically irresponsible to press unwanted 'help' upon a respondent in the course of the interview, it is also wrong to stir up something in a conversation that the interviewee might not be able to cope with afterwards. This is a general guideline for all social science research that involves human participants, but particularly so with the communities that we work with, and the specific subject matter with which we are concerned. Most certainly, we do not want to harm our respondents by unnecessary involvement or interference that might only add to their difficulties.

Community-focused research no doubt has its challenges and its rewards. It can be enjoyable and enriching as well as emotionally and mentally exhausting. What can keep the investigator going, more than anything else, is a feeling that the research is a tool for analysing and exposing power relations in the process of the research itself, as well as in the analysis of the data in order to change the relations that keep people from realizing their full humanity.

REFERENCES

Afshar, H. 1994. Muslim Women in West Yorkshire: Growing Up with Real and Imaginary Values Amidst Conflicting Views of Self and Society. In *The Dynamics of 'Race' and Gender: Some Feminist Interventions*, ed. H. Afshar and M. Maynard. London: Taylor and Francis.

Ali, Y. 1992. Muslim Women and the Politics of Ethnicity and Culture in Northern England. In *Refusing Holy Orders: Women and Fundamentalism in Britain*, ed. G. Sahgal and N. Yuval-Davis. London: Virago Press.

Ashrafi, A., and H. Moghissi. 2002. Afghans in Iran: Asylum Fatigue Overshadows Islamic Brotherhood. *Global Dialogue* 4(4).

Buijs, G., ed. 1996. Introduction to *Migrant Women Crossing Boundaries and Changing Identities*. Washington, DC: BERG.

Cook, J.A., and M.M. Fonow. 1990. Knowledge and Women's Interests: Issues of Epistemology and Methodology in Feminist Sociological Research. In *Feminist Research Methods: Exemplary Readings in the Social Sciences*, ed. J. MacCarl Nielsen. San Francisco; Boulder, CO; and London: Westview.

Eastmond, M. 1996. Reconstructing Life: Chilean Refugee Women and the Dilemmas of Exile. In *Migrant Women: Crossing Boundaries and Changing Identities*, ed. G. Buijs. Oxford and Washington, DC: BERG.

Flynn, K., and C. Crawford. 1998. Committing 'Race Treason': Battered Women and Mandatory Arrest in Toronto's Caribbean Community. In *Unsettling Truths: Battered Women, Policy, Politics, and Contemporary Research in Canada*, ed. K. Bonnycastle and G.S. Rigakos. Vancouver: Collective Press.

Grmela, S. 1991. The Political and Cultural Identity of Second Generation Chilean Exiles in Quebec. In *Immigrant and Refugees in Canada: A National Perspective on Ethnicity, Multiculturalism and Cross-cultural Adjustment*, ed. S.P. Sharma and A.M. Ervin. Saskatoon: University of Saskatchewan.

Kandiyoti, D. 1977. Sex Roles and Social Change: a Comparative Appraisal of Turkish Women. *Signs: Journal of Women in Culture and Society* 3.

Moghissi, H. 1999. Home Away from Home: Iranian Women, Displacement, Cultural Resistance and Change. *Journal of Comparative Family Studies* 30(2).

Mousavi, N. 1999. Afghani Women in Iran. Paper presented to Tenth Annual

Conference of Iranian Women's Studies Association of North America. Montreal, 28 June.

Nielsen, J. 1992. *Muslims in Western Europe*. Edinburgh: Edinburgh University Press.

Ristock, Janice, and Joan Pennell. 1996. *Community Research as Empowerment*. Toronto: Oxford University Press.

Rockhill, Kathleen. 1986. *The Chaos of Subjectivity in the Ordered Halls of Academe*. Toronto: Centre for Women's Studies in Education, OISE.

Scott, J., 1987. Women's History and the Rewriting of History. In *The Impact of Feminist Research in the Academy*, ed. C. Farnham. Bloomington: Indiana University Press.

Walli, S. 1995. Muslim Refugee, Returnee, and Displaced Women: Challenges and Dilemmas. In *Faith and Freedom: Women's Human Rights in the Muslim World*, ed. M. Afkhami. Syracuse, NY: Syracuse University Press.

Young, I. M. 1994. Punishment, Treatment, Empowerment: Three Approaches to Policy for Pregnant Addicts. *Feminist Studies* 20(1).

11 The Quest for the Soul in the Diaspora

VIJAY AGNEW

Hinduism is part of an ancient culture and civilization that inspires particular pride among Hindus who live in the diaspora. When Hindu immigrants are asked to explain the tenets of their faith they sometimes struggle to explain the 'great tradition' that, they believe, is found in sacred texts and incorporates the 'truth' of Hinduism. They give less importance to the many rituals that are practised in specific locales by Hindus either individually at home or with their communities. Disagreements abound, among the faithful, when they attempt to isolate and define that which is an 'authentic' practice or precept of Hinduism from the diverse hybrid, 'inauthentic' practices in the diaspora. Perhaps the faithful are concerned that if they gave importance to the little traditions of Hinduism it would make their religion seem not universal, distinctive, and distinguished. However, in contradiction to such fears, Assayag (2003) argues that all traditions are social inventions, for in essence they are mere practices that have persisted over time and their importance lies in the meaning and significance that they have for their devotees rather than their conformity with any one interpretation of the scriptures.

The practice of religion takes place in a social context that lends its rituals specific meaning and makes its boundaries unstable and fluid. Hinduism is practised in diverse ways in India and in the diaspora. Dynamic acculturation with the norms embedded in the social context of the location gives rise to local practices that take on the tint and flavour of the culture in which they are being practised. Such local and diverse expressions of Hinduism are not static and permanent; rather, they are fluid, temporary, and change over time. Rituals evolve and their interpretation subtly transforms the meaning of the practices for its devotees, preventing the religion from being reduced to an organic set of beliefs in which all cultural manifestations have a fixed and unchanging place. Change resists petrifaction and allows the religion to meet the spiritual and emotional needs of its devotees over time.

In the diaspora the practice of Hinduism is mediated by the politics of race and racism that find expression in queries such as, 'Where do you come from?' or are encoded in talk of Hinduism's mystical and exotic appeal. The binary distinction is between the unworldly, non-materialist, god-loving Hindu and the rational, progressive, and materialistic Westerner. But embedded in such distinctions are hierarchical evaluations about cultures and people that assign some beliefs the status of the norm relegating the rest as 'Other' and also implicitly inferior (Said 1979). Gurus and swamis from India have successfully marketed the belief that they know the secret of attaining nirvana and can impart it to Westerners, at a cost, either in India or elsewhere. Westerners who are disenchanted and alienated from their cultures have been harshly critical of its materialism, and as an alternative have sought solace and comfort in searching for nirvana with and from Indians in ashrams in India and America. In this chapter I describe some of the diverse practices of Hinduism in different locations in India and the diaspora and analyse the fault lines of subscribing to binary distinctions between the materialistic West and the spiritual India.

Varanasi

In the late 1990s, I was in Varanasi (known historically as Banaras and Kashi), one of the prime cities of pilgrimage for Hindus and a favoured place for them to die and be cremated. 'Death in Kashi is not a feared death, for here the ordinary God of Death, frightful Yama, has no jurisdiction. Death in Kashi is death known and faced, transformed and transcended' (Diana Eck, 'Banaras City of Light,' cited in Benaras, India, 2003). The entire city is dedicated to Lord Shiva, and myth has him still living there watching over the twenty-two thousand or so temples build around his worship. Varanasi is 'fierce, full of death, austere yet grandly beautiful, sinister, if not dangerous and singularly attractive' (Roberts 1994, 334), and attracts hordes of pilgrims and Western tourists interested in religious India.

Varanasi is on the banks of the River Ganges, or Ganga Mata (Mother Ganges, as it is called colloquially). The myth is that the waters of Ganga Mata are the fluid medium of Lord Shiva's divine essence;

Hindus believe that a bath in the river will wash away all their sins, that the river:

> sanctifies many cities as she flows from the sacred Himalayan peaks, twisting and turning south through the parched lowlands. Like many rivers in myth and imagination, the meandering of Mother Ganges represents the inexorable wandering of life itself. The image, of course, is in the Vedas, part of that great cycle: sun, cloud, rain, river, ocean, sun, cloud.
>
> The Ganges is not always a gentle mother. Sometimes, she overflow her banks, washing away homes, temples, palaces. Sometimes she withholds her life-giving waters, running so low that the fields shrivel and die, the dhobis wash clothes in mud, corpses get lodged on rocks and tree stumps, vultures circle above, the air stinks of waste and death. (Roberts 1994, 339)

My sister and I were in Varanasi from Toronto as tourists, and we hired a guide, a young man, to show us around. He mistook us for Westerners (which in a way we were), and attempted, in his limited English, to describe the religious significance of the city and tell us myths about the Hindu gods. We asked him to speak to us in Hindi, hoping thereby to get more detailed and nuanced explanations, but we still could not follow what he was saying, for his speech was unlike the colloquial urban Hindi with which we were familiar. He was delighted, however, when he realized he could earn his living comfortably for a day or two, rather than struggling with a foreign language.

One of the most desired spots to visit at Ganga Mata is near the *ghats*, or banks, of the river, and our guide recommended that we watch sunrise there. Accordingly, we went to the river at five o'clock the next morning. We were surprised to find crowds of white Western tourists there, being avidly pursued by local men hoping to sell them religious knickknacks or rent them rickety, dilapidated boats, along with their services as guides-cum-boatmen. We took a boat and went down the river a bit, but the architectural details of the historic buildings along the ghats where the bodies are cremated were obscured, and all we could see were piles of ashes and charred, dirty walls. On stairs leading down from the buildings to the river sat crowds of men, either emerging from a bath or preparing to go into the water. Some stood knee-deep in the river looking up at the sky, their hands folded and totally immersed in their prayers. (Women are assigned a separate and secluded area for bathing, where they go into the river dressed in their saris;

tourists are not encouraged to go into these areas, and we did not do so either.)

The romantic idea of my sister and I enjoying the sunrise while gently gliding down the river in a boat and listening to the chanting of prayers was far from our reality. Any hope of enjoying the morning was marred by the exceedingly filthy waters and the crowd of boats around us, from some of which men were loudly hawking goods. Despite the condition of the dark, green, muddy waters, some of these boatmen still tried to sell us little brass urns of *Ganga jal* (water of the Ganges) to take back with us so that our family, friends, and homes could be purified in a ritual of sprinkling and praying. A dead body wrapped in a sari, apparently a woman, floated in the water while we all went about our affairs nonchalantly. Such apparent suicides by poor, homeless women are common and are taken by the local people as routine.

While we moved along in the rickety boat, our guide pulled out a small, crumpled brown bag from his pocket and threw it into the river. I remonstrated with him for further polluting the water, but he defended himself by saying that the bag contained wilted rose petals and garlands of marigolds from the previous day's prayers in his home. He contended that it would be sacrilegious to dispose of what had been an offering to the gods with the household garbage. He was also knowledgeable enough to argue with me that the flowers were biodegradable and would not further pollute the river.

After watching the sunrise, we went through narrow, winding lanes to see the temples around the ghats. Along these lanes sat many *sadhus* and swamis, holy men who had put on their 'costumes' hoping to profit from the tourist's predilection for photographs of the unusual, quaint, and exotic. Some of them did indeed look very picturesque as they sat with their *dhotis* (plain cloths covering the legs to the knees or ankles) snugly tucked around their waists and their muscular, well-oiled upper torsos nakedly and proudly displayed. They were wearing around them the sacred, woven threads of the Brahmin caste, and had big chunky *malas* (necklaces of wooden beads, akin to a rosary, that are used for praying) around their necks. Their foreheads were lavishly smeared with ashes, and some had put a bit of red powder, considered auspicious, on the middle of their foreheads as well. They sat cross-legged on low stools or on the bare ground, proudly holding up a *trishul* (trident) or a wooden staff. Some who were sitting against a wall had written prayers and stanzas in white chalk or had painted religious symbols behind them. They accommodated tourists, like us, by allow-

ing us to take their pictures, and we handed over the expected obliga-
tory donation to them.

The entire scene was a performance for the benefit of Western tourists
and exploited our stereotypes of the spiritual and religious India. The
sadhus and swamis had sold us their images, and we were free to
impute – or impose – any interpretation or meaning that suited our
fancy. Perhaps it is images like these, along with the history of swamis
and gurus coming to bring enlightenment to Westerners, that have
reinforced stereotypes of the 'spiritual India' and the 'materialistic West.'
Like many other binary distinctions, however, this is a simple caricature
of reality. India's spirituality has a strong vein of materialism embedded in it, and the materialism of the West is envied by many a poor,
religious Indian eking out a living.

Learning about Other Hindus and Hinduisms

When I first came to the University of Toronto in 1971 to study, and
lived at the graduate residence, students there would ask questions
about India's poverty and its religion (by which they almost always
meant Hinduism). India had an exotic appeal for them, and their attitude towards the country and its people was generally empathetic.
They were critical of the British for their colonization of the country, and
a few commented on the common colonial history of India and Canada,
although none of us knew enough about each other's countries to make
critical, comparative comments. (Some British Governors General in
Canada, such as Lord Minto and Marquess of Dufferin, Willingdon,
and Landsdowne, went subsequently to India as viceroys.) The knowledge of these students about India came from their familiarity with the
so-called 'hippies' and the idealistic youth rebellions of the 1960s in the
United States and Canada.

In the mid-to-late sixties, American students who abhorred their
country's involvement in the war in Vietnam were staging massive
protests at university campuses. They were critical of the American
military's use of defoliants, which was wreaking havoc in rural Vietnam and causing the death of Vietnamese civilians. At the residence, I
met several white American males who were called 'draft dodgers,'
though they saw themselves as conscientious objectors to an immoral
war. Some of these students asked me questions about the grass-roots
movements in India; one of them even knew about the Naxalbari movement, a socialist peasant revolt of the 1960s in Bengal. They also asked

me about the caste system, and, although they tried to be discreet, their disapproval of the treatment meted out by Indian society to the untouchables – the casteless and disenfranchised poor – came through.

Other students peppered me with questions about Hindu philosophy and particularly about transcendental meditation, of which I knew little at the time. These students were knowledgeable about the hippies' (and the Beatles') fascination with India (among other things), and so knew a little bit about Hinduism. The hippies, who were disdainful of the establishment and particularly of its materialism and consumerism, were in search of Truth and Happiness. They had lived in communes, experimented with psychedelic drugs, and practised transcendental meditation. In the Orientalist imagination of the hippies, India was exotic, mythical, mystical, and spiritual; it was not materialistic, rational, or scientific.

Some hippies had travelled to India to experience firsthand what they imagined to be its spiritual, nonmaterialistic culture. They were seeking to acquire good karma and enlightenment, but instead were victimized by their own ignorance and enthusiasm for their spiritual quest. The hippies, whose imagination of India was aided to a large extent by drugs, were cheerfully exploited by sadhus, gurus, and the people on the street. 'The seduction lay in the chaos. They [i.e., the hippies] thought they were simple. We thought they were neon. They thought we were profound. We knew we were provincial. Everybody thought everybody else was ridiculously exotic and everybody got it wrong' (Mehta 1979, 5).

I had seen some hippies on the streets of Bombay when I had lived there in the sixties. Their odd combination of Indian and Western clothing made them stand out, even though they were white like other European and North American tourists. Some even walked around barefoot, much like the local beggars, and looked dirty, ragged, and lost. But since I never had an opportunity to speak to them while in Bombay, I had no way of knowing if these hippies were poor, chose to dress that way, or were simply on drugs. I met one hippie in Toronto in 1971, a white Canadian student who had spent time in India. She had been drawn to India by its spirituality, but had lived on an extremely limited budget in unclean surroundings. I don't know if she received spiritual enlightenment from the gurus there, but she did contract the hepatitis that had since been plaguing her. Others were less lucky and had to be flown back by their embassies diseased, malnourished, or 'trapped in inarticulate fears' (Mehta 1979, 22).

One of the earliest attempts to introduce India's spiritual knowledge to the West was by Swami Vivekananda, who set up the Vedanta Society in Chicago in the 1890s. His visit was announced in the *Boston Evening Transcript* with the headline, 'The Hindus at the Fair, Plain Talk of Leading Heathens' (Israel 1994, 47). American intellectual elites who perceived themselves and their society as rational and progressive and Hindus as exotic and esoteric had the opportunity to acquaint themselves with Hinduism from one of its philosophers. Vivekananda spoke of India's spirituality, and argued that it had given India a unique role in a world dominated by the technical, military, and economic prowess of the West (48). He explained that Vedanta philosophy posits a 'non-duality between the divine and the essence of humanity.' Vivekananda eschewed idolatry, and instead focused on Hinduism as a process of spiritual development: 'The Hindu religion does not ... believe in a certain doctrine or dogma, but in realizing; not in believing, but in being and becoming' (cited in Prentiss 2003).

'Transcendentalist poets' such as Ralph Waldo Emerson, Henry David Thoreau, and Walt Whitman saw India as the 'spirit,' and as mysterious, emotional, sentimental, and inscrutable. Thoreau wrote: 'In looking at Menu, Saadi and Bhagvat [ancient Hindu texts], life seems in the east a simple affair, only a tent, a little rice, and ass's milk; and not, as with us, what commerce made it, a feast whose dishes come from the equator and both poles' (cited in Prashad 2000, 16). This distinction between the spiritual India and the materialistic West became widely accepted in both places, even though it was inaccurate, because it glossed over the exploitation of India by colonialism and the consequent poverty of its population.

In the 1960s, however, a different kind of guru came to the United States, drawn by the subculture's need for spiritual enlightenment. The most well known was Maharishi Mahesh Yogi, who popularized transcendental meditation there. Others, such as Swami Satchinananda, introduced hatha yoga; Swami Muktananda brought siddha yoga to North Americans (Knott 1998, 77; Prashad 2000, 51–52). Gita Mehta (1979) describes a session in New York led by an Indian guru who was propagating among his followers, who had located the eyeball as the focal point of all physical and spiritual distress, an unusual meditation technique:

The guru ... had his hands folded serenely over his belly and was rolling his eyeballs. We bowed our heads. After half an hour of bowed heads I got restless and sneaked a glance to see how the faithful were getting on. To my surprise the faithful were emulating the guru, following his eyeballs with their own. Apparently, twice a week these sophisticated urbanites would shed their brushed denims for badly tied saris and come and roll their eyeballs at each other for an hour, in deadly earnest. True believers, convinced that if they rolled their eyes long enough they would, like the guru, acquire healing powers. (55)

Such self-styled Indian gurus and swamis exploited the fascination of American youth with India's spiritual heritage for their personal profit. Their devotees, often young, idealistic, and privileged, played at being poor. Their beneficence enabled the gurus to lead a materialistic, affluent, jet-set life. These entrepreneurial gurus and swamis, many with advanced university degrees in the sciences and the arts, wished to cater to the souls of the Americans by setting up ashrams in the United States and India. The novelist Ruth Prawer Jhabvala (1987; 1998), a Polish-German married to an Indian, often discusses this theme in her writings. Her Western characters are routinely portrayed as idealistic, naïve, well-off, but misguided. They are in India to seek solace and comfort in its spirituality. Instead, their vulnerabilities are exploited by shrewd gurus for profit. The kinds of gurus that came to the West or who gained a following among Westerners in India were quite unlike the mostly poor, humble, and mantra-chanting gurus and swamis that I had known in India.

Some gurus, less flamboyant and media-savvy than Maharishi Mahesh Yogi, came to Toronto, but they did not make a big splash in the newspapers. Sometimes, however, I saw small groups of Hare Krishna devotees on the streets of downtown Toronto, chanting, 'Hare Rama, Hare Krishna,' while clanging small bells and cymbals in rhythm. The men had shaven heads and wore clean, saffron-coloured dhotis and long *kurtas*, or shirts. Ashes were smeared on the centre of their foreheads. The women were also dressed in saffron cotton saris tucked neatly around their waists, their hair pulled back, and a *bindi* (red dot) on each forehead. They would slowly dance to the rhythm of their chanting as they sang. Most times they greeted passersby pleasantly by joining hands in a *namaste*, or greeting, saying 'Hare Krishna' and handing out devotional literature. When I passed them by, they seemed to be smiling at me more broadly and genially as they handed over their flyers and pamphlets. But to me they were not a reminder of 'home' or of my Hinduism, for their rituals were totally unlike any I had seen before.

Being a Hindu Girl in Delhi

During the first few months I was in Toronto, friends introduced me to the Hare Krishna temple on Avenue Road, north of Bloor Street. A fair-sized, impressive stone building that was originally a Baptist church, it housed the devotees who lived an ascetic life of prayer and devotion (Israel 1994, 61). The Hare Krishna movement had been started in North America by A.C. Bhaktivedanta, who created the International Society of Krishna Consciousness in New York City in 1965. He taught young Americans *bhakti*, based on the teachings of a Hindu saint, Chaitanya. *Bhakti* is a Sanskrit word meaning sharing, participation, and devotion. It has three interrelated premises: 'that humankind shares in the nature of divinity; that humankind must participate in the worship of divinity through action – especially chanting God's name; and [that] humankind must be guided by devotion to God and to a spiritual guru' (cited in Prentiss 2003).

I went to the temple on a Sunday, and although I am familiar with Hindu rituals and prayers, I found this to be a most unusual spectacle. A group of believers, almost all white, had gathered in a central hall and were in the throes of a devotional frenzy of singing and dancing. Some were in a trance-like state, their eyes closed as they swayed and loudly chanted. Over the next hour, the volume of the music slowly picked up, and as its rhythm also sped up, so did the accompanying dance of the devotees. I watched, mesmerized, not sure whether I was at a prayer meeting or a dance spectacle. It did not, however, have any resonance for me, and I remained emotionally distant from the proceedings.

The practice of Hinduism in Toronto was quite different from any I had known in Delhi or Bombay, yet it was just one more manifestation of thousands of different rituals and practices throughout the world, and even in different parts of India. There is no authentic or pure Hinduism; rather, it comprises a variety of different philosophical approaches, thousands of deities with their associated mythologies and iconographies, and innumerable ritual practices. Perhaps they are better referred to as Hinduisms.

Religion, itself, is a word of Western origin meaning the bond between people and their gods. *Hinduism* was a term used in the nineteenth century by Orientalist scholars to describe the religion of the 'Hindoos' who lived around the River Indus. Over time, the use of this term was broadened to include the entire population of India. Originally, *Hindoo* signified an ethnic and national identity, but it became synonymous with religion after the discovery by the British of Vedic scriptures and the Brahmin caste and class. British Orientalist Charles Wilkins, an employee of the East India Company, translated the *Bhagavat-Gita* into English in 1785, and William Jones translated the *Manusmriti* (or religious scriptures) in 1789. They presented Hinduism by demonstrating its antiquity and endorsing its ethical and philosophical doctrines. French Jesuit Abbé Dubois wrote an interpretation of Hinduism entitled *Hindu Manners, Customs, and Ceremonies*; it was translated into English in 1815 and became widely used by Europeans who were eager to learn about the religious culture of India.

Hinduism, like some other religions, has been historically described by using the practices of Christianity as the norm, with references to gods, scriptures, institutions or churches, and priests. Using such a mode of description, it could be said that Hinduism has one god – one ultimate reality – but many gods and goddesses, a multitude of scriptures rather than one book, Brahmins but no priests in the Christian sense, and no central institution like the Church. There is no core creed or set of common teachings in Hinduism; importance lies instead with rituals and myths. These descriptions, however, leave out significant aspects of Hinduism, such as its caste system and its popular rituals and practices. The Hindu philosopher Sarvepalli Radhakrishnan declared Hinduism to be 'a way of life,' not separate from society and politics but part of it, and it is in this way that many Hindus live their faith (Knott 1998, 70–71).

The Hinduism that I practised as a child was ritualistic and mythological, not philosophical. Religion permeated the home environment; it was everywhere and nowhere. I was taught to show respect for the tenets of Hinduism, to accept it on faith, and not to question or express scepticism about it (not that I knew enough to do so). Rather, I adopted as a child and young adult an unquestioned, unreflective belief that being a Hindu was an integral aspect of my identity.

My aunt, with whom I made my home as an infant after my mother died, prayed daily and read the scriptures. However, unlike other well-off, devout families, we had no room in our home assigned specifically for praying, and no shrine to the gods and goddesses. (In many homes, idols of Hindu gods and goddesses are decorated with flower garlands, and incense is burnt before them.) Instead, my aunt went to the local temple almost every day, to pray and to visit a guru – *Mataji*, or mother.

There, she read the scriptures and sang devotional songs. Although some of my uncles did so, my father and grandfather observed no religious rituals.

My aunt lived a chaste and austere life of prayer and devotion, which, she explained to me, was part of her karma and *dharma*. Her karma embodied the actions in previous lives that had rewarded her by the transmigration of her soul to a human form and by her birth and marriage into a wealthy family. However, it had been flawed as well, for although she had married and had sons, she had become a widow. Her life as a wife and later as a widow was guided by her dharma, which constituted for her a number of interconnected things such as duty, law, justice, religious merit, and even religion. According to Hinduism, in observing one's dharma by following the 'right conduct,' the individual contributes to the maintenance of the moral and social order of society.

Men and women have different dharma. My aunt's *stri-dharma* (a woman's dharma) was to uphold the honour of the family and lineage, and thereby the moral order of society. Thus, as a widow, my aunt believed that it was her dharma to dress in white clothing as a mark of her austerity, to observe a simple diet at all times, and to forsake all social interactions outside the family. Her strict adherence to her dharma meant that she never questioned the status quo; she accepted her constrained and limited life as her *kismet*, or fate, and an integral aspect of her karma and dharma.

My family observed a vegetarian diet, not because we considered it healthy, as some would claim in the 1990s, but because Hinduism prescribed it. My aunt fasted on days that were religiously significant, such as the day commemorating the birth of Lord Rama, and also every Tuesday, the holy day of Hindus. On that day she went to the neighbourhood temple to make an offering of sweetmeats to the gods and to distribute them to the beggars lined up outside. Sometimes she would donate some money to the lingering children as well. The beggars received plenty of sweetmeats from devotees like my aunt every Tuesday, but eating them on an empty or half-filled stomach probably did not do them much good.

On special occasions, we would go to the Lakshmi Narayan temple, or the Birla Mandir, as it is colloquially referred to in New Delhi. Built by one of the foremost industrial families of India, the Birlas, the temple is dedicated to Lakshmi, the goddess of wealth and prosperity, and to Lord Vishnu. Vishnu is one of the gods of the Hindu trinity: Brahma the creator, Vishnu the preserver, and Shiva the destroyer. The temple is adorned with relief carvings, friezes, and sculptures depicting scenes from Hindu mythology; idols of almost all the gods of the Hindu pantheon are found here. The idols, made of marble, were carved by one hundred and one pundits, or holy men, brought in from Banaras (adding the numeral one to any number is considered auspicious by the Hindus). The iconography of Lakshmi often shows her sitting on a lotus (the lotus represents spiritual authority in Hinduism), and some interpret the image to mean that the goddess has transcended the limitations of the material physical world (the mud of existence) and floats freely in a sphere of purity and spirituality (Lakshmi and Saraswati 2000).

The Birla patriarchs were devoted followers of Mahatma Gandhi, and in 1939 invited him to inaugurate the temple. Gandhi agreed, but as he was an ardent advocate of abolishing untouchability and was leading a movement to eradicate its practice, he insisted that the Birlas open the temple, including the sanctum sanctorum, to all, regardless of their caste. Many Hindu temples have historically prohibited untouchables from entering their premises, and although the Indian constitution made it illegal to do so after 1950, the practice has nevertheless continued in many instances.

When we went to the temple on a Tuesday, we would join a throng of devotees, tourists, children, hawkers, and beggars gathered there. A room at the entrance to the temple was assigned for removing shoes, but as it quickly became crowded, some entrepreneurial men had set up a little business on the street, safe keeping the shoes of the temple-goers. (Since shoes are often made of leather, they are thought to pollute sacred premises, and, therefore, conventionally, one walks barefoot inside a temple.) Young boys were hired to be on the lookout for families heading towards the temple; they would escort them towards the little mat they had set up for the shoes in return for a small tip. At the same time, other vendors would accost us selling garlands of marigolds or flower petals in little cups made up of leaves. Beggars would pleadingly touch the arms of adults, saying, 'In the name of God, I swear, I am hungry,' while rubbing their stomachs. We were accustomed to being importuned and would continue to walk nonchalantly towards the temple, feigning a complete lack of interest in the crowd surrounding us. A word from one of us would only have encouraged the vendors to pursue us more diligently until we bought something from them.

Inside the temple, the atmosphere was one of a *mela*, or village fair: a celebration. Heads were covered and hands folded in salutation to the gods as people prayed to different deities in the various rooms of the *mandir*, or temple. My aunt would go up to the shrine, place some money in front of the gods, prostrate herself for a minute or two, get up, and hold a platter full of food and flowers in front of the pundit for his blessing. Since my aunt was a widow (which was evident by her simple white sari), the pundit would sprinkle some holy water on her. Other women received a bit of red powder on the parting of their hair as he wished them a long married life. If it was sundown, devotees would be heartily reciting the *arti* (a special prayer sung in the evening) to the accompaniment of a harmonium and the clanging of cymbals. Meantime, the children were lined up beside the bell, jumping up high to ring it loudly. All seemed to be enjoying the noisy festivity of the crowd.

My aunt remembered her husband on the anniversary of his death by performing charitable work: feeding and giving alms to the pundits. Although they are holy men like swamis, yogis, and sadhus, pundits are not priests in the Western or Christian sense because they do not study theology and are not ordained. Since Hinduism is not an organized religion, anyone who wishes to take on the occupation of a pundit, sadhu or swami can do so. Pundits are by and large poor men with very limited education. Most likely to have been born into the Brahmin caste, they become pundits by learning prayers and the performance of rituals. If they are lucky, they get assigned by a patron to maintain a temple. The pundits know the rituals of their local Hindu community and are skilled at chanting prayers, reciting the scriptures, and singing devotional songs, but few have an understanding of Hinduism beyond that. Although most Hindus in large urban centres show respect towards them for their nominal holiness, they are also sceptical and do not expect to gain spiritual and moral enlightenment from sadhus and swamis sitting by the roadside or outside temples and other religious sites.

My aunt would invite the local pundits to come to the house for a meal that consisted of several dishes, all prepared under her personal supervision by observing the caste rules of purity and pollution. She would wake up at sunrise, take a ritualistic bath to purify herself, recite prayers, and then go to the kitchen to oversee the preparation of the meal. She fasted all morning and waited to eat until the pundits had finished their meal. The pundits would arrive in freshly washed clothing; some would be wearing the sacred threads of the Brahmins, while others had slung a sacred red cloth over their shoulder. Some had smeared ashes on their foreheads, but other than that, there were no outward symbols of their being different from anyone else.

The pundits would remove their footwear at the entrance of the house and seat themselves on the mat laid out on the floor (as is customary on such occasions) in a room that had been temporarily emptied. A platter made of dried plantain or banana leaves and terracotta cups (all considered both pure and clean) would be placed in front of them. After all the priests had arrived and were seated, the most respected or the eldest would recite a few prayers, and then my aunt would serve their meal. Personal service to the pundits gained the individual religious merit, so sometimes my cousins, sister, and I would assist her in feeding them as well.

After the meal, my aunt would also give the pundits a small monetary donation before they left. They were beholden to my aunt for her generosity on such occasions and were deferential towards her; she in turn respected them for their occupation. She looked to the pundits to perform religious rituals, but not to enlighten her about the meaning of life or guide her in her search for the divine. That quest for *moksha* (liberation of the soul from earthly human desires), or Truth, was an individual undertaking that she could choose to embark upon. My aunt's guru explained the scriptures to her, but its thrust was to observe one's dharma by being moral, dutiful, and accepting of the norms of one's society as being determined by God. Complaints against social and community norms or the injustices of class, caste, and gender could be brushed aside as being the fate or destiny of the individual. Besides, though compassion for those who were unfortunate was encouraged, it was believed these people had brought their fate upon themselves by their karma, and that they provided an example to those who were prone to disregard karma and dharma as inconsequential. Such individuals could, through prayer and devotion, liberate their souls from earthly material concerns and seek to become one with God. No protests and revolution needed here!

Religious festivals were celebrated by following appropriate rituals. My aunt had received a very limited education, but she could read the *Ramayana* and the *Mahabharata* in Hindi, and often read stories from them to me. Through stories such as these, she socialized me into the appropriate gender values for a girl of my community and class. The ideal family relations, she told me, were those of the Hindu gods and goddesses as told in popular epics like the *Ramayana* and the *Mahabharata* (particularly the *Bhagavat-Gita*) and that these guided the behaviour of people. Her favourite, however, was the *Ramayana* as told by Valmiki, although there are many other written and oral versions of it as well.

The story of Ramayana is about the city of Ayodhya's King Dasrath and his wives and children. When Lord Rama, the eldest son, is about to be anointed *yuvaraja*, or crown prince, his stepmother (the number-two queen) asks the king to fulfil an earlier pledge to grant her two wishes. Her first is to have Rama exiled for fourteen years, and her second, to have her son, Bharat, installed as yuvaraja. A tearful King Dasrath conveys the news to Lord Rama, who does not contemplate fighting for his right even momentarily; rather, he insists that his father, on principle, keep his promise to his stepmother.

Lakshman, Lord Rama's brother, is overcome by grief at the news and insists on accompanying him into exile in the forest. Sita, Rama's wife, cries when she hears of his exile and entreats him to let her go with him as well. She says, 'The duty of a wife is to be always by the side of her husband. I will not be able to live in peace without you. This palace will be worse than a forest to me. Allow me, my lord, to follow you.' Lord Rama agrees, and Sita dons the clothes of a hermit to accompany him. In the forest, there are many challenges, but together the three overcome them. The king of demons, however, Ravan, entices Lord Rama away from Sita by sending a beautiful deer to his hut, and while Rama is out trying to capture the animal, Ravan kidnaps Sita.

Sita is Ravan's prisoner for years until she is rescued by Lord Rama with the help of the monkey king, Hanuman, and his army of primates. Lord Rama is overjoyed to have Sita back, and together with Lakshman, they return triumphantly to Ayodhya. Their arrival is marred, however, by the unspoken doubt that hangs in the air regarding Sita's loyalty and fidelity while a prisoner of Ravan. So Sita devises a test to prove her faithfulness. She instructs Lakshman to gather sandalwood and light a fire in a pit. When it is blazing, she walks into the flames, and all wait to see what will happen. As the fire dies down, an unscathed and still beautiful Sita emerges, to the delight of Lord Rama and the citizens of Ayodhya. The festival of Diwali celebrates the return of Lord Rama to Ayodhya; historically, it is one of the most important and loved religious festivals of the Hindus.

Through this story, I was told that the dharma of a woman was to be like Sita – a loyal, devoted wife who upholds the honour of her family and lineage, and thereby the moral order of society. Although Sita is loyal and dutiful, however, she is not necessarily passive. In fact, she is strong, for she argues her case to Rama, resists Ravan, and defends herself against the innuendo of Ayodhya's subjects. There are also lessons in this story about the duty of obedience of sons (and daughters) to the father, brotherly love and support, and, most important, an uncomplaining acceptance of one's fate.

When I was a young girl in the 1960s, some neighbourhoods of Delhi would celebrate the festivals of Dashera (also spelt Dassera), marking the exile of Lord Rama, and Diwali, his return to Ayodhya, with an open air performance called Ramlila. Ramlila began with Dashera and ended two weeks later with Diwali. Each evening, neighbours gathered together to watch a performance of a segment of the Ramayan. Young neighbourhood men – never women – from poor families and of low social status who had a flair for drama acted in the Ramlila. The performance would be on a makeshift stage, if not just an open area, and although there may have been some rehearsals, the acting was amateurish, and the actors, who were very familiar with the storyline, improvised the dialogue as they went along. The audience, sitting on the ground on threadbare mats, would laugh at the inventiveness of the actors; some people would join in as if it were a participatory show. The only light came from the rickety and unsteady wooden poles on which some naked bulbs were entwined. There was some attempt to come up with proper costumes, particularly for the men who had to dress up as women, but on the whole it was a casual and friendly neighbourhood affair. (Ramlila is not performed as much nowadays in large cities, presumably because of the popularity of movies and television. Between 1987 and 1989, the story of Ramayana was produced as a television series that was spectacularly successful and watched by millions of devout Hindus.)

In the early 1980s, the Hare Krishna staged a performance of Ramlila at Massey Hall in Toronto. Massey Hall at that time had recently been renovated and had all the latest technological accoutrements, such as stereo sound and advanced lighting systems. When I went to see Ramlila, I entered a huge centre hall with sparkling chandeliers and plush carpeting that was full of chattering, laughing South Asians milling around and greeting friends. The festive mood of the audience was evident by the women's colourful silk saris and jewellery appropriate to a wedding in India, or a black-tie affair in North America. The actors – men and women – wore vividly coloured silk costumes with lots of gold trimming (a symbol of wealth), depicting Lord Rama and Sita. The actor who played Sita was dressed in a brightly coloured sari with lots of gold jewellery around her neck, forehead, ears, and wrists.

It was a polished performance, in English, and it was obvious that a great deal of preparation and effort had gone into it. Had it not been for the predominantly South Asian diaspora audience, however, we could have been at a performance of *Swan Lake* or *Phantom of the Opera*. Because the context was so different, the show did not evoke memories of my girlhood, despite the familiar storyline. Yet, I was happy, for I was accompanied by my Canadian-born daughter, who was seven, and she got a glimpse of her Hindu culture, even though it was mediated by Western interpretation.

Diwali is celebrated in the family by performing *puja* (the traditional worship of images and idols) to the goddess Lakshmi in the home and at the workplace. In families like mine, adults give their grandchildren, children, nieces, and nephews presents of firecrackers, clothes, and money on Diwali. They also exchange gifts of sweetmeats with other relatives and neighbouring families. Over the years, a convention has emerged to give household help and those who provide services to the family (for example, the mailman) a handsome tip or a present of new clothes – not the hand-me-downs they might receive on another occasion. Traditionally, some well-off families observe Diwali by buying new, preferably silver, utensils for the family. Bonuses to employees are also frequently given during this festival. Some businessmen send gifts on Diwali to associates who have done them a favour. For example, a bank manager might get gifts from clients who hope to be viewed favourably when they apply for loans and other services. This practice has been transplanted into North America. For instance, my brother, a dermatologist in New York State, sends a gift to several family physicians in his area on Diwali to thank them for referring patients to him. Regretfully, the practice has occasionally been tainted by opportunism: in recent times greedy in-laws have taken to demanding lavish presents from their daughter-in-law's parents during this festival.

Religion and Materialism Collide in Life and Death

The images of a spiritual India and a materialistic, consumerist West are simple renditions of a complex reality. Religion provides a reference point and dictates the 'good' and moral behaviour of individuals. It was an integral part of the everyday of my father and grandfather, and an important aspect of their self-identity. My father, grandfather, and other adults accepted the loss of their material possessions consequent to the partition of India and Pakistan as their kismet. But an acceptance of kismet did not make them passive or compliant because they had to fulfil their dharma, as men and householders, to provide for their families. They worked hard to buy homes and re-establish businesses, which in their view was their moral and filial duty towards their families.

Though my father and grandfather lived their lives according to the dictates of Hinduism, they did not ask philosophical questions about the meaning of life and the search for truth, as Maitreyee does in a story from around the eighth century BC from the sacred Sanskrit text *Brihadaranyaka Upanishad*. Maitreyee and her husband, Yajnavalkya, talk about earning more money and the ways and means of becoming wealthy. They move on to discussing the proposition, 'How far would wealth go to help them get what they want?' Maitreyee wonders whether it might be possible that if 'the whole earth full of wealth' were to belong just to her, she could achieve immortality through it. 'No,' responds Yajnavalkya. 'Like the life of rich people will be your life. But there is no hope of immortality by wealth.' Maitreyee remarks, 'What should I do with that by which I do not become immortal?' (cited in Sen 2000).

Unlike Maitreyee, the adults in my family separated everyday, material living from their quest for the soul, salvation, and immortality. The pursuit of these disparate goals, in their view, did not contradict each other; rather, together they formed an integral part of their dharma. Hinduism dictates different conduct at various stages of the life cycle. Ideally, once a man has fulfilled his obligations towards his family, his role is to struggle to detach himself from his love of family and material possessions and to absorb himself in a routine of prayer and meditation. Some, very few, men in the pursuit of moksha, or Truth, leave home and become *sanaysis*, or mendicants, and attempt to become one with God.

When I am in a reflective mood, in my mind's eye I can imagine a scene in which my father is wearing a loose, saffron-coloured robe and sitting cross-legged on a mountaintop, absorbed in prayer and uncaring of the world around him. But then, unwittingly, a whine rises in my throat and I want to say, 'What about me, Dad?'

Devout Hindus wish to have their last death rites performed at Varanasi, or at least have their ashes immersed in the river Ganges there. Cremations in Varanasi are now controlled by the Brahmins and the untouchable caste, the doms, who have profited enormously by it, raising questions about morality, ethics, religion, and materialism. 'Inevitably, those who perform the cremations have a stranglehold on the devout, and some use their power mercilessly. Priests bargain with bereaved families over the price and the quantity of sandalwood and clarified butter to be used for the funeral pyre, to help ignition and salvation. Battles are fought over the price of each verse of the holy Sanskrit scriptures to be recited while the body burns' (Mehta 1979, 142). The doms provide the flame for the fire and come in later to rake the ashes of the dead in search of gold from their tooth fillings (Roberts 1994, 353).

Paul William Roberts (1994), a British-Canadian journalist, in *Empire of the Soul*, published an account of his experiences of 'searching for that vague and tantalizing thing, Truth,' in India in the 1970s and then again in the 1990s (xiii). In the 1970s, as a student fresh out of college, he was in Varanasi to study Hindu religious texts, the *Vedas*, and lived austerely for a few years before returning to the West. In the intervening years he continued to visit India at regular periods, and went back for an extended stay in the 1990s with a different attitude and enough money to live comfortably.

In the 1960s and 1970s, Varanasi was popular among the hippies who became addicted to drugs, and the local population took advantage of them. Even in the 1990s, Roberts is accosted by opportunistic young men trying to con him. One of them takes him 'not to the government's dope emporium' but to a cafe to buy drinks laced with *bhang*, a mild form of hashish. Roberts describes the proprietor thus: 'A skinny old Brahmin in loincloth and sacred thread sat cross-legged by a vast cash register, his well-stocked naked belly like a basketball, selling drinks to passersby, eagerly pouncing on the till's keys, almost smacked aside each time its drawer's maw pinged open and he fed it more rupees' (1994, 342).

While at Varanasi, Roberts wishes to visit 'the untouchable king of death,' who was rumored to have amassed a huge fortune by 'taking upon himself the karma, the sins, the unknown crimes, of the uncountable men and women he burned with the flame from his sacred fire' (1994, 341). Roberts hears the myth of how an untouchable came into the possession of the sacred fire from the king of death, also called king of doms, during a visit to the latter's lavish estate on the banks of the river Ganges. On the day of his visit, he finds the king of doms wearing a 'shimmering, creamy kurta [a loose shirt] that had diamond studs instead of buttons' (346).

A long time ago the king of Banaras, Harischandra, was renowned as a devout and generous man who helped the poor, but the god, Indra, decided to test his generosity and commitment to his faith. Indra demands that Harischandra give him everything he has. Although Harischandra complies, the god finds it unsatisfactory and makes additional demands. Harischandra sells his wife and son to appease Indra, but is unable to do so. In time, the continual demands made by Indra ruin Harischandra, and he becomes destitute and comes to be reviled by his subjects. Having become desperately poor, he looks for a job to survive but is only able to find one with Kalu Chaudri, the untouchable, who is in charge of the cremation grounds. He earns little here and 'the whole society spat on [him] to boot' (Roberts 1994, 347).

Harischandra's humiliation convinces Indra of his devotion, and he raises him to the rank of a god. Kalu Chaudri is also rewarded by being made the keeper of the sacred fire, and at the same time Indra announced that those who were cremated with a flame from this fire would achieve eternal salvation. The original Kalu Chaudri kept the fire burning and so did his descendants. This reward created a contradiction: the Brahmins who are on top of the caste hierarchy can chant prayers and perform rituals for the dead, but they could not provide the fire. Besides, the burning of the body meant that the 'karma of the deceased could be passed on and no one wanted *that* responsibility' (Roberts 1994, 347). Since the job of burning the dead was unpalatable to the caste Hindus, it was passed on to the untouchables. Further, the possession of the sacred fire that everyone needed and no one else had, more or less gave the doms 'a virtual license to print money.'

Roberts has a discussion with the king of doms whether it is possible that one man's sins can be passed to another, and they both agree it could not be so. The ethical issue, for Roberts, was thus profiting by maintaining or at least not discrediting a belief that the individual knows to be erroneous. The king of doms in turn questions the profession of journalism by focusing on journalists' construction of stories that entertain their readers. They both, he notes, 'peddle in lies.' But he goes on to say: 'There is room for all of us between earth and heaven, no? You make your living – I make mine. We all need to live, I think? Yes? Few of us are saints, few are sinners, really. The rest – we live. No?' (1994, 349). Roberts concurs by saying, 'We both lived by peddling lies that pleased, softened the pain of the living. And the dead. The boredom, the pain – that was our business. We were colleagues' (349).

Conclusion

A century ago, Nietzsche wrote:

> Will it be said of us one day that we too,
> steering westward, hope to reach an India,
> but that it was our fate to be wrecked against infinity?
> (Cited in Mehta 1979, 201)

The materialist West and the spiritual India are just one set of binaries. There are similar ones between reason and faith, or between a modern progressive West and a traditional, reactionary India. None of these binaries capture the nuances of the cultures to which they refer – or their vast diversities. The historical record of Western nations exploiting the weaknesses and vulnerabilities of the local population, in countries that eventually became their colonies, is far more extensive than the little revenge that Indians may have perpetrated by using the misconceptions of the West about its spirituality and knowledge of the Truth.

A conversation between a civil servant from the British High Commission and a foreign service Indian man in New Delhi could go like this:

> In my Oxford accent I would ... contradict them – 'yes, but we gave you the railways, the telegraph and the telephone and all the rest of it: where would you be if we hadn't dragged you with us into the twentieth century?'

> 'Where would we be? Listen to her – you gave us Macaulay and denigrated our Indian culture.'

> 'Hey wait a minute! Who was it translated Kalidasa [a poet] and the Upanishads [sacred religious texts]?'

> 'A German! It was Germans, not you people, all you gave us was your steamed pudding and custard!' (Jhabvala 1998, 72–73)

Religion has become a commodity, making those who are able to sell salvation and instant enlightenment, or promise moksha and nirvana, exceedingly wealthy. Varanasi's religiosity attracts Indians and Westerners, and the local population exploits these beliefs to enrich themselves. Such commodification of religion has heightened myths of the industrialized, urbanized, godless West that ruthlessly pursues materialistic goals. Consequently, the more sensitive among its population become alienated by the shallowness and meaninglessness of these pursuits and seek solace in higher spiritual ideals. Capitalists, as sadhus and gurus, have conned their devotees by presenting poverty, filth, hunger, and disease as inconsequential and their alleviation as 'earthly concerns' for lesser beings, while others, more high minded and spiritual, concentrate on the Divine essence, Happiness, and Truth. Thus, religion and culture have become one more commodity for the marketplace, and poverty-stricken Indians, who have little else to fall back on, sell myths about the soul of India.

While Westerners have travelled to India in search of its spiritual treasures, since the 1970s some Indians have immigrated to Canada in pursuit of a better life, defined primarily through the consumption of material goods. In the culturally pluralist environment in Canada, the immigrants are able to practise their religion with others of their faith. They have established a number of temples dedicated to one or several Hindu gods throughout Ontario. Other Hindus, for example those who follow the doctrines of Arya Samaj, content themselves by holding meetings in their homes to study religious scriptures with like-minded people (Israel 1994, 47–71).

An immigrant community's touchstone for determining the authenticity of a belief, value, or practice is comparing it with the ways in which it was practised 'back home.' In the Indian diaspora, groups of people have attempted to reproduce the norms, values, beliefs, and rituals of their specific class, region, and locale, although these are sometimes posited, in more universal terms, as being applicable to all Hindus. The rituals practised by Hindu immigrants best satisfy their desires and needs for a spiritual experience. But some adaptation is inevitable in a society dominated by Christian norms, such as the convenience of holding congregational prayers on a Sunday and allowing some gurus, swamis, and pundits to speak in English rather than in a regional Indian language. Such modifications mean that religion evolves, and its practice is particular to a specific time, place, and social context. Similarly, Hinduism and its practice is not static in India; rather, it is changing and evolving in its present political and social context. Since there are many kinds of Hindus and Hinduisms, the relevant question is not about determining the authenticity of a practice or its conformity with an idealized norm. Rather, significance lies in the nature and practice of the Hinduism that has evolved and developed in its new home in Canada.

Rabindranath Tagore (1921) may provide us with some guidance:

> To study a banyan tree You not
> only must know Its main stem in
> its own soil, But also must trace the
> growth of its greatness in the further
> soil, For then you can know the true
> Nature of its vitality

REFERENCES

Assayag, Jackie. 2003. *At the Confluence of Two Rivers: Muslims and Hindus in South India*. Delhi: Manohar Publications.

Banaras, India. 2003. www.sacredsites.com.

Israel, Milton. 1994. *In the Further Soil: A Social History of Indo-Canadians in Ontario*. Toronto: The Organization for the Promotion of Indian Culture.

Jhabvala, Ruth Prawer. 1987. *Out of India: Selected Stories*. New York: Simon and Schuster.

– 1998. *East into Upper East: Plain Tales from New York and New Delhi*. Washington: Counterpoint.

Knott, Kim. 1998. *Hinduism*. Oxford: Oxford University Press.

Lakshmi and Saraswati. 2000. Tales in Mythology and Art. www.hindupaintings.com

Mehta, Gita. 1979. *Karma Cola: Marketing the Mystic East*. New York: Simon and Schuster.

Prashad, Vijay. 2000. *The Karma of Brown Folk*. Minneapolis: University of Minnesota Press.

Prentiss, Karen Pechilis. 2003. *The Pattern of Hinduism and Hindu Temple Building in the U.S.* (Pluralism Project at Harvard). www.pluralism.org/research.

Roberts, Paul William. 1994. *Empire of the Soul: Some Journeys in India*. Toronto: Stoddart.

Said, Edward. 1979. *Orientalism*. New York: Vintage.

Sen, Amartaya. 2000. *Development as Freedom*. New York: Anchor Books.

Tagore, Rabindranath. 1921. *The Indian Diaspora*. www.Indolink.com.

AFTERWORD
Research Ethics: Philosophy's Role in Interdisciplinary Research

SUSAN E. BABBITT

Philosophy's role in the ethical problems of interdisciplinary research is more interestingly meta-ethical than ethical in the standard sense. When we refer to the role of philosophy in interdisciplinary projects, we think of questions about what ought and what ought not to be done. Yet questions about the meaning of ethical questions themselves may be more challenging or useful. What we refer to as *meta-ethical* questions are questions *about* ethics, about the nature and status of ethical enquiry, and about the meaning of concepts. Meta-ethical enquiry is crucial to interdisciplinary projects, especially those directed to social justice. Unless we agree about what we are referring to when we refer, for instance, to *autonomy, respect, agency,* or *integrity,* we cannot be sure about the conclusions that we draw.

Discussions about cultural differences, such as the ones dealt with in this volume, always depend heavily upon meta-ethical questions. Discussions about exile, memory, identity, resistance, assimilation, or the significance of oral histories have profound philosophical implications. Indeed, such work – especially from feminist and anti-racist scholars with an understanding of systemic injustice – has challenged fundamental conceptions of autonomy, integrity, and even knowledge in the European and North American traditions. But it is important that the relationship between philosophy and the social sciences goes both ways. Philosophy should consider the implications of empirical investigation into the lives of those who have mostly been excluded from academic philosophical traditions; for instance, the lives of women and members of marginalized groups. Nevertheless, scholars involved in studying empirically and explaining the consequences of global injustice should be attentive to the philosophical generalizations that follow from such work.

This volume raises intriguing and worthy philosophical questions that could be pursued further. The task of raising philosophical questions has always been more interesting and challenging than answering them. René Descartes, for instance, raised a question about knowledge in 1641. He didn't answer it well, but his question motivated centuries of research. Raising questions requires vision, because it depends upon seeing what might be. We ask questions when we see that the world could be other than it is, and that what is taken for granted ought not to be.

I do not intend to discuss the specific questions raised by this volume. To do so would require many volumes. I do not even intend to address directly the troublesome issue of ethical relativism, which is the issue for which philosophy is often called into interdisciplinary discussions, although the issues I discuss below are related to this broader one. My purpose here is not so much to address the philosophical issues but rather to suggest that they are important, that they ought to be addressed, and that they can be. The contribution of philosophy to projects in the social sciences is sometimes to show how such projects are important to more general conceptual issues, such as to our understanding of what it means to be human.

Voice and Authority

The first example of a meta-ethical issue involved in discussions about systemic injustice is the question of who speaks, and with what authority. Much research related to social justice relies importantly and correctly upon personal stories. There is a Marxist insight that has to do with the privileged perspective of the oppressed, for instance, a woman is better positioned to identify and interpret sexism than a man, and a person of colour is more likely to understand racism than a white person. Men, for instance, may be unaware of sexist practices simply because they do not run up against them in daily life.

There are important insights here. One idea is that when we understand the world, we rely upon expectations and background beliefs. We understand the world from a particular perspective and if we do not possess certain expectations and concepts, we can look at phenomena in the world and just not see them. Someone who has not lived the experience of exile and displacement, for example, will not raise certain questions about such an experience, even if she may be interested in understanding it. Only someone, whose life expectations are relevantly different, because she is relevantly different, will be able to identify as discriminatory, certain beliefs and practices taken for granted by society at large.

The specific epistemological point, sometimes referred to as the importance of the 'view from below,'[1] is that if a society is systemically discriminatory, we may not see some people as existing as persons at all – thus, the problem of invisibility. Anthropologist Levi Strauss wrote in his report that, 'the whole village left, leaving us alone with the women and children in the abandoned houses.'[2] Evidently Levi Strauss did not expect the women or children to be people.

Yet if someone exists from that invisible position, she can encounter, and identify the error in, the expectation. People who are living a certain social reality are usually better positioned to identify that reality and to make decisions about it. There is a question, though, about what follows logically from such an insight, for researchers investigating the situations of people whose lives and cultures are relevantly different from our own.

What is taken to follow logically from the critical role of personal stories is that, as a 'privileged' researcher, I cannot be justified in criticizing the evaluative perspective of the less privileged person, especially when I do not share her culture. If someone says that a traditional practice is not damaging to her, who am I to dispute that? When the rhetorical response, 'Who's to say?' is offered, the suggested implication is that one ought not *to say*, that one ought not to take authority in such a case. The investigator, correctly aware of the power of her position as investigator, may assume that in order to act respectfully towards the person whose situation is of interest, she should not make evaluative judgments about what is being expressed.

This is an example of a philosophical generalization incorrectly derived from an important insight. There are three reasons for thinking that it does not follow logically from the unique perspective of the oppressed that we should not morally judge someone's evaluation of his or her personal experiences.

The first reason is that the 'Who's to say?' response, by the investigator, is much too easy. It absolves us of making judgments about almost any issue or situation. If we are not justified in criticizing a situation in which we do not participate, we absolve ourselves of any responsibility towards acquiring a proper understanding of that situation. We are then only responsible for that which directly affects us personally. Such a conclusion is counterintuitive. For one thing, if we accept it, we should give up the commitment that motivated the insight about the privileged perspective of the oppressed in the first place; namely, that it matters that we understand the experience of those whose experiences, because of difference, are invisible to us, and, moreover, that it matters to us personally.

A second reason for thinking the conclusion does not follow is that people's expectations for themselves can become diminished as a result of the social expectations informing their lives. People can come to accept injustices if those injustices are considered normal. If it follows from the fact that you experience your life as happy and fulfilling, that your life *is* in fact happy and fulfilling, then I can justify oppressing you as long as I can successfully coerce or persuade you to *think* you are happy and fulfilled. If it is true that as long as you *think* you are doing well, you really *are* doing well, then it would follow that to the extent that a state is successful in indoctrinating its people about the benefits of oppressive, repressive policies, it can claim with good reason to be acting in the interests of its people.

A third reason for resisting the conclusion that the privileged researcher should remain critically removed, and just listen, has to do with respect, and what it means and requires. When we respect people as equals, we engage with them. If I respect you, for one thing I assume that you have at least as much intelligence and ability to reason as I do. So if you say something that sounds implausible, I assume that it is not in fact implausible, and, if it strikes me that way, I must be missing something. So I ask for an explanation because the implausibility, given my expectations about you, is surprising to me. If we respect people whose backgrounds and traditions we do not share, we expect their views also to make sense, to express at least as much intelligence as we ourselves possess. Thus, if the views expressed do not strike us that way, we ask questions, directly of the person or indirectly by research- ing other sources, expecting that something has been missed. The ask- ing of questions, whether or not they are addressed to the individual, assumes a critical perspective. If we respect people, we engage with them and their situation on the assumption that they, as equals, can provide defence and explanation. When we do not engage critically with a view, it is sometimes because we assume that the view has no defence, that it is something less than a reasoned-out view.

When we conclude that, as researchers, we should not take evalua- tive authority over the information that interviewees provide, we make an error. It is true that individuals possess a privileged perspective regarding their own experience. Nevertheless, it may not be true that this privileged perspective provides adequate justification for the specific views expressed. To assume so is, in some cases, irresponsible.

The point is not to deny the primacy of individuals and the significance of their stories; rather, it is to question a certain understanding of individuals' primacy. On the one hand, postmodernism has made it clear that we are always historically situated and that our understanding is always dependent upon this fact. On the other hand, awareness of our historical situation means that we should be more responsible, as investigators, for studying the specific implications of the sorts of institutions and traditions that inform stories and judgments. To ask, 'Who's to say?' as if *we* are not, and cannot be, qualified to judge the relative merits of personal stories and impressions is ingenuous. Certainly, we are sometimes not qualified to judge. By hearing the story in the first place, however, we have already made such a judgment of authority, and the 'Who's to say?' response just leaves unacknowledged and unexamined the role of such implicit presuppositions.

We sometimes think that, as investigators, we should refrain from making value judgments because we possess power over the people whose situation is being investigated. But when we attribute authority to a point of view because of some particular feature of the person's position, we are already making an evaluative judgment that structures the investigation and its interpretation. We need to take responsibility for the judgments we make and our relationship to them. We are already involved, and we already exercise power. We need to be honest about our involvement and take appropriate moral and theoretical responsibility for it.

Generalizations and Particular Stories

An issue about the role of generalizations and the implications for particular stories has arisen in several ways. One way is described as a concern about 'essentialism' – roughly, the idea that entities or phenomena are individuated, or 'picked out,' by specific sets of properties. Although philosophers of science have long recognized that essences, or what makes a thing the thing it is, are changeable, 'essentialists' are taken to be those who presume that essences are somehow fixed and eternal.

There is a view that when we make generalizations about, for instance, women, we make assumptions about the application of the general term *women* that rules out of the realm of consideration the experience of women of less privileged groups. So, famously, the claim of some decades ago, that the problem for women is to get out of the house, was offensive to many Black women whose problem was that they had always had to work in other people's houses, as domestics.

The worry about 'essentialism' is, supposedly, that when we rely upon a category, such as 'women,' we assume a fixed set of properties that defines all women.[3] But, of course, there is no fixed set of properties possessed by all women. There will always be someone who is in fact a woman who does not possess all of the qualities. Perhaps, also, there will be someone with all the specified qualities who is not in fact a woman. This problem of fixed sets of properties has also been much discussed regarding natural kinds – the essences of species, for instance. If we think that there is a set of properties that defines cats, we will surely find something that is a cat that does not have all the properties, or something with all the properties that is not a cat. One of the problems with *natural kinds* – that is, the problem of general categories for sorting natural phenomena – is that species evolve and their defining properties change. We might think this means that species have no essences. Alternatively, we might conclude that we have been mistaken about the fixedness of essential properties.

Although the literature on *natural kinds* in the philosophy of science has shown that essences are not, and ought not to be, fixed sets of properties, the political literature, perhaps largely because of the influence of postmodernism, has continued to conflate the implausibility of fixed, permanent essences with the undesirability of abstract, generalizing concepts.

The worry, then, is that when we make generalizations about 'women,' we preclude the proper appreciation of women's differences. For, in assuming the category 'women,' we presume a fixed set of properties defining all women, and such properties, as defining ones, are bound to be determined by practical and theoretical traditions expressing the arbitrary privileging of some groups of women and the invisibility of others.

The question is whether in fact *essences* are necessarily fixed permanent sets of characteristics. The popular response to worries about 'essences' and 'meta-narratives' has been an emphasis on particular stories, which has been significant. It has become theoretically important to tell, hear, and politically recognize personal stories told from alternative perspectives. Emphasis on stories about *difference*, however, is not necessarily an antidote to ideological domination; it depends *which* stories are considered *different* in which ways. The personal stories that are interesting are those that reflect *difference,* but the differences we are interested in, in trying to understand the consequences or causes of injustice, are those differences that are relevant to that concern. And in order to identify relevant differences, we do in fact make generalizing 'essentialist' claims of all sorts.

Toni Morrison, for instance, has written stories from the perspective of Black women in the United States. But when Toni Morrison describes how she began telling her particular stories, she describes a process of acquiring awareness of *the whole* picture and making a judgment about the general nature of the big picture of American literature. When she first read American literature, she thought that Blacks were just not there in the picture. It was only when she became a writer herself and learned about how meanings are created through stories that she saw that Blacks *are* in fact present in the classics of American literature. They are present, but they are present in a way that suggests that they *ought not* to be present. They are present without names, without physical descriptions, without voice. It was when Morrison understood that American literature *as a whole* was racist in this way, and judged moreover that it was *wrong* that American literature should be so, that she began to tell stories in the way she did. According to Morrison, the telling of the particular stories, in the critically effective way she tells them, is dependent upon a generalized understanding of American literature and American society.[4]

The problem here is that a mistaken understanding of the nature of general concepts and theories is confused with the idea that general concepts and theories are themselves mistaken. It is true that when we rely upon general concepts and theories, we make a mistake if we take such concepts and theories to be absolutist; that is, to be fixed and unrevisable. For then we disregard the empirical evidence before us. But general concepts and theories do not have to be absolute or unrevisable. Biologists do generally assume that species have essences. The properties defining the essence of a species, however, are not fixed.

The philosophical mistake has been to set in opposition reliance upon general concepts and theories and the importance of particular stories, when, in fact, the importance of particular stories depends upon definite, normative judgments of a general sort. The ethical error, similar to the risk identified above, is that in assuming such an opposition, we fail to take responsibility for and to critically examine the general claims we are presupposing.

Responsibility for the Story

There is a popular liberal philosophical view about the virtues of the
'cultural marketplace.' The idea is that if the information is available,
and people are free to deliberate as equals, the best ideas will eventually win out. The motivation behind such views is that it is wrong
to *impose* values and priorities upon a society because everyone's life
is best when directed by values that individuals themselves have
endorsed.

The naivety involved in the 'cultural marketplace' and 'dialogic'
views, as well as in resistance to 'meta-narratives,' 'tyrannical episte-
mologies,' and so on, is that if a society is systemically unjust, then that
society is *already* 'tyrannized' by an inadequate sort of imposed
worldview. For what it means for injustice to be systemic is that such
injustice is expressed in the norms and values of a society, making
injustices acceptable. If the existing national story, the existing meta-
narrative, is already unjust, then the dialogue taking place within it –
within the 'cultural marketplace,' so to speak – is already regulated by
an imposed view that has not been endorsed, because it is barely even
recognized. This is the case, for instance, when certain groups of people
within a society are considered inferior, such as when a society is
systemically and historically racist. It is also the case, as Che Guevara
pointed out, when a certain kind of individualism defines and is expected of human relations within a society.[5]

There are two points here: one is that there already exists a single
story, dominating other stories and generating formative expectations
in the 'cultural marketplace,' so that the market is not relevantly free;
the second point is that national stories are not just intellectual issues,
but are identities, and challenging them requires more than reasons
and argument. Consider the following anecdote from Chinua Achebe's
Anthills of the Savannah:

> Once upon a time the leopard who had been trying for a long time to catch
> the tortoise happened upon him on solitary road. *Aha*, he said; *at long last,
> prepare to die.* And the tortoise said: *Can I ask one favour before you kill me?*
> The leopard saw no harm in that and granted it. But instead of standing
> still as the leopard expected the tortoise went into strange action on the
> road, scratching with hands and feet and throwing sand furiously in all
> directions. *Why are you doing that?* asked the puzzled leopard. The tortoise
> replied, *Because even after I am dead I want anyone passing by this spot to say,
> yes, a fellow and his match struggled here.*[6]

In Achebe's story, the tortoise doesn't fight for his own existence. He knows he's going to die, but he is concerned about the story that will be told. Which story is told makes a difference to what can be understood and acted upon in the future.

Achebe's *Anthills of the Savannah* is a novel about democracy. It suggests that control of the story is more important than politics. There are some who rush to battle, and some who tell the story afterward. Some think it is easy to control the story; according to Achebe's elderly storyteller, they are fools. We often assume that democracy is about choice, about capacity to choose. Achebe's anecdote suggests that more important than an availability of choices, or capacity to choose them, is control of the story that determines the credibility of choices, that determines whether we can expect choices to be important as choices of a certain sort, for us as choosers of a certain sort.

The story that the tortoise wants told is a story about sameness: a *fellow and his match struggled here.* The tortoise expects that a story will be told about the *likeness* between himself and the leopard. The tortoise fights for a story about unity, about similarities. It has been important to be appreciative of differences. But it is important to recognize that differences are always relative to similarities. If Blacks and gays are 'different,' it is because what makes people 'the same' is to be white and heterosexual. If being white were not characteristic of the sameness of 'people,' non-white people would not be considered different in a relevant sense; that is, as regards being people. Achebe's point, in the anecdote, is that *the* story of sameness, of unifying identity, the *single* story, is more important for democracy, for the control of one's destiny, than the political struggles around particular differences.

The ethical issue is that we always interpret the world in terms of moral, political, historical, ontological, and epistemological stories that we are often unaware of. Not only is it important that we acknowledge and take responsibility for such stories, it is also important that we realize that it is hard to do so and that it requires political struggle of an organized, self-conscious sort.

Definitions

There is often discussion in interdisciplinary research about what we mean by central concepts. We might insist, for the sake of the research, on agreement about the issue of how we are to understand, say, 'diaspora,' or we may decide for the sake of the research that it ought not to be defined.

There is an ethical issue involved in decisions to define or not to define central concepts. For when we decide to define a term specifically, we decide to take a position about the specific direction of research. If we decide to define a term, we express confidence in the current theoretical resources and in our perspective upon them. We are making a judgment that in fact the perspective is not in question, and that we are in a position to insist upon specific criteria from the perspective that we now occupy. Sometimes, for instance, it is not appropriate to insist upon a specific definition because it is recognized that the appropriate referent of the term is dependent upon the results of empirical investigation that is still to be undertaken. In science, for instance, research can be carried out effectively in awareness that the referent of a term is still to be discovered. In the case, for instance, of 'black holes,' there was something there to be theorized about, but it would not have been appropriate to try to define the object of investigation. The resources were not available and could not be expected to be available.

To insist prematurely upon a definition can constitute a failure to recognize the importance of the object of investigation. If someone were to insist prematurely that the term *black holes* be precisely defined, one might think such a person had failed to recognize the complexity of the investigation and the importance of that complexity.

Interestingly, Armando Hart argues that *the* biggest mistake made by the leaders of socialist revolutions in Eastern Europe and the Soviet Union was *not* to have taken up seriously the task of redefining terms such as *human rights, freedom*, and *civil society*.[7] How could the failure to redefine concepts be a bigger mistake than all the other mistakes made by the Soviet Union? Philosopher of science Ian Hacking points out that *social* and *human kinds* – that is, categories that classify behaviour and people – have implications for how people understand themselves and for how they behave. For instance, when the term *sexual harassment* was introduced, many women were able to identify disturbing behaviour in the workplace for what it was: wrong! Hart seems to suggest that because terms like human rights and freedom were not redefined and claimed, they were not able to be motivating in practice and theory in the way they might have been.

Because of the essentialist problem mentioned above, it is often assumed we cannot engage critically with social or human categories. This is a mistake. Sometimes it is suggested that because the term *feminist*, say, has no fixed definition, it follows that as long as someone *thinks* she is a feminist, she is a feminist. Or people say that because 'sexual harassment' has no fixed definition, as long as someone thinks she has suffered sexual harassment, she has indeed suffered sexual harassment. I don't need to think there is a fixed definition for 'feminist,' however, in order to think some understandings of the term are wrong. I might well judge, for instance, that being a feminist does not require hating men.

We must distinguish between the requirement that social and human kinds be defined permanently and precisely, and the expectation that there are good reasons for applying such terms in some cases and not in others. It is true that such terms do not possess fixed definitions, applicable to all situations at all times. It does not follow that there are not non-arbitrary criteria for deciding that a term is being applied incorrectly. We do in fact rely upon empirical evidence in arguing that what is *believed* to be sexual harassment is not *in fact* sexual harassment.

In short, definitions raise ethical issues because what we do with them constitutes a commitment to a direction. Decisions about defining a term or not are also, in some cases, judgments about the importance of the research and, in other cases, judgments about the adequacy of a current theoretical or practical perspective. That is, decisions about redefining a term can express a commitment, or not, to critical engagement.

Conclusion

Philosophy has significance in interdisciplinary research, for one reason, because of its role in clarifying questions. Moreover, philosophy can sometimes help to identify the ways in which research ends up assuming the same sorts of mistaken conceptions of individualism and absolute truth – conceptions generally recognized as unfounded. Philosopher Antonio Gramsci, for one, argued that we cannot just stop relying upon mistaken conceptions; we have to examine the ways in which the old conceptions still work to influence our observations and questions, often implicitly. Philosophy is part of that critical investigation.

Moreover, the social sciences have importance for philosophy because stories raise questions that challenge fundamental philosophical conceptions. Academic philosophical traditions are notoriously limited by the fact that those who have participated in and defined such traditions are from more privileged social groups. The intellectual work of more marginalized social groups – women, for one – has often not been

considered philosophy. In the past few decades, academic philosophy
has been challenged, in the United States and Canada, by the work of
feminists and anti-racists in particular, even though much of that work,
arguably, has been done outside of philosophy. The questions raised in
investigating the lives and perspectives of people not often heard in
intellectual debates have been philosophically challenging, showing
that what was before thought to have been understood has not really
been understood.

Achebe's anecdote about the leopard and the tortoise bears upon the
role of philosophy in interdisciplinary research. Achebe's point was that
there are two sorts of struggles: one social and political for global
justice; the other for the philosophical/ideological story that will be
told about that struggle. Today, as we live in a world dominated by a
single ideology about freedom and democracy at risk of being imposed
violently upon 'the dark corners of the earth,'[8] it is important to work
out the conceptual implications of the lived experience of those whose
aspirations have no place in that ideology. The tortoise worked to make
sure that a story was told about his death, one that demonstrated that
his end was not inevitable. He wanted it to be told that 'a fellow and his
match struggled here,' suggesting that the story could have turned out
differently. Only if we do the work to imagine, and to demonstrate, that
things might be different from the way they now are, including the
possibility that we might think of ourselves differently, more humanely,
does it make sense to struggle for the realization of that possibility.

NOTES

I am grateful to Haideh Moghissi, Saeed Rahnema, and Mark Goodman for
the opportunity to first present a version of this essay to those involved in the
Diaspora, Islam, and Gender project at York University in May 2001. I am also
grateful to the Social Sciences and Humanities Research Council of Canada
for funding that project, under Haideh Moghissi's direction, for it has provided an ongoing forum for discussion of philosophical issues, such as those
below, with dedicated social scientists.

1 Donna Haraway (1991) used this phrase in *Simians, Cyborgs and Women: The
  Reinvention of Nature* (New York: Routledge), 86–100.
2 Cited in Lise Noel (1994), *Intolerance: The Parameters of Oppression* (Montreal-
  Kingston: McGill-Queen's University Press), 27.

3 See, for example, Elizabeth V. Spelman (1988), *Inessential Woman: Problems of Exclusion in Feminist Thought* (Boston: Beacon Press).

4 Toni Morrison (1992), *Playing in the Dark: Whiteness and the Literary Imagination* (New York: Vintage Books).

5 Ernesto Che Guevara (2003), Socialism and Man in Cuba, rpt. in David Deutschmann, ed. *Che Guevara Reader: Writings on Politics and Revolution* (Melbourne and New York: Ocean Press), 212–230.

6 Chinua Achebe (1987), *Anthills of the Savannah* (London: Picador), 128.

7 Armando Hart (1988), Roundtable on Sociedad Civil, *Temas: Cultura, Ideología, Sociedad* 16–17 (Havana, Cuba), 157.

8 George W. Bush, 20 May 2002.

Contributors

Vijay Agnew is a professor of social science and the director of the Centre for Feminist Research at York University. Her book, *Resisting Discrimination: Women from Asia, Africa, and the Caribbean and the Women's Movement in Canada* (Toronto: University of Toronto Press, 1996), won the Gustav Myers Award as an 'outstanding book on the subject of human rights in North America.' Her other books are *Where I Come From* (Waterloo: Wilfrid Laurier University Press, 2003), *In Search of a Safe Place: Abused Women and Culturally Sensitive Services* (Toronto: University of Toronto Press, 1998), and *Elite Women in Indian Politics* (Delhi: Vikas, 1979). In 1998, Agnew was appointed to the External Research Advisory Committee of the Status of Women, Canada by Hedy Frye, the minister of multiculturalism.

Susan E. Babbitt received her PhD in philosophy from Cornell University in 1991 and has been teaching at Queen's University in Kingston, Ontario, since 1990. Her research interest, and passion, since 1993 is Cuba, particularly the situation of women there. Since 2001, she has been taking large groups of Queen's students to the University of Havana. She has published two books on rationality and moral imagination, and has co-edited (with Sue Campbell) an anthology on racism and philosophy. She is the author of a number of articles on issues in feminist philosophy and moral psychology.

Rishma Dunlop is an associate professor of literary studies in the Faculty of Education, York University. She has written extensively on women scholars in the arts, and she is the founder of the Red Shoes Collective, a group collective of artist-researchers. She is a poet and fiction writer whose work has won awards and has appeared in numerous books, journals, and anthologies, nationally and internationally. She is the author of three books of poetry: *The Body of My Garden, Reading Like a Girl,* and *Metropolis.* She is co-editor (with Priscila Uppal) of *Red Silk: An Anthology of South Asian Canadian Women Poets.* She also organizes a speakers series at York University, called 'Writers and Artists Without Borders.'

Anh Hua is a doctoral student in women's studies at York University. Her dissertation focuses on diaspora, memory, identity, home, and cultural trauma. She has published in the journals *Canadian Women's Studies, J-Spot,* and *Politics and Culture*

Carl James is a professor in the Faculty of Education at York University. He teaches courses in urban education and foundations of education. His research interests include educational and occupational access and equity for marginalized youth; the complementary and contradictory nature of sports and academics in the schooling attainments of youth; and policies, practices, and implications of multiculturalism, anti-racism, and immigration. His writings include *Seeing Ourselves: Exploring Race, Ethnicity and Culture* (Toronto: Thompson Educational Press, 2003), and *Race in Play: Understanding the Socio-Cultural World of Student Athletes* (Toronto: Canadian Schools' Press, 2005).

Marlene Kadar is professor in Humanities and Women's Studies at York University and is the former director of the graduate program in Interdisciplinary Studies. Her *Essays on Life Writing: From Genre to Critical Practice* (Toronto: University of Toronto Press, 1992) won the Gabrielle Roy Prize in 1993. The editor of Wilfrid Laurier University Press's Life Writing Series, Kadar's research interests include the politics of life writing, including survivor narratives; the construction of privilege and knowledge in women's life writing; and Hungarian and Romani auto/biography in historical accounts, biographical traces, and fragments. Her recent work is published in *Tracing the Autobiographical,* edited by Kadar, Jeanne Perreault, and Susanna Egan (Waterloo: WLUP, 2005).

Atsuko Matsuoka is an associate professor, School of Social Work, Atkinson Faculty of Liberal and Professional Studies, York University. She is co-author of the book *Ghosts and Shadows* (Toronto: University of

Toronto Press, 2001), and has written on the diaspora from the Horn of Africa.

Haideh Moghissi is professor in the Atkinson Faculty of Liberal and Professional Studies and the Faculty of Graduate Studies where she teaches sociology and women's studies. Haideh is the director of the MCRI project Diaspora, Islam, and Gender, and is a widely published scholar on religion, gender, and politics in the Middle East. Before leaving Iran in 1984, she was a founder of the Iranian National Union of Women. Her *Feminism and Islamic Fundamentalism: The Limits of Post-Modern Analysis* (London: Zed Press, 1999; Oxford University Press, 2000) was awarded the 2000 Choice Outstanding Academic Books Award in Sociology. Her publications include articles in referred journals, chapters in edited volumes, and the following books: *Populism and Feminism in Iran* (London: Macmillan, 1994); and *Women and Islam: Critical Concepts in Sociology* (London: Routledge, 2004).

Izumi Sakamoto is an assistant professor at the Faculty of Social Work at the University of Toronto, Canada. Izumi received her MA in social welfare from Sophia University, Japan, and her MSW, MS (psychology), and PhD (social work and social psychology) from the University of Michigan in the United States. With SSHRC and other grants, she is currently conducting multiple research projects focusing on gender and immigration, identities, cultural negotiation processes of newcomers, and anti-oppressive social work.

John Sorenson is a professor in the Department of Sociology at Brock University. He is the author and editor of several books on the Horn of Africa, including *Imagining Ethiopia* (New Brunswick, NJ: Rutgers University Press, 1993) and *Ghosts and Shadows* (Toronto: University of Toronto Press, 2001).

Pamela Sugiman is an associate professor in the Department of Sociology at McMaster University. Her longstanding research interests are in the areas of gender, women's social history, memory, oral history, 'race' and racialization, work and labour. She is currently writing a book on gendered memory and the internment of Japanese Canadians.

Yanqiu Rachel Zhou is a PhD candidate at the Faculty of Social Work at the University of Toronto. Yanqiu received her master's degree in social/cultural anthropology (University of Toronto), and her areas of interest include Chinese diaspora, the impact of social/health policy on socially disadvantaged populations, and international social work. She is currently doing a dissertation on the life experiences of people living with HIV/AIDS in China.